Household Spanish

How to Communicate with Your Spanish Employees

William C. Harvey

BARRON'S

About the Author

William C. Harvey is founder of Language Services Institute, a highly-successful conversation Spanish program aimed specifically at meeting the needs of today's busy adult learner. For the past 12 years he has taught Spanish and ESL (English as a Second Language) in school districts and community colleges, as well as in private industry. He has also traveled extensively throughout the West Coast giving workshops and seminars to teachers and professional organizations. Mr. Harvey holds a bachelor's degree in Spanish and a master's degree in Bilingual-Bicultural Education from Cal State University, Fullerton, where he received the "Project of the Year" award for his work in ESL Curriculum Development.

Three of his books already have been published by Barron's: *Spanish for Gringos, Inglés para Latinos*, and *Spanish for Health Care Professionals*.

All inquiries should be addressed to:
Barron's Educational Series, Inc.
250 Wireless Boulevard
Hauppauge, New York 11788

International Standard Book Number 0-8120-9057-8 (Book Only)
International Standard Book Number 0-8120-8405-5 (Book/Cassettes Package)

Library of Congress Catalog Card Number 95-75398

Printed in the United States of America

78   8800   987654

TABLE OF CONTENTS

A Personal Note   iv

Before We Begin   iv

Good News!   v

Chapter 1 Spanish in a Nutshell   1

Chapter 2 Who Are You? How Are You?   35

Chapter 3 Cleaning   77

Chapter 4 In the Kitchen   110

Chapter 5 Childcare   140

Chapter 6 Out in the Yard   176

Chapter 7 Errands   202

English-Spanish Vocabulary   225

Spanish-English Vocabulary   246

A PERSONAL NOTE

I didn't learn Spanish until I was in my teens. While taking a beginning course in school, I took a part-time job at a local restaurant. None of my fellow workers spoke English, so I was forced to communicate the best I could. It wasn't long before I was imitating their words, phrases, and nonverbal mannerisms. Although I didn't understand everything (and constantly made mistakes), whenever I spoke I was warmly received. Such encouragement led me to more serious studies and eventually a degree in Spanish as a foreign language. I've been teaching other Americans how to speak Spanish ever since.

When people ask what motivates me most as a Spanish teacher, I think back on those days in the restaurant. Those personal experiences — cleaning counters, setting tables, washing dishes — all took place in a rich language environment, which made routine duties exciting and fun.

Household Spanish offers the same opportunity to you. Giving instructions, explaining details, and asking questions in Spanish can do more than help people to communicate. Learning another language often leads to self gratification, new friendships, and meaningful cultural awareness. So enjoy — I certainly did!

BEFORE WE BEGIN

This book provides English-speaking employers with all the Spanish vocabulary and phrases that are needed to communicate with non-English speaking employees in the businesses of housecleaning, child care, food preparation, delivery, gardening, and other related areas of professional service — whether you live in a condo, an apartment, or a private house. Moreover, *Household Spanish* gradually teaches the reader basic Spanish language skills, which are reinforced systematically through practice and review.

To get the most out of this book, either use the convenient specialized dictionary in the back, or try focusing on the icons provided below. They can be helpful when you are working on a specific skill or topic of interest. Simply scan the pages for the corresponding icon, and read up on whatever you need:

 Do It, Please! **¡Hágalo, por Favor!** *('ah-gah-loh, pohr fah-'bohr)* (Spanish commands)

 Culture Clues. **Temas Culturales** *('teh-mahs kool-too-'rah-lehs)* (Insights on Hispanic cultural awareness)

 More Action! **¡Más Acción!** *(mahs ahk-see-'ohn)* (Basic verb tenses)

 Let's Review. **Repasemos** *(reh-pah-'seh-mohs)* (Review practice exercises)

 Super Spanish! **¡El superespañol!** *(ehl soo-pehr-eh-spah-'nyohl)* (Key phrases that combine with verb forms)

 Key Words. **Palabras Claves** *(pah-'lah-brahs 'klah-behs)* (Specialized vocabulary lists)

 There are also sections throughout entitled More Help. **Más Ayuda** *(mahs ah-'yoo-dah)*. These include additional information, tips, and hints.

Bear in mind that using Spanish in familiar settings allows you to pick up more language skills faster. And consistent practice will only accelerate the process. More importantly, close interaction with native Hispanics opens the door to unique and exciting cultural experiences.

GOOD NEWS!
¡Buenas noticias! (buh-'eh-nahs noh-'tee-see-ahs)
Here's some exciting news about learning **español** *(ehs-pahn-'yohl)* as a second language, according to the latest research:

• Grammar and pronunciation don't have to be "perfect" in order to be understood.

• Thousands of words are similar in both Spanish and English, which makes it easier for you to remember vocabulary.

• Messages in Spanish can be communicated with only a few simple expressions.

Feel better? Trust me. Learning the Spanish skills to use around the house is really no **problema** *(proh-'bleh-mah)* at all.

CHAPTER ONE   *Capítulo Uno*
(kah-'pee-too-loh 'oo-noh)

SPANISH IN A NUTSHELL

WHAT'S THAT SOUND?

¿Qué es ese sonido? (keh ehs 'eh-seh soh-'nee-doh)

One of the first things you will discover about speaking Spanish with Hispanic employees is that your poor pronunciation won't really hurt communication. Not only are people generally forgiving, but in reality, there aren't that many differences between the two sound systems. In fact, you need to remember only five sounds in order to speak well enough to be understood. These are the vowels, and unlike their English equivalents, each one is pronounced the way it is written:

a *(ah)* as in yacht
e *(eh)* as in pet
i *(ee)* as in keep
o *(oh)* as in open
u *(oo)* as in spool

Before we practice these new sounds as parts of Spanish words, let's learn how to pronounce all the other letters. And don't forget — these sounds are always the same!

A as in love?
U as in you?

Spanish Letter	English Sound
c (after an e or i)	s as in Sally (**cigarro**) *(see-'gah-rroh)*
g (after an e or i)	h as in Harry (**general**) *(heh-neh-'rahl)*
h	silent, like k in knife (**hombre**) *('ohm-breh)*
j	h as in hot (**Julio**) *('hoo-lee-oh)*
ll	y as in yellow (**tortilla**) *('tohr-tee-yah)*
ñ	ny as in canyon (**señor**) *(seh-'nyohr)*

1

qu	k as in kit (**tequila**) *(teh-'kee-lah)*
rr	the "rolled" r sound (**burro**) *('boo-rroh)*
v	b as in black (**viva**) *('bee-bah)*
z	s as in son (**Sánchez**) *('sahn-chehs)*

Although some dialects may vary slightly, the rest of the letters in Spanish are similar to their equivalents in English:

b	**bueno** *('bweh-noh)*
d	**dinero** *(dee-'neh-roh)*
f	**flan** *(flahn)*
l	**loco** *('loh-koh)*
m	**mucho** *('moo-choh)*
n	**nada** *('nah-dah)*
p	**pronto** *('prohn-toh)*
r	**tres** *(trehs)*
s	**sí** *(see)*
t	**taco** *('tah-koh)*
x	**México** *('meh-hee-koh)*

Now, read the following words aloud and then guess at their meanings. Remember that <u>each</u> <u>letter</u> needs to be pronounced the way it was introduced earlier:

amigo	*(ah-'mee-goh)*
burrito	*(boo-'ree-toh)*
cilantro	*(see-'lahn-troh)*
chiquita	*(chee-'kee-tah)*
español	*(ehs-pah-'nyohl)*
excelente	*(ehk-seh-'lehn-teh)*
Feliz Navidad	*(feh-'lees nah-bee-'dahd)*
Geraldo	*(heh-'rahl-doh)*
grande	*('grahn-deh)*
hola	*('oh-lah)*
muchacho	*(moo-'chah-choh)*
plaza	*('plah-sah)*
pollo	*('poh-yoh)*
vino	*('bee-noh)*

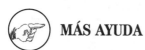 **MÁS AYUDA**

• Any part of a word with an accent mark (´) needs to be pronounced LOUDER and with more emphasis (i.e., María) *(mah-'ree-ah)*. If there's no accent mark, say the last part of the word louder and with more emphasis (i.e., Beatriz) *(beh-ah-'trees)*. For words ending in a vowel, or in **n** or **s**, the next to the last part of word is stressed (i.e., Fernando) *(fehr-'nahn-doh)*.

• In some cases, the letter **u** doesn't make the "oo" sound (i.e., guitarra *[gee-'tah-rrah]* or guerra *['geh-rrah]*).

• If you're having problems with the sounds of Spanish, try listening to the language for a few minutes each day. Spanish radio and TV stations or audio- and videocassettes are fun and effective ways to become familiar with your new pronunciation patterns.

HOW DO YOU SPELL IT?
¿Cómo se deletrea? *('koh-moh seh deh-leh-'treh-ah)*

Because Spanish is written the way it is pronounced, you will not have much trouble writing notes or messages for Spanish-speaking employees. Even if you misspell a few words, they will still be able to figure out what you are trying to say. Take a few moments to look over the Spanish alphabet. Each letter has its own unique name:

a *(ah)*	**e** *(eh)*
b *(beh 'grahn-deh)*	**f** *('eh-feh)*
c *(seh)*	**g** *(heh)*
ch *(cheh)**	**h** *('ah-cheh)*
d *(deh)*	**i** *(ee)*

j *('ho-tah)*	**r** *('eh-reh)*
k *(kah)*	**rr** *('eh-rreh)*
l *('eh-leh)*	**s** *('eh-seh)*
ll *('e-yeh)**	**t** *(teh)*
m *('eh-meh)*	**u** *(oo)*
n *('eh-neh)*	**v** *(beh-'chee-kah)*
ñ *('eh-nyeh)**	**w** *(beh-'doh-bleh)*
o *(oh)*	**x** *('eh-kees)*
p *(peh)*	**y** *(ee-gree-'eh-gah)*
q *(koo)*	**z** *('seh-tah)*

* In 1994 these letters were cut from the "official" Spanish alphabet. However, people still refer to them when spelling out a word.

 REPASEMOS

Can you spell your name in Spanish? How about the city you live in?

WORDS THAT WORK
Las palabras que trabajan
(lahs pah-'lah-brahs keh trah-'bah-hahn)

To begin to communicate in Spanish, you're going to need the basic greetings and courteous exchanges that are heard most often in daily conversations. Although you will hear other phrases that have similar meanings, these will work fine for now:

Excuse me!	**¡Con permiso!** *(kohn pehr-'mee-soh)*
Go ahead!	**¡Pase!** *('pah-seh)*
Good afternoon.	**Buenas tardes** *('bweh-nahs 'tahr-dehs)*
Good evening/ Good night.	**Buenas noches** *('bweh-nahs 'noh-chehs)*
Good morning.	**Buenos días** *('bweh-nohs 'dee-ahs)*
Good-bye.	**Adiós** *(ah-dee-'ohs)*
Hi.	**Hola** *('oh-lah)*
How are you?	**¿Cómo está?** *('koh-moh eh-'stah)*
How may I help you?	**¿Puedo ayudarle?** *('pweh-doh ah-yoo-'dahr-leh)*
How's it going?	**¿Qué tal?** *(keh 'tahl)*
I'm sorry!	**¡Lo siento!** *(loh see-'ehn-toh)*

4

May I come in?	**¿Se puede?** *(seh 'pweh-deh)*
Nice to meet you!	**¡Mucho gusto!** *('moo-choh 'goo-stoh)*
Please!	**¡Por favor!** *('pohr fah-'bohr)*
Thank you!	**¡Gracias!** *('grah-see-ahs)*
Very well.	**Muy bien** *('moo-ee 'bee-ehn)*
What's happening?	**¿Qué pasa?** *(keh 'pah-sah)*
What happened?	**¿Qué pasó?** *(keh pah-'soh)*
You're welcome!	**¡De nada!** *(deh 'nah-dah)*
I am...	**Estoy...** *(ehs-'toh-ee)*
fine	**bien** *('bee-ehn)*
OK	**regular** *(reh-goo-'lahr)*
not bad	**así-así** *(ah-'see ah-'see)*

 ## MÁS AYUDA

• Several words in English are spelled the same in Spanish, and they usually have the same meaning. But, watch out! They are NOT pronounced the same!

chocolate	*(choh-koh-'lah-teh)*
color	*(koh-'lohr)*
doctor	*(dohk-'tohr)*
final	*(fee-'nahl)*
hospital	*(oh-spee-'tahl)*
idea	*(ee-'deh-ah)*
natural	*(nah-too-'rahl)*
terror	*(teh-'rrohr)*

• The upside down exclamation point (¡) and question mark (¿) are found at the beginning of sentences, and must be used when you write in Spanish.

• Scan these other "excuse me" phrases:
Excuse me (if you cough or sneeze) **¡Perdón!** *(pehr-'dohn)*
Excuse me (if you need someone's attention) **¡Disculpe!** *(dees-'kool-peh)*

TEMAS CULTURALES

Friendly greetings in Spanish are used all day long. Being courteous is the key to establishing trust with your employee. Throughout the Spanish-speaking world, a smile and a pleasant word can lead to respect and complete cooperation.

DO YOU UNDERSTAND?
¿Entiende? *(ehn-tee-'ehn-deh)*

Once you finish with the greetings and common courtesies, you will face the inevitable problem of not being able to understand one another. To make things easier, practice a few of these one-liners with yourself. They send the message that you are doing the best you can!

Again.	**Otra vez** *('oh-trah behs)*
Do you speak English?	**¿Habla inglés?** *('ah-blah een-'glehs)*
How do you say it?	**¿Cómo se dice?** *('koh-moh seh 'dee-seh)*
How do you spell it?	**¿Cómo se deletrea?** *('koh-moh seh deh-leh-'treh-ah)*
I don't understand!	**¡No entiendo!** *(noh ehn-tee-'ehn-doh)*
I'm learning Spanish.	**Estoy aprendiendo el español** *(eh-'stoh-ee ah-prehn-dee-'ehn-doh ehl eh-spah-'nyohl)*
I speak little Spanish.	**Hablo poquito español** *('ah-bloh poh-'kee-toh ehs-pah-'nyohl)*
More slowly!	**¡Más despacio!** *(mahs deh-'spah-see·oh)*
Thanks for your patience.	**Gracias por su paciencia** *('grah-see·ahs pohr soo pah-see-'ehn-see·ah)*
What does it mean?	**¿Qué significa?** *(keh seeg-nee-'fee-kah)*
Word by word!	**¡Palabra por palabra!** *(pah-'lah-brah pohr pah-'lah-brah)*

If you get stuck, don't be afraid to communicate with hand gestures or facial expressions. And remember, they're probably having as much trouble understanding you, as you are understanding them!

6

HOW CAN I EXPRESS?
¿Cómo puedo expresar?
('koh-moh 'pweh-doh ehk-spreh-'sahr)

Spanish is full of common expressions that are used regularly in normal conversations. A lot can be communicated simply by saying a few simple phrases. Interject one of these whenever it is appropriate:

Bless you!	**¡Salud!** *(sah-'lood)*
Congratulations!	**¡Felicitaciones!** *(feh-lee-see-tah-see-'oh-nehs)*
Don't worry.	**No se preocupe** *(noh seh preh-oh-'koo-peh)*
Good idea.	**Buena idea** *('bweh-nah ee-'deh-ah)*
Good luck!	**¡Buena suerte!** *('bweh-nah 'swehr-teh)*
Go with God!	**¡Vaya con Dios!** *('bah-yah kohn-dee 'ohs)*
Happy Birthday!	**¡Feliz cumpleaños!** *(feh-'lees koom-pleh-'ah-nyohs)*
Have a nice day!	**¡Qué le vaya bien!** *(keh leh-'vah-yah 'bee-ehn)*
I see.	**Ya veo** *(yah 'beh-oh)*
I think so.	**Creo que sí** *('kreh-oh keh 'see)*
Maybe.	**Quizás** *(kee-'sahs)*
More or less.	**Más o menos** *(mahs oh 'meh-nohs)*
Not yet.	**Todavía no** *(toh-dah-'bee-ah noh)*
Ready?	**¿Listo?** *('lee-stoh)*
Right away!	**¡En seguida!** *(ehn seh-'gee-dah)*
Sure.	**Claro** *('clah-roh)*
Take it easy!	**¡Cúidese bien!** *('kwee-deh-seh 'bee-ehn)*
That depends.	**Depende** *(deh-'pehn-deh)*
That's great!	**¡Qué bueno!** *(keh 'bweh-noh)*
Welcome!	**¡Bienvenidos!** *(bee-ehn beh-'nee-dohs)*
What a shame!	**¡Qué lástima!** *(keh 'lah-stee-mah)*
Wow!	**¡Caramba!** *(kah-'rahm-bah)*

 MÁS AYUDA

• Bear in mind that most idiomatic expressions cannot be translated word for word. Therefore, try to memorize each phrase as one long string of individual sounds.

• Although Spanish expressions and words may differ slightly from region to region, the material in this guidebook is general enough to be understood by most Hispanics worldwide.

 REPASEMOS

Respond to these phrases in Spanish:

Ah-choo!	_____
¿Cómo está?	_____
¿Habla inglés?	_____
¡Adiós!	_____
¡Muchas gracias!	_____

Repasemos exercises are for your personal growth only, so no correct answers will be provided here. You'll have to check back in each section and compare your answers with the material presented.

¿Cómo se dice?

CHILD'S CHATTER
El Lenguaje de los Niños
(ehl lehn-'gwah-heh deh lohs 'nee-nyohs)

As a beginner in a foreign language, you are obviously going to need a selection of basic vocabulary words. The following items are divided into separate lists for easy practice and review. Much like a child whose native language is Spanish, these are probably the words you'll be uttering first:

Everyday Things
Las cosas diarias *(lahs 'koh-sahs dee-'ah-ree·ahs)*

| bathroom | **el baño** *(ehl 'bah-nyoh)* |
| bed | **la cama** *(lah 'kah-mah)* |

book	**el libro** *(ehl 'lee-broh)*
car	**el carro** *(ehl 'kah-rroh)*
chair	**la silla** *(lah 'see-yah)*
door	**la puerta** *(lah 'pwehr-tah)*
floor	**el piso** *(ehl 'pee-soh)*
food	**la comida** *(lah koh-'mee-dah)*
house	**la casa** *(lah 'kah-sah)*
key	**la llave** *(lah 'yah-beh)*
light	**la luz** *(lah loos)*
paper	**el papel** *(ehl pah-'pehl)*
pen	**el lapicero** *(ehl lah-pee-'seh-roh)*
pencil	**el lápiz** *(ehl 'lah-pees)*
room	**el cuarto** *(ehl 'kwahr-toh)*
table	**la mesa** *(lah 'meh-sah)*
trash	**la basura** *(lah bah-'soo-rah)*
water	**el agua** *(ehl 'ah-gwah)*
window	**la ventana** *(lah behn-'tah-nah)*
work	**el trabajo** *(ehl trah-'bah-hoh)*

 MÁS AYUDA

One effective technique to remember your vocabulary words is to write the name of an object in Spanish on a removable sticker, and place it on the object you are trying to learn.

People
La gente (lah 'hehn-teh)

baby	**el bebé** *(ehl beh-'beh)*
boy	**el niño** *(ehl 'nee-nyoh)*
girl	**la niña** *(lah 'nee-nyah)*
man	**el hombre** *(ehl 'ohm-breh)*

person	**la persona** *(lah pehr-'soh-nah)*
teenager (female)	**la muchacha** *(lah moo-'chah-chah)*
teenager (male)	**el muchacho** *(ehl moo-'chah-choh)*
woman	**la mujer** *(lah moo-'hehr)*

THE LAST WORD

Here's a set of vocabulary words that are mandatory for the beginner. These pronouns designate the "who" of a sentence.

I	**Yo** *(yoh)*
We	**Nosotros** *(noh-'soh-trohs)*
You	**Usted** *(oo-'stehd)*
You (plural)	**Ustedes** *(oo-'steh-dehs)*
She	**Ella** *('eh-yah)*
He	**Él** *(ehl)*
They (feminine)	**Ellas** *('eh-yahs)*
They (masculine)	**Ellos** *('eh-yohs)*

Practice:

How are you?	**¿Cómo está usted?** *('koh-moh eh-'stah oo-'stehd)*
He is a friend.	**Él es un amigo** *(ehl ehs oon ah-'mee-goh)*
They have a car.	**Ellos tienen un carro** *('eh-yohs tee-'eh-nehn oon 'kah-rroh)*
We are working.	**Nosotros estamos trabajando** *(noh-'soh-trohs eh-'stah-mohs trah-bah-'hahn-doh)*
I am fine.	**Yo estoy bien** *(yoh eh-'stoh-ee 'bee-ehn)*

 MÁS AYUDA

• **Nosotras** *(noh-'soh-trahs)* is "We" feminine:

We are female doctors. **Nosotras somos doctoras** *(noh'soh-trahs 'soh-mohs dohk-'toh-rahs)*

• You don't have to use the subject pronouns in every sentence. It's usually understood who's involved:

Nosotros somos *(noh-'soh-trohs 'soh-mohs)* and **somos** *('soh-mohs)* both mean "we are."

- **¿Y usted?** *(ee oo-'stehd)*, meaning, "And you?" is a great expression. **¿Como está?** *('koh-moh eh-'stah)* "How are you?" **Bien. ¿Y usted?** *('bee-ehn ee oo-'stehd)* "Fine. And you?"

The Family
La familia *(lah fah-'mee-lee·ah)*

Personal relationships within the Hispanic culture have special meaning, especially between family members. If you are trying to find out more about someone, you will eventually need words from this next list.

aunt	**la tía** *(lah 'tee-ah)*
brother	**el hermano** *(ehl ehr-'mah-noh)*
brother-in-law	**el cuñado** *(ehl koo-'nyah-doh)*
cousin	**el primo** *(ehl 'pree-moh)*
daughter	**la hija** *(lah 'ee-hah)*
daughter-in-law	**la nuera** *(lah 'nweh-rah)*
father	**el padre** *(ehl 'pah-dreh)*
father-in-law	**el suegro** *(ehl 'sweh-groh)*
granddaughter	**la nieta** *(lah nee-'eh-tah)*
grandfather	**el abuelo** *(ehl ah-'bweh-loh)*
grandmother	**la abuela** *(lah ah-'bweh-lah)*
grandson	**el nieto** *(ehl nee-'eh-toh)*
husband	**el marido** *(ehl mah-'ree-doh)*
mother	**la madre** *(lah 'mah-dreh)*
mother-in-law	**la suegra** *(lah 'sweh-grah)*
nephew	**el sobrino** *(ehl soh-'bree-noh)*
niece	**la sobrina** *(lah soh-'bree-nah)*
sister	**la hermana** *(lah ehr-'mah-nah)*
sister-in-law	**la cuñada** *(lah koo-'nyah-dah)*
son	**el hijo** *(ehl 'ee-hoh)*
son-in-law	**el yerno** *(ehl 'yehr-noh)*
uncle	**el tío** *(ehl 'tee-oh)*
wife	**la esposa** *(lah eh-'spoh-sah)*
parents	**los padres** *(lohs 'pah-drehs)*
relatives	**los parientes** *(lohs pah-ree-'ehn-tehs)*

TEMAS CULTURALES

The extended family may include in-laws, friends, or neighbors who have lent their support to family members in the past, so they may be asked to assist in decision-making. They may also want to help out at each other's place of employment.

Hispanic families respect the elderly. Older children, too, are given more responsibilities and are treated differently. When dealing with a large family, it is usually a good idea to find out who is in charge.

Because the traditional Hispanic family includes more that just its immediate members, you may want to consider learning the names for "relations" outside the immediate family:

boyfriend	**el novio** *(ehl 'noh-bee·oh)*
close friend	**el compañero** *(ehl kohm-pah-'nyeh-roh)*
girlfriend	**la novia** *(lah 'noh-bee·ah)*
godchild	**el ahijado** *(ehl ah-ee-'hah-doh)*
godfather	**el compadre** *(ehl kohm-'aph-dreh)*
godmother	**la comadre** *(lah koh-'mah-dreh)*
godparents	**los padrinos** *(lohs pah-'dree-nohs)*

 MÁS AYUDA

• Notice that the names for people, places, and things are either masculine or feminine, and so have either **el** *(ehl)* or **la** *(lah)* in front. **El** and **la** mean "the." Generally, if the word ends in the letter **o** there's an **el** in front (i.e., **el cuarto** *[ehl 'kwahr-toh]*, **el niño** *[ehl 'nee-nyoh]*). Conversely, if the word ends in an **a** there's a **la** in front (i.e., **la mesa** *[lah 'meh-sah]*, **la persona** *[lah pehr-'soh-nah]*). There are some exceptions: **el agua** *(ehl 'ah-gwah)*, **la mano** *(lah 'mah-noh)*, **el sofá** *(ehl soh-'fah)*.

• Words not ending in either an **o** or **a** need to be memorized (i.e., **el amor** *[ehl ah-'mohr]* **la paz** *[lah pahs]*). In the case of single objects, use **el** and **la** much like the word "the" in English: The house is big (**La casa es grande**) *(lah 'kah-sah ehs 'grahn-deh)*.

• Remember too, that **el** and **la** are used in Spanish to indicate a peson's sex. **El doctor** *(ehl dohk-'tohr)* is a male doctor, while **la doctora** *(lah dohk-'toh-rah)* is a female doctor. Here's how we change words to refer to the female gender: **la muchacha** *(lah moo-'chah-chah)*, **la niña** *(lah 'nee-nyah)*, **la bebé** *(lah beh-'beh)*.

The colors
Los colores (lohs koh-'loh-rehs)

black	**negro** *('neh-groh)*
blue	**azul** *(ah-'sool)*
brown	**café** *(kah-'feh)*
gray	**gris** *(grees)*
green	**verde** *('behr-deh)*
orange	**anaranjado** *(ah-nah-rahn-'hah-doh)*
purple	**morado** *(moh-'rah-doh)*
red	**rojo** *('roh-hoh)*
white	**blanco** *('blahn-koh)*
yellow	**amarillo** *(ah-mah-'ree-yoh)*

More Key Words
Más palabras claves (mahs pah-'lah-brahs 'klah-behs)

big	**grande** *('grahn-deh)*
small	**pequeño** *(peh-'keh-nyoh)*
good	**bueno** *('bweh-noh)*
bad	**malo** *('mah-loh)*
many	**muchos** *('moo-chohs)*
a few	**pocos** *('poh-kohs)*
more	**más** *(mahs)*
less	**menos** *('meh-nohs)*
much	**mucho** *('moo-choh)*
a little	**poco** *('poh-koh)*

• Are you ready to form a few phrases? You'll need the following:

for	**para** *('pah-rah)*	**para el niño** *('pah-rah ehl 'nee-nyoh)*
in, on, at	**en** *(ehn)*	**en el cuarto** *(ehn ehl 'kwahr-toh)*
of, from	**de** *(deh)*	**de la persona** *(deh lah pehr-'soh-nah)*
to	**a** *(ah)*	**a la casa** *(ah lah 'kah-sah)*

with	**con** *(kohn)*	**con el agua** *(kohn ehl 'ah-gwah)*
without	**sin** *(seen)*	**sin la comida** *(seen lah koh-'mee-dah)*

¡Sí! EN la cama
EN el libro
EN el trabajo.

- There are only two contractions in Spanish:

to the	**al** *(ahl)*	**al hombre** *(ahl 'ohm-breh)*
of the, from the	**del** *(dehl)*	**del libro** *(dehl 'lee-broh)*

- Use these words to link everything together:

  and **y** *(ee)*   or **o** *(oh)*   but **pero** *('peh-roh)*

- And don't forget:

  Thank you and goodbye!   **¡Gracias y adiós!** *('grah-see·ahs ee ah-dee-'ohs)*

REPASEMOS

- Translate these common objects:

  door   _____

  book   _____

  room   _____

  work   _____

  paper   _____

- Fill in the opposites:

  el niño *(ehl 'nee-nyoh)*   girl

  el hombre *(ehl 'ohm-breh)*   women

  blanco *('blahn-koh)*   black

  malo *('mah-loh)*   good

  bad

- Finish each sentence with the names of your friends:

  El agua es para el _____ *(ehl 'ah-gwah ehs 'pah-rah ehl ____)*

14

El carro es del _____ *(ehl 'kah-rroh ehs dehl ____)*

El trabajo es con el _____ *(ehl trah-'bah-hoh ehs kohn ehl ____)*

The Numbers
Los números *(lohs 'noo-meh-rohs)*

0 **cero** *('seh-roh)*	14 **catorce** *(kah-'tohr-seh)*
1 **uno** *('oo-noh)*	15 **quince** *('keen-seh)*
2 **dos** *(dohs)*	16 **dieciseis** *(dee-ehs-ee-'seh·ees)*
3 **tres** *(trehs)*	17 **diecisiete** *(dee-ehs-ee-see-'eh-teh)*
4 **cuatro** *('kwah-troh)*	18 **dieciocho** *(dee-ehs-ee-'oh-choh)*
5 **cinco** *('seen-koh)*	19 **diecinueve** *(dee-ehs-ee-noo-'eh-beh)*
6 **seis** *('seh·ees)*	20 **veinte** *('beh·een-teh)*
7 **siete** *(see-'eh-teh)*	30 **treinta** *('treh·een-tah)*
8 **ocho** *('oh-choh)*	40 **cuarenta** *(kwah-'rehn-tah)*
9 **nueve** *(noo-'eh-beh)*	50 **cincuenta** *(seen-'kwehn-tah)*
10 **diez** *(dee-'ehs)*	60 **sesenta** *(seh-'sehn-tah)*
11 **once** *('ohn-seh)*	70 **setenta** *(seh-'tehn-tah)*
12 **doce** *('doh-seh)*	80 **ochenta** *(oh-'chehn-tah)*
13 **trece** *('treh-seh)*	90 **noventa** *(noh-'behn-tah)*

For all the numbers in-between, just add **y** *(ee)*, which means "and":

21 **veinte y uno** *('beh·een-teh ee 'oo-noh)*

22 **veinte y dos** *('beh·een-teh ee dohs)*

23 **veinte y tres** *('beh·een-teh ee trehs)*

Sooner or later, you'll also need to know how to say the larger numbers in Spanish. They aren't that difficult, so practice aloud:

100	**cien** *('see-ehn)*
200	**doscientos** *(dohs-see-'ehn-tohs)*
300	**trescientos** *(trehs-see-'ehn-tohs)*

400	**cuatrocientos** *(kwah-troh-see-'ehn-tohs)*
500	**quinientos** *(keen-ee-'ehn-tohs)*
600	**seiscientos** *(seh-ees-see-'ehn-tohs)*
700	**setecientos** *(seh-teh-see-'ehn-tohs)*
800	**ochocientos** *(oh-choh-see-'ehn-tohs)*
900	**novecientos** *(noh-beh-see-'ehn-tohs)*
1000	**mil** *(meel)*
million	**millón** *(mee-'yohn)*

 MÁS AYUDA

The cardinal numbers are valuable around the house, too. Practice:

first	**primero** *(pree-'meh-roh)*
It's my first.	**Es mi primero.** *(ehs mee pree-'meh-roh)*
second	**segundo** *(seh-'goon-doh)*
It's my second.	_____
third	**tercero** *(tehr-'seh-roh)*
It's my third.	_____
fourth	**cuarto** *('kwahr-toh)*
	_____
fifth	**quinto** *('keen-toh)*
	_____
sixth	**sexto** *('sehks-toh)*
	_____
seventh	**séptimo** *('sehp-tee-moh)*
	_____
eighth	**octavo** *(ohk-'tah-boh)*
	_____
ninth	**noveno** *(noh-'beh-noh)*
	_____
tenth	**décimo** *('deh-see-moh)*
	_____

REPASEMOS

• Practice your numbers in Spanish every day. Reciting addresses, phone numbers, and license plate numbers are just a few ways to learn them quickly.

• Can you say these in Spanish?

53	_____	First	_____
12	_____	Third	_____
240	_____	Eighth	_____

THE FLIP-FLOP RULE
La regla del reverso *(lah 'reh-glah dehl reh-'behr-soh)*

As you begin to link your Spanish words together, you will find that sometimes words are positioned in reverse order. This "flip-flop" rule is applied when you give a description. The descriptive word goes *after* the word being described. Study these examples:

The big house.	**La casa grande** *(lah 'kah-sah 'grahn-deh)*
The green chair.	**La silla verde** *('lah 'see-yah 'behr-deh)*
The important man.	**El hombre importante** *(ehl 'ohm-breh eem-pohr-'tahn-teh)*

LET'S AGREE
Vamos a ponernos de acuerdo
('bah-mohs ah poh-'nehr-nohs deh ah-'kwehr-doh)

There are a few additional rules that must be followed when you are referring to more than one item in Spanish. First, the words **el** and **la** (see page 12), become **los** and **las**, respectively:

el baño *(ehl 'bah-nyoh)*
los baños *(lohs 'bah-nyohs)*
el muchacho *(ehl moo-'chah-choh)*
los muchachos *(lohs moo-'chah-hohs)*
la mesa *(lah 'meh-sah)*
las mesas *(lahs 'meh-sahs)*

la niña *(lah 'nee-nyah)*
las niñas *(lahs 'nee-nyahs)*

Also, not only do all the nouns and adjectives need to end in **s** or **es** to make the sentence plural, but when they are used together, the genders (the **o**'s and **a**'s), must match as well:

Two white doors.	**Dos puertas blancas** *(dohs 'pwehr-tahs 'blahn-kahs)*
Many red cars.	**Muchos carros rojos** *('moo-chohs 'kah-rrohs 'roh-hohs)*
Six little children.	**Seis niños pequeños** *('seh·ees 'nee-nyohs peh-'keh-nyohs)*

By the way, to say "a" *(ah)* in Spanish, use **un** *(oon)* for masculine words or **una** *('oo-nah)* for feminine words:

A floor	**Un piso** *(oon 'pee-soh)*
	Un piso azul *(oon 'pee-soh ah-'sool)*
A bed	**Una cama** *('oo-nah 'kah-mah)*
	Una cama grande *('oo-nah 'kah-mah 'grahn-deh)*

And to say "some," use **unos** *('oo-nohs)* or **unas** *('oo-nahs)*:

Some floors	**Unos pisos** *('oo-nohs 'pee-sohs)*
	Unos pisos azules *('oo-nohs 'pee-sohs ah-'soo-lehs)*
Some beds	**Unas camas** *('oo-nahs 'kah-mahs)*
	Unas camas grandes *('oo-nahs 'kah-mahs 'grahn-dehs)*

You will also need to know how to say "this" and "that" in Spanish. Remember to pronounce every letter:

that	ese *('eh-seh)* or esa *('eh-sah)*
	Ese amigo americano *('eh-seh ah-'mee-goh ah-meh-ree-'kah-noh)*
these	estos *('eh-stohs)* or estas *('eh-stahs)*
	Estos tacos malos *('eh-stohs 'tah-kohs 'mah-lohs)*
this	este *('eh-steh)* or esta *('eh-stah)*
	Este papel amarillo *('eh-steh pah-'pehl ah-mah-'ree-yoh)*
those	esos *('eh-sohs)* or esas *('eh-sahs)*
	Esos hombres buenos *('eh-sohs 'ohm-brehs 'bweh-nohs)*

REPASEMOS

• Translate into English:

nueve baños grandes *(noo-'eh-beh 'bah-nyohs 'grahn-dehs)*

nine big bathroom .

unas mesas buenas *('oo-nahs 'meh-sahs 'bweh-nahs)*

Some Tables good

esos cuartos amarillos *('eh-sohs 'kwahr-tohs ah-mah-'ree-yohs)*

Those rooms yellow .

• Put **el, la, los**, or **las** in front of these words:

<u>la</u> **basura** *(bah-'soo-rah)*
<u>los</u> **hombres** *('ohm-brehs)*
<u>el</u> **dinero** *(dee-'neh-roh)*

MÁS AYUDA

In order to accelerate the learning process, try a few of the following suggestions that have helped thousands of Spanish students as they struggle to "get started" in a foreign language:

• Listen to Spanish radio stations, watch a Spanish television station, or rent a Spanish language video.

• As you listen to someone speak Spanish, stop periodically to repeat those words that you understand. This is a tremendous way to figure out the meaning of their message.

• Practice memory exercises like visualization. For a word that is difficult to remember, picture a scene in your mind that relates to its form or meaning. For example, the word "chair," **silla** *('see-yah)*, is easy if you picture someone seated in a chair, flying off a cliff saying, "See-yah!"

ANY QUESTIONS?
¿Tiene preguntas? (tee-'eh-neh preh-'goon-tahs)

In order to survive in any foreign language, one must be aware of the basic question words. If you listen for these carefully, it won't be long before you'll be asking for information all by yourself:

How many?	**¿Cuántos?** *('kwahn-tohs)*
	¿Cuántos amigos? *('kwahn-tohs ah-'mee-gohs)*
How much?	**¿Cuánto?** *('kwahn-toh)*
	¿Cuánto es? *('kwahn-toh ehs)*
How?	**¿Cómo?** *('koh-moh)*
	¿Cómo está? *('koh-moh eh-'stah)*
What?	**¿Qué?** *('keh)*
	¿Qué pasa? *(keh 'pah-sah)*
When?	**¿Cuándo?** *('kwahn-doh)*
	¿Cuándo es la fiesta? *('kwahn-doh ehs lah fee-'eh-stah)*
Where?	**¿Dónde?** *('dohn-deh)*
	¿Dónde está la casa? *('dohn-deh eh-'stah lah 'kah-sah)*
Which?	**¿Cuál?** *('kwahl)*
	¿Cuál piso? *(kwahl 'pee-soh)*
Who?	**¿Quién?** *(kee-'ehn)*
	¿Quién es la señora? *('kee-'ehn ehs lah seh-'nyoh-rah)*

Whose?	**¿De quién?** *(deh kee-'ehn)*
	¿De quién es el libro? *(deh kee-'ehn ehs ehl 'lee-broh)*

We will be working with these words throughout this book. As a warm-up, look over this list again, and then cover up the English translations. Are you able to remember their meanings? As always, try pronouncing your new vocabulary as best you can.

 MÁS AYUDA

• **¿Por qué?** *(pohr keh)* means "why?" in English. To respond, simply repeat the word **porque** because it means "Because." (Note, however, that it is written differently.)

• Combine the words you know to create new questions phrases:

To whom?	**¿A quién?** *(ah kee-'ehn)*
With what?	**¿Con qué?** *(kohn keh)*
From where?	**¿De dónde?** *(deh 'dohn-deh)*
For when?	**¿Para cuándo?** *('pah-rah 'kwahn-doh)*

 REPASEMOS

Match each question word with its translation:

¿Quién? *(kee-'ehn)*	How many?
¿Cuántos? *('kwahn-tohs)*	What?
¿Qué? *(keh)*	Who?

MAKE THE CONNECTION
Haga la conexión ('ah-gah lah koh-nehk-see·'ohn)

Now that you can form short phrases on your own, it's time to join all of your words together. To accomplish this, you'll need to understand the difference between **está** *(eh-'stah)* and **es** *(ehs)*. Both words mean "is," but they're used differently.

The word **está** *(eh-'stah)* expresses a temporary state, condition, or location:

| The girl is fine. | **La niña está bien** *(lah 'nee-nyah eh-'stah 'bee-ehn)* |
| The girl is in the room. | **La niña está en el cuarto** *(lah 'nee-nyah eh-'stah ehn ehl 'kwahr-toh)* |

The word **es** expresses an inherent characteristic or quality, including origin and ownership:

The girl is small.	**La niña es pequeña** *(lah 'nee-nyah ehs peh-'keh-nyah)*
The girl is Maria.	**La niña es María** *(lah 'nee-nyah ehs mah-'ree-ah)*
The girl is American.	**La niña es americana** *(lah 'nee-nyah ehs ah-meh-ree-'kah-nah)*
The girl is my friend.	**La niña es mi amiga** *(lah 'nee-nyah ehs mee ah-'mee-gah)*

Can you see how helpful these two words can be? Countless comments can be made with only a minimum of vocabulary. You'll also need to talk about more than one person, place, or thing. To do so, replace **está** with **están,** and **es** with **son.** And don't forget that words must "agree" when you change to plurals:

The book is on the table.	**El libro está en la mesa** *(ehl 'lee-broh eh-'stah ehn lah 'meh-sah)*
The books are on the table.	**Los libros están en la mesa** *(lohs 'lee-brohs eh-'stahn ehn lah 'meh-sah)*
It's a man.	**Es un hombre** *(ehs oon 'ohm-breh)*
They are men.	**Son hombres** *(sohn 'ohm-brehs)*

Check out these other examples and read them aloud as you focus on their structure and meaning:

The chairs are black.	**Las sillas son negras** *(lahs 'see-yahs sohn 'neh-grahs)*
The papers are in the house.	**Los papeles están en la casa** *(lohs pah-'peh-lehs eh-'stahn ehn lah 'kah-sah)*
They are not important.	**No son importantes** *(noh sohn eem-pohr-'tahn-tehs)*
Are they good?	**¿Están buenos?** *(eh-'stahn 'bweh-nohs)*

The best way to learn how to use these words correctly is to listen to Spanish-speakers in real-life conversations. They constantly use **es**, **está**, **son**, and **están** to communicate simple messages.

Yo estoy aquí.
José está en la silla.
Yo soy mujer.
José es
un hombre.

HERE I AM!
¡Aquí estoy! (ah-'kee eh-'stoh-ee)

To say "I am" and "we are" in Spanish, you must also learn the different forms. As with **está** and **están**, the words **estoy** and **estamos** refer to the location or condition of a person, place, or thing. And just like **es** and **son**, the words **soy** and **somos** are used with everything else:

I am fine.	**Estoy bien** *(eh-'stoh-ee 'bee-ehn)*
We are in the room.	**Estamos en el cuarto** *(eh-'stah-mohs ehn ehl 'kwahr-toh)*
I am Lupe.	**Soy Lupe** *('soh-ee 'loo-peh)*
We are Cuban.	**Somos cubanos** *('soh-mohs koo-'bah-nohs)*

Now let's group all of these forms together. Look over the present tense forms of the verbs "ESTAR" and "SER".

To be	Estar	Ser
I'm	**estoy** *(eh-'stoh-ee)*	**soy** *('soh-ee)*
you're, he's, she's, it's	**está** *(eh-'stah)*	**es** *('ehs)*
they're, you're(plural)	**están** *(eh-'stahn)*	**son** *(sohn)*
we're	**estamos** *(eh-'stah-mohs)*	**somos** *('soh-mohs)*

Two other words, **estás** and **eres**, may also be used to mean "you are" among family, friends, and small children. However, since most of your beginning conversations will be between yourself and an employee, try focusing primarily on the eight words mentioned above.

"There is" and "there are" are very simple. In both cases you use **hay** *('ah·ee)*:

| There's one bathroom. | **Hay un baño** *('ah·ee oon 'bah-nyoh)* |
| There are two bathrooms. | **Hay dos baños** *('ah·ee dohs 'bah-nyohs)* |

I HAVE IT!
¡Lo tengo! (loh 'tehn-goh)

Tener *(teh-'nehr)* is another common linking word in Spanish and it means "to have." Its forms will become more necessary as you begin to create Spanish sentences on your own. Although these words will be discussed in more detail later, here are the basics to get you started:

To have	**Tener**
I have	**tengo** *('tehn-goh)*
you have, he has, she has, it has	**tiene** *(tee-'eh-neh)*
they have, you (plural) have	**tienen** *(tee-'eh-nehn)*
we have	**tenemos** *(teh-'neh-mohs)*

Study these examples:

| I have a problem. | **Tengo un problema** *('tehn-go oon proh-'bleh-mah* |
| She has a white car. | **Tiene un carro blanco** *(tee-'eh-neh oon 'kah-rroh 'blahn-koh)* |

| They have four children. | **Tienen cuatro niños** *(tee-'eh-nehn 'kwah-troh 'nee-nyohs)* |
| We have a big house. | **Tenemos una casa grande** *(teh-'neh-mohs 'oo-nah 'kah-sah 'grahn-deh)* |

Even though **tener** *(teh-'nehr)* literally means "to have," sometimes it is used instead of the verb **estar** *(eh-'stahr)* to express a temporary condition:

(I am) afraid	**(tengo) miedo** *(mee-'eh-doh)*
(we are) at fault	**(tenemos) la culpa** *(lah 'kool-pah)*
(they are) cold	**(tienen) frío** *('free-oh)*
(she is) 15 years old	**(tiene) quince años** *('keen-seh 'ah-nyohs)*
(I am) hot	**(tengo) calor** *(kah-'lohr)*
(they are) hungry	**(tienen) hambre** *('ahm-breh)*
(he is) sleepy	**(tiene) sueño** *('sweh-nyoh)*
(we are) thristy	**(tenemos) sed** *(sehd)*

Yo tengo calor.
Ella tiene calor.
¡ Nosotros tenemos calor !

 MÁS AYUDA

• To say "not" in Spanish, put the word **no** in front of the verb:

José is not my friend.	**José no es mi amigo** *(hoh-'seh noh ehs mee ah-'mee-goh)*
I do not have the job.	**No tengo el trabajo** *(noh 'tehn-goh ehl trah-'bah-hoh)*
There are no more.	**No hay más** *(noh 'ah·ee mahs)*

REPASEMOS

Match each question with the appropriate answer:

¿**Tiene sed?** *(tee-'eh-neh sehd)*
¿**Dónde está usted?** *('dohn-deh eh-'stah oo-'stehd)*
¿**Cuánta agua hay en el baño?** *('kwahn-tah 'ah-gwah 'ah·ee ehn ehl 'bah-nyoh)*
¿**Qué comida es buena?** *(keh koh-'mee-dah ehs 'bweh-nah)*
¿**Cuántas camas están en el cuarto?** *('kwahn-tahs 'kah-mahs eh-'stahn ehn ehl 'kwahr-toh)*

Mucha *('moo-chah)*
Dos *(dohs)*
Estoy en la casa *(eh-'stoh-ee ehn lah 'kah-sah)*
Sí *(see)*
Pizza *('peet-sah)*

¡HÁGALO, POR FAVOR!

As long as we're talking about working with Spanish-speaking employees, why not spend some time reviewing the following important command or request words. They are unique forms of "action verbs" that can be used all by themselves. Try using them in work-related situations — and always say **por favor** *(pohr fah-'bohr)*:

Please...	**Por favor...** *(pohr fah-'bohr)*
come	**venga** *('behn-gah)*
go	**vaya** *('bah-yah)*
hurry up	**apúrese** *(ah-'poo-reh-seh)*
run	**corra** *('koh-rrah)*
sit down	**siéntese** *(see-'ehn-teh-seh)*
stand up	**levántese** *(leh-'bahn-teh-seh)*
stop	**párese** *('pah-reh-seh)*
wait	**espere** *(eh-'speh-reh)*
walk	**camine** *(kah-'mee-neh)*
watch	**mire** *('mee-reh)*

There's no better way to learn than by doing. That's why each chapter in *Household Spanish* includes a section entitled ¡**HÁGALO, POR FAVOR!** where learners receive new lists of command words, followed by tips on how to practice them with Spanish-speakers. Watch out for this icon to learn even more command expressions!

MÁS AYUDA

• Do not try to translate the **se** ending on some commands. It is found throughout Spanish, and has a number of unique meanings. It's probably best if you attempt to say these words now, and ask questions about grammar later!

• Any vocabulary item can be learned quickly if it's practiced in conjunction with a command word. For example, to pick up the names for furniture, have a native Spanish-speaker command you to touch, look at, or point to things throughout the house. This exercise really works, and more importantly, it can be lots of fun:

Touch... **Toque** *('toh-keh)*
Look at... **Mire** *('mee-reh)*
Point to... **Señale** *(seh-'nyah-leh)*

...the table **(la mesa)**
(lah 'meh-sah)

REPASEMOS

Can you translate the following command phrases?

Siéntese en la silla. _____
Espere en la casa. _____
Apúrese, por favor. _____

SPANISH IN ACTION!

El español en acción (ehl eh-spah-'nyohl ehn ahk-see-'ohn)
Putting a few words together in a new language is a thrilling experience, but real communication begins once you start to use verbs or action words. Although **estar** *(eh-'stahr)*, **ser** *(sehr)*, and **tener** *(teh-'nehr)* are extremely useful, they do not express action. Learning how to use Spanish verbs will allow us to talk about what's going on in the world around us.

Spend a few moments memorizing this brief list of helpful beginning verbs. Notice that Spanish action words end in the letters **ar**, **er**, or **ir**, and they aren't to be confused with the command forms you learned earlier:

to clean   **limpiar** *(leem-pee-'ahr)*
to drive   **manejar** *(mah-neh-'hahr)*
to eat   **comer** *(koh-'mehr)*

to go	**ir** *(eer)*
to read	**leer** *(leh-'ehr)*
to run	**correr** *(koh-'rrehr)*
to sleep	**dormir** *(dohr-'meer)*
to speak	**hablar** *(ah-'blahr)*
to sweep	**barrer** *(barr-'ehr)*
to wash	**lavar** *(lah-'vahr)*
to work	**trabajar** *(trah-bah-'hahr)*
to write	**escribir** *(eh-skree-'beer)*

You can never learn enough action words in Spanish. Over one hundred verbs are listed in the specialized dictionary at the end of this book, so use it as a reference tool. When you come across a verb as you study and practice, look it up in Spanish or English to learn its base form and meaning.

 MÁS AYUDA

Many Spanish verb infinitives that relate to household Spanish are similar to English. Look at these examples:

plant	**plantar** *(plahn-'tahr)*
disinfect	**desinfectar** *(dehs-een-fehk-'tahr)*
install	**instalar** *(een-stah-'lahr)*
repair	**reparar** *(reh-pah-'rahr)*
move	**mover** *(moh-'behr)*

Can you add any others?

_____   _____

_____   _____

_____   _____

 ¡EL SUPERESPAÑOL!

One of the most effective ways to put your verbs into action is to combine them with simple phrases that create complete commands. For example, look what happens when you add these verb infinitives to **Favor de...** *(fah-'bohr deh)*, which implies, "Would you please...":

Please...   **Favor de...** *(fah-'bohr deh)*
  clean the bathroom   **limpiar el baño** *(leem-pee-'ahr ehl 'bah-nyoh)*
  go to the party   **ir a la fiesta** *(eer ah lah fee-'eh-stah)*
  speak in English   **hablar en inglés** *(ah-'blahr ehn een-'glehs)*

Here's another tip. By adding the word **no** in front of the verb, you communicate the command "don't."

Please don't clean the bathroom   **Favor de no limpiar el baño** *(fah-'bohr deh noh leem-pee-'ahr ehl 'bah-nyoh)*

Favor de is one of several key expressions that can be found in chapter segments entitled **EL SUPERESPAÑOL**. These phrases are combined with basic verb forms in order to raise your language skills to a whole new level.

 TEMAS CULTURALES

"Spanglish" is a universal trend to blend Spanish words with English words. All across America, millions of immigrants have come to realize that it's easier to communicate in "Spanglish" than in "Spanish." Notice the trend:

English	Spanglish	Spanish
carpet	**la carpeta**	**la alfombra**
	(lah kahr-'peh-tah)	*(lah ahl-'fohm-brah)*
lunch	**el lonche**	**el almuerzo**
	(ehl 'lohn-cheh)	*(ehl ahl-moo-'ehr-soh)*
muffler	**el mofle**	**el silenciador**
	(ehl 'moh-fleh)	*(ehl see-lehn-see-ah-'dohr)*
pie	**el pay**	**el pastel**
	(ehl 'pah·ee)	*(ehl pah-'stehl)*
truck	**la troca**	**el camión**
	(lah 'troh-kah)	*(ehl kah-mee-'ohn)*
typing	**el taipin**	**escribir a máquina**
	(ehl tah·ee-'peen)	*(eh-skree-'beer ah 'mah-kee-nah)*

Sometimes, all you need is English:

el break
el manager
el overtime
la happy hour
la party

MÁS AYUDA

Beware of "false cognates," or words that look similar in both languages but don't mean the same thing. Here are a few of my favorites:

conteste *(kohn-'teh-steh)* means answer, *not* contest
embarazada *(ehm-bah-rah-'sah-dah)* means pregnant, *not* embarrassed
pan *(pahn)* means bread, *not* pan
papa *('pah-pah)* means potato, *not* dad
pie *('pee-eh)* means foot, *not* pie

¡MÁS ACCIÓN!

In order to clearly express your thoughts in Spanish, you'll need to learn as many verb tenses as possible. Throughout this book, in sections entitled **¡MÁS ACCIÓN!**, you will be introduced to a variety of conjugated verb forms. By practicing the patterns, you'll soon be able to discuss past, present, and future events.

Let's begin with one of the easiest verb forms to use. It's the present progressive tense, and it refers to actions that are taking place at this moment. It is similar to our "-ing" form in English. Simply change the base verb ending slightly, and then combine the new form with the four forms of the verb **estar** *(eh-'stahr)*. The **ar** verbs become **-ando** *('ahn-doh)*, while the **er** and **ir** verbs become **-iendo** *(ee-'ehn-doh)*. Study these examples closely:

clean   **limpiar** *(leem-pee-'ahr)*
cleaning   **limpiando** *(leem-pee-'ahn-doh)*
We're cleaning the bathroom.   **Estamos limpiando el baño** *(eh-'stah-mohs leem-pee-'ahn-doh ehl 'bah-nyoh)*

eat	**comer** *(koh-'mehr)*
eating	**comiendo** *(koh-mee-'ehn-doh)*
The baby is eating.	**El bebé está comiendo** *(ehl beh-'beh eh-'stah koh-mee-'ehn-doh)*
write	**escribir** *(eh-skree-'beer)*
writing	**escribiendo** *(eh-skree-bee-'ehn-doh)*
I'm writing on the paper.	**Estoy escribiendo en el papel** *(eh-'stoh-ee eh-skree-bee-'ehn-doh ehn ehl pah-'pehl)*

 MÁS AYUDA

Some verbs change in spelling and pronunciation when you add the **-ndo** ending. Look at these examples:

follow	**seguir** *(seh-'geer)*
following	**siguiendo** *(see-gee-'ehn-doh)*
sleep	**dormir** *(dohr-'meer)*
sleeping	**durmiendo** *(duhr-mee-'ehn-doh)*
read	**leer** *(leh-'ehr)*
reading	**leyendo** *(leh-'yehn-doh)*

 REPASEMOS

Read the following story. How much of it can you understand?

Yo soy María. Estoy en mi cuarto *(yoh 'soh-ee mah-' ree-ah. eh-' stoh-ee ehn mee 'kwahr-toh)*

Estoy escribiendo en el libro de inglés *(eh-' stoh-ee eh-skree-bee-' ehn-doh ehn ehl 'lee-broh deh een-' glehs)*

Hay una mesa y dos sillas en el cuarto *('ah-ee 'oo-nah 'meh-sah ee dohs 'see-yahs ehn ehl 'kwahr-toh)*

El cuarto tiene una puerta y dos ventanas *(ehl 'kwahr-toh tee-' eh-neh 'oo-nah 'pwehr-tah ee dohs behn-' tah-nahs)*

WHOSE IS IT?
¿De quién es? (deh kee-'ehn ehs)

A similar group of Spanish words is used to indicate possession. They tell us "whose" it is:

It's my house.	**Es mi casa** *(ehs mee 'kah-sah)*
It's your, his, her or their house	**Es su casa** *(ehs soo 'kah-sah)*
It's our house.	**Es nuestra casa** *(ehs 'nweh-strah 'kah-sah)*

Notice what happens when you talk about more than one.

mi casa *(mee 'kah-sah)*	**mis casas** *(mees 'kah-sahs)*
su casa *(soo 'kah-sah)*	**sus casas** *(soos 'kah-sahs)*
nuestra casa *('nweh-strah 'kah-sah)*	**nuestras casas** *('nweh-strahs 'kah-sahs)*

Now try these other possessive words. Are you able to translate?

mine	**mío or mía** *('mee-oh, 'mee-ah)*
	Es mío *(ehs 'mee-oh)*
yours, his, hers, theirs	**suyo or suya** *('soo-yoh, 'soo-yah)*
	Es suya *(ehs 'soo-yah)*

 MÁS AYUDA

If something "belongs to " someone else, use **de** to indicate possession:

It's Mary's.	**Es de María** *(ehs deh mah-'ree-ah)*

| It's the hotel's. | Es del hotel *(ehs dehl oh-'tehl)* |
| It's his. | Es de él *(ehs deh ehl)* |

 TEMAS CULTURALES

Spanish verbs also have an informal **tú** *(too)* form, which is used between family members, small children, and friends. Since your relationship with Hispanics in the household will be at a professional level, the only form you'll need for now is the **usted** *(oo-'stehd)* or formal form. Notice these examples:

	Formal	Informal
Come	**Venga usted**	**Ven tú**
	('behn-gah oo-'stehd)	*(behn too)*
Sit	**Siéntese usted**	**Siéntate tú**
	(see-'ehn-teh-seh oo-'stehd)	*(see-'ehn-tah-teh too)*
You're working	**Usted está trabajando**	**Tú estás trabajando**
	(oo-'stehd eh-'stah trah-bah-'hahn-doh)	*(too eh-'stahs trah-bah-'hahn-doh)*

CHAPTER TWO

Capítulo Dos
(kah-'pee-too-loh dohs)

WHO ARE YOU? HOW ARE YOU?
¿Quién es usted? ¿Cómo está usted?
(kee-'ehn ehs oo-'stehd, 'koh-moh ehs-'tah oo-'stehd)

I NEED INFORMATION.
Necesito información.
('neh-seh-'see-toh lah een-fohr-mah-see·'ohn)

Hopefully, you've taken some time to read over and practice the basic language material found in Chapter One, for this next series of skills builds upon the fundamentals. We are going to develop sentences that meet our specific needs as we try to communicate with our Spanish-speaking help. Let's open with those questions that you'd ask anyone who was interested in employment. Pay close attention to the patterns:

What is your...?	**¿Cuál es su...?** *(kwahl ehs soo)*
address	**dirección** *(dee-rehk-see·'ohn)*
date of birth	**fecha de nacimiento** *('feh-chah deh nah-see-mee-'ehn-toh)*
first language	**primer lenguaje** *(pree-'mehr lehn-'gwah-heh)*
first name	**primer nombre** *(pree-'mehr 'nohm-breh)*
full name	**nombre completo** *('nohm-breh kohm-'pleh-toh)*
insurance company	**compañía de seguros** *(kohm-pah-'nyee-ah deh seh-'goo-rohs)*
last name	**apellido** *(ah-peh-'yee-doh)*
last place of employment	**último lugar de empleo** *('ool-tee-moh loo-'gahr deh ehm-'pleh-oh)*
license number	**número de licencia** *('noo-meh-roh deh lee-'sehn-see·ah)*

maiden name	**nombre de soltera** (*'nohm-breh deh sohl-'teh-rah*)
marital status	**estado civil** (*eh-'stah-doh see-'beel*)
middle initial	**segunda inicial** (*seh-'goon-dah ee-nee-see-'ahl*)
name	**nombre** (*'nohm-breh*)
nationality	**nacionalidad** (*nah-see·oh-nah-lee-'dahd*)
place of birth	**lugar de nacimiento** (*loo-'gahr deh nah-see-mee-'ehn-toh*)
relationship	**relación** (*reh-lah-see·'ohn*)
religion	**religión** (*reh-lee-hee·'ohn*)
social security number	**número de seguro social** (*'noo-meh-roh deh seh-'goo-roh soh-see-'ahl*)
telephone number	**número de teléfono** (*'noo-meh-roh deh teh-'leh-foh-noh*)
zip code	**zona postal** (*'soh-nah poh-'stahl*)

 ## MÁS AYUDA

Understanding and using question words in Spanish is crucial in gathering information. The best way to learn how to use question words in a foreign language is to focus on the first word of each sentence, and then try to get a general feel for what the person might be asking. Attempting to translate every word will only lead to frustration.

DO YOU KNOW?
¿Sabe? (*'sah-beh*)

In Spanish, there are two primary ways to say "to know." "To know something" requires the verb **saber** (*sah-'behr*), while "to know someone" requires the verb **conocer** (*koh-noh-'sehr*). Instead of working on all the conjugated forms of these new verbs, try to put them to practical use. Next time you need "to know," pull a line from the sentences below:

I don't know.	**No sé** (*noh seh*)
I don't know him.	**No lo conozco** (*noh loh koh-'nohs-koh*)
Do you know English?	**¿Sabe usted inglés?** (*'sah-beh oo-'stehd een-'glehs*)

Do you know her?	**¿La conoce a ella?** *(lah koh-'noh-seh ah 'eh-yah)*
I didn't know it.	**No lo sabía** *(noh loh sah-'bee-ah)*
I didn't know him.	**No lo conocía a él** *(noh loh koh-noh-'see-ah ah ehl)*

Obviously, **saber** *(sah-'behr)* works wonders at an interview. Ask your helpers about their professional skills:

Do you know how to speak English?	**¿Sabe hablar inglés?** *('sah-beh ah-'blahr een-'glehs)*
Do you know how to read and write?	**¿Sabe leer y escribir?** *('sah-beh leh-'ehr ee ehs-kree-'beer)*
Do you know how to...?	**¿Sabe...?** *('sah-beh)*
clean a house	**limpiar una casa** *(leem-pee-'ahr 'oo-nah 'kah-sah)*
cook	**cocinar** *(koh-see-'nahr)*
take care of children	**cuidar a los niños** *(kwee-'dahr ah lohs 'nee-nyohs)*
repair cars	**reparar los carros** *(reh-pah-'rahr lohs 'kah-rrohs)*
answer the phone	**contestar el teléfono** *(kohn-teh-'stahr ehl teh-'leh-foh-noh)*
iron	**planchar** *(plahn-'chahr)*
sew	**coser** *(koh-'sehr)*
take care of animals	**cuidar los animales** *(kwee-'dahr lohs ah-nee-'mah-lehs)*
mow the lawn	**cortar el pasto** *(kohr-'tahr ehl 'pah-stoh)*

TEMAS CULTURALES

There are numerous ways to find an outstanding housekeeper, babysitter, or gardener. While most are found through referrals from friends, some churches, schools, and employment agencies can provide you with names of potential employees. Still, the best method might be to run an English-Spanish ad in the local newspaper.

When referring to others by name, it really helps if you are able to pronounce the names correctly, as it makes them feel much more at ease. Always remember that Spanish is pronounced the way it is written. Also, it is not uncommon for someone in Spain or Latin America to have two last names. Don't get confused. Here's the order:

First name
primer nombre *(pree-'mehr 'nohm-breh)*

Father's last name
apellido paterno *(ah-peh-'yee-doh pah-'tehr-noh)*

Mother's last name
apellido materno *(ah-peh-'yee-doh mah-'tehr-noh)*

Juan Carlos	**Espinoza**	**García**
(wahn 'kahr-lohs)	*(ehs-pee-'noh-sah)*	*(gahr-'see-ah)*

 MÁS AYUDA

• The popular phrase "**¿Cómo se llama?**" *('koh-moh seh'yah-mah)* is usually translated to mean "What's your name?" However, you may also hear "**¿Cuál es su nombre?**" *(kwahl ehs soo 'nohm-breh)*, which means "Which is your name?"

• Not all Hispanic people have two first names, and there is no middle name as we know it.

• When a woman marries, she keeps her father's last name, followed by her husband's.

• Learn these abbreviations:

Mr.	**Sr.** *(seh-'nyohr)*
Mrs.	**Sra.** *(seh-'nyoh-rah)*
Miss	**Srta.** *(seh-nyoh-'ree-tah)*

 REPASEMOS

Translate and answer these questions about yourself:

¿Cuál es su...

date of birth	_____
last name	_____
telephone number	_____

¿Sabe...

sew	_____
cook	_____
speak English	_____

MORE QUESTIONS!
¡Más preguntas! (mahs preh-'goon-tahs)

Continue gathering information with more question words. Pronounce these next sentences correctly, and try to memorize any unfamiliar vocabulary.

Who?	**¿Quién?** *(kee-'ehn)*
Who is the boss?	**¿Quién es el jefe?** *(kee-'ehn ehs ehl 'heh-feh)*
Who is the owner?	**¿Quién es el dueño?** *(kee-'ehn ehs ehl 'dweh-nyoh)*

Who is the supervisor?	**¿Quién es el supervisor?** *(kee-'ehn ehs ehl soo-pehr-bee-'sohr)*
What?	**¿Qué?** *(keh)*
What number?	**¿Qué número?** *(keh 'noo-meh-roh)*
What time?	**¿Qué hora?** *(keh 'oh-rah)*
What type?	**¿Qué tipo?** *(keh 'tee-poh)*
How much?	**¿Cuánto?** *('kwahn-toh)*
How much does it cost?	**¿Cuánto cuesta?** *('kwahn-toh 'kweh-stah)*
How much experience?	**¿Cuánta experiencia?** *('kwahn-tah ehks-peh-ree-'ehn-see-ah*
How much time?	**¿Cuánto tiempo?** *('kwahn-toh tee-'ehm-poh)*
How many?	**¿Cuántos?** *('kwahn-tohs)*
How many bathrooms	**¿Cuántos baños?** *('kwahn-tohs 'bah-nyohs)*
How many children?	**¿Cuántos niños?** *('kwahn-tohs 'nee-nyohs)*
How many times?	**¿Cuántas veces?** *('kwahn-tahs 'beh-sehs)*
Why?	**¿Por qué?** *(pohr keh)*
Why are you applying?	**¿Por qué está aplicando?** *(pohr keh eh-'stah ah-plee-'kahn-doh)*
Why are you quitting?	**¿Por qué está renunciando?** *(pohr keh eh-'stah reh-noon-see-'ahn-doh)*
Why aren't you working?	**¿Por qué no está trabajando?** *(pohr keh noh eh-'stah trah-bah-'hahn-doh)*

Tengo un marido,
dos niñas,
tres niños,
y cuatro trabajos.

MÁS AYUDA

- Note the translation of this common question:

How old are you?   **¿Cuántos años tiene?** *('kwahn-tohs 'ah-nyohs tee-'eh-neh)*

- "Time" in general is **el tiempo** *(ehl tee-'ehm-poh)*. The specific "time" is **la hora** *(lah 'oh rah)*. "Time" in reference to an occurrence is **la vez** *(lah behs)*. Note the differences in the sentences above.

- Two of the most common question words used in a job interview are "when" and "where." As you practice the samples below, avoid focusing on how the sentences are structured or what the words mean — we'll learn all about those things later. For the time being, just have them available at an interview, and read aloud the ones you need:

¿Cuándo? *('kwahn-doh)*

When can you start?   **¿Cuándo puede empezar?** *('kwahn-doh 'pweh-deh ehm-peh-'sahr)*

When can you work?   **¿Cuándo puede trabajar?** *('kwahn-doh 'pweh-deh trah-bah-'hahr)*

When did you quit?   **¿Cuándo renunció?** *('kwahn-doh reh-noon-see-'oh)*

When did you work there?   **¿Cuándo trabajó allí?** *('kwahn-doh trah-bah-'hoh ah-'yee)*

When were you born?   **¿Cuándo nació?** *('kwahn-doh nah-see-'oh)*

¿Dónde? *('dohn-deh)*

Where are you from?   **¿De dónde es?** *(deh 'dohn-deh ehs)*

Where did you go to school?   **¿Adónde fue a la escuela?** *(ah-'dohn-deh fweh ah lah eh-'skweh-lah)*

Where did you work before?   **¿Dónde trabajó antes?** *('dohn-deh trah-bah-'hoh 'ahn-tehs)*

Where do you work now?   **¿Dónde trabaja ahora?** *('dohn-deh trah-'bah-hah ah-'oh-rah)*

Where do you live?   **¿Dónde vive?** *('dohn-deh 'bee-beh)*

 **REPASEMOS**

Match each question with its appropriate answer:

¿Quién es el dueño? *(kee-'ehn ehs ehl 'dweh-nyoh)*	Miami
¿Qué marca de carro? *(keh 'mahr-kah deh 'kah-rroh)*	21
¿Cuánto cuesta? *('kwahn-toh 'kweh-stah)*	11/24/53
¿Cuántos años? *('kwahn-tohs 'ah-nyohs)*	$10.00
¿Cuándo nació? *('kwahn-doh nah-see-'oh)*	Honda
¿Dónde vive? *('dohn-deh 'bee-beh)*	Sr. Brown

WHERE IS IT?
¿Dónde está? *('dohn-deh eh-'stah)*

Answering "where" questions is easy, because in most cases all you need is the name of a particular place. However, you'll probably have to specify an exact location once in awhile. As you vocalize the following words and phrases, feel free to point:

Where is the...?	¿Dónde está...? *('dohn-deh eh-'stah)*
apartment	**el apartamento** *(ehl ah-pahr-tah-'mehn-toh)*
condominium	**el condominio** *(ehl kohn-doh-'mee-nee-oh)*
house	**la casa** *(lah 'kah-sah)*
It's...	Está... *(eh-'stah)*
above	**encima** *(ehn-'see-mah)*
at the bottom	**en el fondo** *(ehn ehl 'fohn-doh)*
behind	**detrás** *(deh-'trahs)*
down	**abajo** *(ah-'bah-hoh)*
far	**lejos** *('leh-hohs)*
the first floor	**el primer piso** *(ehl pree-'mehr 'pee-soh)*
here	**aquí** *(ah-'kee)*
in front of	**en frente de** *(ehn 'frehn-teh deh)*
inside	**adentro** *(ah-'dehn-troh)*
next to	**al lado de** *(ahl 'lah-doh deh)*
outside	**afuera** *(ah-'fweh-rah)*
over there	**allá** *(ah-'yah)*
the second floor	**el segundo piso** *(ehl seh-'goon-doh 'pee-soh)*
straight ahead	**adelante** *(ah-deh-'lahn-teh)*
there	**allí** *(ah-'yee)*

to the left	**a la izquierda** *(ah lah ees-kee-'ehr-dah)*
near	**cerca** *('sehr-kah)*
to the right	**a la derecha** *(ah lah deh-'reh-chah)*
up	**arriba** *(ah-'rree-bah)*
east	**este** *('eh-steh)*
west	**oeste** *(oh-'eh-steh)*
north	**norte** *('nohr-teh)*
south	**sur** *(soor)*

By the way, **en** *(ehn)* (in, on, at) is one of the most commonly used words in Spanish. Watch:

She's at her house, on the second floor, in her room.

Está en su casa *(eh-'stah ehn soo 'kah-sah)*, **en el segundo piso** *(ehn ehl seh-'goon-doh 'pee-soh)*, **en su cuarto** *(ehn soo 'kwar-toh)*.

And always use **estar** *(eh-'stahr)* instead of **ser** *(sehr)* to tell where someone is located.

The man is here.	**El hombre está aquí** *(ehl 'ohm-breh eh-'stah ah-'kee)*

Be familiar with as many location words as you can:

face down	**boca abajo** *('boh-kah ah-'bah-hoh)*
face up	**boca arriba** *('boh-kah ah-'rree-bah)*
on its way	**en camino** *(ehn kah-'mee-noh)*
toward the back	**hacia atrás** *('ah-see-ah ah-'trahs)*

 MÁS AYUDA

• During an interview, try to use all the words that refer to one's location:

city	**la ciudad** *(lah see-ooh-'dahd)*
country	**el país** *(ehl pah-'ees)*
county	**el condado** *(ehl kohn-'dah-doh)*
state	**el estado** *(ehl eh-'stah-doh)*

(By the way, the U.S.A. **(Los Estados Unidos)** *(lohs eh-'stah-dohs oo-'nee-dohs)* is written **E.E.U.U.** in Spanish!)

REPASEMOS

Translate the following:

Estoy en mi cuarto *(eh-'stoh-ee ehn mee 'kwahr-toh)*
El cuarto está adentro de un apartamento *(ehl 'kwahr-toh eh-'stah ah-'dehn-troh deh oon ah-pahr-tah-'mehn-toh)*
El apartamento está encima de una casa *(ehl ah-pahr-tah-'mehn-toh eh-'stah ehn-'see-mah deh 'oo-nah 'kah-sah)*
La casa está enfrente de un hotel *(lah 'kah-sah eh-'stah ehn-'frehn-teh deh oon oh-'tehl)*

SAY WHEN

Diga cuándo ('dee-gah 'kwahn-doh)

Without a doubt, one of the most frequently asked questions in Spanish is **¿Cuándo?** *('kwahn-doh)*, so you'll need to be prepared when it comes time to answer. Begin by learning a few of the most popular responses:

A.M.	**de la mañana** *(deh lah mah-'nyah-nah*
P.M.	**de la tarde** *(deh lah 'tahr-deh)*
afterward	**después** *(deh-'spwehs)*
already	**ya** *(yah)*
always	**siempre** *(see-'ehm-preh)*
at dawn	**a la madrugada** *(ah lah mah-droo-'gah-dah)*
at dusk	**al anochecer** *(ahl ah-noh-cheh-'sehr)*
at sunset	**a la puesta del sol** *(ah lah 'pweh-stah dehl sohl)*
before	**antes** *('ahn-tehs)*
daily	**a diario** *(ah dee-ah-ree·oh)*

44

each day	**cada día** *('kah-dah 'dee-ah)*
early	**temprano** *(tehm-'prah-noh)*
every day	**todos los días** *('toh-dohs lohs 'dee-ahs)*
in a moment	**en un momento** *(ehn ehl moh-'mehn-toh)*
in a while	**en un rato** *(ehn oon 'rah-toh)*
just	**apenas** *(ah-'peh-nahs)*
last month	**el mes pasado** *(ehl mehs pah-'sah-doh)*
last night	**anoche** *(ah-'noh-cheh)*
last week	**la semana pasada** *(lah seh-'mah-nah pah-'sah-dah)*
late	**tarde** *('tahr-deh)*
later	**luego** *(loo-'eh-goh)*
lots of times	**muchas veces** *('moo-chahs 'beh-sehs)*
never	**nunca** *('noon-kah)*
next month	**el próximo mes** *(ehl 'prohk-see-moh mehs)*
next week	**la próxima semana** *(lah 'prohk-see-mah seh-'mah-nah)*
now	**ahora** *(ah-'oh-rah)*
once	**una vez** *('oo-nah behs)*
right now	**ahorita** *(ah-oh-'ree-tah)*
sometimes	**a veces** *(ah 'beh-sehs)*
soon	**pronto** *('prohn-toh)*
the day after tomorrow	**pasado mañana** *(pah-'sah-doh mah-'nyah-nah)*
the day before yesterday	**anteayer** *(ahn-teh-ah-'yehr)*
then	**entonces** *(ehn-'tohn-sehs)*
today	**hoy** *('oh-ee)*
tomorrow	**mañana** *(mah-'nyah-nah)*
tomorrow morning	**mañana por la mañana** *(mah-'nyah-nah pohr lah mah-'nyah-nah)*
tonight	**esta noche** *('eh-stah 'noh-cheh)*
until	**hasta** *('ah-stah)*
yesterday	**ayer** *(ah-'yehr)*
yet	**todavía** *(toh-dah-'bee-ah)*

Now practice:

¿Está trabajando hoy? *(eh-'stah trah-bah-'hahn-doh 'oh-ee)*
Are you working today?

¡Venga ahorita! *('behn-gah ah-oh-'ree-tah)*
Come right now!

A veces tengo problemas con mi carro *(ah 'beh-sehs 'tehn-goh proh-'bleh-mahs kohn mee 'kah-rroh)*
Sometimes I have problems with my car.

 MÁS AYUDA

Read over this next set of useful expressions. You never know when you'll need them:

Above all...	**Sobre todo...** *('soh-breh 'toh-doh)*
At first...	**Al principio...** *(ahl preen-'see-pee·oh)*
At last...	**Por fin...** *(pohr feen)*
At least...	**Por lo menos...** *(pohr loh 'meh-nohs)*
By the way...	**A propósito...** *(ah proh-'poh-see-toh)*
For example...	**Por ejemplo...** *(pohr eh-'hehm-ploh)*
In general...	**En general...** *(ehn heh-neh-'rahl)*
In other words...	**Es decir...** *(ehs deh-'seer)*
On the other hand...	**En cambio...** *(ehn 'kahm-bee·oh)*

Practice:

En general, estoy bien *(ehn heh-neh-'rahl eh-'stoh-ee 'bee-ehn)*
A propósito, _____ *(ah proh'-poh-see-toh)* (fill blank)

Al principio, venga a la casa *(ahl preen-'see-pee·oh 'behn-gah ah lah 'kah-sah)*

En cambio, _____ *(ehm 'kahm-bee·oh)* (fill blank)

AT WHAT TIME?
¿A qué hora? (ah keh 'oh-rah)

You can't discuss employment without mentioning the clock. Everyone has to check in or out sometime. To read the clock in Spanish, simply give the hour, followed by the word **y** *(ee)* (and), and the minutes. For example, 8:15 is **ocho y quince** *('oh-choh ee 'keen-seh)*. (Numbers were given on page 15.) Closely examine these other examples:

It's...	**Son las...** *(sohn lahs)*
At...	**A las...** *(ah lahs)*
10:40	**diez y cuarenta** *(dee-'ehs ee kwah-'rehn-tah)*
3:25	**tres y veinte y cinco** *(trehs ee 'bee·een-teh ee 'seen-koh)*
12:05 A.M.	**doce y cinco de la mañana** *('doh-seh ee 'seen-koh deh lah mah-'nyah-nah)*
4:00 P.M.	**cuatro de la tarde** *('kwah-troh deh lah 'tahr-deh)*
9:30 P.M.	**nueve y treinta de la noche** *(noo-'eh-beh ee 'treh·een-tah deh lah 'noh-cheh)*

 MÁS AYUDA

For 1:00 – 1:59, use **Es la...** *(ehs lah)* instead of **Son las...** *(sohn lahs)*. For example:

It's one o'clock.	**Es la una** *(ehs lah 'oo-nah)*.
It's one-thirty.	**Es la una y treinta** *(ehs lah 'oo-nah ee 'treh·een-tah)*.

 TEMAS CULTURALES

Not all folks panic when it comes to tardiness — some cultures put less emphasis on "beating the clock" than others. Be direct, and explain the importance of punctuality in certain areas of employment. But be sensitive to those who believe that personal health, family, and friends are valid reasons for being a little late. If you're a stickler for punctuality, inform your help of the concern:

You have to arrive early.
Tiene que llegar temprano *(tee-'eh-neh keh yeh-'gahr tehm-'prah-noh)*
Don't be late!
¡No llegue tarde! *(noh 'yeh-geh 'tahr-deh)*
If you're late again, I'll have to let you go.
Si llega tarde otra vez, tendré que despedirle *(see 'yeh-gah 'tahr-deh 'oh-trah behs, tehn-'dreh keh dehs-peh-'deer-leh)*

If missing work is a problem, or if there's a request for a day off, the best way to handle things is to ask **¿Cuál es el problema?** *('kwahl ehs ehl proh-'bleh-mah)* (What's the problem?) and focus only on the key words as you both work out a solution.

DO YOU KNOW THE DATE?
¿Sabe la fecha? *('sah-beh lah 'feh-chah)*
Spend a few minutes looking over the following Spanish words. They'll allow you to say things about the calendar and work schedules. Then stress each sound as you pronounce them aloud:

The days of the week
Los días de la semana
(lohs 'dee-ahs deh lah seh-'mah-nah)

Monday	**lunes** *('loo-nehs)*
Tuesday	**martes** *('mahr-tehs)*
Wednesday	**miércoles** *(mee-'ehr-koh-lehs)*
Thursday	**jueves** *(hoo-'eh-behs)*
Friday	**viernes** *(bee-'ehr-nehs)*
Saturday	**sábado** *('sah-bah-doh)*
Sunday	**domingo** *(doh-'meen-goh)*

Read these questions and answers. See how **los días** function as one-word responses to "when" questions:

When do I get paid?   **¿Cuándo me pagan?** *('kwahn-doh meh 'pah-gahn)*
Viernes *(bee-'ehr-nehs)*

48

When do I start?	**¿Cuándo empiezo?** *('kwahn-doh ehm-pee-'eh-soh)*
	Sábado *('sah-bah-doh)*
When do I work?	**¿Cuándo trabajo?** *('kwahn-doh trah-'bah-hoh)*
	Martes y jueves *('mahr-tehs ee joo-'eh-behs)*

 MÁS AYUDA

Most students of Spanish get confused when using the words **por** *(pohr)* and **para** *('pah-rah)* because they are similar in meaning. The differences between the two are not easy to explain, so it may be best to listen to Spanish-speakers as they use them, and then try them out in short, practical phrases. The worse that could happen is that you'd be wrong and might be corrected. Are you willing to take that risk? Here are a few common examples:

by Friday	**para el viernes** *('pah-rah ehl bee-'ehr-nehs)*
for two days	**por dos días** *(pohr dohs 'dee-ahs)*
in order to clean	**para limpiar** *('pah-rah leem-pee-'ahr)*
throughout the afternoon	**por la tarde** *(pohr lah 'tahr-deh)*

The months of the year
Los meses del año (lohs 'meh-sehs dehl 'ah-nyoh)

As far as the months are concerned, just remember that most words are similar in both Spanish and English.

49

January	**enero** *(eh-'neh-roh)*
February	**febrero** *(feh-'breh-roh)*
March	**marzo** *('mahr-soh)*
April	**abril** *(ah-'breel)*
May	**mayo** *('mah-yoh)*
June	**junio** *('hoo-nee·oh)*
July	**julio** *('hoo-lee·oh)*
August	**agosto** *(ah-'goh-stoh)*
September	**septiembre** *(sehp-tee-'ehm-breh)*
October	**octubre** *(ohk-'too-breh)*
November	**noviembre** *(noh-bee-'ehm-breh)*
December	**diciembre** *(dee-see-'ehm-breh)*

What's the date?
¿Cuál es la fecha? (kwahl ehs lah 'feh-chah)

To give the date, reverse the order of your words. For example, February 2nd becomes "the 2 of February," **el dos de febrero** *(ehl dohs deh feh-'breh-roh)*.

This is how you say "the first" in Spanish:

el primero *(ehl pree-'meh-roh)*.

January 1st   **el primero de enero** *(ehl pree-'meh-roh deh eh-'neh-roh)*

The year is often read as one large number:

1996   **mil novecientos noventa y seis** *(meel noh-beh-see-'ehn-tohs noh-'behn-tah ee 'seh·ees)*

Can you give today's date in Spanish? Use a calendar to practice all of your new vocabulary.

 MÁS AYUDA

- "On Friday" is **el viernes** *(ehl bee-'ehr-nehs)*, but "on Fridays" (every Friday) is **los viernes** *(lohs bee-'ehr-nehs)*.

- If you want, you can interject the following expressions:

the next one	**el próximo** *(ehl 'prohk-see-moh)*
the past one	**el pasado** *(ehl pah-'sah-doh)*
the weekend	**el fin de semana** *(ehl feen deh seh-'mah-nah)*

• Use **¿Hace cuánto?** *('ah-seh 'kwahn-toh)* for "How long ago?"

 REPASEMOS

Read these times and dates aloud in Spanish:

4:30, Friday, November 5
8:00, Monday, June 22
11:10, Sunday, April 14

Are you able to interpret the sample phrases below?

ago	**hace** *('ah-seh)*
	hace una semana *('ah-seh 'oo-nah seh-'mah-nah)*
between	**entre** *('ehn-treh)*
	entre las tres y las cuatro *('ehn-treh lahs trehs ee lahs 'kwah-troh)*
the following	**el siguiente** *(ehl see-gee-'ehn-teh)*
	el siguiente día *(ehl see-gee-'ehn-teh 'dee-ah)*
within	**dentro de** *('dehn-troh deh)*
	dentro de dos horas *('dehn-troh deh dohs 'oh-rahs)*

Read these sentences aloud as you continue to translate:

Estoy trabajando en una casa ahorita *(eh-'stoh-ee trah-bah-'hahn-doh ehn 'oo-nah 'kah-sah ah-oh-'ree-tah)*

Hay mucho trabajo aquí todos los días *('ah-ee 'moo-choh trah-'bah-hoh ah-'kee 'toh-dohs lohs 'dee-ahs)*

Estoy trabajando hoy en un cuarto grande *('eh-stoh-ee trah-bah-'hahn-doh 'oh-ee ehn oon 'kwahr-toh 'grahn-deh)*

51

Match the words on the left with their opposites.

temprano *(tehm-'prah-noh)*	**muchas veces** *('moo-chahs 'beh-sehs)*
mañana *(mah-'nyah-nah)*	**siempre** *(see-'ehm-preh)*
el próximo *(ehl 'prohk-see-moh)*	**tarde** *('tahr-deh)*
una vez *('oo-nah behs)*	**después** *(dehs-'pwehs)*
nunca *('noon-kah)*	**ayer** *(ah-'yehr)*
antes *('ahn-tehs)*	**el pasado** *(ehl pah-'sah-doh)*

 TEMAS CULTURALES

Learn the following expressions to greet your Spanish-speaking helper on special occasions:

Happy Easter!	**¡Felices Pascuas!** *(feh-lee-sehs 'pah-skahs)*
Happy New Year!	**¡Feliz Año Nuevo!** *(feh-'lees 'ah-nyoh noo-'eh-boh)*
Merry Christmas!	**¡Feliz Navidad!** *(feh-'lees nah-bee-'dahd)*

One tip concerning holidays is to mark on a calendar all the important dates that everyone plans to recognize or celebrate. Include birthdays, vacations, and all other special events. By inviting your employees to participate, you will have an opportunity to learn about major celebrations in other cultures.

EASY ANSWERS
Respuestas simples *(reh-'spweh-stahs 'seem-plehs)*

Another simple way to get personal information from potential employees is to ask questions that they can answer with **sí** or **no**:

Do you have the (a, an)...?	**¿Tiene...?** *(tee-'eh-neh)*
application	**la solicitud** *(lah soh-lee-see-'tood)* or **la aplicación** *(lah ah-plee-kah-see·'ohn)*
appointment	**la cita** *(lah 'see-tah)*
benefits	**los beneficios** *(lohs beh-neh-'fee-see·ohs)*
contract	**el contrato** *(ehl kohn-'trah-toh)*

criminal record	**los antecedentes penales** *(lohs ahn-teh-seh-'dehn-tehs peh-'nah-lehs)*
diploma	**el título** *(ehl 'tee-too-loh)*
driver's license	**la licencia de manejar** *(lah lee-'sehn-see·ah deh mah-neh-'hahr)*
employment	**el empleo** *(ehl ehm-'pleh-oh)*
equipment	**el equipo** *(ehl eh-'kee-poh)*
experience	**la experiencia** *(lah ehk-spoh roo 'ehn-see·ah)*
forms	**los formularios** *(lohs fohr-moo-'lah-ree-ohs)*
identification	**la identificación** *(lah ee-dehn-tee-fee-kah-see·'ohn)*
insurance	**el seguro** *(ehl seh-'goo-roh)*
interview	**la entrevista** *(lah ehn-treh-'bee-stah)*
medical problems	**los problemas médicos** *(lohs proh-'bleh-mahs 'meh-dee-kohs)*
meeting	**la reunión** *(lah reh-oo-nee-'ohn)*
question	**la pregunta** *(lah preh-'goon-tah)*
references	**las referencias** *(lahs reh-feh-'rehn-see·ahs)*
schedule	**el horario** *(ehl oh-'rah-ree·oh)*
time card	**la tarjeta de trabajo** *(lah tahr-'heh-tah deh trah-'bah-hoh)*
training	**el entrenamiento** *(ehl ehn-treh-nah-mee-'ehn-toh)*
transportation	**el transporte** *(ehl trahns-'pohr-teh)*
uniform	**el uniforme** *(ehl oo-nee-'fohr-meh)*
workman's compensation	**la compensación de obrero** *(lah kohm-pehn-sah-see·'ohn deh oh-'breh-roh)*

Keep going, but this time check on their current status or condition. Remember that every one of the words ending in "o" is in masculine mode, that is, **¿Está ocupado?** means that you are asking a *male* employee if he is busy or not. To address a female change the "o" ending into an "a" (**¿Está ocupada?**). Also, do use the word **está** with these adjectives:

Are you...?	**¿Está usted...?** *(eh-'stah oo-'stehd)*
available	**disponible** *(dees-poh-'nee-bleh)*
bored	**aburrido** *(ah-boo-'ree-doh)*
busy	**ocupado** *(oh-koo-'pah-doh)*
excited	**excitado** *(ehk-see-'tah-doh)*
happy	**contento** *(kohn-'tehn-toh)*
interested	**interesado** *(een-teh-reh-'sah-doh)*
nervous	**nervioso** *(nehr-bee-'oh-soh)*
sad	**triste** *('tree-steh)*
sick	**enfermo** *(ehn-'fehr-moh)*
surprised	**sorprendido** *(sohr-prehn-'dee-doh)*
tired	**cansado** *(kahn-'sah-doh)*
upset	**enojado** *(eh-noh-'hah-doh)*
well	**bien** *('bee-ehn)*
worried	**preocupado** *(preh-oh-koo-'pah-doh)*

Two important expressions to learn are:

You are...	**Usted está...** *(oo-'stehd eh-'stah)*
fired	**despedido** *(deh-speh-'dee-doh)*
hired	**contratado** *(kohn-trah-'tah-doh)*

In place of current status or condition questions with **está** *(eh-'stah)*, move on to more personal and serious concerns with **es** *(ehs)*:

 PALABRAS CLAVES

Are you...?	¿Es usted...? *(ehs oo-'stehd)*
divorced	**divorciado** *(dee-bohr-see-'ah-doh)*
married	**casado** *(kah-'suh-doh)*
separated	**separado** *(seh-pah-'rah-doh)*
single	**soltero** *(sohl-'teh-roh)*
widowed	**viudo** *(bee-'oo-doh)*
Argentinian	**argentino** *(ahr-hehn-'tee-noh)*
Bolivian	**boliviano** *(boh-lee-bee-'ah-noh)*
Brazilian	**brasileño** *(brah-see-'leh-nyoh)*
Chilean	**chileno** *(chee-'leh-noh)*
Costa Rican	**costarricense** *(koh-stah-ree-'sehn-seh)*
Cuban	**cubano** *(koo-'bah-noh)*
Dominican	**dominicano** *(doh-mee-nee-'kah-noh)*
Ecuadorean	**ecuatoriano** *(eh-kwah-toh-ree-'ah-noh)*
Guatemalan	**guatemalteco** *(gwah-teh-mahl-'teh-koh)*
Haitian	**haitiano** *(ah-ee-tee-'ah-noh)*
Honduran	**hondureño** *(ohn-doo-'reh-nyoh)*
Mexican	**mexicano** *(meh-hee-'kah-noh)*
Nicaraguan	**nicaragüense** *(nee-kah-rah-'gwehn-seh)*
Panamanian	**panameño** *(pah-nah-'meh-nyoh)*
Paraguayan	**paraguayo** *(pah-rah-'gwah-yoh)*
Peruvian	**peruano** *(peh-roo-'ah-noh)*
Puerto Rican	**puertorriqueño** *(pwehr-toh-rree-'keh-nyoh)*
Salvadorean	**salvadoreño** *(sahl-bah-doh-'reh-nyoh)*
Spanish	**español** *(eh-spah-'nyohl)*
Uruguayan	**uruguayo** *(oo-roo-'gwah-yoh)*
Venezuelan	**venezolano** *(beh-neh-soh-'lah-noh)*
a legal resident	**un residente legal** *(oon reh-see-'dehn-teh leh-'gahl)*
a U.S. citizen	**un ciudadano de los Estados Unidos** *(oon see-oo-dah-'dah-noh deh lohs eh-'stah-dohs oo-'nee-dohs)*
a veteran	**un veterano** *(oon beh-teh-'rah-noh)*

55

Again, all of the above words ending in "o" are meant for males. Change the ending to "a" to address females. See both choices when we learn about religious affiliation:

I am...	Soy *('soh-ee)...*
Catholic	**católico** *(kah-'toh-lee-koh)* or **católica** *(kah-'toh-lee-kah)*
Christian	**cristiano** *(krees-tee-'ah-noh)* or **cristiana** *(krees-tee-'ah-nah)*
Jewish	**judío** *(hoo-'dee-oh)* or **judía** *(hoo-'dee-ah)*
Moslem	**musulmán** *(moo-sool-'mahn)* or **musulmana** *(moo-sool-'mah-nah)*

 TEMAS CULTURALES

Most of Latin America is Roman Catholic, so you may notice the religious influence during your association with some Hispanics. Using God, **Dios** *(dee-'ohs)* in conversation, attending daily Mass, **la misa** *(lah 'mee-sah)* or observing Catholic traditions are simple signs of their devout faith. Remember that respect and sensitivity are always in demand when topics center around cultural and religious beliefs or personal opinions.

PLEASE DESCRIBE
Describa, por favor *(dehs-'kree-bah)*

Care to know more about the person you're hiring? Ask around, and use the words below. Remember that descriptive word endings change from an "o" to an "a" when they refer to females:

Is he...?	¿Es...? *(ehs)*
ambitious	**ambicioso** *(ah-bee-see-'oh-soh)*
brave	**valiente** *(bah-lee-'ehn-teh)*
bright	**brillante** *(bree-'yahn-teh)*
clean	**limpio** *('leem-pee-oh)*
cruel	**cruel** *(kroo-'ehl)*
famous	**famoso** *(fah-'moh-soh)*
fast	**rápido** *('rah-pee-doh)*
fat	**gordo** *('gohr-doh)*

funny	**chistoso** *(chees-'toh-soh)*
good-looking	**guapo** *('gwah-poh)*
healthy	**saludable** *(sah-loo-'dah-bleh)*
imaginative	**imaginativo** *(ee-mah-hee-nah-'tee-boh)*
industrious	**trabajador** *(trah-bah-hah-'dohr)*
intelligent	**inteligente** *(een-teh-lee-'hehn-teh)*
lazy	**perezoso** *(peh-reh-'soh-soh)*
mature	**maduro** *(mah-'doo-roh)*
new	**nuevo** *(noo-'eh-boh)*
nice	**simpático** *(seem-'pah-tee-koh)*
old	**viejo** *(bee-'eh-hoh)*
older	**mayor** *(mah-'yohr)*
patient	**paciente** *(pah-see-'ehn-teh)*
polite	**cortés** *(kohr-'tehs)*
poor	**pobre** *('poh-breh)*
prompt	**puntual** *(poon-too-'ahl)*
quiet	**quieto** *(kee-'eh-toh)*
rich	**rico** *('ree-koh)*
short (in height)	**bajo** *('bah-hoh)*
slow	**lento** *('lehn-toh)*
strange	**raro** *('rah-roh)*
strong	**fuerte** *('fwehr-teh)*
sure	**seguro** *(seh-'goo-roh)*
tall	**alto** *('ahl-toh)*
thin	**delgado** *(dehl-'gah-doh)*
valuable	**valioso** *('bah-lee-'oh-soh)*

weak	**débil** *('deh-beel)*
young	**joven** *('hoh-behn)*
younger	**menor** *(meh-'nohr)*

 ## REPASEMOS

Can you guess at the meanings of these?

fantástico *(fahn-'tahs-tee-koh)*
horrible *(oh-'rree-bleh)*
magnífico *(mahg-'nee-fee-koh)*
maravilloso *(mah-rah-bee-'yoh-soh)*
necesario *(neh-seh-'sah-ree·oh)*
posible *(poh-'see-bleh)*
probable *(proh-'bah-bleh)*
terrible *(teh-'rree-bleh)*

Work on expanding your descriptive vocabulary by reading the list of opposites below. They will help as you try to explain things in detail.

It's...	**Es...** *(ehs)*
	Está... *(eh-'stah)*
cheap	**barato** *(bah-'rah-toh)*
clean	**limpio** *('leem-pee·oh)*
deep	**profundo** *(proh-'foon-doh)*
difficult	**difícil** *(dee-'fee-seel)*
dirty	**sucio** *('soo-see·oh)*
dry	**seco** *('seh-koh)*
easy	**fácil** *('fah-seel)*
expensive	**caro** *('kah-roh)*
hard	**duro** *('doo-roh)*
long	**largo** *('lahr-goh)*
narrow	**estrecho** *(eh-'streh-choh)*
pretty	**bonito** *(boh-'nee-toh)*
rough	**áspero** *('ahs-peh-roh)*
shallow	**bajo** *('bah-hoh)*
short (in length)	**corto** *('kohr-toh)*
smooth	**liso** *('lee-soh)*
soft	**blando** *('blahn-doh)*
thick	**grueso** *(groo-'eh-soh)*

ugly	**feo** *('feh-oh)*
wet	**mojado** *(moh-'hah-doh)*
wide	**ancho** *('ahn-choh)*

Keep in mind that in Spanish, the descriptive adjective usually goes after the noun:

It's an _____ job.	**Es un trabajo** _____ *(ehs oon trah-'bah-hoh)*
excellent	**excelente** *(ehk-seh-'lehn-teh)*
important	**importante** *(eem-pohr-'tahn-teh)*
interesting	**interesante** *(een-teh-reh-'sahn-teh)*
He's a _____ man.	**Es un hombre** _____ *(ehs oon 'ohm-breh)*
bald	**calvo** *('kahl-boh)*
blond	**rubio** *('roo-bee·oh)*
dark-haired	**moreno** *(moh-'reh-noh)*
red-headed	**pelirrojo** *(peh-lee-'rroh-hoh)*

 MÁS AYUDA

• Some descriptive words change a little and go immediately in front of the noun.

Él es un buen amigo *(ehl ehs oon bwehn ah-'mee-goh)*
He's a very good friend.

Ella es una gran persona *('eh-yah ehs 'oo-nah grahn pehr-'soh-nah)*
She's a great person.

Ella está mal preparada *('eh-yah eh-'stah mahl preh-pah-'rah-dah)*
She is poorly prepared.

• Not all descriptive words change because of the **o** or **a** endings.

For example:

| It's a big taco. | **Es un taco grande** *(ehs oon 'tah-koh 'grahn-deh)* |
| It's a big enchilada. | **Es una enchilada grande** *(ehs 'oo-nah ehn-chee-'lah-dah 'grahn-deh)* |

• Description words that begin with **des** or **in** often refer to an opposite:

| correct | **(correcto)** *('koh-'rrehk-toh)* |
| incorrect | **(incorrecto)** *(een-koh-'rrehk-toh)* |

| employed | (**empleado**) *(ehm-pleh-'ah-doh)* |
| unemployed | (**desempleado**) *(dehs-ehm-pleh-'ah-doh)* |

• Use these little words to compare things:

a little big	**un poco grande** *(oon 'poh-koh 'grahn-deh)*
as big as	**tan grande como** *(tahn 'grahn-deh)*
bigger than	**más grande que** *(mahs 'grahn-deh keh)*
biggest	**el** (or **la**) **más grande** *(ehl* (or *lah) mahs 'grahn-deh)*
so big	**tan grande** *(tahn 'grahn-deh)*
too big	**demasiado grande** *(deh-mah-see-'ah-doh 'grahn-deh)*
very big	**muy grande** *('moo-ee 'grahn-deh)*

Practice:

Carlos es más grande que Pedro *('kahr-lohs ehs mahs 'grahn-deh keh 'peh-droh)*

Carlos es tan grande como una casa *('kahr-lohs ehs tahn 'grahn-deh 'koh-moh 'oo-nah 'kah-sah)*

Carlos es el más grande *('kahr-lohs ehs ehl mahs 'grahn-deh)*

Juana:
un poco
grande

María:
másgrande
que Juana

Luisa:
La,
más
grande

 **REPASEMOS**

Match the opposites:

barato	**difícil** *(dee-'fee-seel)*
bonito	**rico** *('ree-koh)*
fácil	**caro** *('kah-roh)*
nuevo	**viejo** *(bee-'eh-hoh)*
pobre	**lento** *('lehn-toh)*
rápido	**feo** *('feh-oh)*
sucio	**limpio** *('leem-pee·oh)*

Translate:

¿Tiene usted...	**horario?** *(oh-'rah-ree·oh)*
	cita? *('see-tah)*
	seguro? *(seh-'goo-roh)*
¿Está usted...	**triste?** *('trees-teh)*
	cansado? *(kahn-'sah-doh)*
	contratado? *(kohn-'trah-doh)*
¿Es usted...	**casado?** *(ehs oo-'stehd kah-'sah-doh)*
	ciudadano? *(see-oo-dah-'dah-noh)*
	simpático? *(seem-'pah-tee-koh)*

GOOD JOB!

¡Buen trabajo! *(bwehn trah-'bah-hoh)*

Besides giving a description, the word **es** *(ehs)* is also used to identify a person's occupation. Continue interviewing people about their areas of expertise, and switch to the **a** ending when it's a female:

Have you ever been a (an)...?	**¿Ha sido usted un (una)...?** *(ah 'see-doh oo-'stehd oon ('oo-nah)*
artist	**artista** *(ahr-'tees-tah)*
assistant	**asistente** *(ah-sees-'tehn-teh)*
babysitter	**niñero** *(nee-'nyeh-roh)*
bartender	**cantinero** *(kahn-tee-'neh-roh)*
bellhop	**botones** *(boh-'toh-nehs)*

busboy	ayudante de camarero *(ah-yoo-'dahn-teh deh kah-mah-'reh-roh)*
carpenter	carpintero *(kahr-peen-'teh-roh)*
cashier	cajero *(kah-'heh-roh)*
chauffeur	chofer *(cho-'fehr)*
clerk	dependiente *(deh-pehn-dee-'ehn-teh)*
client	cliente *(klee-'ehn-teh)*
cook	cocinero *(koh-see-'neh-roh)*
dishwasher	lavaplatos *(lah-vah 'plah-tohs)*
driver	chofer *(choh-'fehr)*
employee	empleado *(ehm-pleh-'ah-doh)*
farmer	campesino *(kahm-peh-'see-noh)*
gardener	jardinero *(hahr-dee-'neh-roh)*
guide	guía *('gee-ah)*
helper	ayudante *(ah-yoo-'dahn-teh)*
janitor	conserje *(kohn-'sehr-heh)*
laborer	obrero *(oh-'breh-roh)*
mail carrier	cartero *(kahr-'teh-roh)*
manager	gerente *(heh-'rehn-teh)*
mechanic	mecánico *(meh-'kah-nee-koh)*
musician	músico *('moo-see-koh)*
nurse	enfermero *(ehn-fehr-'meh-roh)*
painter	pintor *(peen-'tohr)*
plumber	plomero *(ploh-'meh-roh)*
priest	cura *('koo-rah)*
salesman	vendedor *(behn-deh-'dohr)*
secretary	secretario *(seh-kreh-'tah-ree·oh)*
servant	criado *(kree-'ah-doh)*
soldier	soldado *(sohl-'dah-doh)*
student	estudiante *(ehs-too-dee-'ahn-teh)*
tailor	sastre *('sahs-treh)*
teacher	maestro *(mah-'eh-stroh)*
truck driver	camionero *(kah-mee-oh-'neh-roh)*
waiter	mesero *(meh-'seh-roh)*
worker	trabajador *(trah-bah-hah-'dohr)*

Here are some more standard professions. Try them with **soy** *('soh-ee)* instead of **es** *(ehs):*

I'm the (a, an)...	**Soy...** *('soh-ee)*
architect	**arquitecto** *(ahr-kee-'tehk-toh)*
dentist	**dentista** *(dehn-'tees-tah)*
doctor	**doctor** *(dohk-'tohr)*
engineer	**ingeniero** *(een-heh-nee-'eh-roh)*
firefighter	**bombero** *(bohm-'beh-roh)*
lawyer	**abogado** *(ah-boh-'gah-doh)*
librarian	**bibliotecario** *(bee-blee-oh-teh-'kah-ree·oh)*
pilot	**piloto** *(pee-'loh-toh)*
police officer	**policía** *(poh-lee-'see-ah)*
receptionist	**recepcionista** *(reh-sehp-see·oh-'nees-tah)*
secretary	**secretario** *(seh-kreh-'tah-ree-oh)*
surgeon	**cirujano** *(see-roo-'hah-noh)*
telephone operator	**telefonista** *(teh-leh-foh-'nee-stah)*
typist	**mecanógrafo** *(meh-kah-'noh-grah-foh)*

Practice these new words in sentences:

- boss **el jefe** *(ehl 'heh-feh)* or **la jefa** *(lah 'heh-fah)*

Carlos es el jefe importante *('kahr-lohs ehs ehl 'heh-feh eem-pohr-'tahn-teh)*

María es la jefa en el banco *(María ehs lah 'heh-fah ehn ehl 'bahn-koh)*

- employer **el empresario** *(ehl ehm-preh-'sah-ree·oh)* or **la empresaria** *(lah ehm-preh-'sah-ree-ah)*

¿Quién es el empresario? *(kee-'ehn ehs ehl ehm-preh-'sah-ree·oh)*

La empresaria es importante *(lah ehm-preh-'sah-ree-ah ehs eem-pohr-'tahn-teh)*

- owner **el dueño** *(ehl 'dweh-nyoh)* or **la dueña** *(lah 'dweh-nyah)*

Soy el dueño de la casa *('soh-ee ehl 'dweh-nyoh deh lah 'kah-sah)*

Ana es la dueña de la silla *(Anah ehs lah 'dweh-nyah deh lah 'see-ya)*

 TEMAS CULTURALES

It's no surprise that some occupations can be spoken in Spanglish:

la babysitter
el manager
la nurse
el principal
la security

Your worker may be shy or have difficulty in expressing his or her need. Learn these expressions and use them!

Do you need...?	**¿Necesita...?** *(neh-seh-'see-tah)*
bus fare	**dinero para el autobús** *(dee-'neh-roh 'pah-rah ehl ow-toh-'boos)*
day off	**un día de descanso** *(oon 'dee-ah deh dehs-'kahn-soh)*
fixed salary	**un sueldo fijo** *(oon 'swehl-doh 'fee-hoh)*
free time	**tiempo libre** *(tee-'ehm-poh 'lee-breh)*
full-time work	**trabajo completo** *(trah-'bah-hoh kohm-'pleh-toh)*

64

holiday	**un día de fiesta** *(oon 'dee-ah deh fee-'ehs-tah)*
more privileges	**más privilegios** *(mahs pree-bee-'leh-hee·ohs)*
part-time work	**trabajo parcial** *(trah-'bah-hoh pahr-see-'ahl)*
private bathroom	**un baño privado** *(oon 'bah-nyoh pree-'bah-doh)*
raise	**un aumento del sueldo** *(oon ow-'mehn-toh dehl 'swehl-doh)*
ride	**alguien que le lleve** *('ahl-gee-ehn keh leh 'yeh-beh)*
to have visitors	**tener visitantes** *(teh-'nehr bee-see-'tahn-tehs)*
to live with us	**vivir con nosotros** *(bee-'beer kohn noh-'soh-trohs)*
to use the telephone	**usar el teléfono** *(oo-'sahr ehl teh-'leh-foh-noh)*
It's (a, an)...	**Es...** *(ehs)*
childcare	**el cuidado de los niños** *(ehl kwee-'dah-doh deh lohs 'nee-nyohs)*
chore	**una tarea** *('oo-nah tah-'reh-ah)*
domestic service	**el servicio doméstico** *(ehl sehr-'bee-see·oh doh-'meh-stee-koh)*
errand	**un mandado** *(oon mahn-'dah-doh)*
floor waxing	**el encerado del piso** *(ehl ehn-seh-'rah-doh dehl 'pee-soh)*
housecleaning	**la limpieza de la casa** *(lah leem-pee-'eh-sah deh-lah 'kah-sah)*
housework	**el trabajo general de la casa** *(ehl trah-'bah-hoh heh-neh-'rahl deh lah 'kah-sah)*
window washing	**el lavado de las ventanas** *(ehl lah-'bah-doh deh lahs behn-'tah-nahs)*

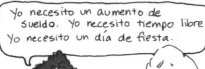

 MÁS AYUDA

- Don't forget the most important questions of all!

Do you drink?	**¿Toma licor?** (*'toh-mah lee-'kohr*)
Do you smoke?	**¿Fuma?** (*'foo-mah*)
Do you take drugs?	**¿Toma drogas?** (*'toh-mah 'droh-gahs*)
Have you ever been in jail?	**¿Ha estado alguna vez en la cárcel?** (*ah eh-'stah-doh ahl-'goo-nah behs ehn lah 'kahr-sehl*)

- And, don't leave them hanging:

I'll let you know soon!	**¡Le aviso pronto!** (*leh ah-'bee-soh 'prohn-toh*)

 REPASEMOS

Change the following to the feminine:

el enfermero   **la enfermera**
(*ehl ehn-fehr-'meh-roh*)   (*lah ehn-fehr-'meh-rah*)
el cocinero (*ehl koh-see-'neh-roh*)   la cocinera
el secretario (*ehl seh-kreh-'tah-ree-oh*) _____
el empleado (*ehl ehm-pleh-'ah-doh*)   _____
el niñero (*ehl nee-'nyeh-roh*)

- Can you figure out what's going on here?

¿Cómo se llama? (*'koh-moh seh 'yah-mah*)
   María Torres (*mah-'ree-ah 'toh-rrehs*)
¿Cuántos años tiene? (*'kwahn-tohs 'ah-nyohs tee-'eh-neh*)
   Tengo treinta años (*'tehn-goh 'tree-een-tah 'ah-nyohs*)

¿Cuánto tiempo tiene en los Estados Unidos? *('kwahn-toh tee-'ehm-poh tee-'eh-neh ehn lohs eh-'stah-dohs oo-'nee-dohs)*
Tengo cinco años aquí *('tehn-goh 'seen-koh 'ah-nyohs ah-'kee)*
¿De dónde es? *(deh 'dohn-deh ehs)*
Soy de Nicaragua *('soh-ee deh nee-kah-'rah-gwah)*
¿Dónde vive ahora? *('dohn-deh 'bee-beh ah-'oh-rah)*
Vivo en Chicago *('bee-boh ehn chee-'kah-goh)*
¿Tiene teléfono? *(tee-'eh-neh toh-'leh-foh-noh)*
Sí, tengo uno *(see 'tehn-goh 'oo-noh)*
¿Tiene familia aquí? *(tee-'eh-neh fah-'mee-lee·ah ah-'kee)*
No, mi familia no está aquí *(noh, mee fah-mee-lee·ah noh eh-'stah ah-'kee)*
¿Cuánta experiencia tiene? *('kwahn-tah ehk-speh-ree-'ehn-see·ah tee-'eh-neh)*
Tengo tres años de experiencia. *('tehn-goh trehs 'ah-nyohs deh ehk-speh-ree-'ehn-see·ah)*
¿Es soltera o casada? *(ehs sohl-'teh-rah oh kah-'sah-dah)*
Soy casada *('soh-ee kah-'sah-dah)*
¿Cuántos niños tiene? *('kwahn-tohs 'nee-nyohs)*
Tengo dos hijos *('tehn-goh dohs 'nee-nyohs)*

- Answer these questions about your family tree:

¿Quién es el padre de su padre? *(kee-'ehn ehs ehl 'pah-dreh deh soo 'pah-dreh)* _____

¿Quién es la hija de su hija? *(kee-'ehn ehs lah 'ee-hah deh soo 'ee-hah)* _____

¿Quién es la esposa de su tío? *(kee-'ehn ehs lah eh-'spoh-sah deh soo 'tee-oh)* _____

¿Quién es el hijo de su hermano? *(kee-'ehn ehs ehl 'ee-hoh deh soo ehr-'mah-noh)* _____

 ## ¡HÁGALO, POR FAVOR!

Conducting interviews in Spanish requires a number of language skills. In addition to formulating questions and answers, you will also need to give clear instructions. To do so, internalize as many of these request words as you can, and then combine them with all of your other vocabulary:

answer	**conteste** *(kohn-'teh-steh)*
	Conteste en inglés *(kohn-'teh-steh ehn een-'glehs)*
bring	**traiga** *('trah·ee-gah)*
	Traiga el formulario *('trah·ee-gah ehl fohr-moo-'lah-ree·oh)*
call	**llame** *('yah-meh)*
	Llame a su madre *('yah-meh ah soo 'mah-dreh)*
listen	**escuche** *(eh-'skoo-cheh)*
	Escuche, por favor *(eh-'skoo-cheh pohr fah-'bohr)*
read	**lea** *('leh-ah)*
	Lea la solicitud *('leh-ah lah soh-lee-see-'tood)*
return	**devuelva** *(deh-voo-'ehl-vah)*
	Devuelva los papeles *(deh-voo-'ehl-vah lohs pah-'peh-lehs)*
sign	**firme** *('feer-meh)*
	Firme su nombre *('feer-meh soo 'nohm-breh)*
speak	**hable** *('ah-bleh)*
	Hable con el jefe *('ah-bleh kohn ehl 'heh-feh)*
take	**tome** *('toh-meh)*
	Tome una silla *('toh-meh 'oo-nah 'see-yah)*
write	**escriba** *('eh-skree-bah)*

Escriba el número *(eh-skree-bah ehl 'noo-meh-roh)*

These Spanish words are actually complete phrases:

give me   **deme**   *('deh-meh)*

             Deme la dirección *('deh-meh lah dee-rehk-see·'ohn)*

show me   **enséñeme** *(ehn-'seh-nyeh-me)*

             Enséñeme la licencia *(ehn-'seh-nyeh-meh lah lee-'sehn-soo·ah)*

tell me   **dígame** *('dee-gah-meh)*

             Dígame su apellido *('dee-gah-meh ehl ah-peh-'yee doh)*

 REPASEMOS

Translate these commands, some of which we learned in Chapter One:

Please, come here. Sit down. Tell me your name.

Please, stand up. Show me the paper. Write your address.

GET TO WORK!

¡Vaya a trabajar! *('bah-yah ah trah-bah-'hahr)*

It's not easy to discuss employment without the appropriate work-related terms and expressions. The words in the list below are sure to come in handy to find out where the person you are interviewing worked previously and what they worked with:

Did you work in the...?   **¿Trabajó usted en...?** *(trah-bah-'hoh oo-'stehd en...)*

agency   **la agencia** *(lah ah-'hehn-see·ah)*

business   **el negocio** *(ehl ne-'goh-see·oh)*

factory   **la fábrica** *(lah 'fah-bree-kah)*

office   **la oficina** *(lah oh-fee-'see-nah)*

parking lot   **el estacionamiento** *(ehl eh-stah-see·oh-'nah-mee-'ehn-toh)*

restroom   **el servicio** *(ehl sehr-'bee-see·oh)*

showroom   **el salón de demostraciones** *(ehl sah-'lohn deh deh-moh-strah-see·'oh-nehs)*

warehouse   **el almacén** *(ehl ahl-mah-'sehn)*

Can you use the...?	**¿Puede usted usar...?** *('pweh-deh oo-'stehd oo-'sahr...)*
computer	**la computadora** *(lah kohm-poo-tah-'doh-rah)*
copier	**la copiadora** *(lah koh-pee-ah-'doh-rah)*
machine	**la máquina** *(lah 'mah-kee-nah)*
sewing machine	**la máquina de coser** *(lah 'mah-kee-nah deh koh-'sehr)*
tool	**la herramienta** *(lah eh-rrah-mee-'ehn-tah)*
typewriter	**la máquina de escribir** *(lah 'mah-kee-nah deh eh-skree-'beer)*
Were you the...?	**¿Era usted el (la)...?** *('eh-rah oo-'stehd ehl, lah...)*
custodian	**el guardián** *(gwahr-dee-'ahn)*
doorman	**el portero** *(pohr-'teh-roh)*
janitor	**el conserje** *(kohn-'sehr-heh)*
seamstress	**la costurera** *(koh-stoo-'reh-rah)*
You need the...	**Usted necesita...** *(oo-'stehd neh-seh-'see-tah...)*
benefits	**los beneficios** *(lohs beh-neh-'fee-see·ohs)*
bill	**la cuenta** *(lah 'kwehn-tah)*
paycheck	**el cheque** *(ehl 'cheh-keh)*
receipt	**el recibo** *(ehl reh-'see-boh)*
salary	**el salario** *(ehl sah-'lah-ree·oh)*
career	**la carrera** *(lah kah-'rreh-rah)*
opportunity	**la oportunidad** *(lah oh-pohr-too-nee-'dahd)*
position	**el puesto** *(ehl 'pweh-stoh)*

TEMAS CULTURALES

Trust is very important in the Hispanic culture. Once you've followed up on references and asked enough personal questions, feel free to open up about yourself, your family, your work, and your home. Since language is a barrier, begin letting your hair down by showing your new help where everything is located. Don't be shy, always be honest, and make them feel at home.

¡EL SUPERESPAÑOL!

Turn back to pages 27 and 28 and look over the list of Spanish verbs. Do you remember any of them? We learned also that these base forms can be used as instructional phrases when followed by "Please..." (**Favor de...**) or "Don't... " (**No...**):

Please write your name. **Favor de escribir su nombre** *(fah-'bohr deh eh-skree-'beer soo 'nohm-breh)*

Don't clean. **No limpiar** *(noh leem-pee-'ahr)*

Consider this next set of super-expressions. By adding the word **que** *(keh)* to the verb **tener** *(teh-'nehr)* you create a new action phrase — "to have to":

To have to	Tener que
I have to	**tengo que** *('tehn-goh keh)*
you have to, he or she has to	**tiene que** *(tee-'eh-neh keh)*
they have to, you (plural) have to	**tienen que** *(tee-'eh-nehn keh)*
we have to	**tenemos que** *(teh-'meh-mohs keh)*

Now bring in a few verbs from the base form list, and look what you can say:

I have to go to the house. **Tengo que ir a la casa** *('tehn-goh keh eer ah lah 'kah-sah)*

You have to work on Saturday. **Tiene que trabajar el sábado** *(tee-'eh-neh keh trah-bah-'hahr ehl 'sah-bah-doh)*

They have to move the chair.	**Tienen que mover la silla** *(tee-'eh-nehn keh moh-'behr lah 'see-yah)*
We have to clean the room.	**Tenemos que limpiar el cuarto** *(teh-'neh-mohs keh leem-pee-'ahr ehl 'kwahr-toh)*

 ## MÁS AYUDA

These next two phrases may also be used in place of **tiene que** *(tee-'eh-neh keh)*:

One must...	**(Hay que...)** *('ah·ee keh)*
One must work.	**Hay que trabajar** *('ah·ee kehtrah-bah-'hahr)*
You should...	**(Debe...)** *('deh-beh)*
You should read.	**Debe leer** *('deh-beh lee-'ehr)*

 ## ¡MÁS ACCIÓN!

We have learned that our Spanish verbs change when we talk about current action. Just like English, we alter our endings slightly:

speak	**Hablar** *(ah-'blahr)*
I'm speaking.	**Estoy hablando** *(eh-'stoh-ee ah-'blahn-doh)*
eat	**Comer** *(koh-'mehr)*

We're eating.	**Estamos comiendo** *(eh-'stah-mohs koh-mee-'ehn-doh)*
write	**Escribir** *(eh-skree-'beer)*
He's writing.	**Está escribiendo** *(eh-'stah eh-skree-bee-'ehn-doh)*

The same thing happens consistently when we refer to every day activities. However, this time the verbs shift the one who completes the action. This next pattern is the same for most action words:

To speak	**Hablar** *(ah-'blahr)*
I speak	**hablo** *('ah-bloh)*
you speak, he, she speaks	**habla** *('ah-blah)*
you (plural), they speak	**hablan** *('ah-blahn)*
we speak	**hablamos** *(ah-'blah-mohs)*

To eat	**Comer** *(koh-'mehr)*
I eat	**como** *('koh-moh)*
you eat; he, she eats	**come** *('koh-meh)*
you (plural), they eat	**comen** *('koh-mehn)*
we eat	**comemos** *(koh-'meh-mohs)*

To write	**Escribir** *(eh-skree-'beer)*
I write	**escribo** *(eh-'skree-boh)*
you write; he, she writes	**escribe** *(eh-'skree-beh)*
you (plural), they write	**escriben** *(eh-'skree-behn)*
we write	**escribimos** *(eh-skree-'bee-mohs)*

Notice how in the **ar** verb, **hablar**, the endings are different from those in the **er** and **ir** verbs. This tip will be helpful as you pick up more action forms later on.

 MÁS AYUDA

To describe an action word in Spanish, try one of these.
Do you note any pattern?

completely	**completamente** *(kohm-pleh-tah-'mehn-teh)*
quickly	**rápidamente** *('rah-pee-dah-'mehn-teh)*
slowly	**lentamente** *(lehn-tah-'mehn-teh)*

REPASEMOS

Using the proper verb forms you have just learned, answer these questions about yourself with **sí** or **no**:

    ¿Habla usted inglés todos los días? *('ah-blah oo-'stehd een-'glehs 'toh-dohs lohs 'dee-ahs)* _____

    ¿Vive usted con su familia? *('bee-beh oo-'stehd kohn soo fah-'mee-lee·ah)* _____

    ¿Tiene que dormir mucho? *(tee-'eh-neh keh dohr-'meer 'moo-choh)*

_____

PALABRAS CLAVES

As a beginning Spanish student, try to acquire as much vocabulary as you can because you are going to need a variety of practical one-word responses to communicate with people who work for you. Scan this list, and choose those that suit you best.

alone	**solo** *('soh-loh)*
also	**también** *(tahm-bee-'ehn)*
anyone	**cualquier persona** *(kwahl-kee-'ehr pehr-'soh-nah)*
anything	**cualquier cosa** *(kwahl-kee-'ehr 'koh-sah)*
anywhere	**en cualquier sitio** *(ehn kwahl kee-'ehr 'see-tee·oh)*
enough	**bastante** *(bah-'stahn-teh)*
everybody	**todos** *('toh-dohs)*
everything	**todo** *('toh-doh)*
everywhere	**por todas partes** *(pohr 'toh-dahs 'pahr-tehs)*

74

no one	**nadie** *('nah-dee·eh)*
nowhere	**en ningún sitio** *(ehn neen-'goon 'see-tee·oh)*
none	**ninguno** *(neen-'goo-noh)*
nothing	**nada** *('nah-dah)*
only	**solamente** *(soh-lah-'mehn-teh)*
same	**mismo** *('mees-moh)*
someone	**alguien** *('ahl-gee·ehn)*
something	**algo** *('ahl-goh)*
somewhere	**en algún sitio** *(ehl ah-'goon 'see-tee·oh)*
too much	**demasiado** *(deh-mah-see'ah-doh)*

 REPASEMOS

Match the opposites:

nada *('nah-dah)*	**diferente** *(dee-feh-'rehn-teh)*
mismo *('mees-moh)*	**nadie** *('nah-dee·eh)*
alguien *('ahl-gee·ehn)*	**todos** *('toh-dohs)*

 MÁS AYUDA

My Schedule
Mi horario (mee oh-'rah-ree·oh)

Set up a schedule using the following guide words as examples. They can be useful no matter what the job is:

You start _____	**Empieza** _____	*(ehm-pee-'eh-sah)*
You finish _____	**Termina** _____	*(tehr-'mee-nah)*
Day in _____	**Día de entrada**_____	*('dee-ah deh ehn-'trah-dah)*
Day out _____	**Día de salida** _____	*('dee-ah deh sah-lee-dah)*
Day off _____	**Día de descanso** _____	*('dee-ah deh dehs-'kahn-soh)*
From _____	**De** _____	*(deh)*
Until _____	**Hasta** _____	*('ah-stah)*
Chores _____	**Las tareas** _____	*(lahs tah-'reh-ahs)*

TELEPHONE LINES

Once you have hired a Spanish-speaker, it is essential that you make sure that person is able to handle your telephone calls for you. Practice your Spanish, while they learn these basic expressions in English:

He/she is not home.	**No está en casa** *(no eh-'stah ehn 'kah-sah)*
Hello!	**¡Aló!** *(ah-'loh)*
I'll call back later.	**Llamaré más tarde** *(yah-mah-'reh mahs 'tahr-deh)*
I am going to transfer you.	**Le voy a transferir** *(leh 'boh·ee ah trahs-feh-'reer)*
Is there someone there who speaks English?	**¿Hay alguien allí que hable inglés?** *('ah·ee 'ahl-gee-ehn ah-'yee keh 'ah-bleh een-'glehs)*
May I leave (take) a message?	**¿Puedo dejar (tomar) un mensaje?** *('pweh-doh deh-'hahr (toh-'mahr) oon mehn-'sah-heh)*
Please call me at _____.	**Favor de llamarme al número** _____ *(fah-'bohr deh yah-'mahr-meh ahl 'noo-meh-roh)*
Please don't hang up.	**No cuelgue, por favor** *(noh 'kwehl-geh, pohr fah-'bohr)*
Please wait a moment.	**Espere un momento, por favor** *(eh-'speh-reh oon moh-'mehn-toh, pohr fah-'bohr)*
More slowly, please.	**Más despacio, por favor** *(mahs deh-'spah-see·oh, pohr fah-'bohr*
Thanks a lot, and good-bye.	**Muchas gracias, y adiós** *('moo-chahs 'grah-see·ahs ee ah-dee-'ohs)*
This is _____.	**Este es** _____ *('eh-steh ehs)*
When will he/she return?	**¿Cuándo regresa?** *('kwahn-doh reh-'greh-sah)*

 ## TEMAS CULTURALES

Many Americans work with new immigrants who are unfamiliar with local, state, or federal laws and regulations. If you plan to establish a long-term relationship, you can prevent potential problems by giving them as much legal information as possible. By contacting a variety of service agencies, one can pick up literature in Spanish concerning citizenship, taxes, health care, education, transportation, and residence, as well as personal rights and privileges.

CHAPTER THREE

Capítulo Tres
('kah-'pee-too-loh trehs)

CLEANING
La limpieza (lah leem-pee-'eh-sah)

TOOLS OF THE HOME TRADE
Las herramientas del trabajo casero
(lahs eh-rrah-mee-'ehn-tahs dehl trah-'bah-hoh kah-'seh-roh)
Now that everyone has been hired, are you ready to get to work? Let's begin by cleaning the home from top to bottom! In order to train or instruct anyone involved in housecleaning, you'll need the important words below.

Why not place labels or stickers on these items around the house? Write both the Spanish and the English on each label, and practice naming everything in both languages.

Bring the...	**Traiga...** *('trah-ee-gah)*
box	**la caja** *(lah 'kah-hah)*
broom	**la escoba** *(lah eh-'skoh-bah)*
brush	**el cepillo** *(ehl seh-'pee-yoh)*
bucket	**el balde** *(ehl 'bahl-deh)*
dustpan	**la pala de recoger basura** *(lah 'pah-lah deh reh-koh-'hehr bah-'soo-rah)*
feather duster	**el plumero** *(ehl ploo-'meh-roh)*
glove	**el guante** *(ehl 'gwahn-teh)*
hose	**la manguera** *(lah mahn-'geh-rah)*
mask	**la máscara** *(lah 'mahs-kah-rah)*
mop	**el trapeador** *(ehl trah-peh-ah-'dohr)*
rag	**el trapo** *(ehl 'trah-poh)*
scouring pad	**el estropajo** *(ehl eh-stroh-'pah-hoh)*
scraper	**el raspador** *(ehl rah-spah-'dohr)*
scrub brush	**el cepillo limpiasuelos** *(ehl seh-pee-'yoh 'leem-pee·ah-'sweh-lohs)*
sponge	**la esponja** *(lah eh-'spohn-hah)*

stepladder	**la escalera** *(lah eh-skah-'leh-rah)*
towel	**la toalla** *(lah toh-'ah-yah)*
trashbag	**la bolsa para basura** *(lah 'bohl-sah 'pah-rah bah-'soo-rah)*
trashcan	**el cesto de basura** *(ehl 'sehs-toh deh bah-'soo-rah)*
	el basurero *(ehl bah-soo-'reh-roh)*
vacuum cleaner	**la aspiradora** *(lah ah-spee-rah-'doh-rah)*
wastepaper basket	**el papelero** *(ehl pah-peh-'leh-roh)*

CLEANING SUPPLIES
Los productos para limpiar
(lohs proh-'dook-tohs 'pah-rah leem-pee-'ahr)

The following products can easily be identified by name brands, and sometimes all you have to mention is the color of the container. However, to avoid confusion, try to be as specific as you can:

Please use...	Favor de usar...
cleaner	**el limpiador** *(ehl leem-pee-ah-'dohr)*
powder	**el polvo** *(ehl 'pohl-boh)*
soap	**el jabón** *(ehl hah-'bohn)*
ammonia	**el amoníaco** *(ehl ah-moh-'nee-ah-koh)*
bleach	**el blanqueador** *(ehl blahn-keh-ah-'dohr)*
cleanser	**el agente de limpieza** *(ehl ah-'gehn-teh deh leem-pee-'eh-zah)*
cream	**la crema** *(lah 'kreh-mah)*

foam	la espuma *(lah eh-'spoo-mah)*
liquid	el líquido *(ehl 'lee-kee-doh)*
paste	la pasta *(lah 'pah-stah)*
polish	el lustrador *(ehl loo-strah-'dohr)*
spray	la rociada *(lah roh-see-'ah-dah)*
suds	las jabonaduras *(lahs hah-boh-nah-'doo-rahs)*
wax	la cera *(lah 'seh-rah)*

Can you guess what these words mean?

el detergente *(ehl deh-tehr-'hehn-teh)*

_____

el desinfectante *(ehl dehs-een-fehk-'tahn-teh)*

_____

el jabón de platos *(ehl hah-'bohn deh 'plah-tohs)*

_____

el limpiador de metal *(ehl leem-pee-ah-'dohr deh meh-'tahl)*

_____

la solución *(lah soh-loo-see-'ohn)*

_____

 MÁS AYUDA

To be specific in your instructions, combine as many words as you can to get your point across:

back door	la puerta de atrás *(lah 'pwehr-tah deh ah-'trahs)*
front window	la ventana de enfrente *(lah behn-'tah-nah deh ehn-'frehn-teh)*
side wall	la pared del lado *(lah pah-'rehd dehl 'lah-doh)*
cleaning powder	el polvo para limpiar *(ehl 'pohl-boh 'pah-rah leem-pee-'ahr)*
liquid soap	el jabón líquido *(ehl hah-'bohn 'lee-kee-doh)*
paper towel	la toalla de papel *(lah toh-'ah-yah deh pah-'pehl)*
glass table	la mesa de vidrio *(lah 'meh-sah deh 'veed-ree-oh)*
hot water	el agua caliente *(ehl 'ah-gwah kah-lee-'ehn-teh)*
wet sponge	la esponja mojada *(lah eh-'spohn-hah moh-'hah-dah)*

79

TEMAS CULTURALES

• In the housekeeping profession, many household products are simply referred to by their brand name or **marca del producto**. Here's just a sample:

el Palmolive
el Brillo
el Clorox
el Comet
el Kleenex

• By the way, you do not translate names of businesses, brands, and streets. Nor do you have to change your name to Spanish in order to communicate. All over the world, most formal titles in English remain the same.

 REPASEMOS

Remember what you're not supposed to do with chemicals (**los químicos**). Go ahead and fill in the blanks:

Don't use _____.
No use _____. *(noh 'oo-seh)*
Don't mix _____ with _____.
No mezcle *(noh 'mehs-'kleh)* _____ **con** *(kohn)* _____.
Don't put _____ on _____.
No ponga *(noh 'pohn-gah)* _____ **en** *(ehn)* _____.
And be careful with chemicals!
¡Y tenga cuidado con _____! *(ee 'tehn-gah kwee-'dah-doh kohn)*

Translate:

Bring the...
    bleach   _____
    broom   _____
    hose   _____
    soap   _____
    towel   _____

IT'S NOT CLEAN!

¡No está limpio! (noh eh-'stah 'leem-pee·oh)

Now that all our supplies are in order, it's time to learn about the job ahead of us. Although we've already chatted a bit about descriptive words in Spanish, check over this next list of "unclean" vocabulary. Think of different ways to describe the unpleasant sights around you!

There is (are)...	**Hay...** *(ehs)*
ash	**la ceniza** *(lah seh-'nee-sah)*
crumbs	**las migas** *(lahs 'mee-gahs)*
dirt	**la tierra** *(lah tee-'eh-rrah)*
dust	**el polvo** *(ehl 'pohl-boh)*
filth	**la suciedad** *(lah soo-see-eh-'dahd)*
fungus	**el hongo** *(ehl 'hon-goh)*
grime	**la mugre** *(lah 'moo-greh)*
mold	**el moho** *(ehl 'moh-oh)*
mud	**el lodo** *(ehl 'loh-doh)*
rust	**la herrumbre** *(lah eh-'rroom-breh)*
scum	**el desecho** *(ehl dehs-'eh-choh)*
sewage	**el desague** *(ehl dehs-'ah-gweh)*
silt	**el cieno** *(ehl see-'eh-noh)*
soot	**el tizne** *(ehl 'tees-neh)*
trash	**la basura** *(lah bah-'soo-rah)*
waste	**los desperdicios** *(lohs dehs-pehr-'dee-see·ohs)*

It's...	Está... *(eh-'stah)*
broken	**roto** *('roh-toh)*
corroded	**corroído** *(koh-rroh-'ee-doh)*
cracked	**trizado**
damaged	**dañado** *(dah-'nyah-doh)*
dangerous	**peligroso** *(peh-lee-'groh-soh)*
dirty	**sucio** *('soo-see·oh)*
dusty	**polvoriento** *(pohl-boh-ree-'ehn-toh)*
faded	**descolorido** *(dehs-koh-loh-'ree-doh)*
filthy	**muy sucio** *('moo-ee 'soo-se·oh)*
marked	**marcado** *(mahr-'kah-doh)*
poisonous	**venenoso** *(beh-neh-'noh-soh)*
rotten	**podrido** *(poh-'dree-doh)*
ruined	**arruinado** *(ah-rroo-ee-'nah-doh)*
rusty	**herrumbrado** *(eh-rroom-'brah-doh)*
scuffed	**rayado** *(rah-'yah-doh)*
spoiled	**estropeado** *(eh-stroh-peh-'ah-doh)*
stained	**manchado** *(mahn-'chah-doh)*
torn	**rasgado, roto** *(rahs-'gah-doh, 'roh-toh)*
warped	**torcido** *(tohr-'see-doh)*
worn	**gastado** *(gah-'stah-doh)*

Bear in mind that **está** refers to the current condition of things. For work around the house, here are a few others that you'll need:

It's...	Está... *(eh-'stah)*
closed	**cerrado** *(seh-'rrah-doh)*
cold	**frío** *('free-oh)*
comfortable	**cómodo** *('koh-moh-doh)*
correct	**correcto** *(koh-'rrehk-toh)*
dark	**oscuro** *(oh-'skoo-roh)*
dull	**romo** *('roh-moh)*
empty	**vacío** *(bah-'see-oh)*
full	**lleno** *('yeh-noh)*
hot	**caliente** *(kah-lee-'ehn-teh)*
light (color)	**claro** *('klah-roh)*
loose	**flojo** *('floh-hoh)*
lost	**perdido** *(pehr-'dee-doh)*
open	**abierto** *(ah-bee-'ehr-toh)*

prohibited	**prohibido** *(proh-ee-'bee-doh)*
rough	**áspero** *('ahs-peh-roh)*
sharp	**afilado** *(ah-fee-'lah-doh)*
soft	**suave** *('swah-beh)*
tight	**apretado** *(ah-preh-'tah-doh)*
wrong	**equivocado** *(eh-kee-boh-'kah-doh)*

 REPASEMOS

Translate the key words:

The <u>mud</u> is <u>filthy</u>. _____ _____

The <u>trash</u> is <u>rotten</u>. _____ _____

The <u>sewage</u> is <u>contaminated</u>. _____ _____

FROM ROOM TO ROOM
De cuarto a cuarto *(deh 'kwahr-toh ah 'kwahr-toh)*

Learning the parts of the house can be fun, whether you are busy cleaning, or just going through your daily routine. Simply place printed stickers, signs, or notes on objects and doors throughout the house, and label each one in Spanish. Then walk around pronouncing all the items you come into contact with. You can even call out the name of each room as you wander through it. In no time at all, you'll be remembering words easily, and won't have to depend on the labels any more!

As you practice a particular item, make comments using various descriptive words.

- The bedroom **el dormitorio** *(ehl dohr-mee-'toh-ree-oh)*
  ...**es grande** *(ehs 'grahn-deh)*
- The basement **El sótano** *(ehl 'soh-tah-noh)*
  ...**está sucio** *(eh-'stah 'soo-see·oh)*
- The attic **El desván** *(ehl dehs-'bahn)*
  ...**es pequeño** *(ehs peh-'kehn-yoh)*
- The hallway **El pasillo** *(ehl pah-'see-yoh)*
  ...**está frío** *(eh-'stah 'free-oh)*
- The bathroom **El cuarto de baño** *(ehl 'kwahr-toh deh 'bah-nyoh)*
  ...**es nuevo** *(ehs noo-'eh-boh)*
- The kitchen **La cocina** *(lah koh-'see-nah)*
  ...**está limpia** *(eh-'stah 'leem-pee·ah)*

- The dining room **El comedor** *(ehl koh-meh-'dohr)*
  ...es viejo *(ehs bee-'eh-hoh)*
- The garage **El garaje** *(ehl gah-'rah-heh)*
  ...está lleno *(eh-'stah 'yeh-noh)*
- The living room **La sala** *(lah 'sah-lah)*
  ...es bonita *(ehs boh-'nee-tah)*

PARTS OF THE HOUSE
Las partes de la casa *(lahs 'pahr-tehs deh lah 'kah-sah)*

Here are important words for you to know for parts of the house —
inside and out!

backyard	**el patio** *(ehl 'pah-tee·oh)*
bar	**el bar** *(ehl bahr)*
bathroom	**el baño** *(ehl 'bah-nyoh)*
breakfast room	**el ante-comedor** *(ehl ahn-teh-koh-meh-'dohr)*
ceiling	**el techo** *(ehl 'teh-choh)*
chimney	**la chimenea** *(lah chee-meh-'neh-ah)*
door	**la puerta** *(lah 'pwehr-tah)*
dressing room	**el vestuario** *(ehl beh-stoo-'ah-ree·oh)*
driveway	**la entrada para carros** *(lah ehn-'trah-dah 'pah-rah 'kah-rrohs)*
family room	**la sala de familia** *(lah 'sah-lah deh fah-'mee-lee·ah)*
fence	**la cerca** *(lah 'sehr-kah)*
fireplace	**el fogón** *(ehl foh-'gohn)*
floor	**el piso** *(ehl 'pee-soh)*
gate	**el portón** *(ehl pohr-'tohn)*
guest room	**el cuarto de visitas** *(ehl 'kwahr-toh deh bee-'see-tahs)*

library	la biblioteca *(lah beeb-lee-oh-'teh-kah)*
playroom	la sala de juegos *(lah 'sah-lah deh joo-'eh-gohs)*
pool	la piscina *(lah pee-'see-nah)*
porch	el portal *(ehl pohr-'tahl)*
roof	el tejado *(ehl teh-'hah-doh)*
spa	el balneario *(ehl bahl-neh-'ah-ree·oh)*
storeroom	el depósito *(ehl deh-'poh-see-toh)*
terrace	la terraza *(lah teh-'rrah-sah)*
wall	la pared *(luh pah-'rehd)*
window	la ventana *(lah behn 'tah-nah)*

 MÁS AYUDA

From the very first day, let everyone on the premises know where the emergency items are located. Before moving forward, memorize these essential words:

alarm	la alarma *(lah ah-'lahr-mah)*
fire extinguisher	el extintor *(ehl ehks-teen-'tohr)*
first aid kit	la caja de primeros auxilios *(lah 'kah-hah deh pree-'meh-rohs owk-'see-lee·ohs)*
fuse box	la caja de fusibles *(lah 'kah-hah deh foo-'see-blehs)*
gas meter	el medidor de gas *(ehl meh-dee-'dohr deh gahs)*
water valve	la válvula de agua *(lah 'bahl-boo-lah deh 'ah-gwah)*

FIXTURES AND FURNITURE
Instalaciones y Muebles
(een-stah-lah-see·'oh-nehs ee 'mweh-blehs)

While learning the names for household items, create practical phrases to use with your Spanish-speaking help. For example:

Please clean the...	**Por favor, limpie...** *(pohr fah-'bohr 'leem-pee·eh)*
Where is the...?	**¿Dónde está...?** *('dohn-deh eh-'stah)*
It's next to the...	**Está al lado de...** *(eh-'stah ahl 'lah-doh deh)*

bathroom sink	**el lavabo** *(ehl lah-'bah-boh)*
bathtub	**la tina** *(lah 'tee-nah)*
cabinet	**el gabinete** *(ehl gah-bee-'neh-teh)*
closet	**el ropero** *(ehl roh-'peh-roh)*
counter	**el mostrador** *(ehl moh-strah-'dohr)*
fireplace	**la chimenea** *(lah chee-meh-'neh-ah)*
kitchen sink	**el fregadero** *(ehl freh-gah-'deh-roh)*
medicine chest	**el botiquín** *(ehl boh-tee-'keen)*
shower	**la ducha** *(lah 'doo-chah)*
toilet	**el excusado** *(ehl ehks-koo-'sah-doh)*
windowsill	**el antepecho** *(ehl ahn-teh-'peh-choh)*

And don't forget these important parts of your home:

- air conditioning **el aire acondicionado** *(ehl 'ah·ee-reh ah-kohn-dee-see·oh-'nah-doh)*
- electrical outlet **el enchufe** *(ehl ehn-'choo-feh)*
- heating **la calefacción** *(lah kah-lee-fahk-see·'ohn)*
- light switch **el interruptor** *(ehl een-teh-roop-'tohr)*
- plumbing **la tubería** *(lah too-beh-'ree-ah)*

Label these to help you learn their names:

bannister	**la baranda** *(lah bah-'rahn-dah)*
baseboards	**las bases de las paredes** *(lahs 'bah-sehs deh lahs pah-'reh-dehs)*
blinds	**las persianas** *(lahs pehr-see-'ah-nahs)*
curtains	**las cortinas** *(lahs kohr-'tee-nahs)*
draperies	**las colgaduras** *(lahs kohl-gah-'doo-rahs)*
drawers	**los cajones** *(lohs kah-'hoh-nehs)*

faucets	los grifos *(lohs 'gree-fohs)*
lampshades	las pantallas *(lahs pahn-'tah-yahs)*
lights	las luces *(lahs 'loo-sehs)*
rugs	las alfombras *(lahs ahl-'fohm-brahs)*
shelves	las repisas *(lahs reh-'pee-sahs)*
shutters	los postigos *(lohs poh-'stee-gohs)*
stairs	las escaleras *(lahs eh-skah-'leh-rahs)*
steps	los escalones *(lohs eh-skah-'loh-nehs)*
wall-to-wall carpeting	las alfombras de pared a pared *('lahs ahl-'fohm-brahs deh pah-'rehd ah pah-'rehd)*

MÁS AYUDA

- These are special:

French doors	las puertas francesas *(lahs 'pwehr-tahs frahn-'seh-sahs)*
glass doors	las puertas de vidrio *(lahs 'pwehr-tahs deh 'bee-dree·oh)*
screen doors	las puertas de malla *(lahs 'pwehr-tahs de 'mah-yah)*

- Notice this pattern when you talk about "racks":

magazine rack	el revistero *(ehl reh-bee-'steh-roh)*
shoe rack	el zapatero *(ehl sah-pah-'teh-roh)*
towel rack	el toallero *(ehl toh-ah-'yeh-roh)*

TEMAS CULTURALES

In order to learn the names in Spanish for items not mentioned in this book, ask the question **¿Qué es esto?** *(keh ehs 'eh-stoh)* which means "What is this? Most Hispanic employees will be delighted to share a little of their native language with you. Be patient with yourself, because they may ask you to practice!

¡HÁGALO, POR FAVOR!

Let's take a break from our labeling activities and learn how to put our new terminology into action.

Teaching others how to clean requires a unique set of Spanish command words. Although there are several new phrases to study and remember, these promise to help get the job done (and be sure to add **por favor**):

carry	**lleve** *('yeh-beh)*
	Lleve el balde *('yeh-beh ehl 'bahl-deh)*
clean	**limpie** *('leem-pee-'eh)*
	Limpie el baño *('leem-pee-'eh ehl 'bah-nyoh)*
close	**cierre** *(see-'eh-rreh)*
	Cierre la puerta *(see-'eh-rreh lah 'pwehr-tah)*
dust	**desempolve** *(deh-sehn-'pohl-veh)*
	Desempolve el gabinete *(deh-sehn-'pohl-veh ehl gah-bee-'neh-teh)*
lift	**levante** *(leh-'bahn-teh)*
	Levante la mesa *(leh-'bahn-teh lah 'meh-sah)*
lower	**baje** *('bah-heh)*
	Baje la escalera *('bah-heh lah eh-skah-'leh-rah)*
move	**mueva** *(moo·'eh-bah)*
	Mueva el sofá *(moo·'eh-bah ehl soh-'fah)*
open	**abra** *('ah-brah)*
	Abra la ventana *(ah-brah lah behn-'tah-nah)*
pick up	**recoja** *(reh-'koh-hah)*
	Recoja la tierra *(eh-'koh-hah lah tee-'eh-rrah)*
put	**ponga** *('pohn-gah)*
	Ponga la silla aquí *('pohn-gah lah 'see-yah ah-'kee)*
sweep	**barra** *('bah-rrah)*
	Barra el piso *('bah-rrah ehl 'pee-soh)*
throw away	**tire** *('tee-reh)*
	Tire la basura *('tee-reh lah bah-'soo-rah)*
turn off	**apague** *(ah-'pah-geh)*
	Apague la luz *(ah-'pah-geh lah loos)*
turn on	**prenda** *('prehn-dah)*
	Prenda la aspiradora *('prehn-dah lah ah-spee-rah-'doh-rah)*

vacuum	**limpie con aspiradora** (*'leem-pee-eh kohn-ah-spee-rah-'doh-rah*)
	Limpie con aspiradora la sala (*'leem-pee-eh kohn ah-spee-rah-'doh-rah lah 'sah-lah*)
wash	**lave** (*'lah-beh*)
	Lave con el cepillo (*'lah-beh kohn ehl seh-'pee-yoh*)

Here's a reminder. To say "don't," just put **no** in front of the command:

Don't open the door to strangers!

¡No abra la puerta para desconocidos! (*noh 'ah-brah lah 'pwehr-tah 'pah-rah dehs-koh-noh-'see-dohs*)

PAY ATTENTION!
¡Preste atención! (*'preh-steh ah-tehn-see-'ohn*)

Before anyone touches anything in or around your home, learn the following phrases.

All of these should be memorized and practiced right away!

Be very careful.	**Tenga mucho cuidado** (*'tehn-gah 'moo-choh kwee-'dah-doh*)
Do it by hand.	**Hágalo a mano** (*'ah-gah-loh ah 'mah-noh*)
Do not touch it.	**No lo toque** (*noh loh 'toh-keh*)
It doesn't work.	**No funciona** (*noh foonk-see-'oh-nah*)
Like this.	**Así** (*ah-'see*)
Remember this.	**Recuerde esto** (*reh-'kwehr-deh 'eh-stoh*)
This is the procedure.	**Este es el procedimiento** (*'eh-steh ehs ehl proh-seh-dee-mee-'ehn-toh*)
This is what I want.	**Esto es lo que quiero** (*'eh-stoh ehs loh keh kee-'eh-roh*)
This way.	**De esta manera** (*deh 'eh-stah mah-'neh-rah*)

FURNITURE
Los muebles (*lohs 'mweh-blehs*)

You can't ask someone to thoroughly clean your home unless you know how to say the Spanish words for your furniture. Put labels on everything to practice. Then try them out with all your furnishings.

Dust...	**Sacuda...** *(sah-'koo-dah)*
Clean...	**Limpie...** *('leem-pee'eh)*
Move...	**Mueva...** *(moo·'eh-bah)*
the armchair	**el sillón** *(ehl see-'yohn)*
armoire	**el armario** *(ehl ahr-'mah-ree·oh)*
bed	**la cama** *(lah 'kah-mah)*
bookshelf	**el librero** *(ehl lee-'breh-roh)*
chair	**la silla** *(lah 'see-yah)*
chest	**el baúl** *(ehl bah-'ool)*
desk	**el escritorio** *(ehl eh-skree-'toh-ree·oh)*
dresser	**el tocador** *(ehl toh-kah-'dohr)*
nightstand	**la mesita de noche** *(lah meh-'see-tah deh 'noh-cheh)*
piano	**el piano** *(ehl pee-'ah-noh)*
sofa	**el sofá** *(ehl soh-'fah)*
stool	**el banquillo** *(ehl bahn-'kee-yoh)*
table	**la mesa** *(lah 'meh-sah)*

 MÁS AYUDA

Not all home furnishings stay indoors. You may want to consider labeling some outdoor pieces as well:

barbeque grill	**la parrilla** *(lah pah-'rree-yah)*
beach chair	**la silla de playa** *(lah 'see-yah deh 'plah-yah)*

hammock	**la hamaca** *(lah ah-'mah-kah)*
lawn chair	**la silla de patio** *(lah 'see-yah deh 'pah-tee oh)*
screens	**las pantallas** *(lahs pahn-'tah-yahs)*
umbrella	**la sombrilla** *(lah sohm-'bree-yah)*

ELECTRICAL APPLIANCES
Los electrodomésticos
(loho oh lohk troh doh-'mch-stee-kohs)

Appliances are there to make our lives easier. Learn how to refer to them in Spanish:

Plug in...	**Enchufe...** *(ehn-'choo-feh)*
Unplug...	**Desenchufe...** *(dehs-ehn-'choo-feh)*
air conditioner	**el acondicionador de aire** *(ehl ah-kohn-dee-see·oh-nah-'dohr deh 'ah·ee-reh)*
answering machine	**el contestador telefónico** *(ehl kohn-teh-stah-'dohr teh-leh-'foh-nee-koh)*
cassette	**el casete** *(ehl kah-'seh-teh)*
clock	**el reloj** *(ehl reh-'loh)*
computer	**la computadora** *(lah kohm-poo-tah-'doh-rah)*
dishwasher	**el lavaplatos** *(ehl lah-bah-'plah-tohs)*
dryer	**la secadora** *(lah seh-kah-'doh-rah)*
fan	**el ventilador** *(ehl behn-tee-lah-'dohr)*
freezer	**el congelador** *(ehl kohn-heh-lah-'dohr)*
fusebox	**la caja de fusibles** *(lah 'kah-hah deh foo-'see-blehs)*
garage door opener	**el abridor de garajes** *(ehl ah-bree-'dohr deh gah-'rah-hehs)*
hairdryer	**el secador de pelo** *(ehl seh-kah-'dohr deh 'peh-loh)*
heater	**el calentador** *(ehl kah-lehn-tah-'dohr)*
hot water heater	**el calentador para el agua** *(ehl kah-lehn-tah-'dohr 'pah-rah ehl 'ah-gwah)*
lamp	**la lámpara** *(lah 'lahm-pah-rah)*
microwave	**el horno de microonda** *(ehl 'ohr-noh deh mee-kroh-'ohn-dah)*
oven	**el horno** *(ehl 'ohr-noh)*

radio	**el radio** *(ehl 'rah-dee·oh)*
record player	**el tocadiscos** *(ehl toh-kah-'dees-kohs)*
refrigerator	**el refrigerador** *(ehl reh-free-heh-rah-'dohr)*
scale	**la báscula** *(lah 'bahs-koo-lah)*
security system	**el sistema de seguridad** *(ehl sees-'teh-mah deh seh-goo-ree-'dahd)*
sewing machine	**la máquina de coser** *(lah 'mah-kee-nah deh koh-'sehr)*
smoke alarm	**el detector de humo** *(ehl deh-tehk-'tohr de 'oo-moh)*
stereo	**el estéreo** *(ehl eh-'steh-reh-oh)*
stove	**la estufa** *(lah eh-'stoo-fah)*
telephone	**el teléfono** *(ehl teh-'leh-foh-noh)*
thermostat	**el termostato** *(ehl tehr-moh-'stah-toh)*
toaster	**la tostadora** *(lah toh-stah-'doh-rah)*
TV	**el televisor** *(ehl teh-leh-bee-'sohr)*
VCR	**la videocasetera** *(lah bee-deh-oh-kah-seh-'teh-rah)*
washer	**la lavadora** *(lah lah-bah-'doh-rah)*

 MÁS AYUDA

The location words fit in with most household vocabulary, especially when you're asking someone to do something. For example:

Change the sheets in the room.

Cambie las sábanas en el cuarto *('kahm-bee'eh lahs 'sah-bah-nahs ehn el 'cwahr-toh)*

Clean behind the sofa.
Limpie detrás del sofá (*'leem-pee-eh deh-'trahs dehl soh-'fah*)
Make the bed over there.
Haga la cama allá (*'ah-gah lah 'kah-mah ah-'yah*)
Sweep next to the stove.
Barra al lado de la estufa (*'bah-rrah ahl 'lah-doh deh lah eh-'stoo-fah*)
Vacuum under the bed.
Limpie con aspiradora debajo de la cama (*'leem-pee-eh kohn ah-spee-rah-'doh-rah deh-'bah-hoh deh lah 'kah-mah*)

 REPASEMOS

- Match the furniture with the appropriate room:

  la cama (*lah 'kah-mah*)
  la sala (*lah 'sah-lah*)
  la estufa (*lah eh-'stoo-fah*)
  la cocina (*lah koh-'see-nah*)

  el excusado (*ehl ehks-koo-'sah-doh*)
  el dormitorio (*ehl dohr-mee-'toh-ree-oh*)
  el sofá (*ehl soh-'fah*)
  el cuarto de baño (*ehl 'kwahr-toh deh 'bah-nyoh*)

- Translate:

  Limpie el mostrador (*'leem-pee-eh ehl moh-strah-'dohr*) _____
  Apague la lámpara (*ah-'pah-geh lah 'lahm-pah-rah*) _____
  Mueva el librero (*'moo-eh-beh ehl lee-'breh-roh*) _____
  Lave el espejo (*'lah-beh ehl eh-'speh-hoh*) _____
  Abra el buzón (*'ah-brah ehl boo-'sohn*) _____

HOUSE DECOR
La decoración *(lah deh-koh-rah-see·'ohn)*

Look at all these other items that we may have overlooked. Are you repeating each new word so that you won't forget? You can try the label trick with these words too.

Lift the...	**Levante...** *(leh-'bahn-teh)*
Dust the...	**Desempolve...** *(deh-sehm-'pohl-veh)*
artificial plant	**la planta artificial** *(lah 'plahn-tah ahr-tee-fee-see-'ahl)*
ashtray	**el cenicero** *(ehl seh-nee-'seh-roh)*
basket	**la canasta** *(lah kah-'nah-stah)*
candelabra	**el candelabro** *(ehl kahn-deh-'lah-broh)*
firewood	**la leña** *(lah 'leh-nyah)*
flowerpot	**la maceta** *(lah mah-'seh-tah)*
mat	**el tapete** *(ehl tah-'peh-teh)*
mirror	**el espejo** *(ehl eh-'speh-hoh)*
ornament	**el ornamento** *(ehl ohr-nah-'mehn-toh)*
painting	**el cuadro** *(ehl 'kwah-droh)*
pedestal	**el pedestal** *(ehl peh-deh-'stahl)*
photograph	**el retrato** *(ehl reh-'trah-toh)*
picture frame	**el marco** *(ehl 'mahr-koh)*
pottery	**la alfarería** *(lah ahl-fah-reh-'ree-ah)*
statue	**la estatua** *(lah eh-'stah-too-ah)*
tapestry	**el tapiz** *(ehl tah-'peez)*
vase	**el florero** *(ehl floh-'reh-roh)*

 MÁS AYUDA

You can never learn enough vocabulary! Try out this next set of key words and try to translate these simple sentences:

alarm	**la alarma** *(lah ah-'lahr-mah)*
	¿Dónde está la alarma? *('dohn-deh eh-'stah lah ah-'lahr-mah)*
doorbell	**el timbre** *(ehl 'teem-breh)*
	Favor de usar el timbre *(fah-'bohr deh oo-'sahr ehl 'teem-breh)*
knob, handle	**el tirador** *(ehl tee-rah-'dohr)*

94

	La puerta no tiene tirador *(lah 'pwehr-tah noh tee-'eh-neh tee-'rah-dohr)*
lock	**la cerradura** *(lah seh-rrah-'doo-rah)*
	La cerradura es grande *(lah seh-rrah-'doo-rah ehs 'grahn-deh)*
mailbox	**el buzón** *(ehl boo-'sohn)*
	Vaya al buzón *('bah-yah ahl boo-'sohn)*

 TEMAS CULTURALES

As we have already learned, "Spanglish" is everywhere. Here are some others:

C.D.	**el C.D.**
closet	**el closet**
spray	**el spray**
switch	**el switch**

WASH DAY
El día de lavar la ropa
(ehl 'dee-ah deh lah-'bahr lah 'roh-pah)

The subject of housecleaning would be incomplete without mentioning the washer (**la lavadora**) *(lah lah-bah-'doh-rah)* and the dryer (**la secadora**) *(lah seh-kah-'doh-rah)*. Clothing, beddings, blankets, rugs, curtains — as well a countless other items — get dirty, and need to be cleaned as soon as possible. Fortunately, just like our home furnishings, these items are everywhere, and the names for them can be practiced daily as you come into contact with them. Begin by naming the clothing (**la ropa**) *(lah 'roh-pah)* that you're wearing right now!

I'm wearing...	**Estoy usando...** *(eh-'stoh-ee oo-'sahn-doh)*
Please wash, dry, and put away...	**Favor de lavar, secar, y guardar...** *(fah-'bohr deh lah-'bahr, seh-'kahr ee gwahr-'dahr)*
a bathing suit	**un traje de baño** *(oon 'trah-heh deh 'bah-nyoh)*
a bathrobe	**una bata de baño** *('oo-nah 'bah-tah deh 'bah-nyoh)*
a belt	**un cinturón** *(oon seen-too-'rohn)*

a blouse	**una blusa** *('oo-nah 'bloo-sah)*
a brassiere	**un sostén** *(oon soh-'stehn)*
a cap	**una gorra** *('oo-nah 'goh-rrah)*
a dress	**un vestido** *(oon beh-'stee-doh)*
a girdle	**una faja** *('oo-nah 'fah-hah)*
gloves	**unos guantes** *('oo-nohs 'gwahn-tehs)*
a jacket	**una chaqueta** *('oo-nah chah-'keh-tah)*
mittens	**unos mitones** *('oo-nohs mee-'toh-nehs)*
an overcoat	**un abrigo** *(oon ah-'bree-goh)*
pajamas	**un pijama** *(oon pee-'hah-mah)*
panties	**unas bragas** *('oo-nahs 'brah-gahs)*
pants	**unos pantalones** *('oo-nohs pahn-tah-'loh-nehs)*
a raincoat	**un impermeable** *(oon eem-pehr-meh-'ahb-leh)*
a scarf	**una bufanda** *('oo-nah boo-'fahn-dah)*
a shirt	**una camisa** *('oo-nah cah-'mee-sah)*
shorts	**unos calzoncillos** *('oo-nohs kahl-sohn-'see-yos)*
a skirt	**una falda** *('oo-nah 'fahl-dah)*
a slip	**un fondo** *(oon 'fohn-doh)*
slippers	**unas zapatillas** *('oo-nahs sah-pah-'tee-yahs)*
socks	**unos calcetines** *('oo-nohs kahl-seh-'tee-nehs)*
a sportcoat	**un saco** *(oon 'sah-koh)*
stockings	**unas medias** *('oo-nahs 'meh-dee·ahs)*
a suit	**un traje** *(oon 'trah-heh)*
a sweater	**un suéter** *(oon 'sweh-tehr)*
a sweatsuit	**una sudadera** *('oo-nah soo-dah-'deh-rah)*
a T-shirt	**una camiseta** *('oo-nah kah-mee-'seh-tah)*
a tie	**una corbata** *('oo-nah kohr-'bah-tah)*
underpants	**unos calzoncillos** *('oo-nohs kahl-sohn-'see-yohs)*
underwear	**ropa interior** *('roh-pah een-teh-ree-'ohr)*
a uniform	**un uniforme** *(oon oo-nee-'fohr-meh)*
a vest	**un chaleco** *(oon chah-'leh-koh)*

DIRTY LAUNDRY

La ropa sucia *(lah 'roh-pah 'soo-see·ah)*

Now that you're ready to have the laundry done, did you bring everything into the laundry room?

I have the...	Tengo... *('tehn-goh)*
bleach	**el blanqueador** *(ehl blahn-keh-ah-'dohr)*
clothesline	**la tendedera** *(lah tehn-deh-'deh-rah)*
clothespins	**las pinzas** *(lahs 'peen-sahs)*
detergent	**el detergente** *(ehl deh-tehr-'hehn-teh)*
fabric softener	**el suavizador** *(ehl swah-bee-sah-'dohr)*
hangers	**los ganchos** *(lohs 'gahn-chohs)*
iron	**la plancha** *(lah 'plahn-chah)*
ironing board	**la tabla de planchar** *(lah 'tah-blah deh plahn-'chahr)*
laundry basket	**la canasta para la ropa** *(lah kah-'nah-stah 'pah-rah lah 'roh-pay)*
spot remover	**el quitamanchas** *(ehl kee-tah-'mahn-chahs)*
starch	**el almidón** *(ehl ahl-mee-'dohn)*

Not everything being washed is clothing. Notice these other common articles that aren't always as clean as they should be:

Please rinse, fold, and hang the...

Favor de enjuagar, doblar, y colgar... *(fah-'bohr deh ehn-hoo·ah-'gahr, doh-'blahr ee kohl-'gahr)*

bedspread	**la cubrecama** *(lah koo-breh-'kah-mah)*
blanket	**la cobija** *(lah koh-bee-hah)*
drape	**la cortina** *(lah kohr-'tee-nah)*
mattress	**el colchón** *(ehl kohl-'chohn)*
napkin	**la servilleta** *(lah sehr-bee-'yeh-tah)*
pillow	**la almohada** *(lah ahl-moh-'ah-dah)*
pillowcase	**la funda** *(lah 'foon-dah)*
quilt	**la colcha** *(lah 'kohl-chah)*
rug	**el tapete** *(ehl tah-'peh-teh)*
sheet	**la sábana** *(lah 'sah-bah-nah)*
towel	**la toalla** *(lah toh-'ah-yah)*
washcloth	**el paño** *(ehl 'pah-nyoh)*

And you may need a tailor or professional cleaning service when it comes to these, but you should still learn the words:

boots	**las botas** *(lahs 'boh-tahs)*
buckle	**la hebilla** *(lah eh-'bee-yah)*
button	**el botón** *(ehl boh-'tohn)*
collar	**el cuello** *(ehl 'kweh-yoh)*
cuff	**el puño** *(ehl 'poo-nyoh)*
embroidery	**el bordado** *(ehl bohr-'dah-doh)*
hat	**el sombrero** *(ehl sohm-'breh-roh)*
hem	**el ruedo** *(ehl roo-'eh-doh)*
pocket	**el bolsillo** *(ehl bohl-'see-yoh)*
raincoat	**el impermeable** *(ehl eem-pehr-meh-'ah-bleh)*
sandals	**las sandalias** *(lahs sahn-'dah-lee·ahs)*
shoes	**los zapatos** *(lohs sah-'pah-tohs)*
shoulder pad	**la hombrera** *(lah ohm-'breh-rah)*
sleeve	**la manga** *(lah 'mahn-gah)*
strap	**la correa** *(lah koh-'rreh-ah)*
tennis shoes, sneakers	**los tenis** *(lohs 'teh-nees)*
zipper	**el cierre** *(ehl see-'eh-rreh)*

 REPASEMOS

Match the Spanish word with its translation:

el vestido *(ehl beh-'stee-doh)*	towel
el cinturón *(ehl seen-too-'rohn)*	suit

el traje *(ehl 'trah-heh)*	belt
la plancha *(lah 'plahn-chah)*	sleeve
la manga *(lah 'mahn-gah)*	dress
la toalla *(lah toh-'ah-yah)*	iron

WASH AND DRY
Lavar y secar (lah-'bahr ee seh-'kahr)

Have you ever looked closely at the dials on a washer or dryer? Most of us get confused when it comes to setting all of the appropriate switches. Here are a few words that will help you explain the various functions of these household devices. But don't forget to read your owner's manual first!

Program it for...	**Prográmelo para...** *(proh-'grah-meh-loh 'pah-rah)*
Set it at...	**Póngalo en...** *('pohn-gah-loh ehn)*
Press...	**Oprima...** *('oh-pree-mah)*
automatic	**automático** *(ow-toh-'mah-tee-koh)*
cold	**frío** *('free-oh)*
color	**color** *(koh-'lohr)*
cool	**fresco** *('frehs-koh)*
damp	**húmedo** *('oo-meh-doh)*
delicate	**delicado** *(deh-lee-'kah-doh)*
dry	**seco** *('seh-koh)*
forward	**adelante** *(ah-deh-'lahn-teh)*
gentle	**delicado** *(deh-lee-'kah-doh)*
heavy	**pesado** *(peh-'sah-doh)*
high	**alto** *('ahl-toh)*
hot	**caliente** *(kah-lee-'ehn-teh)*
light	**ligero** *(lee-'heh-roh)*
low	**bajo** *('bah-hoh)*
low heat	**llama baja** *('yah-mah 'bah-hah)*
medium	**mediano** *(meh-dee-'ah-noh)*
off	**apagado** *(ah-pah-'gah-doh)*
on	**prendido** *(prehn-'dee-doh)*
permanent press	**planchado permanente** *(plahn-'chah-doh pehr-mah-'nehn-teh)*
reverse	**retroceder** *(reh-troh-deh-'sehr)*

rinse	**enjuagar** *(ehn-joo·ah-'gahr)*
soak	**remojar** *('reh-moh-'hahr)*
spin	**girar** *(gee-'rahr)*
start	**empezar** *(ehm-peh-'sahr)*
stop	**parar** *(pah-'rahr)*
warm	**tibio** *('tee-bee·oh)*
wet	**mojado** *(moh-'hah-doh)*
white	**blanco** *('blahn-koh)*
What's the...?	**¿Cuál es...?** *(kwahl ehs)*
level	**el nivel** *(ehl nee-'behl)*
load	**la carga** *(lah 'kahr-gah)*
temperature	**la temperatura** *(lah tehm-peh-rah-'too-rah)*
time	**el tiempo** *(ehl tee-'ehm-poh)*
weight	**el peso** *(ehl 'peh-soh)*

 MÁS AYUDA

Lo, La, and Le *(loh, lah, leh)*

• Generally speaking, the words **lo** *(loh)* or **la** *(lah)* refer to "it" in Spanish (**lo** for masculine, **la** for feminine). They can be very useful when they are added to your commands:

Bring **(Traiga)** *('trah·ee-gah)*
Bring it. **(Tráigala)** *('trah·ee-gah-lah)*
Repeat **(Repita)** *(reh-'pee-tah)*
Repeat it. **(Repítalo)** *(reh-'pee-tah-loh)*
Do **(Haga)** *('ah-gah)*
Do it. **(Hágalo)** *('ah-gah-loh)*

Please pick it up and put it in the trash!

¡**Recójalo** y **métalo en la basura!** *(reh-'koh-hah-loh ee 'meh-tah-loh ehn lah bah-'soo-rah)*

• The word **le** *(leh)* refers to "him, her, and you." Use it when you're working with an interpreter or when you're instructing your help regarding messages:

Tell him/her.	**Dígale** *('dee-gah-leh)*
Ask him/her.	**Pregúntele** *(preh-'goon-teh-leh)*
Explain to him/her.	**Explíquele** *(ehks-'plee-keh-leh)*

- Other words that may give you trouble sometimes include **me** *(meh)*, **les** *(lehs)*, **nos** *(nohs)*, and **se** *(seh)*. The best way to learn them is to practice using them in complete expressions. Try to memorize these:

We lost it.	**Se nos perdió** *(seh nohs pehr-dee-'oh)*
I forgot it.	**Se me olvidó** *(seh meh ohl-bee-'doh)*
They broke it.	**Se les quebró** *(seh lehs keh-'broh)*

IN NEED OF REPAIR
Necesita reparación
(neh-seh-'see-tah reh-pah-rah-see·'ohn)

In the midst of all these activities involving housecleaning, another problem arises. A variety of objects are in need of repair and/or restoration. Before you put them in the garage or the basement, send them to the repair shop, or throw them away, spend a minute or two describing each item **en español** *(ehn eh-spah-'nyohl)*:

It's...	**Está...** *(eh-'stah)*
bent	**doblado** *(doh-'blah-doh)*
broken	**quebrado** *(keh-'brah-doh)*
crushed	**aplastado** *(ah-plah-'stah-doh)*
disposable	**desechable** *(deh-seh-chab-leh)*
loose	**flojo** *('floh-hoh)*
missing parts	**faltando piezas** *(fahl-'tahn-doh pee-'eh-sahs)*

out of service	**fuera de servicio** *('fweh-rah deh sehr-'bee-see·oh)*
stained	**manchado** *(mahn-'chah-doh)*
torn	**rasgado** *(rahs-'gah-doh)*
twisted	**torcido** *(tohr-'see-doh)*
It's (the)...	**Es...** *(ehs)*
antique	**el objeto antiguo** *(ehl ob-'heh-toh ahn-'tee-goo-oh)*
family heirloom	**la herencia de familia** *(lah eh-'rehn-see·ah deh fah-'mee-lee·ah)*
junk	**la basura** *(lah bah-'soo-rah)*
valuable	**valioso** *(bah-lee-'oh-soh)*
worthless	**sin valor** *(seen bah-'lohr)*

 MÁS AYUDA

Most beginners in Spanish use the command words all the time. Try to keep things simple by using the words "this" (**esto**) *('eh-stoh)* and "that" (**eso**) *('eh-soh)*:

Clean this.	**Limpie esto** *('leem-pee-eh 'eh-stoh)*
Wash that.	**Lave eso** *('lah-beh 'eh-soh)*

Here are some new ones:

Spray this.	**Rocíe esto** *(roh-'see-eh 'eh-stoh)*
Scrub that.	**Friegue eso** *(free-'eh-geh 'eh-soh)*
Empty this.	**Vacíe esto** *(bah-'see-eh 'eh-stoh)*
Turn that over.	**Voltée eso** *(bohl-'teh-ee 'eh-soh)*

• And feel free to converse about the material:

It's made of...	**Está hecho de...** *(eh-'stah 'eh-choh deh)*
asphalt	**el asfalto** *(ehl ahs-'fahl-toh)*
brick	**el ladrillo** *(ehl lah-'dree-yoh)*
cardboard	**el cartón** *(ehl kahr-'tohn)*
cement	**el cemento** *(ehl seh-'mehn-toh)*
china	**la porcelana** *(lah pohr-seh-'lah-nah)*
clay	**el barro** *(ehl 'bah-rroh)*
floor tile	**la baldosa** *(lah bahl-'doh-sah)*
glass	**el vidrio** *('bee-dree·oh)*

plastic	**el plástico** *(ehl 'plah-stee-koh)*
rubber	**la goma** *(lah 'goh-mah)*
stone	**la piedra** *(lah pee-'eh-drah)*
wire	**el alambre** *(ehl ah-'lahm-breh)*
wood	**la madera** *(lah mah-'deh-rah)*
metals:	**los metales** *(lohs meh-'tah-lehs)*
brass	**el latón** *(ehl lah-'tohn)*
copper	**el cobre** *(ehl 'koh-breh)*
gold	**el oro** *(ehl 'oh-roh)*
iron	**el hierro** *(ehl 'yeh-rroh)*
silver	**la plata** *(lah 'plah-tah)*
steel	**el acero** *(ehl ah-'seh-roh)*

CHECK THE FABRICS
Las telas *(lahs 'teh-lahs)*

To further help you to describe an item in Spanish, you need the following:

It's made of...	**Está hecho de...** *(eh-'stah 'eh-choh deh)*
acrylic	**el acrílico** *(ehl ah-'kree-lee-koh)*
canvas	**la lona** *(lah 'loh-nah)*
corduroy	**la pana** *(lah 'pah-nah)*
cotton	**el algodón** *(ehl ahl-goh-'dohn)*
denim	**el dril** *(ehl dreel)*
fur	**la piel** *(lah pee-'ehl)*
gabardine	**la gabardina** *(lah gah-bahr-'dee-nah)*

knit	el **tejido** *(ehl teh-'hee-doh)*
lace	el **encaje** *(ehl ehn-'kah-heh)*
leather	el **cuero** *(ehl 'kweh-roh)*
linen	el **lino** *(ehl 'lee-noh)*
rayon	el **rayón** *(ehl rah-'yohn)*
satin	el **raso** *(ehl 'rah-soh)*
silk	la **seda** *(lah 'seh-dah)*
suede	la **gamuza** *(lah gah-'moo-sah)*
velvet	el **terciopelo** *(ehl tehr-see·oh-'peh-loh)*
wool	la **lana** *(lah 'lah-nah)*

REPASEMOS

Fill in the blanks with the appropriate word:

La pelota está hecha de ⟨goma⟩
(lah peh-'loh-tah eh-'stah 'eh-chah deh)

La ventana está hecha de ⟨vidrio⟩
(lah behn-'tah-nah eh-'stah 'eh-chah deh)

El anillo está hecho de ⟨oro⟩
(ehl ah-'nee-yoh eh-'stah 'eh-choh deh)

El suéter está hecho de ⟨lana⟩
(ehl 'sweh-tehr eh-'stah 'eh-chah deh)

lana *('lah-nah)*
goma *('goh-mah)*
vidrio *('bee-dree·oh)*
oro *('oh-roh)*

TEMAS CULTURALES

Still more "Spanglish" — try it out:

el **"jean"**
el **"nailon"**
el **"polyester"**
el **"velcro"**

PRECIOUS STONES
Las piedras preciosas
(lahs pee-'eh-drahs preh-see-'oh-sahs)

We certainly don't want to lose any of these around the house! If one should turn up, make sure it gets back to the rightful owner:

diamond	**el diamante** *(ehl dee-ah-'mahn-teh)*
emerald	**la esmeralda** *(lah ehs-meh-'rahl-dah)*
onyx	**el ónix** *(ehl 'oh-neeks)*
opal	**el ópalo** *(ehl 'oh-pah-loh)*
pearl	**la perla** *(lah 'pehr-lah)*
ruby	**el rubí** *(ehl roo-'bee)*
sapphire	**el zafiro** *(ehl sah-'fee-roh)*
topaz	**el topacio** *(ehl toh-'pah-see·oh)*
turquoise	**la turquesa** *(lah toor-'keh-sah)*

Mi casa está hecha de piedras preciosas. Las escaleras están hechas de esmeraldas y el tejado está hecho de perlas.

¡EL SUPERESPAÑOL!

Are you still combining the Spanish infinitives with these "super" phrases?

Please...	**Favor de...** *(fah-'bohr deh)*
...work	**...trabajar** *(trah-bah-'hahr)*
Don't...	**No...**
...clean	**...limpiar** *(leem-pee-'ahr)*
You have to...	**Tiene que...** *(tee-'eh-neh keh)*
...sweep	**...barrer** *(bah-'rrehr)*

Helpful, aren't they? You can say even more with this next set of words. These are forms of the verb "to need" **(necesitar)** *(neh-seh-see-'tahr)*:

I need	**necesito...** *(neh-seh-'see-toh)*
to wash	**lavar** *(lah-'bahr)*
You need, he, she needs	**necesita...** *(neh-seh-'see-tah)*
to dust	**desempolvar** *(deh-sehm-pohl-'vahr)*
they, you (plural) need	**necesitan...** *(neh-seh-'see-tahn)*
to sweep	**barrer** *(bahr-'rehr)*
we need	**necesitamos...** *(neh-seh-see-'tah-mohs)*
to scrub	**fregar** *(freh-'gahr)*

REPASEMOS

Now translate the following sentences:

Carlos y Juan necesitan limpiar el apartamento grande *('kahr-lohs ee wahn neh-seh-'see-tahn leem-pee-'ahr ehl ah-pahr-tah-'mehn-toh 'grahn-deh)*

Usted necesita barrer y sacudir todos los cuartos *(oo-'stehd neh-seh-'see-tah bah-'rrehr ee sah-koo-'deer 'toh-dohs lohs 'kwahr-tohs)*

Necesito hablar más español con mis amigos *(neh-seh-'see-toh ah-'blahr mahs eh-spah-'nyohl kohn mees ah-'mee-gohs)*

 ¡MÁS ACCIÓN!

The last time we looked at Spanish infinitive verb forms, we learned how to talk about everyday activities. We discovered that the endings of action words must change according to the tense and the person, and that most forms follow a familiar pattern.

AR verbs: to clean	***Limpiar** (leem-pee-'ahr)*
I clean	**limpio** *('leem-pee·oh)*
you clean, he, she cleans	**limpia** *('leem-pee·ah)*
they, you (plural) clean	**limpian** *('leem-pee-ahn)*
we clean	**limpiamos** *(leem-pee-'ah-mohs)*

ER, IR verbs: to sweep	***Barrer** (bah-'rrehr)*
I sweep	**barro** *('bah-rroh)*
You sweep, he, she sweeps	**barre** *('bah-rreh)*
They, you (plural) sweep	**barren** *('bah-rrehn)*
we sweep	**barremos** *(bah-'rreh-mohs)*

However, some verbs have irregular changes that you may have to study a little more carefully. The following examples will help you talk about more everyday actions around the house.

Notice that the four forms below each infinitive refer to the same persons as the translated forms above. And remember that this is only a brief selection of irregular patterns. To learn more, consider buying a Spanish grammar textbook, or take a class in Spanish language structures:

To hang **colgar** *(kohl-'guhr)*
cuelgo *('kwehl-goh)*
cuelga *('kwehl-gah)*
cuelgan *('kwehl-gahn)*
colgamos *(kohl-'gah-mohs)*

To close **cerrar** *(seh 'rrahr)*
cierro *(see-'eh-rroh)*
cierra *(see-'eh-rrah)*
cierran *(see-'eh-rrahn)*
cerramos *(seh-'rrah-mohs)*

To go **ir** *(eer)*
voy *('boh-ee)*
va *(bah)*
van *(bahn)*
vamos *('bah-mohs)*

To laugh **reír** *(reh-'eer)*
río *('ree-oh)*
ríe *('ree-eh)*
ríen *('ree-ehn)*
reímos *(reh-'ee-mohs)*

To hear **oír** *(oh-'eer)*
oigo *(oh·ee-goh)*
oye *('oh-yeh)*
oyen *('oh-yehn)*
oímos *(oh-'ee-mohs)*

To do **hacer** *(ah-'sehr)*
hago *('ah-goh)*
hace *('ah-seh)*
hacen *('ah-sehn)*
hacemos *(ah-'seh-mohs)*

CAR WASH!

El lavado de carros (ehl lah-'bah-doh deh 'kah-rrohs)

Many Spanish-speakers are able to translate the basic parts of an automobile from Spanish into English. So, you shouldn't have too much trouble in dialogues about washing and taking care of a car. In an emergency, however, refer to this bonus list of pertinent command words:

Clean (the)...	**Limpie...** *('leem-pee-eh)*
Wash (the)...	**Lave...** *('lah-beh)*
Wax (the)...	**Encere...** *(ehn-'seh-reh)*
Replace (the)...	**Reemplace...** *(eh-ehm-'plah-seh)*
Repair (the)...	**Repare...** *(reh-'pah-reh)*

brakes	**los frenos** *(lohs 'freh-nohs)*
bumper	**el parachoques** *(ehl pah-rah-'choh-kehs)*
carseat	**el asiento** *(ehl ah-see-'ehn-toh)*
dashboard	**el tablero** *(ehl tah-'bleh-roh)*
door	**la puerta** *(lah 'pwehr-tah)*
engine	**el motor** *(ehl moh-'tohr)*
glove compartment	**la guantera** *(lah gwahn-'teh-rah)*
hood	**la cubierta** *(lah koo-bee-'ehr-tah)*
horn	**la bocina** *(lah boh-'see-nah)*
hubcap	**el tapacubos** *(ehl tah-pah-'koo-bohs)*
lights	**las luces** *(lahs 'loo-sehs)*
mirror	**el espejo** *(ehl eh-'speh-hoh)*
muffler	**el silenciador** *(ehl see-lehn-see·ah-'dohr)*
roof	**el techo** *(ehl 'teh-choh)*
steering wheel	**el volante** *(ehl boh-'lahn-teh)*
tire	**el neumático** *(ehl neh-oo-'mah-tee-koh*
spare tire	**el neumático de repuesto** *(ehl neh-oo-'mah-tee-koh deh reh-'pweh-stoh)*
trunk	**la maletera** *(lah mah-leh-'teh-rah)*
windshield	**el parabrisas** *(ehl pah-rah-'bree-sahs)*

 **MÁS AYUDA**

Specify your needs by adding words to the phrases below. These also work well as parts of written notes or messages:

When you finish...	**Cuando termine...** *('kwahn-doh tehr-'mee-neh)*
If it's possible...	**Si es posible...** *(see ehs poh-'see-bleh)*
Before you go...	**Antes de irse...** *('ahn-tehs deh 'eer-seh)*
...call me.	**...llámeme.** *('yah-meh-meh)*

_____   _____

_____   _____

I told you that...	**Le dije que...** *(leh 'dee-heh keh)*
Remember that...	**Recuerde que...** *(reh-'kwehr-deh)*
It's important that...	**Es importante que...** *(ehs eem-pohr-'tahn-teh)*
...the door is locked.	**...la puerta está cerrada.** *(lah 'pwehr-tah eh-'stah seh-'rrah-dah)*

_____   _____

_____   _____

 REPASEMOS

Escriba tres partes de un carro *(eh-'skree-bah trehs 'pahr-tehs deh oon 'kah-rroh)*

_____   _____   _____

CHAPTER FOUR *Capítulo Cuatro*
(kah-'pee-too-loh 'kwah-troh)

IN THE KITCHEN
En la cocina
(ehn lah koh-'see-nah)

MEALTIME
La hora de comer (lah 'oh-rah deh koh-'mehr)

In homes all over the world, there's no room quite like the kitchen. Sights, smells, and tastes continue to attract family members, and hungry stomachs are satisfied. Mealtimes often differ, however, from one culture to the next. Guide your Spanish-speaking assistant through a few key words before anyone actually cooks anything:

Here is the...	**Aquí está...** *(ah-'kee eh-'stah)*
meal	**la comida** *(lah koh-'mee-dah)*
breakfast	**el desayuno** *(ehl deh-sah-'yoo-noh)*
dessert	**el postre** *(ehl 'poh-streh)*
dinner	**la cena** *(lah 'seh-nah)*
lunch	**el almuerzo** *(ehl ahl-moo-'ehr-soh)*
snack	**la merienda** *(lah meh-ree-'ehn-dah)*

Now practice:

La comida es muy buena *(lah koh-'mee-dah ehs 'moo·ee 'bweh-nah)*

¿Dónde está el desayuno? *('dohn-deh eh-'stah ehl deh-sah-'yoo-noh)*

Ponga el almuerzo en la mesa *('pohn-gah ehl ahl-moo-'ehr-soh ehn lah 'meh-sah)*

Ella prepara la cena a las seis *('eh-yah preh-'pah-rah lah 'seh-nah ah lahs 'seh·ees)*

Favor de sacar el postre del refrigerador *(fah-'bohr deh sah-'kahr ehl 'poh-streh dehl reh-free-heh-rah-'dohr)*

MÁS AYUDA

"Groceries" are **los comestibles** *(lohs koh-meh-'stee-blehs)*

"Hors d'oeuvres" are **los entremeses** *(lohs ehn-treh-'meh-sehs)*

"To go shopping" is **ir de compras** *(eer deh 'kohm-prahs)*

FOOD!
¡La comida! *(lah koh-'mee-dah)*

Obviously, some of the first words that you'll need in the kitchen are the names of the foods. Go ahead and "feast" on the following:

MEAT	***La carne*** *(lah 'kahr-neh)*
bacon	**el tocino** *(ehl toh-'see-noh)*
beef	**la carne de vaca** *(lah 'kahr-neh deh 'bah-kah)*
chicken	**el pollo** *(ehl 'poh-yoh)*
ground beef	**la carne molida** *(lah 'kahr-neh moh-'lee-dah)*
ham	**el jamón** *(ehl hah-'mohn)*
hamburger	**la hamburguesa** *(lah ahm-boor-'geh-sah)*
hot dog	**el perro caliente** *(ehl 'peh-rroh kah-lee-'ehn-teh)*
lamb	**el cordero** *(ehl kohr-'deh-roh)*
meatball	**la albóndiga** *(lah ahl-'bohn-dee-gah)*
pork	**el cerdo** *(ehl 'sehr-doh)*

111

roast beef	el rosbif *(ehl rohs-'beef)*
sausage	la salchicha *(lah sahl-'chee-chah)*
steak	el bistec *(ehl bees-'tehk)*
turkey	el pavo *(ehl 'pah-boh)*
veal	la ternera *(lah tehr-'neh-rah)*

 ## MÁS AYUDA

How do you like your meat?	¿Cómo le gusta la carne? *('koh-moh leh 'goo-stah lah 'kahr-neh)*
medium	medio cocida *('meh-dee·oh koh-'see-dah)*
rare	poco cocida *('poh-koh koh-'see-dah)*
well-done	bien cocida *('bee-ehn koh-'see-dah)*

SEAFOOD *Los mariscos (lohs mah-'rees-kohs)*

clam	la almeja *(lah ahl-'meh-hah)*
crab	el cangrejo *(ehl kah-'greh-hoh)*
fish	el pescado *(ehl peh-'skah-doh)*
lobster	la langosta *(lah lahn-'goh-stah)*
salmon	el salmón *(ehl sahl-'mohn)*
seafood	el marisco *(ehl mah-'rees-koh)*
shrimp	el camarón *(ehl kah-mah-'rohn)*
tuna	el atún *(ehl ah-'toon)*

VEGETABLES *Los vegetales (lohs beh-heh-'tah-lehs)*
When it comes to the preparation of a healthy meal, the addition of fresh vegetables is a must. Enjoy!

artichoke	la alcachofa *(lah ahl-kah-'choh-fah)*
asparagus	el espárrago *(ehl eh-'spah-rrah-goh)*
beans	los frijoles *(lohs free-'hoh-lehs)*
beet	el betabel *(ehl beh-tah-'behl)*
broccoli	el brocolí *(ehl broh-koo-'lee)*
cabbage	el repollo *(ehl reh-'poh-yoh)*
carrot	la zanahoria *(lah sah-nah-'oh-ree·ah)*
cauliflower	el coliflor *(ehl koh-lee-'flohr)*
celery	el apio *(ehl 'ah-pee·oh)*
corn	el maíz *(ehl mah-'ees)*

cucumber	**el pepino** *(ehl peh-'pee-noh)*
eggplant	**la berenjena** *(lah beh-rehn-'heh-nah)*
green bean	**la judía verde** *(lah hoo-'dee-ah 'behr-deh)*
green onion	**el cebollino** *(ehl seh-boh-'yee-noh)*
lettuce	**la lechuga** *(lah leh-'choo-gah)*
mushroom	**el champiñón** *(ehl chahm-pee-'nyohn)*
onion	**la cebolla** *(lah seh-'boh-yah)*
peas	**las arvejitas** *(lahs ahr-beh-'hee-tahs)*
potato	**la papa** *('lah 'pah-pah)*
mashed potato	**el puré de papa** *(ehl poo-'reh deh 'pah-pah)*
pumpkin	**la calabaza** *(lah kah-lah-'bah-sah)*
radish	**el rábano** *(ehl 'rah-bah-noh)*
spinach	**la espinaca** *(lah eh-spee-'nah-kah)*
sweet potato	**el camote** *(ehl kah-'moh-teh)*
tomato	**el tomate** *(ehl toh-'mah-teh)*
turnip	**el nabo** *(ehl 'nah-boh)*
watercress	**el berro** *(ehl 'beh-rroh)*
zucchini	**la calabacita verde** *(lah kah-lah-bah-'see-tah 'behr-deh)*

FRUIT *La fruta (lah 'froo-tah)*

Food words go great with your commands. As you give instructions —
and don't forget **por favor** — touch each item and call out its name in
Spanish.

Bring the...	**Traiga...** *(trah-'ee-gah)*
apple	**la manzana** *(lah mahn-'sah-nah)*
apricot	**el durazno** *(ehl doo-'rahs-noh)*
banana	**el plátano** *(ehl 'plah-tah-noh)*
blackberry	**la mora** *(lah 'moh-rah)*
blueberry	**el arándano** *(ehl ah-'rahn-dah-noh)*
cantaloupe	**el melón** *(ehl meh-'lohn)*
cherry	**la cereza** *(lah seh-'reh-sah)*
coconut	**el coco** *(ehl 'koh-koh)*
fig	**el higo** *(ehl 'ee-goh)*
grape	**la uva** *(lah 'oo-bah)*
grapefruit	**la toronja** *(lah toh-'rohn-hah)*
lemon/lime	**el limón** *(ehl lee-'mohn)*

orange	**la naranja** *(lah nah-'rahn-hah)*
peach	**el melocotón** *(ehl meh-loh-koh-'tohn)*
pear	**la pera** *(lah 'peh-rah)*
pineapple	**la piña** *(lah 'pee-nyah)*
plum	**la ciruela** *(lah see-roo-'eh-lah)*
prune	**la ciruela pasa** *(lah see-roo-'eh-lah 'pah-sah)*
raisin	**la pasita** *(lah pah-'see-tah)*
strawberry	**la fresa** *(lah 'freh-sah)*

DAIRY PRODUCTS
Productos lácteos (proh-'dook-tohs 'lahk-teh-ohs)

butter	**la mantequilla** *(lah mahn-teh-'kee-yah)*
cheese	**el queso** *(ehl 'keh-soh)*
cottage cheese	**el requesón** *(ehl reh-keh-'sohn)*
cream cheese	**el queso crema** *(ehl 'keh-soh 'kreh-mah)*
Parmesan cheese	**el queso parmesano** *(ehl 'keh-soh pahr-meh-'sah-noh)*
cream	**la crema** *(ehl 'kreh-mah)*
egg	**el huevo** *(ehl 'weh-boh*
hard-boiled egg	**el huevo duro** *(ehl 'weh-boh 'doo-roh)*
scrambled egg	**el huevo revuelto** *(ehl 'weh-boh reh-'bwehl-toh)*
margarine	**la margarina** *(lah mahr-gah-'ree-nah)*
milk	**la leche** *(lah 'leh-cheh)*
condensed milk	**la leche condensada** *(lah 'leh-cheh kohn-'dehn-sah-dah)*
evaporated milk	**la leche evaporada** *(lah 'leh-cheh eh-bah-poh-'rah-dah)*

MISCELLANEOUS

bread	**el pan** *(ehl pahn)*
cake	**la torta** *(lah 'tohr-tah)*
candy	**los dulces** *(lohs 'dool-sehs)*
cereal	**el cereal** *(ehl seh-reh-'ahl)*
chewing gum	**el chicle** *(ehl 'chee-kleh)*
cookie	**la galleta** *(lah gah-'yeh-tah)*
cracker	**la galleta salada** *(lah gah-'yeh-tah sah-'lah-dah)*
ice cream	**el helado** *(ehl eh-'lah-doh)*
jello	**la gelatina** *(lah heh-lah-'tee-nah)*
noodles	**los fideos** *(lohs fee-'deh-ohs)*
oatmeal	**la avena** *(lah ah-'beh-nah)*
pie	**el pastel** *(ehl pah-'stehl)*
rice	**el arroz** *(ehl ah-'rrohs)*
roll	**el panecillo** *(ehl pah-neh-'see-yoh)*
salad	**la ensalada** *(lah ehn-sah-'lah-dah)*
soup	**la sopa** *(lah 'soh-pah)*
toast	**el pan tostado** *(ehl pahn toh-'stah-doh)*
yogurt	**el yogurt** *(ehl yoh-'goor)*

Cuando como frijoles, tengo mucho gas.

 MÁS AYUDA

You may want to refer to your favorite ethnic foods. Use the words below:

Chinese food	**la comida china** *(lah koh-'mee-dah 'chee-nah)*
French food	**la comida francesa** *(lah koh-'mee-dah frahn-'seh-sah)*

Italian food	**la comida italiana** *(lah koh-'mee-dah ee-tah-lee-'ah-nah)*
Japanese food	**la comida japonesa** *(lah koh-'mee-dah hah-poh-'neh-sah)*
Mexican food	**la comida mexicana** *(lah koh-'mee-dah meh-hee-'kah-nah)*

You may need to ask your Spanish-speaking help to place a food order over the phone. Rehearse the various items, beforehand, and practice this phrase in English:

I'd like to order...	**Quisiera ordenar...** *(kee-see-'eh-rah or-deh-'nahr)*

 REPASEMOS

Answer these questions in Spanish:

¿Qué come usted para desayuno? *(keh 'koh-meh oo-'stehd 'pah-rah deh-sah-'yoo-noh)*

¿Qué tipo de carne compra usted? *(keh 'tee-poh deh 'kahr-neh 'kohm-prah oo-'stehd)*

¿Cuál es su fruta favorita? *(kwahl ehs soo 'froo-tah fah-boh-'ree-tah)*

¿Cuáles vegetales son deliciosos? *('kwah-lehs beh-heh-'tah-lehs sohn deh-lee-see-'oh-sohs)*

INGREDIENTS, SPICES AND CONDIMENTS
Los ingredientes, las especias y los condimentos *(lohs een-greh-dee-'ehn-tehs, lahs eh-'speh-see-ahs ee lohs kohn-dee-'mehn-tohs)*

Making sure that you have all the basic foods on hand is important, but to properly prepare the best dish possible, you need to know the following words:

Put in more...	**Ponga más...**
baking powder	**el polvo de hornear** *(ehl 'pohl-boh deh ohr-neh-'ahr)*
baking soda	**el bicarbonato de soda** *(ehl bee-kahr-boh-'nah-toh deh 'soh-dah)*
barbecue sauce	**la salsa de barbacoa** *(lah 'sahl-sah deh bahr-bah-'koh-ah)*

broth	**el caldo** *(ehl 'kahl-doh)*
chocolate	**el chocolate** *(ehl choh-koh-'lah-teh)*
cinnamon	**la canela** *(lah kah-'neh-lah)*
cornstarch	**el almidón de maíz** *(ehl ahl-mee-'dohn deh mah-'ees)*
flour	**la harina** *(lah ah-'ree-nah)*
garlic	**el ajo** *(ehl 'ah-hoh)*
honey	**la miel** *(lah mee-'ehl)*
hot pepper	**el chile** *(ehl 'chee-leh)*
lard	**la manteca** *(lah mahn-'teh-kah)*
marmalade	**la mermelada** *(lah mehr-meh-'lah-dah)*
mayonnaise	**la mayonesa** *(lah mah-yoh-'neh-sah)*
mint	**la menta** *(lah 'mehn-tah)*
mustard	**la mostaza** *(lah moh-'stah-sah)*
nuts	**las nueces** *(lahs noo-'eh-sehs)*
oil	**el aceite** *(ehl ah-'seh-ee-teh)*
olive	**la aceituna** *(lah ah-seh-ee-'too-nah)*
parsley	**el perejil** *(ehl peh-reh-'heel)*
peanut butter	**la crema de maní** *(lah 'kreh-mah deh mah-'nee)*
pepper	**la pimienta** *(lah pee-mee-'ehn-tah)*
pickle	**el encurtido** *(ehl ehn-koor-'tee-doh)*
salad dressing	**la salsa para la ensalada** *(lah 'sahl-sah 'pah-rah lah ehn-sah-'lah-dah)*
salt	**la sal** *(lah sahl)*
sauce	**la salsa** *(lah 'sahl-sah)*
soy sauce	**la salsa de soja** *(lah 'sahl-sah deh 'soh-yah)*
sugar	**el azúcar** *(ehl ah-'soo-kahr)*
teriyaki sauce	**la salsa japonesa** *(lah 'sahl-sah hah-poh-'neh-sah)*
tomato sauce	**la salsa de tomate** *(lah 'sahl-sah deh toh-'mah-teh)*
vanilla	**la vainilla** *(lah bah-ee-'nee-yah)*
vinegar	**el vinagre** *(ehl bee-'nah-greh)*
Worcestershire sauce	**la salsa inglesa** *(lah 'sahl-sah een-'gleh-sah)*

If you don't want to include certain parts of the food, say:

We don't eat the... **No comemos...** *(noh koh-'meh-mohs)*

bone	**el hueso** *(ehl 'weh-soh)*
fat	**la grasa** *(lah 'grah-sah)*
leaf	**la hoja** *(lah 'oh-hah)*
seed	**la semilla** *(lah seh-'mee-yah)*
skin	**el cuero** *(ehl 'kweh-roh)*
stem	**el tallo** *(ehl 'tah-yoh)*
yolk	**la yema** *(lah 'yeh-mah)*

 ## MÁS AYUDA

Several foods are pronounced almost the same in both Spanish and English:

broccoli	**el brocolí** *(ehl broh-koh-'lee)*
macaroni	**los macarrones** *(lohs mah-kah-'roh-nehs)*
pancake	**el panqueque** *(ehl pahn-'keh-keh)*
pizza	**la pizza** *(lah 'peet-sah)*
pudding	**el pudín** *(ehl poo-'deen)*
spaghetti	**el espagueti** *(ehl eh-spah-'geh-tee)*

 ## ¡HÁGALO, POR FAVOR!

Training a person how to cook, using Spanish terms, involves more than calling out the different names for foods and drinks. The trick is to utilize as many "cooking commands" as possible. Say each phrase aloud as you translate.

add	**añada** *(ah-'nyah-dah)*
Añada más sal *(ah-'nyah-dah mahs sahl)*	
bake	**hornee** *(ohr-'neh-ee)*
Hornee el pastel *(ohr-'neh-ee ehl pah-'stehl)*	
barbecue	**ase** *('ah-seh)*
Ase la carne en las brasas *('ah-seh lah-'kahr-neh ehn lahs 'brah-sahs)*	
beat	**bata** *('bah-tah)*
Bata los huevos *('bah-tah lohs 'weh-bohs)*	
boil	**hierva** *('yehr-bah)*

Hierva el agua *('yehr-bah ehl 'ah-gwah)*
broil, brown **dore** *('doh-reh)*
Dore el pescado *('doh-reh ehl peh-'skah-doh)*
cook **cocine** *(koh-'see-neh)*
Cocine por dos horas *(koh-'see-neh pohr dohs 'oh-rahs)*
cover **cubra** *('koo-brah)*
Cubra el sartén *('koo-brah ehl sahr-'tehn)*
cut **corte** *('kohr-teh)*
Corte la lechuga *('kohr-teh lah leh-'choo-gah)*
defrost **descongele** *(dehs-kohn-'heh-leh)*
Descongele la hamburguesa *(dehs-kohn-'heh-leh lah ahm-boor-'geh-sah)*
fry **fría** *('free-ah)*
Fría las papas *('free-ah lahs 'pah-pahs)*
heat **caliente** *(kah-lee-'ehn-teh)*
Caliente el pan *(kah-lee-'ehn-teh ehl pahn)*
measure **mida** *('mee-dah)*
Mida el agua *('mee-dah ehl 'ah-gwah)*
mix **mezcle** *('mehs-kleh)*
Mezcle con aceite *('mehs-kleh kohn ah-'seh·ee-teh*
peel **pele** *('peh-leh)*
Pele las papas *(peh-'leh lahs 'pah-pahs)*
prepare **prepare** *(preh-'pah-reh)*
Prepare el desayuno *(preh-'pah-reh ehl deh-sah-'yoo-noh)*
put inside **meta** *('meh-tah)*
Meta el pollo en el horno *('meh-tah ehl 'poh-yoh ehl ehl 'ohr-noh)*
remove **quite** *('kee-teh)*
Quite la carne *('kee-teh lah 'kahr-neh)*
roast **ase** *('ah-seh)*
Ase el pavo *('ah-seh ehl 'pah-boh)*
serve **sirva** *('seer-bah)*
Sirva con arroz *('seer-bah ehl ah-'rrohs)*
stir **revuelva** *(reh-boo-'ehl-bah)*
Revuelva rápidamente *(reh-boo-'ehl-bah rah-pee-dah-'mehn-teh)*
take out **saque** *('sah-keh)*
Saque todo del refrigerador *('sah-keh 'toh-doh dehl reh-free-heh-rah-'dohr)*

Use the standard "Don't" phrase to avoid chaos in the kitchen:

Don't put...   **No poner...** *(noh poh-'nehr)*

bones in the disposal   **los huesos en el desechador** *(lohs 'weh-sohs ehn ehl dehs-eh-chah-'dohr)*

metal in the microwave   **el metal en el horno de microonda** *(ehl meh-'tahl ehn ehl 'ohr-noh deh mee-kroh-'ohn-dah)*

plastic in the oven   **el plástico en el horno** *(ehl 'plah-stee-koh ehn ehl 'ohr-noh)*

 ## REPASEMOS

Can you figure out what's going on here?

Corte el pollo en cuatro partes *('kohr-teh ehl 'poh-yoh ehn 'kwah-troh 'pahr-tehs)*

Prepare el pollo con ajo y limón *(preh-'pah-reh ehl 'poh-yoh kohn 'ah-hoh ee lee-'mohn)*

Meta el pollo en el horno *('meh-tah ehl 'poh-yoh ehn ehl 'ohr-noh)*

Cocínelo por una hora *(koh-'see-neh-loh pohr 'oo-nah 'oh-rah)*

HAVE A DRINK

Tome una bebida *('toh-meh 'oo-nah beh-'bee-dah)*

Thirsty? Wash down your meals with the appropriate beverage. While giving instructions, use either "to take" (**tomar**) *(toh-'mahr)* or "to drink" (**beber**) *(beh-'behr)*:

Is she drinking tea?	¿Está bebiendo té? *(eh-'stah beh-bee-'ehn-doh teh)*
No, she takes coffee.	No, toma café *(noh, 'toh-mah kah-'feh)*
I drink...	Tomo... *('toh-moh)*
alcoholic drink	la bebida alcóholica *(lah beh-'bee-dah ahl-koh-'oh-lee-kah)*
beer	la cerveza *(lah sehr-'beh-sah)*
coffee	el café *(ehl kah-'feh)*
decaffeinated coffee	el café descafeinado *(ehl kah-'feh dehs-kah-feh·ee-'nah-doh)*
diet soda	la soda de dieta *(lah 'soh-dah deh dee-'eh-tah)*
hot chocolate	el chocolate caliente *(ehl choh-koh-'lah-teh kah-lee-'ehn-teh)*
iced coffee	el café helado *(ehl kah-'feh eh-'lah-doh)*
iced tea	el té helado *(ehl teh eh-'lah-doh)*
juice	el jugo *(ehl 'hoo-goh)*
lemonade	la limonada *(lah lee-moh-'nah-dah)*
milk	la leche *(lah 'leh-cheh)*
shake	el batido *(ehl bah-'tee-doh)*
skim milk	la leche descremada *(lah 'leh-cheh dehs-kreh-'mah-dah)*
soft drink	el refresco *(ehl reh-'frehs-koh)*
tea	el té *(ehl teh)*
water	el agua *(ehl 'ah-gwah)*
wine	el vino *(ehl 'bee-noh)*

 **REPASEMOS**

¿Cuál es su bebida favorita? *(kwahl ehs soo beh-'bee-dah fah-boh-'ree-tah)* _____

Translate:

cream and sugar   _____

salt and pepper   _____

oil and vinegar   _____

NOW YOU'RE COOKING!
¡Ahora está cocinando!
(ah-'oh-rah eh-'stah koh-see-'nahn-doh)

Of course, you can't prepare and eat meals without the proper equipment. Become familiar with the following items:

Dishes, silverware, and utensils
La vajilla, los cubiertos, y los utensilios
(lah bah-'hee-yah, lohs koo-bee-'ehr-tohs, ee lohs oo-tehn-'see-lee·ohs)

Take out the...	**Saque...** *('sah-keh)*
bowl	**el plato hondo** *(ehl 'plah-toh 'ohn-doh)*
butter dish	**la mantequillera** *(lah mahn-teh-kee-'yeh-rah)*
china	**la loza de porcelana** *(lah 'loh-sah deh pohr-seh-'lah-nah)*
coffeepot	**la cafetera** *(lah kah-feh-'teh-rah)*
creamer	**la cremera** *(lah kreh-'meh-rah)*
cup	**la taza** *(lah 'tah-sah)*
fork	**el tenedor** *(ehl teh-neh-'dohr)*
fruit dish	**el frutero** *(ehl froo-'teh-roh)*
funnel	**el embudo** *(ehl ehm-'boo-doh*
glass	**el vaso** *(ehl 'bah-soh)*
grater	**el rallador** *(ehl rah-yah-'dohr)*
gravy boat	**la salsera** *(lah sahl-'seh-rah)*
griddle	**el comal** *(ehl koh-'mahl)*
grill	**la parrilla** *(lah pah-'rree-yah)*

knife	el cuchillo *(ehl koo-'chee-yoh)*
ladle	el cucharón *(ehl koo-chah-'rohn)*
mold/cutter	el molde *(ehl 'mohl-deh)*
pan	el sartén *(ehl sahr-'tehn)*
peeler	el pelador *(ehl peh-'lah-dohr)*
pepper shaker	el pimentero *(ehl pee-mehn-'teh-roh)*
pitcher	el cántaro *(ehl 'kahn-tah-roh)*
plate	el plato *(ehl 'plah-toh)*
platter	la fuente *(lah 'fwehn-teh)*
pot	la olla *(lah 'oh-yah)*
rack	el estilador *(ehl eh-stee-lah-'dohr)*
roasting pan	el asador *(ehl ah-sah-'dohr)*
rolling pin	el rodillo *(ehl roh-'dee-yoh)*
salad bowl	la ensaladera *(lah ehn-sah-lah-'deh-rah)*
salt shaker	el salero *(ehl sah-'leh-roh)*
saucepan	la cacerola *(lah kah-seh-'roh-lah)*
saucer	el platillo *(ehl plah-'tee-yoh)*
spatula	la espátula *(lah eh-'spah-too-lah)*
spoon	la cuchara *(lah koo-'chah-rah)*
strainer	el colador *(ehl koh-lah-'dohr)*
sugar bowl	la azucarera *(lah ah-soo-kah-'reh-rah)*
tea kettle	la tetera *(lah teh-'teh-rah)*
thermos	el termo *(ehl 'tehr-moh)*
tongs	las tenazas *(lahs teh-'nah-sahs)*
tray	la bandeja *(lah bahn-'deh-hah)*
wooden spoon	la cuchara de madera *(lah koo-'chah-rah deh mah-'deh-rah)*

To practice these words, create useful comments using your **Super-español** skills. For example:

Favor de limpiar los platos y los vasos *(fah-'bohr deh leem-pee-'ahr lohs 'plah-tohs ee lohs 'bah-sohs)*

Tiene que poner la limonada en el cántaro *(Tee-'eh-neh keh poh-'nehr lah lee-moh-'nah-dah ehn ehl 'kahn-tah-roh)*

Necesita usar las tenazas con la carne *(neh-seh-'see-tah oo-'sahr lahs teh-'nah-sahs kohn lah 'kahr-neh)*

TEMAS CULTURALES

Keep up with the latest "kitchen Spanglish:"

el ketchup
el nutra-sweet
el pyrex
el sandwich
el tupper

THE MACHINES
Las máquinas (*lahs 'mah-kee-nahs*)

Modern kitchens are full of machines that help speed up the process of meal preparation. Here are a few of the most common:

We use the...	**Usamos...** (*oo-'sah-mohs*)
blender	**la licuadora** (*lah lee-kwah-'doh-rah*)
can opener	**el abrelatas** (*ehl ah-breh-'lah-tahs*)
dishwasher	**el lavaplatos** (*ehl lah-bah-'plah-tohs*)
food processor	**el procesador de comida** (*ehl proh-seh-sah-'dohr deh koh-'mee-dah*)
gargage disposal	**el desechador** (*ehl dehs-eh-chah-'dohr*)
ice maker	**la hielera** (*lah yeh-'leh-rah*)
microwave	**el horno de microonda** (*lehl 'ohr-noh deh mee-kroh-'ohn-dah*)
mixer	**la batidora** (*lah bah-tee-'doh-rah*)
popcorn popper	**la máquina para hacer palomitas** (*lah 'mah-kee-nah 'pah-rah ah-'sehr pah-loh-'mee-tahs*)
timer	**el reloj de cocina** (*ehl reh-'loh deh koh-'see-nah*)
toaster	**el tostador** (*ehl toh-stah-'dohr*)
trash compacter	**el comprimidor de basura** (*ehl kohm-pree-mee-'dohr deh bah-'soo-rah*)

TURN IT ON! *¡Préndalo!* (*'prehn-dah-loh*)

Help out your Spanish-speaking assistant with those kitchen appliances. Knowing this selection can prevent problems and clear up confusion.

Touch on the...	**Toque...** *('toh-keh)*
button	**el botón** *(ehl boh-'tohn)*
clock	**el reloj** *(ehl reh-'lohj)*
dial	**el marcador** *(ehl mahr-kah-'dohr)*
knob	**la perilla** *(lah peh-'ree-yah)*
meter	**el medidor** *(ehl meh-dee-'dohr)*
switch	**el interruptor** *(ehl een-teh-rroop-'tohr)*
thermometer	**el termómetro** *(ehl tehr-'moh-meh-troh)*
thermostat	**el termostato** *(ehl tehr-moh-'stah-toh)*
Press...	**Oprima...** *(oh-'pree-mah)*
off	**apagado** *(ah-pah-'gah-doh)*
on	**prendido** *(prehn-'dee-doh)*
automatic	**automático** *(ow-toh-'mah-tee-koh)*
bake	**hornear** *(ohr-neh-'ahr)*
blend	**mezclar** *(mehs-'klahr)*
boil	**hervir** *(ehr-'beer)*
broil	**asar** *(ah-'sahr)*
cancel	**cancelar** *(kahn-seh-'lahr)*
cycle	**ciclo** *('see-kloh)*
dark	**oscuro** *(oh-'skoo-roh)*
defrost	**descongelar** *(dehs-kohn-heh-'lahr)*
erase	**borrar** *(boh-'rrahr)*
front	**enfrente** *(ehn-'frehn-teh)*
grate	**rallar** *(rah-'yahr)*
grind	**moler** *(moh-'lehr)*
high	**alto** *('ahl-toh)*
ignite	**prender** *(prehn-'dehr)*
level	**nivel** *(nee-'behl)*
light	**claro** *('klah-roh)*
liquefy	**licuar** *(lee-koo-'ahr)*
liquid	**liviano** *(lee-vee-'ah-noh)* *(weight)*
low	**bajo** *('bah-hoh)*
mash	**machacar** *(mah-chah-'kahr)*
normal	**normal** *(nohr-'mahl)*
pause	**pausa** *('pah-oo-sah)*
power	**activar** *(poh-'dehr)*
pulse	**pulsar** *('ahk-tee-vahr)*

rear	**atrás** *(ah-'trahs)*
simmer	**hervir a fuego lento** *(ehr-'beer ah 'fweh-goh 'lehn-toh)*
speed	**velocidad** *(beh-loh-see-'dahd)*
start	**empezar** *(ehm-peh-'sahr)*
stir	**revolver** *(reh-bohl-'behr)*
temperature	**temperatura** *(tehm-peh-rah-'too-rah)*
toast	**tostar** *(toh-'stahr)*
tune	**tono** *('toh-noh)*
volume	**volumen** *(boh-'loo-mehn)*
warm	**calentar** *(kah-lehn-'tahr)*
whip	**batir** *(bah-'teer)*

MORE KITCHEN VOCABULARY
Más vocabulario para la cocina
(mahs boh-kah-boo-'lah-ree·oh 'pah-rah lah koh-'see-nah)

Learn the Spanish words for the following useful items:

Give me the...	**Deme...** *('deh-meh)*
apron	**el delantal** *(ehl deh-lahn-'tahl)*
coffee filter	**el filtro de café** *(ehl 'feel-troh deh kah-'feh)*
cutting board	**la tabla para cortar** *(lah 'tah-blah 'pah-rah kohr-'tahr)*
dishwashing detergent	**el jabón de platos** *(ehl ha-'bohn deh 'plah-tohs)*
glove	**el guante** *(ehl 'gwahn-teh)*
kitchen towel	**el paño de cocina** *(ehl 'pah-nyoh deh koh-'see-nah)*
matches	**los fósforos** *(lohs 'fohs-foh-rohs)*
napkin	**la servilleta** *(lah sehr-bee-'yeh-tah)*
paper napkin	**la servilleta de papel** *(lah sehr-bee-'yeh-tah deh pah-'pehl)*
placemat	**el mantel individual** *(ehl mahn-'tehl een-dee-bee-doo-'ahl)*
plastic bag	**la bolsa de plástico** *(lah 'bohl-sah deh 'plahs-tee-koh)*
potholder	**el portaollas** *(ehl pohr-tah-'oh-yahs)*
tablecloth	**el mantel** *(ehl mahn-'tehl)*

FOLLOW THE RECIPE!

¡Siga la receta! *('see-gah lah reh-'seh-tah)*

In countries all over the world, food recipes follow the same basic pattern. Although the food items, instructions, and cooking tools may differ, the format is somewhat universal. We have already been introduced to hundreds of "cooking" words in Spanish. The only terms missing are those that refer to the amount of food we're using. As always, read both the word and the sample phrase:

dough **la masa** *(lah 'mah-sah)*
La masa del pan *(lah 'mah-sah dehl pahn)*
grain **el grano** *(ehl 'grah-noh)*
El grano de sal *(ehl 'grah-noh deh sahl)*
powder **el polvo** *(ehl 'pohl-boh)*
El polvo de chile *(ehl 'pohl-boh deh 'chee-leh)*

chop **la chuleta** *(lah choo-'leh-tah)*
La chuleta de puerco *(lah choo-'leh-tah deh 'pwehr-koh)*
cube **el cubito** *(ehl koo-'bee-toh)*
El cubito de azúcar *(ehl koo-'bee-toh deh ah-'soo-kahr)*
filet **el filete** *(ehl fee-'leh-teh)*
El filete de pescado *(ehl fee-'leh-teh deh peh-'skah-doh)*
piece **el pedazo** *(ehl peh-'dah-soh)*
El pedazo de carne *(ehl peh-'dah-soh deh 'kahr-neh)*
portion **la porción** *(lah pohr-see·'ohn)*
La porción de ensalada *(lah pohr-see·'ohn deh ehn-sah-'lah-dah)*
slice **la tajada** *(lah tah-'hah-dah)*
La tajada de jamón
stick **el palo** *(ehl 'pah-loh)*
El palo de canela *(ehl 'pah-loh deh kah-'neh-lah)*

These terms refer to the various containers you need in the kitchen:

bag **la bolsa** *(lah 'bohl-sah)*
La bolsa de arroz *(lah 'bohl-sah deh ah-'rrohs)*
bottle **la botella** *(lah boh-'teh-yah)*
La botella de vino *(lah boh-'teh-yah deh 'bee-noh)*
box **la caja** *(lah 'kah-hah)*
La caja de galletas *(lah 'kah-hah deh gah-'yeh-tahs)*
can **la lata** *(lah 'lah-tah)*

La lata de leche *(lah 'lah-tah deh 'leh-cheh)*

jar   **el frasco** *(ehl 'frah-skoh)*

   El frasco de mermelada *(ehl 'frah-skoh deh mehr-meh-'lah-dah)*

package   **el paquete** *(ehl pah-'keh-teh)*

   El paquete de tomates *(ehl pah-'keh-teh deh toh-'mah-tehs)*

 MÁS AYUDA

Take the words you already know and combine them to form meaningful food items:

chicken leg   **la pierna de pollo** *(lah pee-'ehr-nah deh 'poh-yoh)*

orange juice   **el jugo de naranja** *(ehl 'hoo-goh deh nah-'rahn-hah)*

pork chops   **la chuleta de cerdo** *(lah choo-'leh-tah deh 'sehr-doh)*

- Match the utensil with the food item:

la parrilla *(lah pah-'rree-yah)*   **el café** *(ehl kah-'feh)*

la taza *(lah 'tah-sah)*   **la sopa** *(lah 'soh-pah)*

la olla *(lah 'oh-yah)*   **la hamburguesa** *(lah ahm-boor-'geh-sah)*

el tostador *(ehl toh-stah-'dohr)*   **el pan** *(ehl pahn)*

- Match the Spanish with the English:

la batidora *(lah bah-tee-'doh-rah)*   blender

la servilleta *(lah sehr-bee-'yeh-tah)*   mixer

la licuadora *(lah lee-kwah-'doh-rah)* napkin

TEMAS CULTURALES

Ask your employee to prepare an occasional traditional home-cooked meal, and get ready for a culinary treat! Contrary to popular belief, not all Latin Americans eat spicy foods, many dishes resemble traditional U.S. meals, and many more will be welcome additions to your kitchen.

MEASUREMENTS
Las medidas (lahs meh-'dee-dahs)

To properly measure the necessary ingredients, you'll need a few measuring tools. These are the most common:

measuring cup	**la taza de medir** *(lah 'tah-sah deh meh-'deer)*
measuring spoon	**la cuchara de medir** *(lah koo-'chah-rah deh meh-'deer)*
one cup	**una taza** *('oo-nah 'tah-sah)*
1/4 cup	**un cuarto de taza** *(oon 'kwahr-toh deh 'tah-sah)*
1/2 cup	**media taza** *('meh-dee-ah 'tah-sah)*
tablespoon	**la cucharada** *(lah koo-chah-'rah-dah)*
teaspoon	**la cucharadita** *(lah koo-chah-rah-'dee-tah)*

Describe specific amounts with these useful expressions:

It's...	**Es...** *(ehs)*
a bunch	**un ramo** *(oon 'rah-moh)*
a centimeter	**un centímetro** *(oon sehn-'tee-meh-troh)*
double	**doble** *('doh-bleh)*
a dozen	**una docena** *('oo-nah doh-'seh-nah)*
enough	**bastante** *(bah-'stahn-teh)*
a gallon	**un galón** *(oon gah-'lohn)*
a gram	**un gramo** *(oon 'grah-moh)*
half	**la mitad** *(lah mee-'tahd)*
an inch	**una pulgada** *('oo-nah pool-'gah-dah)*
a kilogram	**un kilo** *(oon 'kee-loh)*
a liter	**un litro** *(oon 'lee-troh)*
a pair	**un par** *(oon pahr)*
a pinch	**un poquito** *(oon poh-'kee-toh)*

a pint	una pinta (*'oo-nah 'peen-tah*)
a portion	una porción (*'oo-nah pohr-see-'ohn*)
a quart	una cuarta (*'oo-nah 'kwahr-tah*)
a quarter	un cuarto (*oon 'kwahr-toh*)
a third	un tercero (*oon tehr-'seh-roh*)

 MÁS AYUDA

• Continue to combine words to express detail:

aluminum foil	el papel de aluminio (*ehl pah-'pehl deh ah-loo-'mee-nee·oh*)
cutting knife	el cuchillo de cortar (*ehl koo-'chee-yoh deh kohr-'tahr*)
plastic wrap	el papel de plástico (*ehl pah-'pehl deh 'plah-stee-koh*)
serving dish	el plato de servir (*ehl 'plah-toh deh sehr-'beer*)
wax paper	el papel de cera (*ehl pah-'pehl deh 'seh-rah*)
wine glass	la copa de vino (*lah 'koh-pah deh 'bee-noh*)

• Are any of your Spanish-speaking employees good with numbers? Get some help with your shopping list as you go over the "latest figures":

adding machine	la máquina de sumar (*lah 'mah-kee-nah deh soo-'mahr*)
calculator	la calculadora (*lah kahl-koo-lah-'doh-rah*)
cash register	la registradora (*lah reh-hee-strah-'doh-rah*)
computer	la computadora (*lah kohm-poo-tah-'doh-rah*)
add	sumar (*soo-'mahr*)
divide	dividir (*dee-bee-'deer*)
multiply	multiplicar (*mool-tee-plee-'kahr*)
subtract	restar (*reh-'stahr*)

 REPASEMOS

Fill in the blanks with words that you know:

una bolsa de (*'oo-nah 'bohl-sah deh*) _____

una botella de (*'oo-nah boh-'teh-yah deh*) _____

un pedazo de *(oon peh-'dah-soh deh)* _____

una docena de *('oo-nah doh-'seh-nah deh)* _____

KITCHEN COMMENTS
Los comentarios en la cocina
(lohs koh-mehn-'tah-ree·ohs ehn lah koh-'see-nah)

There's so much to say about food! Practice these comments, which describe how everything looks, smells, and tastes!

It's...	**Está...** *(eh-'stah)*
baked	**horneado** *(ohr-neh-'ah-doh)*
bitter	**amargo** *(ah-'mahr-goh)*
blended	**licuado** *(lee-'kwah-doh)*
broiled	**asado** *(ah-'sah-doh)*
burned	**quemado** *keh-'mah-doh)*
cooked	**cocido** *(koh-'see-doh)*
delicious	**delicioso** *(deh-lee-see-'oh-soh)*
dry	**seco** *('seh-koh)*
fresh	**fresco** *('frehs-koh)*
fried	**frito** *('free-toh)*
frozen	**congelado** *(kohn-heh-'lah-doh)*
grated	**rallado** *(rah-'yah-doh)*
ground	**molido** *(moh-'lee-doh)*
hard	**duro** *('doo-roh)*

131

minced	**picado** *(pee-'kah-doh)*
moist	**húmedo** *('oo-meh-doh)*
natural	**natural** *(nah-too-'rahl)*
pre-cooked	**pre-cocido** *(preh-koh-'see-doh)*
raw	**crudo** *('kroo-doh)*
rehashed	**refrito** *(reh-'free-toh)*
ripe	**maduro** *(mah-'doo-roh)*
rotten	**podrido** *(poh-'dree-doh)*
salty	**salado** *(sah-'lah-doh)*
sliced	**rebanado** *(reh-bah-'nah-doh)*
soft	**suave** *('swah-beh)*
sour	**agrio** *('ah-gree·oh)*
spicy	**picante** *(pee-'kahn-teh)*
steamed	**al vapor** *(ahl bah-'pohr)*
stuffed	**relleno** *(reh-'yeh-noh)*
sweet	**dulce** *('dool-seh)*
tasty	**sabroso** *(sah-'broh-soh)*
warm	**tibio** *('tee-bee·oh)*

 MÁS AYUDA

Hang around a kitchen where Spanish is spoken, and you're bound to hear some of the following words. More and more people are being cautious about what they're putting into their bodies. Can you add to these comments?

It's...	**Es...** *(ehs)*
diet	**de dieta** *(deh dee-'eh-tah)*
fat-free	**desgrasado** *(dehs-grah-'sah-doh)*
kosher	**preparado conforme a la ley judía** *(preh-pah-'rah-doh kohn-'fohr-meh ah lah leh hoo-'dee-ah)*
light	**ligero** *(lee-'heh-roh)*
natural	**natural** *(nah-too-'rahl)*
organic	**orgánico** *(ohr-'gah-nee-koh)*
sugar-free	**sin azúcar** *(seen ah-'soo-kahr)*
vegetarian	**vegetariano** *(beh-heh-tah-ree-'ah-noh)*

REPASEMOS

Match the opposites:

suave *('swah-beh)*	claro *('klah-roh)*
maduro *(mah-'doo-roh)*	dulce *('dool-seh)*
agrio *('ah-gree·oh)*	apagado *(ah-pah-'gah-doh)*
prendido *(prehn-'dee-doh)*	duro *('doo-roh)*
oscuro *(oh-'skoo-roh)*	podrido *(poh-'dree-doh)*

TEMAS CULTURALES

We're having a party! **una fiesta** *('oo-nah fee-'eh-stah)*:

anniversary	**aniversario** *(ah-nee-behr-'sah-ree·oh)*
birth	**nacimiento** *(nah-see-mee-'ehn-toh)*
birthday	**cumpleaños** *(koom-pleh-'ah-nyohs)*
engagement	**compromiso** *(kohm-proh-'mee-soh)*
wedding	**casamiento** *(kah-sah-mee-'ehn-toh)*

It's a surprise party. **Es una fiesta de sorpresa** *(ehs 'oo-nah fee-'eh-stah deh sohr-'preh-sah)*

If guests are coming, use the proper Spanish to describe them to your help:

We're having...	**Vamos a tener...** *('bah-mohs ah teh-'nehr)*
co-workers	**los compañeros del trabajo** *(lohs kohm-pah-'nyeh-rohs dehl trah-'bah-hoh)*
good friends	**los buenos amigos** *(lohs 'bweh-nohs ah-'mee-gohs)*
guests	**los huéspedes** *(lohs 'weh-speh-dehs)*
relatives	**los parientes** *(lohs pah-ree-'ehn-tehs)*
visitors	**los visitantes** *(lohs bee-see-'tahn-tehs)*

When discussing cooking temperatures, remember that people from Spanish-speaking countries may be more familiar with **centígrados** (C°) *(sehn-'tee-grah-dohs)* instead of "Fahrenheit" (F°).

¡EL SUPERESPAÑOL!

Ready for another tip on how to use Spanish action words? Try out this new pattern with the words **querer** *(keh-'rehr)* (to want) and **preferir** *(preh-feh-'reer)* (to prefer). Can you translate each sample sentence all by yourself?

To want   **Querer**

I want   **quiero** *(kee-'eh-roh)*

  Quiero cocinar los huevos *(kee-'eh-roh koh-see-'nahr lohs 'weh-bohs)*

you want, he/she wants   **quiere** *(kee-'eh-reh)*

  Quiere prender la estufa *(kee-'eh-reh prehn-'dehr lah eh-'stoo-fah)*

you (plural) want, they want   **quieren** *(kee-'eh-rehn)*

  Quieren servir las frutas *(kee-'eh-rehn sehr-'beer lahs 'froo-tahs)*

we want   **queremos** *(keh-'reh-mohs)*

  Queremos preparar la crema *(keh-'reh-mohs preh-pah-'rahr lah 'kreh-mah)*

To prefer   **Preferir**

I prefer   **prefiero** *(preh-fee-'eh-roh)*

  Prefiero comer la pasta *(preh-fee-'eh-roh koh-'mehr lah 'pah-stah)*

you prefer, he/she prefers   **prefiere** *(preh-fee-'eh-reh)*

Prefiere descongelar la carne *(preh-fee-'eh-reh dehs-kohn-heh-'lahr lah 'kahr-neh)*

you (plural) prefer, they prefer **prefieren** *(preh-fee-'eh-rehn)*
   Prefieren tostar el pan *(preh-fee-'eh-rehn toh-'stahr ehl pahn)*

we prefer   **preferimos** *(preh-feh-'ree-mohs)*
   Preferimos ordenar el desayuno *(preh-feh-'ree-mohs ohr-deh-'nahr ehl deh-sah-'yoo-noh)*

 MÁS AYUDA

Here are three other ways to discuss one's likes and dislikes. Note how unique each form is:

Do you like...?	**¿Le gusta...?** *(leh 'goo-stah)*
Yes, I like...	**Sí, me gusta...** *(see, meh 'goo-stah)*
Would you like...?	**¿Quisiera...?** *(kee-see-'eh-rah)*
Yes, I'd like...	**Sí, quisiera...** *(see, kee-see-'eh-rah)*
Do you desire...?	**¿Desea..?** *(deh-'seh-ah)*
Yes, I desire...	**Sí, deseo...** *(see, deh-'seh-oh)*

 ¡MÁS ACCIÓN!

Up to now, we've been given the skills on how to converse about current, everyday activities around the home.

We know the pattern for discussing current action:

Estoy preparando una ensalada *(eh-'stoh·ee preh-pah-'rahn-doh 'oo-nah ehn-sah-'lah-dah)*

And we know the pattern for everyday, ongoing activities:

Preparo ensaladas todos los días *(preh-'pah-roh ehn-sah-'lah-dahs 'toh-dohs lohs 'dee-ahs)*

Now, let's check out a simple formula for changing basic verb forms to refer to *past* action. First, change all the verb endings to **-ndo**, just as you did when you talked about current action:

tomar *(toh-'mahr)*	**tomando** *(toh-'mahn-doh)*
comer *(koh-'mehr)*	**comiendo** *(koh-mee-'ehn-doh)*
escribir *(eh-skree-'beer)*	**escribiendo** *(eh-skree-bee-'ehn-doh)*

Next, in place of **estoy, está, están,** and **estamos** *(eh-'stoh-ee, eh-'stahs, eh-'stah, eh-'stah-mohs)* which refer to present time, combine the following past action words with the **-ndo** verb forms:

I was   **estaba** *(eh-'stah-bah)*

Estaba hablando por teléfono *(eh-'stah-bah ah-'blahn-doh pohr teh-'leh-foh-noh)* (I was talking on the phone.)

you were, he/she was   **estaba** *(eh-'stah-bah)*

Estaba tomando la leche *(eh-'stah-bah toh-'mahn-doh lah 'leh-cheh)* (He was drinking the milk.)

you (plural) were, they were   **estaban** *(eh-'stah-bahn)*

Estaban abriendo las ventanas *(eh-'stah-bahn ah-bree-'ehn-doh lahs behn-'tah-nahs)* (They were opening the windows.)

we were   **estábamos** *(eh-'stah-bah-mohs)*

Estábamos comprando la comida *(eh-'stah-bah-mohs kohm-'prahn-doh lah koh-'mee-dah)* (We were buying the food.)

 MÁS AYUDA

It's quite common for one word in Spanish to mean many words in English:

calentar *(kah-lehn-'tahr)*   -   heat, warm, brew
cortar *(kohr-'tahr)*   -   cut, clip, slice
mezclar *(mehs-'klahr)*   -   mix, blend, combine

 **REPASEMOS**

Answer these questions:

¿Qué quiere comer en la noche? *(keh kee-'eh-reh koh-'mehr ehn lah 'noh-cheh)*

¿Qué prefiere tomar en una fiesta? *(keh preh-fee-'eh-reh toh-'mahr ehn 'oo-nah fee-'eh-stah)*

¿Qué estaba comiendo ayer? *(keh eh-'stah-bah koh-mee-'ehn-doh ah-'yehr)*

Read the examples and follow the pattern:

To work	**Trabajar** *(trah-bah-'hahr)*
Samuel is working.	**Samuel está trabajando** *(Sah-moo-'ehl eh-'stah trah-bah-'hahn-doh)*
Samuel works.	**Samuel trabaja** *(Sah-moo-'ehl trah-'bah-hah)*
Samuel was working.	**Samuel estaba trabajando** *(Sah-moo-'ehl eh-'stah-bah trah-bah-'hahn-doh)*

To cook	**Cocinar** *(koh-see-'nahr)*
Tina cooks.	_____
Tina was cooking.	_____
Tina is cooking.	_____

To clean	**Limpiar** *(leem-pee-'ahr)*
Arturo is cleaning.	_____
Arturo cleans.	_____
Arturo was cleaning.	_____

THE BAR
El Bar (ehl bahr)

In some cases, it might be necessary to train a Spanish-speaker to tend bar. Although several of the commands, phrases, and vocabulary that we've already learned will help, there are some terms that relate specifically to the world of alcoholic beverages. Cheers! **¡Salud!** *(sah-'lood)*:

I need...	**Necesito...** *(neh-seh-'see-toh)*
a bottle	**una botella** *('oo-nah boh-'teh-yah)*
a drink	**un trago** *(oon 'trah-goh)*
a mug	**un vasito** *(oon bah-'see-toh)*
a pitcher	**una jarra** *('oo-nah 'hah-rrah)*
a wine glass	**un vaso de vino** *(oon 'bah-soh deh 'bee-noh)*
crushed ice	**el hielo molido** *(ehl 'yeh-loh moh-'lee-doh)*
cubed ice	**el hielo en cubitos** *(ehl 'yeh-loh ehn koo-'bee-tohs)*
Beer	**la cerveza** *(lah sehr-'beh-sah)*
domestic beer	**la cerveza doméstica** *(lah sehr-'beh-sah doh-'meh-stee-kah)*
imported beer	**la cerveza importada** *(lah sehr-'beh-sah eem-pohr-'tah-dah*
Wine	**el vino** *(ehl 'bee-noh)*
burgundy	**el borgoña** *(ehl bohr-'goh-nyah)*
champagne	**el champán** *(ehl chahm-'pahn)*
house wine	**el vino de la casa** *(ehl 'bee-noh deh lah 'kah-sah)*
red wine	**el vino tinto** *(ehl 'bee-noh 'teen-toh)*
rosé wine	**el vino rosado** *(ehl 'bee-noh roh-'sah-doh)*
white wine	**el vino blanco** *(ehl 'bee-noh 'blahn-koh)*
Other beverages	**otras bebidas** *('oh-trahs beh-'bee-dahs)*
bourbon	**el whisky americano** *(ehl 'wees-kee-ah-meh-ree-'kah-noh)*
cocktail	**el coctel** *(ehl kohk-'tehl)*
gin	**la ginebra** *(lah hee-'neh-brah)*
liquor, liqueur	**el licor** *(ehl lee-'kohr)*
nonalcoholic drink	**la bebida sin alcohol** *(lah beh-'bee-dah seen ahl-koh-'ohl)*
rum	**el ron** *(ehl rohn)*
rye	**el whisky de centeno** *(ehl 'wees-kee deh sehn-'teh-noh)*
scotch	**el escocés** *(ehl eh-skoh-'sehs)*
soda water	**el agua mineral** *(ehl 'ah-gwah mee-neh-'rahl)*
vermouth	**el vermut** *(ehl behr-'moot)*

These drinks are the same in both English and Spanish:

brandy
club soda
Coca-Cola
ginger ale
Pepsi
Seven-Up
tequila
vodka
whisky

Here are some additional useful words around the bar:

Add...	Añada... *(ah-'nyah-dah)*
celery	**apio** *('ah-pee·oh)*
cherries	**cerezas** *(seh-'reh-sahs)*
fruit juice	**jugo de fruta** *('hoo-goh deh 'froo-tah)*
lemon	**limón** *(lee-'mohn)*
lime juice	**jugo de lima** *('hoo-goh deh 'lee-mah)*
olives	**aceitunas** *(ah-seh·ee-'too-nahs)*
onions	**cebollas** *(seh-'boh-yahs)*
orange juice	**jugo de naranja** *('hoo-goh deh nah-'rahn-hah)*
pineapple juice	**jugo de piña** *('hoo-goh deh 'pee-nyah)*
strawberries	**fresas** *('freh-sahs)*
tomato juice	**jugo de tomate** *('hoo-goh deh toh-'mah-teh)*

CHAPTER FIVE

Capítulo Cinco
(kah-'pee-too-loh 'seen-koh)

CHILDCARE
El cuidado de los niños
(ehl kwee-'dah-doh deh lohs 'nee-nyohs)

DO YOU HAVE CHILDREN?
¿Tiene usted niños? (tee-'eh-neh oo-'stehd 'nee-nyohs)

Giving instructions in a foreign language can be a difficult task, especially in the field of child care. Because you are dealing with the lives of children, it is crucial that all orders are kept simple and clear.

If you need to speak Spanish with a nurse, nanny, babysitter, or anyone else who cares for your children, pay close attention to the special vocabulary introduced throughout this chapter.

In order to discuss **los niños** *('nee-nyohs)*, you'll need a few basic terms and phrases first. As you pronounce each word, envision a scenario where you'll be using it:

Where is the...	**¿Dónde está...** *('dohn-deh eh-'stah)*
ball	**la pelota** *(lah peh-'loh-tah)*
bassinet	**el bacinete** *(ehl bah-see-'neh-teh)*
bib	**el babero** *(ehl bah-'beh-roh)*
blanket	**la cobija** *(lah koh-'bee-hah)*
changing table	**la mesa de muda** *(lah 'meh-sah deh 'moo-dah)*
crib	**la cuna** *(lah 'koo-nah)*
diaper	**el pañal** *(ehl pah-'nyahl)*
doll	**la muñeca** *(lah moo-'nyeh-kah)*
game	**el juego** *(ehl hoo-'eh-goh)*
infant car seat	**el asiento para infantes** *(ehl ah-see-'ehn-toh 'pah-rah een-'fahn-tehs)*
nursing bottle	**el biberón** *(ehl bee-beh-'rohn)*
pacifier	**el chupete** *(ehl choo-'peh-teh)*
stroller	**el cochecillo** *(ehl koh-cheh-'see-yoh)*

talcum powder	**el talco** *(ehl 'tahl-koh)*
toy	**el juguete** *(ehl hoo-'geh-teh)*

¿Dónde está el talco?

 REPASEMOS

Add descriptions to all your vocabulary:

The disposable diaper **El pañal desechable** *(ehl pah-'nyahl deh-seh-'chah-bleh)*

The dirty diaper _____

The white diaper _____

The clean diaper _____

The new diaper _____

WHAT HAPPENED?
¿Qué pasó? (keh pah-'soh)

The first thing to learn is that, sooner or later, one of the children is going to get hurt. Scratches, bumps, and bruises are all a part of growing up. Obviously, whether it's putting on a bandage, or giving the child a bath, you will have to know how to say the body parts in Spanish. As always, try to combine these words with practical sentence patterns:

What's wrong with the _____ ?	**¿Qué pasó con** _____**?** *(keh pah-'soh kohn)*
His _____ hurts.	**Le duele** _____ *(leh 'dweh-leh)*
Wash the _____.	**Lave** _____ *('lah-beh)*
ankle	**el tobillo** *(ehl toh-'bee-yoh)*
arm	**el brazo** *(ehl 'brah-soh)*
back	**la espalda** *(lah eh-'spahl-dah)*

bone	el **hueso** *(ehl 'hwe-soh)*
buttock	la **nalga** *(lah 'nahl-gah)*
check	la **mejilla** *(lah meh-'hee-yah)*
chest	el **pecho** *(ehl 'peh-choh)*
chin	la **barbilla** *(lah bahr-'bee-yah)*
ear	el **oído** *(ehl oh-'ee-doh)*
elbow	el **codo** *(ehl 'koh-doh)*
eye	el **ojo** *(ehl 'oh-hoh)*
face	la **cara** *(lah 'kah-rah)*
finger, toe	el **dedo** *(ehl 'deh-doh)*
foot	el **pie** *(ehl pee-'eh)*
gum	la **encía** *(lah ehn-'see-ah)*
hand	la **mano** *(lah 'mah-noh)*
head	la **cabeza** *(lah kah-'beh-sah)*
hip	la **cadera** *(lah kah-'deh-rah)*
knee	la **rodilla** *(lah roh-'dee-yah)*
leg	la **pierna** *(lah pee-'ehr-nah)*
lip	el **labio** *(ehl 'lah-bee·oh)*
mouth	la **boca** *(lah 'boh-kah)*
navel	el **ombligo** *(ehl ohm-'blee-goh)*
neck	el **cuello** *(ehl 'kweh-yoh)*
nose	la **nariz** *(lah nah-'rees)*
penis	el **pene** *(ehl 'peh-neh)*
rib	la **costilla** *(lah koh-'stee-yah)*
shoulder	el **hombro** *(ehl 'ohm-broh)*
skin	la **piel** *(lah 'pee-ehl)*
stomach	el **estómago** *(ehl eh-'stoh-mah-goh)*
throat	la **garganta** *(lah gahr-'gahn-tah)*
tongue	la **lengua** *(lah 'lehn-gwah)*
tooth	el **diente** *(ehl dee-'ehn-teh)*
vagina	la **vagina** *(lah bah-'hee-nah)*
waist	la **cintura** *(lah seen-'too-rah)*
wrist	la **muñeca** *(lah moo-'nyeh-kah)*

HE/SHE DOESN'T FEEL WELL

No se siente bien (noh seh see-'ehn-teh 'bee-ehn)

He/She has trouble with the...	Tiene problemas con... *(tee-'eh-neh proh-'bleh-mahs kohn)*
bladder	la vejiga *(lah beh-'hee-gah)*
brain	el cerebro *(ehl seh-'reh-broh)*
genitals	los genitales *(lohs heh-nee-'tah-lehs)*
heart	el corazón *(ehl koh-rah-'sohn)*
liver	el hígado *(ehl 'ee-gah-doh)*
lung	el pulmón *(ehl pool-'mohn)*
He/She has (a, an)...	Tiene... *(tee-'eh-neh)*
allergy	la alergia *(lah ah-'lehr-hee·ah)*
belch	el eructo *(ehl eh-'rook-toh)*
blister	la ampolla *(lah ahm-'poh-yah)*
bruise	la contusión *(lah kohn-too-see-'ohn)*
chicken pox	la varicela *(lah bah-ree-'seh-lah)*
chill	el escalofrío *(ehl eh-skah-loh-'free-oh)*
cold	el resfriado *(ehl rehs-free-'ah-doh)*
colic	el cólico *(ehl 'koh-lee-koh)*
constipation	el estreñimiento *(ehl eh-streh-nyee-mee-'ehn-toh)*
cough	la tos *(lah tohs)*
cut	el corte *(ehl 'kohr-teh)*
diarrhea	la diarrea *(lah dee-ah-'rreh-ah)*
fever	la fiebre *(lah fee-'eh-breh)*
flatulation	el flato *(ehl 'flah-toh)*
flu	el resfriado *(ehl rehs-free-'ah-doh)*
gas	el gas *(ehl gahs)*
headache	el dolor de cabeza *(ehl doh-'lohr deh kah-'beh-sah)*
indigestion	la indigestión *(lah een-dee-heh-stee-'ohn)*
injury	la herida *(lah eh-'ree-dah)*
measles	el sarampión *(ehl sah-rahm-pee-'ohn)*
mumps	las paperas *(lahs pah-'peh-rahs)*
nausea	la náusea *(lah 'now-seh-ah)*
pain	el dolor *(ehl doh-'lohr)*
phlegm	flema *(lah 'fleh-mah)*

rash	**la erupción** *(lah eh-roop-see-'ohn)*
scratch	**el rasguño** *(ehl rahs-'goo-nyoh)*
sore throat	**el dolor de garganta** *(ehl doh-'lohr deh gahr-'gahn-tah)*
sneeze	**el estornudo** *(ehl eh-stohr-'noo-doh)*
sprain	**la torcedura** *(lah tohr-seh-'doo-rah)*
stomachache	**el dolor de estómago** *(ehl doh-'lohr deh eh-'stoh-mah-goh)*
temperature	**la temperatura** *(lah tehm-peh-rah-'too-rah)*
toothache	**el dolor de muela** *(ehl doh-'lohr deh 'mweh-lah)*
yawn	**el bostezo** *(ehl boh-'steh-soh)*
It's...	**Está...** *(eh-'stah)*
broken	**roto** *('roh-toh)*
burned	**quemado** *(keh-'mah-doh)*
infected	**infectado** *(een-fehk-'tah-doh)*
swollen	**hinchado** *(een-'chah-doh)*
twisted	**torcido** *(tohr-'see-doh)*

REPASEMOS

- Name five parts of the body.
- Name three major internal organs.
- Name five common ailments.

IN CASE OF EMERGENCY!
¡En caso de emergencia!
(ehn 'kah-soh deh eh-mehr-'hehn-see·ah)

In those rare cases when a child needs professional medical attention, it will become necessary to discuss more serious maladies. To be on the safe side, get acquainted with these expressions:

He/She is bleeding.	**Está sangrando** *(ehs-'tah sahn-'grahn-doh)*
He/She is vomiting.	**Está vomitando** *(ehs-'tah voh-mee-'tahn-doh)*
Where is the...	**Dónde está...** *('dohn-deh ehs-'tah)*
accident	**el accidente** *(ehl ahk-see-'dehn-teh)*
bad fall	**la mala caída** *(lah 'mah-lah kah-'ee-dah)*
burn	**la quemadura** *(lah keh-mah-'doo-rah)*
choking	**la sofocación** *(lah soh-foh-kah-see-'ohn)*
contagious disease	**la enfermedad contagiosa** *(lah ehn-fehr-meh-'dahd kohn-tah-hee-'oh-sah)*
convulsion	**la convulsión** *(lah kohn-bool-see-'ohn)*
dehydration	**la deshidratación** *(lah dehs-hee-drah-tah-see-'ohn)*
dog bite	**la mordedura de perro** *(lah mohr-deh-'doo-rah deh 'peh-rroh)*
drowning	**el ahogo** *(ehl ah-'oh-goh)*
fatigue	**la fatiga** *(lah fah-'tee-gah)*
frostbite	**el congelamiento** *(ehl kohn-heh-lah-mee-'ehn-toh)*
heat stroke	**la postración por calor** *(lah poh-strah-see-'ohn pohr kah-'lohr)*
insect bite	**la mordedura de insecto** *(lah mohr-deh-'doo-rah deh een-'sehk-toh)*
poisoning	**el envenenamiento** *(ehl ehn-beh-neh-nah-mee-'ehn-toh)*
shock	**la postración nerviosa** *(lah pohs-trah-see-'ohn nehr-bee-'oh-sah)*
seizure	**el ataque** *(ehl ah-'tah-keh)*
snake bite	**la mordedura de culebra** *(lah mohr-deh-'doo-rah deh koo-'leh-brah)*
sunstroke	**la insolación** *(lah een-soh-lah-see-'ohn)*

It's in the...	Está en... *(eh-'stah ehn)*
blood	la **sangre** *(lah 'sahn-greh)*
body	el **cuerpo** *(ehl 'kwehr-poh)*
bone	el **hueso** *(ehl 'weh-soh)*
hair	el **pelo** *(ehl 'peh-loh)*
skin	la **piel** *(lah pee-'ehl)*
system	el **sistema** *(ehl see-'steh-mah)*
Call (the)...	Llame al... *('yah-meh ahl)*
911	**nueve-uno-uno** *(noo-'eh-beh 'oo-noh oo-'noh)*
ambulance	la **ambulancia** *(lah ahm-boo-'lahn-see·ah)*
clinic	la **clínica** *(lah 'klee-nee-kah)*
dentist	el **dentista** *(ehl dehn-'tees-tah)*
doctor	el **doctor** *(ehl dohk-'tohr)*
fire department	el **departamento de bomberos** *(ehl deh-pahr-tah-'mehn-toh deh bohm-'beh-rohs)*
hospital	el **hospital** *(ehl oh-spee-'tahl)*
neighbor	el **vecino** *(ehl beh-'see-noh)*
operator	la **operadora** *(lah oh-peh-rah-'doh-rah)*
paramedic	el **paramédico** *(ehl pah-rah-'meh-dee-koh)*
pediatrician	el **pediatra** *(ehl peh-dee-'ah-trah)*
pharmacist	el **farmacéutico** *(ehl fahr-mah-'seh·oo-tee-koh)*
pharmacy	la **farmacia** *(lah fahr-'mah-see·ah)*
police	la **policía** *(lah poh-lee-'see-ah)*
relative	el **pariente** *(ehl pah-ree-'ehn-teh)*
tow truck	la **grúa** *(lah 'groo-ah)*
work number	el **número de trabajo** *(ehl 'noo-meh-roh deh trah-'bah-hoh)*

PALABRAS CLAVES

Making a phone call can sometimes be the difference between life and death. Each time you leave the house, sit down with your Spanish-speaking help and go over the steps they'll need to take in order to reach you by phone or to get help in an emergency. Especially rehearse any unfamiliar English words:

Wait for the tone.
> **Espere por el tono** *(eh-'speh-reh pohr ehl 'toh-noh)*

Say, "I need to speak with..."
> **Diga** *('dee-gah)* **"I need to speak with..."**

Say, "It's an emergency".
> **Diga** *('dee-gah)* **"It's an emergency."**

Ask for extension...
> **Pida la extensión...** *('pee-dah lah ehks-tehn-see-'ohn)*

Press this number.
> **Oprima este número** *(oh-'pree-mah 'eh-steh 'noo-meh-roh)*

Dial this number.
> **Marque este número** *('mahr-keh 'eh-steh 'noo-meh-roh)*

BE CAREFUL WITH THE... !

¡Tenga cuidado con...! *('tehn-gah kwee-'dah-doh kohn)*

Make sure you have reviewed these potentially dangerous items with the person watching your child:

bleach	**el cloro** *(ehl 'kloh-roh)*
chemicals	**los productos químicos** *(lohs proh-'dook-tohs 'kee-mee-kohs)*
detergent	**el detergente** *(ehl deh-tehr-'hehn-teh)*
electricity	**la electricidad** *(lah eh-lehk-tree-see-'dahd)*
fire	**el fuego** *(ehl 'fweh-goh)*
flames	**las llamas** *(lahs 'yah-mahs)*
gas	**el gas** *(ehl gahs)*
grease	**la grasa** *(lah 'grah-sah)*
hot water	**el agua caliente** *(ehl 'ah-gwah kah-lee-'ehn-teh)*
insecticide	**el insecticida** *(ehl een-sehk-tee-'see-dah)*

oil	**el aceite** *(ehl ah-'see-ee-teh)*
paint	**la pintura** *(lah peen-'too-rah)*
smoke	**el humo** *(ehl 'oo-moh)*
remedies	**los remedios** *(lohs reh-'meh-dee-ohs)*

The doctor or emergency room personnel may advise the following:

He/She needs...	Necesita... *(neh-seh-'see-tah)*
aspirin	**la aspirina** *(lah ah-spee-'ree-nah)*
Band-Aid®	**la curita** *(lah coo-'ree-tah)*
a bandage	**un vendaje** *(oon behn-'dah-heh)*
capsules	**las cápsulas** *(lahs 'kahp-soo-lahs)*
a cast	**una armadura de yeso** *('oo-nah ahr-mah-'doo-rah deh 'yeh-soh)*
cough syrup	**el jarabe para la tos** *(ehl hah-'rah-beh 'pah-rah lah tohs)*
CPR	**la respiración artificial** *(lah reh-spee-rah-see-'ohn ahr-tee-fee-see-'ahl)*
cream	**la pomada** *(lah poh-'mah-dah)*
crutches	**las muletas** *(lahs moo-'leh-tahs)*
a disinfectant	**un desinfectante** *(oon dehs-een-fehk-'tahn-teh)*
drops	**las gotas** *(lahs 'goh-tahs)*
iodine	**el yodo** *(ehl 'yoh-doh)*
liniment	**el linimento** *(ehl lee-nee-'mehn-toh)*
lotion	**la loción** *(lah loh-see-'ohn)*
lozenges	**las pastillas** *(lahs pah-'stee-yahs)*
medicine	**la medicina** *(lah meh-deh-'see-nah)*
penicillin	**la penicilina** *(lah peh-nee-see-'lee-nah)*

pills	**las píldoras** *(lahs 'peel-doh-rahs)*
powder	**el talco** *(ehl 'tahl-koh)*
a prescription	**una receta** *('oo-nah reh-'seh-tah)*
a shot	**una inyección** *('oo-nah een-yehk-see-'ohn)*
stitches	**unas puntadas** *('oo-nahs poon-'tah-dahs)*
tablets	**las tabletas** *(lahs tah-'bleh-tahs)*
a cane	**un bastón** *(oon bah-'stohn)*
a wheelchair	**una silla de ruedas** *('oo-nah 'see-yah deh roo-'eh-dahs)*
a thermometer	**un termómetro** *(oon tehr-'moh-meh-troh)*
vaseline	**la vaselina** *(lah bah-seh-'lee-nah)*
vitamins	**las vitaminas** *(lahs bee-tah-'mee-nahs)*
X-rays	**los rayos equis** *(lohs 'rah-yohs 'eh-kees)*

 REPASEMOS

You can see how many medical words in Spanish resemble their equivalents in English. Try to translate these:

antiácido *(ahn-tee-'ah-see-doh)*
antibiótico *(ahn-tee-bee-'oh-tee-koh)*
antídoto *(ahn-'tee-doh-toh)*
antihistamínicos *(ahn-tee-ees-tah-'mee-nee-kohs)*
antiséptico *(ahn-tee-'sehp-tee-koh)*

MEDICATION LA MEDICINA

If your child requires medicine, you will have to explain the following:

HOW MUCH?
¿Cuánto? *('kwahn-toh)*

a cup	**una taza** *('oo-nah 'tah-sah)*
double	**doble** *('doh-bleh)*
half	**la mitad** *(lah mee-'tahd)*
a tablespoon	**una cucharada** *('oo-nah koo-chah-'rah-dah)*
a teaspoon	**una cucharadita** *('oo-nah koo-chah-rah-'dee-tah)*

WHEN?

¿Cuándo? *('kwahn-doh)*

at night	**en la noche** *(ehn lah 'noh-cheh)*
before breakfast	**antes del desayuno** *('ahn-tehs dehl deh-sah-'yoo-noh)*
between meals	**entre las comidas** *('ehn-treh lahs koh-'mee-dahs)*
every four hours	**cada cuatro horas** *('kah-dah 'kwah-troh 'oh-rahs)*
twice a day	**dos veces por día** *(dohs 'beh-sehs pohr 'dee-ah)*

MÁS AYUDA

• Be very careful when it comes to medication! Let your help know what's best for the child:

Don't give it to him/her.	**No se lo dé** *(noh seh loh deh)*
Don't take it.	**No la tome** *(noh lah 'toh-meh)*
It isn't for children.	**No es para niños** *(noh ehs 'pah-rah 'nee-nyohs)*

• Although we don't like to think about it, there's a chance that our helpers could be witnesses or victims of a crime. To be on the safe side, look over this next set of Spanish words and phrases:

It's a (an)...	**Es...** *(ehs)*
accident	**un accidente** *(oon ahk-see-'dehn-teh)*
crime	**un crimen** *(oon 'kree-mehn)*
gang	**una pandilla** *('oo-nah pahn-'dee-yah)*
rape	**una violación** *('oo-nah bee-oh-lah-see-'ohn)*
robbery	**un robo** *(oon 'roh-boh)*

shooting	un disparo *(oon dees-'pah-roh)*
suspect	un sospechoso *(oon soh-speh-'choh-soh)*
thief	un ladrón *(oon lah-'drohn)*
victim	una víctima *('oo-nah 'beek-tee-mah)*
weapon	un arma *(oon 'ahr-mah)*
witness	un testigo *(oon teh-'stee-goh)*
Are you hurt?	¿Está lastimado? *(eh-'stah lah-stee-'mah-doh)*
Did you see anything?	¿Vio algo? *(bee-'oh 'ahl-goh)*

Should I call the police? **¿Debo llamar a la policía?** *('deh-boh yah-'mahr ah lah poh-lee-'see-ah)*

TEMAS CULTURALES

Throughout history, we have discovered that certain herbs and spices work wonders on common ailments. In Latin America, the practice of home remedies—**los remedios caseros** *(lohs reh-'meh-dee·ohs kah-'seh-rohs)* is quite popular, so don't be surprised if your Hispanic employee offers to prepare something when your child gets sick.

NATURAL DISASTERS
Los desastres naturales
(lohs deh-'sah-strehs nah-too-'rah-lehs)

Not every problem is under your control. Natural disasters occur, and you may need to take precautions. As you train the child care professional, clearly outline the steps to be taken if trouble strikes. Are you both prepared to handle the following?

earthquake	el terremoto *(ehl teh-rreh-'moh-toh)*
epidemic	la epidemia *(lah eh-pee-'deh-mee·ah)*
flood	la inundación *(lah een-oon-dah-see-'ohn)*
hurricane	el huracán *(ehl oo-rah-'kahn)*
rain	la lluvia *(lah 'yoo-bee·ah)*
snow	la nieve *(lah nee-'eh-beh)*
storm	la tormenta *(lah tohr-'mehn-tah)*
tornado	el tornado *(ehl tohr-'nah-doh)*

 REPASEMOS

Match the English word with its translation:

burn	**el vecino** *(ehl beh-'see-noh)*
smoke	**la sangre** *(lah 'sahn-greh)*
bandaid	**las muletas** *(lahs moo-'leh-tahs)*
neighbor	**la tirita** *(lah tee-'ree-tah)*
blood	**la quemadura** *(lah keh-mah-'doo-rah)*
crutches	**el humo** *(ehl 'oo-moh)*
weapon	**el terremoto** *(ehl teh-rreh-'moh-toh)*
earthquake	**el arma** *(ehl 'ahr-mah)*

 MÁS AYUDA

• Freak accidents require steady nerves and quick reactions. Make sure your help knows what to do the moment things suddenly go wrong. Your instructions should include:

Cover the children with a blanket!

¡Cubra a los niños con una frazada! *('koo-brah ah lohs 'nee-nyohs kohn 'oo-nah frah-'sah-dah)*

Go to the neighbors and ask for help!

¡Vaya a los vecinos y pida su ayuda! *('bah-yah ah lohs beh-'see-nohs ee 'pee-dah soo ah-'yoo-dah)*

Grab the children and run outside!

¡Agarre los niños y corra hacia afuera! *(ah-'gah-rreh lohs 'nee-nyohs ee 'koh-rrah 'ah-see·ah ah-'fweh-rah)*

Keep the children away from windows!

¡Deje a los niños muy lejos de las ventanas! *('deh-heh ah lohs 'nee-nyohs 'moo-ee 'leh-hohs deh lahs behn-'tah-nahs)*

Put the children under the table!

¡Ponga a los niños debajo de la mesa! *('pohn-gah ah lohs 'nee-nyohs deh-'bah-hoh deh lah 'meh-sah)*

• You should be familiar with these:

Danger!	**¡Peligro!** *(peh-'lee-groh)*
Fire!	**¡Fuego!** *('fweh-goh)*
Help!	**¡Socorro!** *(soh-'koh-rroh)*

 REPASEMOS

Name three animals that might be considered dangerous:

_____

_____

_____

 TEMAS CULTURALES

• Don't hesitate to teach your help everything there is to know about handling emergencies — especially if they happen at night. Study this list so that no one will be left in the dark:

candle	**la vela** *(lah 'beh-lah)*
flashlight	**la linterna** *(lah leen-'tehr-nah)*
fuse	**el fusible** *(ehl foo-'see-bleh)*

• When emergencies arise, illnesses or injury aren't the only causes for alarm. Sometimes a personal problem or family conflict can lead to anxiety, pain, and emotional outbursts. It's always best to share such information with anyone who sees your child on a regular basis. Will any of these words be necessary?

abuse	el abuso *(ehl ah-'boo-soh)*
death	la muerte *(lah 'mwehr-teh)*
depression	el desánimo *(ehl dehs-'ah-nee-moh)*
divorce	el divorcio *(ehl dee-'bohr-see·oh)*
nightmare	la pesadilla *(lah peh-sah-'dee-yah)*
trauma	el trauma *(ehl 'trah·ooh-mah)*

 ## TEMAS CULTURALES

Don't expect Spanish speakers to communicate in English with your children. Though they may try, their native language will come out first. Simple commands, and even songs, will emerge naturally during childcare activities. And, don't worry about your child's English skills. Research indicates that exposure to more than one language makes children smarter!

PLAYTIME
La hora de jugar (lah 'oh-rah deh hoo-'gahr)

All children like to play. Here are some terms to help your caregiver and you discuss your child at play.

He/She likes to play with (the)...	Le gusta jugar con... *(leh 'goo-stah hoo-'gahr kohn)*
balloon	el globo *(ehl 'gloh-boh)*
blocks	los bloques de madera *(lohs 'bloh-kehs deh mah-'deh-rah)*
cards	la baraja *(lah bah-'rah-hah)*
cartoons	los dibujos animados *(lohs dee-'boo-hohs ah-nee-'mah-dohs)*
checkers	el juego de damas *(ehl hoo·'eh-goh deh 'dah-mahs)*
chess	el ajedrez *(ehl ah-heh-'drehs)*
coloring book	el libro de pintar *(ehl 'lee-broh deh peen-'tahr)*
costume	el disfraz *(ehl dees-'frahs)*
crayons	los gises *(lohs 'gee-sehs)*
game	el juego *(ehl hoo·'eh-goh)*
joke	el chiste *(ehl 'chee-steh)*

jump rope	**la cuerda para brincar** *(lah 'kwehr-dah 'pah-rah breen-'kahr)*
kite	**la cometa** *(lah koh-'meh-tah)*
marble	**la canica** *(lah kah-'nee-kah)*
model	**el modelo** *(ehl moh-'deh-loh)*
monopoly	**el monopolio** *(ehl moh-noh-'poh-lee·oh)*
parade	**el desfile** *(ehl dehs-'fee-leh)*
puppet	**el títere** *(ehl 'tee-teh-reh)*
puzzle	**el rompecabezas** *(ehl rohm-peh-kah-'beh-sah)*
radio	**la radio** *(lah 'rah-dee·oh)*
skateboard	**la patineta** *(lah pah-tee-'neh-tah)*
skate	**el patín** *(ehl pah-'teen)*
sled	**el trineo** *(ehl tree-'neh-oh)*
slide	**el resbalador** *(ehl rehs-bah-lah-'dohr)*
song	**la canción** *(lah kahn-see-'ohn)*
story	**el cuentito** *(ehl kwehn-'tee-toh)*
swing	**el columpio** *(ehl koh-'loom-pee·oh)*
tea set	**el juego de té** *(ehl 'hwe-goh deh teh)*
television	**la televisión** *(lah teh-leh-bee-see-'ohn)*
top	**el trompo** *(ehl 'trohm-poh)*
toy train	**el tren de juguete** *(ehl 'trehn deh hoo-'geh-teh)*
toy truck	**el camión de juguete** *(ehl kah-mee-'oh deh hoo-'geh-teh)*
trick	**el truco** *(ehl 'troo-koh)*
tricycle	**el triciclo** *(ehl tree-'see-kloh)*
videos	**los vídeos** *(lohs 'bee-deh-ohs)*
wagon	**el carreton** *(ehl kah-rreh-'tohn)*

 TEMAS CULTURALES

Young children are sacred creatures in most cultures. In some Hispanic homes, the traditions and rituals of childrearing are not easily changed. Many customs are centuries old and may contradict your own practices, so keep these things in mind as you give advice to Spanish-speaking nannies and babysitters.

Notice how the babysitter loves to hold your child! In some Spanish-speaking countries, many people believe that children can get sick if you stare at them without making physical contact. A brief stroke, hug, or light caress makes everyone feel more comfortable.

HOBBIES

Los pasatiempos *(lohs pah-sah-tee-'ehm-pohs)*

He/She prefers...	**Prefiere...** *(preh-fee-'eh-reh)*
art	**el arte** *(ehl 'ahr-teh)*
ballet	**el ballet** *(ehl bah-'yeht)*
coins	**las monedas** *(lahs moh-'neh-dahs)*
computers	**las computadoras** *(lahs kohm-poo-tah-'doh-rahs)*
magic	**la magia** *(lah 'mah-gee·ah)*
movies	**las películas** *(lahs peh-'lee-koo-lahs)*
music	**la música** *(lah 'moo-see-kah)*
photography	**la fotografía** *(lah foh-toh-grah-'fee-ah)*
stamps	**los sellos** *(lohs 'seh-yohs)*
video games	**los juegos de vídeo** *(lohs hoo-'eh-gohs deh 'bee-deh-oh)*

Yo prefiero música. Ella prefiere películas.

Notice how many of these words are for fun activities:

boating	**el paseo en bote** *(ehl pah-'seh-oh ehn 'boh-teh)*
dancing	**el baile** *(ehl bah-ee-'leh)*
drawing	**el dibujo** *(ehl dee-boo-'hoh)*
fishing	**la pesca** *(lah peh-'skah)*
hiking	**la caminata** *(lah kah-mee-'nah-tah)*
horseback riding	**la equitación** *(lah eh-kee-tah-see·'ohn)*

jogging	**el trote** *(ehl 'troh-teh)*
painting	**la pintura** *(lah peen-'too-rah)*
playing music	**la música** *(lah 'moo-see-kah)*
reading	**la lectura** *(lah lehr-'too-rah)*
riding bikes	**andar en bicicleta** *(ahn-'dahr ehn bee-see-'kleh-tah)*
running	**la carrera** *(lah kah-'re-rah)*
sailing	**la navegación a vela** *(lah nah-veh-gah-see-'ohn ah 'beh-lah)*
skating	**el patinaje** *(ehl pah-tee-'nah-heh)*
skiing	**el esquí** *(ehl ehs-'kee)*
sports	**los deportes** *(lohs deh-'pohr-tehs)*
swimming	**la natación** *(lah nah-tah-see-'on)*
playing "dress-up"	**el juego de disfraces** *(ehl hoo-'eh-goh deh dees-'frah-sehs)*
playing "house"	**el juego a la casita** *(ehl hoo-'eh-goh ah lah kah-'see-tah)*
playing "soldiers"	**el juego a los soldados** *(ehl hoo-'eh-goh ah lohs sohl-'dah-dohs)*

 REPASEMOS

Match each word with its translation:

kite	**el globo** *(ehl 'gloh-boh)*
movies	**las cometas** *(lahs koh-'meh-tahs)*
balloon	**la película** *(lahpeh-'lee-koo-lah)*

MORE FUN!
¡Más diversión! *(mahs dee-behr-see-'ohn)*

Stuffed animals
Los animales de peluche *(lohs ah-nee-'mah-lehs deh peh-'loo-cheh)*

He/She has a...	**Tiene...** *(tee-'eh-neh)*
bear	**el oso** *(ehl 'oh-soh)*
cat	**el gato** *(ehl 'gah-toh)*
dinosaur	**el dinosaurio** *(ehl dee-noh-'sah·oo-ree-oh)*
dog	**el perro** *(ehl 'peh-rroh)*

duck	el **pato** *(ehl 'pah-toh)*
elephant	el **elefante** *(ehl eh-leh-'fahn-teh)*
giraffe	la **jirafa** *(lah hee-'rah-fah)*
horse	el **caballo** *(ehl kah-'bah-yoh)*
monkey	el **mono** *(ehl 'moh-noh)*
mouse	el **ratón** *(ehl rah-'tohn)*
pig	el **puerco** *(ehl 'pwehr-koh)*
pony	el **caballito** *(ehl kah-bah-'yee-toh)*
puppy	el **perrito** *(ehl peh-'rree-toh)*
rabbit	el **conejo** *(ehl koh-'neh-hoh)*
sheep	la **oveja** *(lah oh-'beh-hah)*
zebra	la **cebra** *(lah 'seh-brah)*

Musical instruments
Los instrumentos musicales
(lohs een-stroo-'mehn-tohs moo-see-'kah-lehs)
He/She plays the... **Toca...** *('toh-kah)*

clarinet	el **clarinete** *(ehl klah-ree-'neh-teh)*
drum	el **tambor** *(ehl tahm-'bohr)*
guitar	la **guitarra** *(lah gee-'tah-rrah)*
organ	el **órgano** *(ehl 'ohr-gah-noh)*
piano	el **piano** *(ehl pee-'ah-noh)*
saxophone	el **saxófono** *(ehl sahk-'soh-foh-noh)*
trombone	el **trombón** *(ehl trohm-'bohn)*
trumpet	la **trompeta** *(lah trohm-'peh-tah)*
violin	el **violín** *(ehl bee-oh-'leen)*

Sports

Los deportes *(lohs deh-'pohr-tehs)*
Notice that these words sound just like English!

He/she wants to play...	**Quiere jugar...** *(kee-'eh-reh hoo-'gahr)*
baseball	**el béisbol** *(ehl 'beh·ees-bohl)*
basketball	**el básquetbol** *(ehl 'bahs-keht-bohl)*
bowling	**el boliche** *(ehl boh-'lee-cheh)*
boxing	**el boxeo** *(ehl bohk-'seh-oh)*
football	**el fútbol americano** *(ehl 'foot-bohl ah-meh-ree-'kah-noh)*
golf	**el golf** *(ehl gohlf)*
lacrosse	**el lacrosse** *(ehl lah-'kroh-seh)*
soccer	**el fútbol** *(ehl 'foot-bohl)*
tennis	**el tenis** *(ehl 'teh-nees)*
volleyball	**el vóleibol** *(ehl boh-leh-ee-'bohl)*

They go to the...	**Van a...** *(bahn ah)*
court	**la cancha** *(lah 'kahn-chah)*
field	**el campo** *(ehl 'kahm-poh)*
game	**el juego** *(ehl hoo-'eh-goh)*
golf course	**el campo de golf** *(ehl 'kahm-poh deh 'gohlf)*
gymnasium	**el gimnasio** *(ehl heem-'nah-see·oh)*
match	**el partido** *(ehl pahr-'tee-doh)*
playground	**el campo de recreo** *(ehl 'kahm-poh deh reh-'kreh-oh)*
pool	**la piscina** *(lah pee-'see-nah)*
practice	**la práctica** *(lah 'prahk-tee-kah)*
stadium	**el estadio** *(ehl eh-'stah-dee·oh)*

 REPASEMOS

• Answer these questions with either **sí** or **no**:

¿Puede usted jugar tenis? *('pweh-deh oo-'stehd hoo-'gahr 'teh-nees)*

¿Puede usted bailar el tango? *('pweh-deh oo-'stehd bah·ee-'lahr ehl 'tahn-goh)*

¿Puede usted leer este libro? *('pweh-deh oo-'stehd leh-'ehr 'eh-steh 'lee-broh)*

- List three items under each category:

Los deportes *(lohs deh-'pohr-tehs)*

_____

_____

_____

Los instrumentos musicales *(lohs een-stroo-'mehn-tohs moo-see-'kah-lehs)*

_____

_____

_____

Los pasatiempos *(lohs pah-sah-tee-'ehm-pohs)*

_____

_____

_____

 TEMAS CULTURALES

Here we go again — Spanglish!

el surf
el hockey
el Nintendo
el golf
la Barbie
el hockey
el rollerblading

TELL THEM!
¡Dígales! *('dee-gah-lehs)*

Regardless of the activity, children generally need to be told what to do and what not to do. Even when they are at play, certain guidelines need to be established. Read over the following sentence pattern and figure out ways to substitute phrases with other key vocabulary.

Tell them that...   **Dígales que...** *('dee-gah-lehs keh)*
   they have to calm down   **tienen que calmarse** *(tee-'eh-nehn keh kahl-'mahr-seh)*

they have to share	**tienen que compartir** *(tee-'eh-nehn keh kohm-pahr-'teer)*
they must obey the rules	**tienen que obedecer las reglas** *(tee-'eh-nehn keh oh-beh-deh-'sehr lahs 'reh-glahs)*
they must return the toys	**tienen que devolver los juguetes** *(tee-'eh-nehn keh deh-bohl-'behr lohs hoo-'geh-tehs)*
they need to be careful	**necesitan tener cuidado** *(neh-seh-'see-tahn teh-'nehr kwee-'dah-doh)*
they need to rest	**necesitan descansar** *(neh-seh-'see-tahn dehs-kahn-'sahr)*
they should ask permission	**deben pedir permiso** *('deh-behn peh-'deer pehr-'mee-soh)*
they should come home	**deben regresar a la casa** *('deh-behn reh-greh-'sahr ah lah 'kah-sah)*
they can't fight	**no pueden pelear** *(noh 'pweh-dehn peh-leh-'ahr)*
they can't hit	**no pueden golpear** *(noh 'pweh-dehn gohl-peh-'ahr)*
they can't kick	**no pueden patear** *(noh 'pweh-dehn pah-teh-'ahr)*
they can't play here	**no pueden jugar aquí** *(noh 'pweh-dehn hoo-'gahr ah-'kee)*
they can't push	**no pueden empujar** *(noh 'pweh-dehn ehm-poo-'hahr)*
they can't run	**no pueden correr** *(noh 'pweh-dehn koh-'rrehr)*
they can't say bad words	**no pueden decir groserías** *(noh 'pweh-dehn deh-'seer groh-seh-'ree-ahs)*
they can't watch that	**no pueden mirar eso** *(noh 'pweh-dehn mee-'rahr 'eh-soh)*
they can't yell	**no pueden gritar** *(noh 'pweh-dehn gree-'tahr)*
I love them	**les quiero mucho** *(lehs kee-'eh-roh 'moo-choh)*
it is a punishment	**es un castigo** *(ehs oon kah-'stee-goh)*

| it is their bedtime | **es la hora de acostarse** *(ehs lah 'oh-rah deh ah-koh-'stahr-seh)* |
| we will be home soon! | **¡regresaremos pronto!** *(reh-greh-sah-'reh-mohs 'prohn-toh)* |

Dígale a John que tiene que vestirse.
Dígales a Jenny y Pamela que tienen que bañarse.

HOUSE RULES

Las reglas de la casa

(lahs 'reh-glahs deh lah 'kah-sah)

Since you have the final say, let everyone — child and nanny/babysitter — know in both languages what the rules are. Consider creating your own bilingual "do's and don'ts" list so that there are no misunderstandings. These will get you started:

You/He/She must...	**Tiene que...** *(tee-'eh-neh keh)*
go to bed at _____	**acostarse a** _____ *(ah-koh-'stahr-seh ah)*
wake up at _____	**despertarse a** _____ *(deh-spehr-'tahr-seh ah)*
ask for permission	**pedir permiso** *(peh-'deer pehr-'mee-soh)*
behave	**portarse bien** *(pohr-'tahr-seh 'bee-ehn)*
brush hair	**cepillarse el pelo** *(seh-pee-'yahr-seh ehl 'peh-loh)*

brush teeth	**cepillarse los dientes** *(seh-pee-'yahr-seh lohs dee-'ehn-tehs)*
clean the room	**limpiar el cuarto** *(leem-pee-'ahr ehl 'kwahr-toh)*
clean up the mess	**limpiar la basura** *(leem-pee-'ahr lah bah-'soo-rah)*
do the homework	**hacer la tarea de escuela** *(ah-'sehr lah tah-'reh-ah deh eh-'skweh-lah)*
finish the chores	**terminar las tareas** *(tehr-mee-'nahr lahs tah-'reh-ahs)*
follow the schedule	**seguir el horario** *(seh-'geer ehl oh-'rah-ree·oh)*
get dressed	**vestirse** *(beh-'steer-seh)*
have good manners	**tener buenos modales** *(teh-'nehr 'bweh-nohs moh-'dah-lehs)*
limit the phone calls	**limitar las llamadas** *(lee-mee-'tahr lahs yah-'mah-dahs)*
make the bed	**tender la cama** *(tehn-'dehr lah 'kah-mah)*
put everything away	**guardar todo** *(gwahr-'dahr 'toh-doh)*
put on a sweater	**ponerse un suéter** *(poh-'nehr-seh oon 'sweh-tehr)*
stay in the nursery	**quedarse en la guardería** *(keh-'dahr-seh ehn lah gwahr-deh-'ree-ah)*
study	**estudiar** *(eh-stoo-dee-'ahr)*
take a bath	**bañarse** *(bah-'nyahr-seh)*
take a nap	**tomar una siesta** *(toh-'mahr 'oo-nah see-'ehs-tah)*
turn off the lights	**apagar las luces** *(ah-pah-'gahr lahs 'loo-sehs)*
turn off the TV	**apagar la televisión** *(ah-pah-'gahr lah teh-leh-bee-see-'ohn)*
use this bathroom	**usar este baño** *(oo-'sahr 'eh-steh 'bah-nyoh)*
wash hands	**lavarse las manos** *(lah-'bahr-seh lahs 'mah-nohs)*
wash up	**lavarse** *(lah-'bahr-seh)*
wear a helmet	**ponerse el casco** *(poh-'nehr-seh ehl 'kah-skoh)*

Are there any others that you'd care to add?

 **MÁS AYUDA**

Some children tend to misbehave around strangers. You may ask the nanny/babysitter a few basic questions:

They argued?	**¿Discutieron?** *(dees-kuh-tee-'eh-rohn)*
They misbehaved?	**¿Se comportaron mal?** *(seh kohm-pohr-'tah-rohn mahl)*
They refused?	**¿Se negaron?** *(seh neh-'gah-rohn)*
They would not obey you?	**¿Se negaron a obedecerla?** *(seh neh-'gah-rohn ah oh-beh-deh-'sehr-lah)*

 TEMAS CULTURALES

One of the most difficult things to discuss in a foreign language concerns family values. Your personal feelings, attitudes, and beliefs cannot be communicated in a few short sentences. Therefore, the best way to express any serious matter is either through an interpreter or by preparing a written note. Be sure that your help knows exactly what you consider is "right" or "wrong."

 ¡HÁGALO, POR FAVOR!

Although the duties of childcare professionals may vary, most of the following commands will meet your specific needs. Remember that these words tell an employee what to do, and are usually combined with **le**, which means "him" or "her."

Accompany	him/her.	**Acompáñele** *(ah-kohm-'pah-nyeh-leh)*
Allow	him/her.	**Permítale** *(pehr-'mee-tah-leh)*
Bathe	him/her.	**Báñele** *('bah-nyeh-leh)*
Call	him/her.	**Llámele** *('yah-meh-leh)*
Dress	him/her.	**Vístale** *('bee-stah-leh)*
Give	him/her.	**Dele** *('deh-leh)*
Help	him/her.	**Ayúdele** *(ah-'yoo-deh-leh)*
Keep	him/her.	**Manténgale** *(mahn-'tehn-gah-leh)*
Let/leave	him/her.	**Déjele** *('deh-heh-leh)*
Pick up	him/her.	**Recójale** *(reh-'koh-hah-leh)*

Put	him/her.	**Póngale** *('pohn-gah-leh)*
Scold	him/her.	**Regáñele** *(reh-'gah-nyeh-leh)*
Serve	him/her.	**Sírvale** *('seer-bah-leh)*
Show	him/her.	**Muéstrele** *('mwehs-treh-leh)*
Tell	him/her.	**Dígale** *('dee-'gah-leh)*
Undress	him/her.	**Desvístale** *(dehs-'bee-stah-leh)*
Wake up	him/her.	**Despiértele** *(dehs-pee-'ehr-teh-leh)*
Wash	him/her.	**Lávele** *('lah-beh-leh)*

Tell your Spanish-speaking assistant exactly what you expect. Here are some expressions that every parent needs:

Make sure that you...	**Asegúrese de...** *(ah-seh-'goo-reh-seh deh)*
ask me if you don't understand	**preguntarme si no entiende** *(preh-goon-'tahr-meh see noh ehn-tee-'ehn-deh)*
call me later	**llamarme más tarde** *(yah-'mahr-meh mahs 'tahr-deh)*
check on the children	**vigilar a los niños** *(bee-hee-'lahr ah lohs 'nee-nyohs)*
don't leave them alone	**no dejarles solos** *(noh deh-'hahr-lehs 'soh-lohs)*
don't talk to strangers	**no hablar con desconocidos** *(noh ah-'blahr kohn dehs-koh-noh-'see-dohs)*
lock the doors	**cerrar las puertas** *(seh-'rrahr lahs 'pwehr-tahs)*
put it out of his/her reach	**ponerlo fuera del alcance del niño** *(poh-'nehr-loh 'fweh-rah dehl ahl-'kahn-seh dehl 'nee-nyoh)*
read the labels carefully	**leer las etiquetas con cuidado** *(leh-'ehr lahs eh-tee-'keh-tahs kohn kwee-'dah-doh)*
take messages	**tomar los mensajes** *(toh-'mahr lohs mehn-'sah-hehs)*
turn off the machine	**apagar la máquina** *(ah-pah-'gahr lah 'mah-kee-nah)*

 **MÁS AYUDA**

Still, the easiest way to ask someone to help you is to use the phrase,
Favor de... *(fah-'bohr deh)*:

Please...	**Favor de...** *(fah-'bohr deh)*
bathe the children.	**bañar a los niños** *(bah-'nyahr ah lohs 'nee-nyohs)*
change their clothes.	**cambiarles la ropa** *(kahm-bee-'ahr-lehs lah 'roh-pah)*
feed the kids.	**alimentar a los niños** *(ah-lee-mehn-'tahr ah lohs 'nee-nyohs)*
leave it here.	**dejarlo aquí** *(deh-'hahr-loh ah-'kee)*
make a list.	**hacerme una lista** *(ah-'sehr-meh 'oo-nah 'lees-tah)*
tell me in English.	**decirme en inglés** *(deh-'seer-meh ehn een-'glehs)*
wash their clothes.	**lavar su ropa** *(lah-'bahr soo 'roh-pah)*

Ejercicio para gente de oficina.

 TEMAS CULTURALES

In terms of discipline, be very clear about what you want. There is no traditional method of punishment for children in Latin America, so there is
nothing to fear. However, your caregiver does need specific instructions

concerning disciplinary consequences. Use drawings, written notes, or drama to clarify details, and follow up everything with, **¿Entiende?** *(ehn-tee-'ehn-deh)* (Understand?).

SITTER'S SPANISH
El español para la niñera
(ehl eh-spah-'nyohl 'pah-rah lah nee-'nyeh-rah)

There's a lot more to childcare than assigning rules and handing out commands. Loving, encouraging remarks are also necessary. Listen carefully as a Spanish speaker communicates kindly to your little ones.

How cute!	**¡Qué precioso!** *(keh pre-see-'oh-soh)*
How funny!	**¡Qué cómico!** *(keh 'koh-mee-koh)*
How pretty!	**¡Qué bonito!** *(keh boh-'nee-toh)*
What a beautiful face!	**¡Qué linda cara!** *(keh 'leen-dah 'kah-rah)*
What a beautiful outfit!	**¡Qué linda ropa!** *(keh 'leen-dah 'roh-pah)*
What a beautiful smile!	**¡Qué linda sonrisa!** *(keh 'leen-dah sohn-'ree-sah)*
What a beautiful voice!	**¡Qué linda voz!** *(keh 'leen-dah vohs)*

Be aware that action words change a bit when you chat with children. Hispanics use the "informal" or "tú" *(too)* form:

Come here, darling	**Ven acá, mi querido** *(behn ah-'kah mee keh-'ree-doh)*
Come her, my love	**Ven acá, mi amor** *(behn ah-'kah, mee ah-'mohr)*
Come here, sweetie	**Ven acá, mi dulce** *(behn ah-'kah mee 'dool-seh)*
Don't be afraid.	**No tengas miedo** *(noh 'tehn-gahs mee-'eh-doh)*
Don't cry.	**No llores** *(noh 'yoh-rehs)*
Give me a hug.	**Deme un abrazo** *('deh-meh oon ah-'brah-soh)*
Give me a kiss.	**Deme un beso** *('deh-meh oon 'beh-soh)*
It's lots of fun.	**Es muy divertido** *(ehs 'moo-ee dee-behr-'tee-doh)*
It's for you.	**Es para ti** *(ehs 'pah-rah tee)*

REPASEMOS

Translate:

> They have to share.
> They can't fight.
> You have to behave.
> Make sure that you lock the doors.

¡Qué preciosa la rubia!
¡Qué bonita la morena!
(¡Qué feo el perro!)

 TEMAS CULTURALES

• It's not uncommon for native Hispanics to use nicknames when referring to other people. This is especially true with children. It is meant to show intimacy, so it might be fun to look up the translations for any terms of endearment that you hear.

• In every language, people use slang to chitchat about routine activities. If you're having trouble understanding certain words or expressions, continue to use the phrase, **¿Qué significa eso?** *(keh seeg-nee-'fee-kah 'eh-soh)*, which translates, "What does that mean?". Chances are they'll come up with the Spanish words that are more familiar to you.

• Slang might include some not-so-nice words as well. Foul language exists in every country, so make it clear that none of it will be allowed around your home. Use this line.

> Please don't use foul language.
> **Por favor, no diga groserías** *(pohr fah-'bohr, noh 'dee-gah groh-seh-'ree-ahs)*

168

- Talk about your children in Spanish! Do any of these descriptions fit a child of yours?

She's...	Es... *(ehs)*
bald	**calvita** *(kahl-'bee-tah)*
blonde	**rubia** *('roo-bee-ah)*
brunette	**morena** *(moh-'reh-nah)*
chubby	**gordita** *(gohr-'dee-tah)*
dark-skinned	**prieta** *(pree-'eh-tah)*
a redhead	**pelirroja** *(peh-lee-'roh-hah)*
skinny	**flaquita** *(flah-'kee-tah)*
a twin	**una gemela** *('oo-nah heh-'meh-lah)*

Study these phrases and terms:

How much does the baby weigh?
> **¿Cuánto pesa el bebé?** *('kwahn-toh 'peh-sah ehl beh-'beh)*

Is it a boy or a girl?
> **¿Es un niño o una niña?** *(ehs oon 'nee-nyoh oh 'oo-nah 'nee-nyah)*

When was it born?
> **¿Cuándo nació?** *('kwahn-doh nah-see-'oh)*

It's _____.	**Tiene** _____. *(tee-'eh-neh)*
inches	**pulgadas** *(pool-'gah-dahs)*
ounces	**onzas** *('ohn-sahs)*
pounds	**libras** *('lee-brahs)*
a birth defect	**un defecto de nacimiento** *(oon deh-'fehk-toh deh nah-see-mee-'ehn-toh)*
He is a diabetic	**Es diabético** *(Ehs dee-ah-'beh-tee-koh)*
She is handicapped	**Es minusválida** *(Ehs mee-noos-'bah-lee-dah)*

 ¡MÁS ACCIÓN!

Although there are a variety of ways to state a *past* tense in Spanish, you need to start by learning the more commonly used form. Read the following examples and, just a you did with *present* actions, make the changes in your verbs. You won't be perfect at first, but Spanish speakers will know what you're trying to say.

• AR verbs

To speak	**Hablar** *(ah-'blahr)*
I spoke with the child.	**Hablé con el niño** *(ah-'bleh kohn ehl 'nee-nyoh)*
You/he/she spoke a lot.	**Habló mucho** *(ah-'bloh 'moo-choh)*
You (plural) or they spoke in English.	**Hablaron en inglés** *(ah-'blah-rohn ehn een-'glehs)*
We spoke a little.	**Hablamos un poquito** *(ah-'blah-mohs oon poh-'kee-toh)*

• ER/IR verbs

To drink	**Beber** *(beh-'behr)*
To leave	**Salir** *(sah-'leer)*
I left at eight.	**Salí a las ocho** *(sah-'lee ah lahs 'oh-choh)*
I drank the milk.	**Bebí la leche** *(beh-'bee lah 'leh-cheh)*
You/he/she left late.	**Salió tarde** *(sah-lee-'oh 'tahr-deh)*
You/he/she drank all of it.	**Bebió todo** *(beh-bee-'oh 'toh-doh)*
You (plural), they left happy.	**Salieron contentos** *(sah-lee-'eh-rohn kohn-'tehn-tohs)*
You (plural), they drank water.	**Bebieron agua** *(beh-bee-'eh-rohn 'ah-gwah)*
We left in a car.	**Salimos en el carro** *(sah-'lee-mohs ehn ehl 'kah-rroh)*
We drank yesterday.	**Bebimos ayer** *(beh-'bee-mohs ah-'yehr)*

Ella habló de su divorcio. ¡Qué pesadilla!

• Some common verbs have irregular past tenses, so be on the look-out! These three are common:

To be	**Ser** *(sehr)*
To go	**Ir** *(eer)*
I was or went	**fui** *(fwee)*
you were or went and	
he, she was or went	**fue** *(fweh)*
you (plural), they	**fueron** *('fweh-rohn)*
were or went	
we were or went	**fuimos** *('fwee-mohs)*

To have	**Tener** *(teh-'nehr)*
I had	**tuve** *('too-beh)*
you, he, she had	**tuvo** *('too-boh)*
you(plural), they had	**tuvieron** *(too-bee-'eh-rohn)*
we had	**tuvimos** *(too-'bee-mohs)*

This past tense action form is probably the most practical when it comes to childcare. How else can you find out what happened with the children? Whenever you need an update, use the question ¿**Qué pasó?** *(keh pah-'soh)*, which means, "What happened?":

They went to the park.	**Fueron al parque** *('fweh-rohn ahl 'pahr-keh)*
He played in the house.	**Jugó en la casa** *(hoo-'goh ehn lah 'kah-sah)*
They behaved well.	**Se portaron bien** *(seh pohr-'tah-rohn 'bee-ehn)*
We had an accident.	**Tuvimos un accidente** *(too-'bee-mohs oon ahk-see-'dehn-teh)*
I put the toys in the box.	**Metí los juguetes en la caja** *(meh-'tee lohs hoo-'geh-tehs ehn lah 'kah-hah)*
She saw a video.	**Vio un vídeo** *(bee-'oh oon 'bee-deh-oh)*

This isn't the only verb form you're going to need. Although these phrases won't be discussed in detail, check out the spellings and meanings of the examples below:

I used to have	**tenía** *(teh-'nee-ah)*
I would have	**tendría** *(tehn-'dree-ah)*
I will have	**tendré** *(tehn-'dreh)*

Follow the pattern below:

I speak.	**Hablo** *('ah-bloh)*
I spoke.	**Hablé** *(ah-'bleh)*
I work.	**Trabajo** *(trah-'bah-hoh)*
I worked.	_____
I drive.	**Manejo** *(mah-'neh-hoh)*
I drove.	_____
I run.	**Corro** *('koh-rroh)*
I ran.	_____
I eat.	**Como** *('koh-moh)*
I ate.	_____
I promise.	**Prometo** *(proh-'meh-toh)*
I promised.	_____

 ¡EL SUPERESPAÑOL!

Here's still another one of those incredible verb patterns that makes speaking Spanish so much easier. Combine your verbs with the forms of the work **poder** *(poh-'dehr)*, which means "to be able to":

To be able to	**Poder** *(poh-'dehr)*
I can	**Puedo** *('pweh-doh)*
I can begin.	**Puedo comenzar** *('pweh-doh koh-mehn-'sahr)*
you, she, he can	**Puede** *('pweh-deh)*
She can play.	**Puede jugar** *('pweh-deh hoo-'gahr)*
you (plural), they can	**Pueden** *('pweh-dehn)*
They can rest.	**Pueden descansar** *('pweh-dehn dehs-kahn-'sahr)*
we can	**Podemos** *(poh-'deh-mohs)*
We can eat.	**Podemos comer** *(poh-'deh-mohs koh-'mehr)*

 **REPASEMOS**

Practice your skills by adding these verb infinitives to the phrases below:

Trabajar *(trah-bah-'hahr)*   Comer *(koh-'mehr)*
Cocinar *(koh-see-'nahr)*   Limpiar *(leem-pee-'ahr)*
Ir *(eer)* Caminar *(kah-mee-'nahr)* Hablar *(ah-'blahr)*
Favor de... *(fah-'bohr deh)*
No... *(noh)*
Tiene que... *(tee-'eh-neh keh)*
Debe... *('deh-beh)*
Necesita... *(neh-seh-'see-tah)*
¿Quiere...? *(kee-'eh-reh)*
¿Le gusta...? *(leh 'goo-stah)*
¿Puede...? *('pweh-deh)*

 PALABRAS CLAVES

Youngsters who are old enough to attend school need special attention at home. Their needs go beyond food, clothing, and shelter. They require certain instructions regarding their schoolwork and studies. The following words refer to education, and can be used with all of your other Spanish skills to discuss those issues relating to students.

absent   **ausente** *(ow-'sehn-teh)*
   No puede estar ausente *(noh 'pweh-deh eh-'stahr ow-'sehn-teh)*
academic grade   **la calificación** *(lah kah-lee-fee-kah-see-'ohn)*
   Tiene buenas calificaciones *(tee-'eh-neh 'bweh-nahs kah-lee-fee-kah-see-'oh-nehs)*
attendance   **la asistencia** *(ah-sees-'tehn-see·ah)*
   Su asistencia es importante *(soo ah-sees-'tehn-see·ah ehs eem-pohr-'tahn-teh)*
class   **la clase** *(lah 'klah-seh)*
   Tiene una clase grande *(tee-'eh-neh 'oo-nah 'klah-seh 'grahn-deh)*
counselor   **el consejero** *(ehl kohn-seh-'heh-roh)*
   ¿Quién es su consejero? *(kee-'ehn ehs soo kohn-seh-'heh-roh)*

grade level **el grado** *(ehl 'grah-doh)*
Está en el segundo grado *(eh-'stah ehn ehl seh-'goon-doh 'grah-doh)*

homework **la tarea** *(lah tah-'reh-ah)*
Tiene que hacer su tarea *(tee-'eh-neh keh ah-'sehr soo tah-'reh-ah)*

meeting **la reunión** *(lah reh-uh-nee-'ohn)*
Está en la reunión *(eh-'stah ehn lah reh-oo-nee-'ohn)*

notebook **el cuaderno** *(ehl kwah-'dehr-noh)*
Escribe en el cuaderno *(eh-'skree-beh ehn ehl kwah-'dehr-noh)*

playground **el campo de recreo** *(ehl 'kahm-ph deh reh-'kreh-oh)*
El campo de recreo es bueno *(ehl 'kahm-poh deh reh-'kreh-oh ehs 'bweh-noh)*

principal **el director** *(ehl dee-rehk-'tohr)*
Necesito llamarle al director *(neh-seh-'see-toh yah-'mahr-leh ahl dee-rehk-'tohr)*

school **la escuela** *(lah eh-'skweh-lah)*
Su escuela está muy cerca *(soo eh-'skweh-lah eh-'stah 'moo-ee 'sehr-kah)*

student **el estudiante** *(ehl eh-stoo-dee-'ahn-teh)*
Es un estudiante inteligente *(ehs oon eh-stoo-dee-'ahn-teh een-teh-lee-'hehn-teh)*

subject **la asignatura** *(lah ah-seeg-nah-'too-rah)*
Es su asignatura favorita *(ehs soo ah-seeg-nah-'too-rah fah-boh-'ree-tah)*

teacher **el maestro** *(ehl mah-'eh-stroh)*
Sr. Smith es su maestro *(seh-'nyohr Smith ehs soo mah-'eh-stroh)*

test **el examen** *(ehl ehk-'sah-mehn)*
El examen es importante *(ehl ehk-'sah-mehn ehs eem-pohr-'tahn-teh)*

 **REPASEMOS**

When dealing with the care of children, all kinds of vocabulary will be needed. You'll be mentioning furniture, food, and clothing on a daily basis, so you may want to review them first. Speaking of review, can you list three items under the following?

colors   **los colores** *(lohs koh-'loh-rehs)*

_____   _____   _____

months   **los meses** *(lohs 'meh-sehs)*

_____   _____   _____

numbers   **los números** *(lohs 'noo-meh-rohs)*

_____   _____   _____

CHAPTER SIX

Capítulo Seis
(kah-'pee-too-loh 'seh·ees)

OUT IN THE YARD
Afuera en el Jardín
(ah-'fweh-rah ehn ehl hahr-'deen)

THE OUTDOORS
Al aire libre *(ahl 'ah-ee-reh 'lee-breh)*

Life around the house can be hectic at times, with plenty to do at every turn. That's why we hire some people to lend us a hand, and then learn how to communicate with them in their native language.

However, caring for one's property doesn't simply mean keeping the home in order. We still need to talk about responsibilities outdoors. Whether it's providing care for the family pet, doing a little landscaping, or even taking on some light construction, many times we can't do everything by ourselves.

Since we all reside in different geographical locations, it's probably best to start off with words that describe the land around us.

I live near the...	**Vivo cerca de...** *('bee-boh 'sehr-kah deh)*
beach	**la playa** *(lah 'plah-yah)*
desert	**el desierto** *(ehl deh-see-'ehr-toh)*
field	**el campo** *(ehl 'kahm-poh)*
forest	**el bosque** *(ehl 'boh-skeh)*
gulch	**la barranca** *(lah bah-'rrahn-kah)*
hill	**el cerro** *(ehl 'seh-rroh)*
jungle	**la selva** *(lah 'sehl-bah)*
lake	**el lago** *(ehl 'lah-goh)*
mountain	**la montaña** *(lah mohn-'tah-nyah)*
pond	**la charca** *(lah 'chahr-kah)*
river	**el río** *(ehl 'ree-oh)*
sea	**el mar** *(ehl mahr)*
stream	**el arroyo** *(ehl ah-'rroh-yoh)*
swamp	**el pantano** *(ehl pahn-'tah-noh)*
valley	**el valle** *(ehl 'bah-yeh)*

El cerro es más bajo que la montaña.

THE GARDEN

El jardín (ehl hahr-'deen)

Regardless of where you live, there's probably outdoor work to be done. But before anyone gets dirty, let's practice the words that you'll need to share with Spanish-speakers out in the garden. Read them as part of the phrase below:

We're working with the...	**Estamos trabajando con...** *(eh-'stah-mohs trah-bah-'hahn-doh kohn)*
bark	**la corteza** *(lah kohr-'teh-sah)*
branch	**la rama** *(lah 'rah-mah)*
bud	**el botón** *(ehl boh-'tohn)*
bulb	**el bulbo** *(ehl 'bool-boh)*
bush	**el arbusto** *(ehl ahr-'boo-stoh)*
dirt	**la tierra** *(lah tee-'eh-rrah)*
dust	**el polvo** *(ehl 'pohl-boh)*
flower	**la flor** *(lah flohr)*
foliage	**el follaje** *(ehl foh-'yah-heh)*
grass	**el pasto** *(ehl 'pah-stoh)*
gravel	**la grava** *(lah 'grah-bah)*
land	**el terreno** *(ehl teh-'rreh-noh)*
lawn	**el césped** *(ehl sehs-'pehd)*
leaf	**la hoja** *(lah 'oh-hah)*
mud	**el lodo** *(ehl 'loh-doh)*
plant	**la planta** *(lah 'plahn-tah)*
rock	**la piedra** *(ehl 'pee-'eh-drah)*
root	**la raíz** *(lah rah-'ees)*
sand	**la arena** *(lah ah-'reh-nah)*

seed	**la semilla** *(lah seh-'mee-yah)*
stem	**el tallo** *(ehl 'tah-yoh)*
tree	**el árbol** *(ehl 'ahr-bohl)*
trunk	**el tronco** *(ehl 'trohn-koh)*
twig	**la ramita** *(lah rah-'mee-tah)*
water	**el agua** *(ehl 'ah-gwah)*
weeds	**la mala hierba** *(lah 'mah-lah 'yehr-bah)*
We have a...	**Tenemos...** *(teh-'neh-mohs)*
crop	**la cosecha** *(lah koh-'seh-chah)*
flowerbed	**el cuadro** *(ehl 'kwah-droh)*
greenhouse	**el invernadero** *(ehl een-behr-nah-'deh-roh)*
grove	**la arboleda** *(lah ahr-boh-'leh-dah)*
nursery	**el criadero** *(ehl kree-ah-'deh-roh)*
orchard	**la huerta** *(lah 'wehr-tah)*

 REPASEMOS

Connect the words that relate to each other:

el árbol	**la arena** *(lah ah-'reh-nah)*
la playa	**el tronco** *(ehl 'trohn-koh)*
el campo	**la hierba** *(lah 'yehr-bah)*

 MÁS AYUDA

Learn the following words for trees, flowers, and plants on your grounds:

Trees
Los árboles (los 'ahr-boh-lehs)

birch	**el abedul** *(ehl ah-beh-'dool)*
cedar	**el cedro** *(ehl 'seh-droh)*
elm	**el olmo** *(ehl 'ohl-moh)*
fir	**el abeto** *(ehl ah-'beh-toh)*
maple	**el arce** *(ehl 'ahr-seh)*
oak	**el roble** *(ehl 'roh-bleh)*
palm	**la palmera** *(lah pahl-'meh-rah)*
pine	**el pino** *(ehl 'pee-noh)*
walnut	**el nogal** *(ehl noh-'gahl)*
willow	**el sauce** *(ehl 'sow-seh)*

Plants

Las Plantas *(lahs 'plahn-tahs)*

azalea	**la azalea** *(lah ah-sah-'leh-ah)*
cactus	**el cacto** *(ehl 'kahk-toh)*
daisy	**la margarita** *(lah mahr-gah-'ree-tah)*
dandelion	**el diente de león** *(ehl dee-'ehn-teh deh leh-'ohn)*
fern	**el helecho** *(ehl eh-'leh-choh)*
forsythia	**la forsitia** *(lah fohr-'see-tee-ah)*
geranium	**el geranio** *(ehl heh-'rah-nee-oh)*
holly	**el acebo** *(ehl ah-'seh-boh)*
ivy	**la hiedra** *(lah 'yeh-drah)*
marigold	**la caléndula** *(lah kah-'lehn-doo-lah)*
petunia	**la petunia** *(lah peh-'too-nee-ah)*
poppy	**la amapola** *(lah ahm-ah-'poh-lah)*
rhododendron	**el rododendro** *(ehl roh-doh-'dehn-droh)*
rose	**la rosa** *(lah 'roh-sah)*
sunflower	**el girasol** *(ehl hee-rah-'sohl)*
tulip	**el tulipán** *(ehl too-lee-'pahn)*
violet	**la violeta** *(lah bee-oh-'leh-tah)*

¿Qué es un roble y qué es un geranio?

El roble es un árbol y el geranio es una planta.

Fruit

Las frutas *(lohs 'froo-tahs)*

apple	**la manzana** *(lah mahn-'sah-nah)*
apricot	**el albaricoque** *(ehl ahl-bah-ree-'koh-keh)*
avocado	**el aguacate** *(ehl ah-gwah-'kah-teh)*
cherry	**la cereza** *(lah seh-'reh-sah)*
grapefruit	**la toronja** *(lah toh-'rohn-hah)*

lemon	**el limón** *(ehl lee-'mohn)*
lime	**la lima** *(lah 'lee-mah)*
nectarine	**la nectarina** *(lah nehk-tah-'ree-nah)*
orange	**la naranja** *(lah nah-'rahn-hah)*
peach	**el durazno** *(ehl doo-'rahs-noh)*
tangerine	**la mandarina** *(lah mahn-dah-'ree-nah)*

(For the names of other fruits and vegetables, look on pages 112–114 in Chapter Four, where all the food words are presented.)

 REPASEMOS

Name three kinds of wood.
Name three kinds of flowers.
Name three kinds of fruit trees.

CALL THE GARDENER!
¡Llame al jardinero! *('yah-meh ahl hahr-dee-'neh-roh)*

As your garden grows, so does the responsibility of proper maintenance and care; however, yard work and landscaping can be very demanding. That's why homeowners worldwide contract the services of professional gardeners. If your help speaks Spanish, here are the one-liners you may need:

I need the...	**Necesito...** *(neh-seh-'see-toh)*
channel	**el canal** *(ehl kah-'nahl)*
ditch	**la zanja** *(lah 'sahn-hah)*
divider	**el divisor** *(ehl dee-bee-'sohr)*
drainage	**el drenaje** *(ehl dreh-'nah-heh)*
fence	**la cerca** *(lah 'sehr-kah)*
furrow	**el surco** *(ehl 'soor-koh)*
hole	**el hoyo** *(ehl 'oh-yoh)*
irrigation	**la irrigación** *(lah ee-rree-gah-see-'ohn)*
path	**el camino** *(ehl kah-'mee-noh)*
pipe	**el tubo** *(ehl 'too-boh)*
post	**el poste** *(ehl 'poh-steh)*
pot	**la maceta** *(lah mah-'seh-tah)*
slope	**el declive** *(ehl deh-'klee-beh)*

sprinklers	**las rociadoras** *(lahs roh-see-ah-'doh-rahs)*
stake	**la estaca** *(lah eh-'stah-kah)*
stone	**la piedra** *(lah pee-'eh-drah)*

 ¡HÁGALO, POR FAVOR!

Working with Spanish-speakers in an outdoor setting requires a unique set of command words. How many of these helpful phrases can you put to good use?

arrange   **arregle** *(ah-'rreh-gleh)*
Arregle las plantas *(ah-'rreh-gleh lahs 'plahn-tahs)*
build   **construya** *(kohn-'stroo-yah)*
Construya la cerca *(kohn-'stroo-yah lah 'sehr-kah)*
dig   **excave** *(ehks-'kah-beh)*
Excave una zanja *(ehks-'kah-beh 'oo-nah 'sahn-hah)*
install   **instale** *(een-'stah-leh)*
Instale el poste *(een-'stah-leh ehl 'poh-steh)*
kill   **mate** *('mah-teh)*
Mate los insectos *('mah-teh lohs een-'sehk-tohs)*
load   **cargue** *('kahr-geh)*
Cargue el camión *('kahr-geh ehl kah-mee-'ohn)*
mow   **corte el pasto** *('kohr-teh ehl 'pah-stoh)*
Corte el pasto hoy *('kohr-teh ehl 'pah-stoh 'oh-ee)*
pile   **amontone** *(ah-mohn-'toh-neh)*
Amontone las hojas *(ah-mohn-'toh-neh lahs 'oh-hahs)*
plant   **plante** *('plahn-teh)*
Plante el arbusto aquí *('plahn-teh ehl ahr-'boo-stoh ah-'kee)*
rake   **rastrille** *(rah-'stree-yeh)*
Rastrille el jardín *(rah-'stree-yeh ehl hahr-'deen)*
spray   **rocíe** *(roh-'seh-ee)*
Rocíe la huerta *(roh-'see-ee lah 'wehr-tah)*
transplant   **transplante** *(trahns-'plahn-teh)*
Transplante el cacto *(trahns-'plahn-teh ehl 'kahk-toh)*
trim   **pode** *('poh-deh)*
Pode el árbol *('poh-deh ehl 'ahr-bohl)*
unload   **descargue** *(dehs-'kahr-gue)*
Descargue las cajas *(dehs-'kahr-gue lahs 'kah-hahs)*
water   **riegue** *(ree-'eh-geh)*

Riegue las flores *(ree-'eh-geh lahs 'floh-rehs)*

And, don't forget any command words that we learned earlier:

carry **lleve** *('yeh-beh)*
Lleve la maceta *('yeh-beh lah mah-'seh-tah)*

change **cambie** *('kahm-bee-eh)*
Cambie las flores *('kahm-bee-eh lahs 'floh-rehs)*

clean **limpie** *('leem-pee-eh)*
Limpie el patio *('leem-pee-eh ehl 'pah-tee·oh)*

dump **tire** *('tee-reh)*
Tire la basura *('tee-reh lah bah-'soo-rah)*

sweep **barra** *('bah-rrah)*
Barra la tierra *('bah-rrah lah tee-'eh-rrah)*

 MÁS AYUDA

Are you ready to create your own command word?

A simple approach to forming a command in Spanish requires knowledge of the three different action word (verb) endings:

ar as in **hablar** *(ah-'blahr)* (to speak)
er as in **comer** *(koh-'mehr)* (to eat)
ir as in **escribir** *(eh-skree-'beer)* (to write)

To make a command, drop the last two letters of the infinitive form and replace them as follows.

AR

To speak **hablar** *(ah-'blahr)*

E

Speak **Hable** *('ah-bleh)*

ER

To eat **comer** *(koh-'mehr)*

A

Eat **Coma** *('koh-mah)*

IR

To write **escriber** *(eh-skree-'beer)*

A

Write **Escriba** *(eh-'skree-bah)*

But beware. Some verbs are strange and simply have to be memorized:

To go	**ir** *(eer)*	Go	**Vaya** *('bah-yah)*
To come	**venir** *(beh-'neer)*	Come	**Venga** *('behn-gah)*
To speak	**decir** *(deh-'seer)*	Speak	**Diga** *('dee-gah)*

 REPASEMOS

Fill in the blanks with the correct and conjugated verb.

Abrir _____ el tubo *('too-boh)*

Instalare _____ el piso *(ehl 'pee-soh)*

Barrer _____ la zanja *(lah 'sahn-hah)*

TOOLS OF THE HOME TRADE
Las herramientas del trabajo casero
(lahs eh-rrah-mee-'ehn-tahs dehl trah-'bah-hoh kah-'seh-roh)

Anyone who works around your house will need to use specific tools and supplies. Here is a list for you to refer to:

You have to use (the)... **Tiene que usar...** *(tee-'eh-neh keh oo-'sahr)*

ax	**el hacha** *(ehl 'ah-chah)*
bag	**la bolsa** *(lah 'bohl-sah)*
blower	**el soplador** *(ehl soh-plah-'dohr)*
box	**la caja** *(lah 'kah-hah)*
chainsaw	**la motosierra** *(lah 'moh-toh-see-eh-rah)*
clippers	**las tijeras podadoras** *(lahs tee-'heh-rahs poh-dah-'doh-rahs)*

183

fertilizer	**el abono** *(ehl ah-'boh-noh)*
gloves	**los guantes** *(lohs 'gwahn-tehs)*
hoe	**el azadón** *(ehl ah-sah-'dohn)*
hose	**la manguera** *(lah mahn-'geh-rah)*
insecticide	**el insecticida** *(ehl een-sehk-tee-'see-dah)*
lawn mower	**la cortadora de césped** *(lah kohr-tah-'doh-rah deh 'sehs-pehd)*
manure	**el estiércol** *(ehl eh-stee-'ehr-kohl)*
pick	**el pico** *(ehl 'pee-koh)*
pitchfork	**la horquilla** *(lah ohr-'kee-yah)*
poison	**el veneno** *(ehl beh-'neh-noh)*
potting soil	**la tierra abonada** *(lah tee-'eh-rrah ah-boh-'nah-dah)*
rake	**el rastrillo** *(ehl rah-'stree-yoh)*
rope	**la soga** *(lah 'soh-gah)*
rototiller	**el aflojador de tierra** *(ehl ah-floh-hah-'dohr deh tee-'eh-rah)*
shovel	**la pala** *(lah 'pah-lah)*
sprayer	**el rociador** *(ehl roh-see-ah-'dohr)*
tractor	**el tractor** *(ehl trahk-'tohr)*
trimmer	**el podador** *(ehl poh-dah-'dohr)*
trowel	**el desplantador** *(ehl dehs-plahn-tah-'dohr)*
vitamins	**las vitaminas** *(lah bee-tah-'mee-nahs)*
wheelbarrow	**la carretilla** *(lah kah-rreh-'tee-yah)*

Escriba a José y diga que venga con el tractor.

José no tiene tractor, él tiene una carretilla.

DIRTY POOL

La piscina sucia *(lah pee-'see-nah 'soo-see·ah)*

Since we're outside, let's wander over to the pool area! For those who are fortunate enough to have a private spa or swimming pool, check out this next vocabulary list. Repeat a few as you give instructions to the pool maintenance personnel:

Move the...	**Mueva...** *('mweh-bah)*
Where's the...?	**¿Dónde está...** *('dohn-deh eh-'stah)*
acid	**el ácido** *(ohl 'ah-see-doh)*
brush	**el cepillo** *(ehl seh-'pee-yoh)*
chemical	**el compuesto químico** *(ehl kahm-'pwes-toh 'kee-mee-koh)*
chlorine	**el cloro** *(ehl 'kloh-roh)*
cover	**la funda** *(lah 'foon-dah)*
deck	**la terraza** *(lah teh-'rrah-sah)*
diving board	**el trampolín** *(ehl trahm-poh-'leen)*
drain	**el desaguadero** *(ehl dehs-ah-gwah-'deh-roh)*
filter	**el filtro** *(ehl 'feel-troh)*
fountain	**la fuente** *(lah 'fwehn-teh)*
heater	**el calentador** *(ehl kah-lehn-tah-'dohr)*
hose	**la manguera** *(lah mahn-'geh-rah)*
ladder	**la escala** *(lah eh-skah-'lah)*
light	**la luz** *(lah loos)*
pilot	**el piloto** *(ehl pee-'loh-toh)*
pump	**la bomba** *(lah 'bohm-bah)*
slide	**el resbaladero** *(ehl rehs-bah-lah-'deh-roh)*
thermometer	**el termómetro** *(ehl tehr-'moh-meh-troh)*
tile	**la loceta** *(lah loh-'seh-tah)*
tube	**el tubo** *(ehl 'too-boh)*
vacuum	**la aspiradora** *(lah ah-spee-rah-'doh-rah)*
valve	**la válvula** *(lah 'bahl-boo-lah)*
There's a problem with...	**Hay un problema con...** *('ah·ee oon proh-'bleh-mah kohn)*
algae	**las algas** *(lahs 'ahl-gahs)*
corrosion	**la corrosión** *(lah koh-roh-see·'ohn)*
cracks	**las grietas** *(lahs gree-'eh-tahs)*
holes	**los hoyos** *(lohs 'oh-yohs)*
odors	**los olores** *(lohs oh-'loh-rehs)*

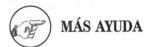
Make a comment or two about the outside world. Look over the yard and describe what you see, beginning with those terms you've used before:

It's...	**Está...** *(eh-'stah)*
up	**arriba** *(ah-'rree-bah)*
down	**abajo** *(ah-'bah-hoh)*
wet	**mojado** *(moh-'hah-doh)*
dry	**seco** *('seh-koh)*
clean	**limpio** *('leem-pee·oh)*
dirty	**sucio** *('soo-see·oh)*
tall	**alto** *('ahl-toh)*
short	**bajo** *('bah-hoh)*

Now, build some on your vocabulary:

cultivated	**cultivado** *(kool-tee-'bah-doh)*
cut	**cortado** *(kohr-'tah-doh)*
dying	**muriendo** *(moo-ree-'ehn-doh)*
growing	**creciendo** *(kreh-see-'ehn-doh)*
in the shade	**en la sombra** *(ehn lah 'sohm-brah)*
in the sun	**al sol** *(ahl sohl)*
lovely	**lindo** *('leen-doh)*

on the ground	**en el suelo** *(ehn ehl 'sweh-loh)*
raw	**crudo** *('kroo-doh)*
ripe	**maduro** *(mah-'doo-roh)*
rotten	**podrido** *(poh-'dree-doh)*
trimmed	**podado** *(poh-'dah-doh)*
underground	**subterráneo** *(soob-teh-'rrah-neh-oh)*
well-kept	**bien mantenido** *('bee-ehn mahn-teh-'nee-doh)*

BUGS!

Los insectos *(lohs een-'sehk-tohs)*

Insects and gardens go hand in hand, so study this next list as soon as you can and, if necessary, call the exterminator.

There's the...	**Allí está...** *(ah-'yee eh-'stah)*
Kill the...	**Mate...** *('mah-teh)*
ant	**la hormiga** *(lah ohr-'mee-gah)*
bee	**la abeja** *(lah ah-'beh-hah)*
beetle	**el escarabajo** *(ehl eh-skah-rah-'bah-hoh)*
butterfly	**la mariposa** *(lah mah-ree-'poh-sah)*
cricket	**el grillo** *(ehl 'gree-yoh)*
dragonfly	**la libébula** *(lah lee-'beh-boo-lah)*
flea	**la pulga** *(lah 'pool-gah)*
fly	**la mosca** *(lah 'moh-skah)*
grasshopper	**el saltamontes** *(ehl sahl-tah-'mohn-tehs)*
hornet	**el avispón** *(ehl ah-bees-'pohn)*
ladybug	**la mariquita** *(lah mah-ree-'kee-tah)*
mosquito	**el zancudo** *(ehl sahn-'koo-doh)*
moth	**la polilla** *(lah poh-'lee-yah)*
scorpion	**el escorpión** *(ehl ehs-kohr-pee-'ohn)*
slug	**la babosa** *(lah bah-'boh-sah)*
snail	**el caracol** *(ehl kah-rah-'kohl)*
spider	**la araña** *(lah ah-'rah-nyah)*
wasp	**la avispa** *(lah ah-'bees-pah)*
worm	**el gusano** *(ehl goo-'sah-noh)*

List three words under each category:

garden tools   parts of swimming pool   insects

_____   _____   _____

_____   _____   _____

_____   _____   _____

WILD ANIMALS!
¡Los animales salvajes!
(lohs ah-nee-'mah-lehs sahl-'bah-hehs)

Have you seen any of these lately? Let your Spanish-speaking help know that they're around.

Did you see the...?   **¿Vio...?** (bee-'oh)

The _____ did it.   _____ **lo hizo** (___ loh 'ee-soh)

bear	**el oso** (ehl 'oh-soh)
beaver	**el castor** (ehl kah-'stohr)
coyote	**el coyote** (ehl koh-'yoh-teh)
deer	**el venado** (ehl beh-'nah-doh)
fox	**el zorro** (ehl 'soh-rroh)
frog	**el sapo** (ehl 'sah-poh)
lizard	**el lagarto** (ehl lah-'gahr-toh)
mole	**el topo** (ehl 'toh-poh)
moose	**el alce** (ehl 'ahl-seh)
mouse	**el ratón** (ehl rah-'tohn)
opossum	**el zarigüeya** (ehl sah-ree-'gweh-yah)
porcupine	**el puerco espín** (ehl 'pwehr-koh eh-'speen)
rabbit	**el conejo** (ehl koh-'neh-hoh)
raccoon	**el mapache** (ehl mah-'pah-cheh)
rat	**la rata** (lah 'rah-tah)
skunk	**el zorrillo** (ehl soh-'rree-yoh)
snake	**la culebra** (lah koo-'leh-brah)
squirrel	**la ardilla** (lah ahr-'dee-yah)
turtle	**la tortuga** (lah tohr-'too-gah)
wolf	**el lobo** (ehl 'loh-boh)

And for the birdwatcher...

Look at the...	**Mire...** *('mee-reh)*
bird	**el pájaro** *(ehl 'pah-hah-roh)*
crow	**el cuervo** *(ehl 'kwehr-boh)*
duck	**el pato** *(ehl 'pah-toh)*
hawk	**el halcón** *(ehl ahl-'kohn)*
owl	**el buho** *(ehl 'boo-oh)*
robin	**el petirrojo** *(ehl peh-tee-'rroh-hoh)*
sparrow	**el gorrión** *(ehl goh-rree-'ohn)*
swan	**el cisne** *(ehl 'sees-neh)*
woodpecker	**el picaposte** *(ehl pee-kah-'poh-steh)*
wren	**el reyezuelo** *(ehl reh-yeh-soo-'eh-loh)*

PET CARE
El cuidado de las mascotas
(ehl kwee-'dah-doh deh lahs mah-'skoh-tahs)

Not all animals show up uninvited. Many people provide food and shelter for their own pets. Keeping pets is a big responsibility, so you may need some assistance from time to time, especially if you're planning to be away from your home at times. If your helper speaks Spanish, try communicating with a couple of these:

Do you like (the)...?	**¿Le gusta...?** *(leh 'goo-stah)*
Give food to the...	**Dé comida a...** *(deh koh-'mee-dah ah)*
The___needs water.	_____ **necesita agua** *(neh-seh-'see-tah 'ah-gwah)*
canary	**el canario** *(ehl kah-'nah-ree-oh)*
cat	**el gato** *(ehl 'gah-toh)*

chicken	**la gallina** *(lah gah-'yee-nah)*
cow	**la vaca** *(lah 'bah-kah)*
dog	**el perro** *(ehl 'peh-rroh)*
duck	**el pato** *(ehl 'pah-toh)*
fish	**el pez** *(ehl pehs)*
goat	**el chivo** *(ehl 'chee-boh)*
hamster	**el hámster** *(ehl 'ahm-stehr)*
horse	**el caballo** *(ehl kah-'bah-yoh)*
parakeet	**el perico** *(ehl peh-'ree-koh)*
pig	**el puerco** *(ehl 'pwehr-koh)*
rabbit	**el conejo** *(ehl koh-'neh-hoh)*
sheep	**la oveja** *(lah oh-'beh-hah)*
turtle	**la tortuga** *(lah tohr-'too-gah)*
Put it in the...	**Póngalo en...** *('pohn-gah-loh ehn)*
aquarium	**el acuario** *(ehl ah-'kwah-ree·oh)*
box	**la caja** *(lah 'kah-hah)*
cage	**la jaula** *(lah 'hah·oo-lah)*
doghouse	**la casa de perros** *(lah 'kah-sah deh 'peh-rrohs)*
pen	**el corral** *(ehl koh-'rrahl)*
stable	**el establo** *(ehl eh-'stah-bloh)*
yard	**el patio** *(ehl 'pah-tee-oh)*
It likes to...	**Le gusta...** *(leh 'goo-stah)*
bark	**ladrar** *(lah-'drahr)*
bite	**morder** *(mohr-'dehr)*
climb	**subir** *(soo-'beer)*
do tricks	**hacer trucos** *(ah-'sehr 'troo-kohs)*
eat this	**comer esto** *(koh-'mehr 'eh-stoh)*
hunt	**cazar** *(kah-'sahr)*
make noise	**hacer ruido** *(ah-'sehr roo-'ee-doh)*
play	**jugar** *(hoo-'gahr)*
run	**correr** *(koh-'rrehr)*
scratch	**rascar** *(rah-'skahr)*
sit here	**sentarse aquí** *(sehn-'tahr-seh ah-'kee)*
sleep	**dormir** *(dohr-'meer)*
swim	**nadar** *(nah-'dahr)*

It eats...	**Come...** *('koh-meh)*
anything	**cualquier cosa** *(kwahl-kee-'ehr 'koh-sah)*
cat food	**comida para gatos** *(koh-'mee-dah 'pah-rah 'gah-tohs)*
dog food	**comida para perros** *('koh-mee-dah 'pah-rah 'peh-rrohs)*
fish food	**comida para peces** *(koh-'mee-dah 'pah-rah 'peh-sehs)*
grain	**grano** *('grah-noh)*
hay	**heno** *('eh-noh)*
meat	**carne** *('kahr-neh)*
plants	**plantas** *('plahn-tahs)*
seeds	**semillas** *(seh-'mee-yahs)*

Keep talking about your special animal friend:

Its name is _____.	**Su nombre es** _____ *(soo 'nohm-breh ehs)*
It's _____ years old.	**Tiene** _____ años *(tee-'eh-neh ___ 'ah-nyohs)*
It's a female.	**Es hembra** *(ehs 'ehm-brah)*
It's a male.	**Es macho** *(ehs 'mah-choh)*
It's friendly.	**Es amistoso** *(ehs ah-mee-'stoh-soh)*
It's trained.	**Está entrenado** *(eh-'stah ehn-'treh-'nah-doh)*

It needs...	
a bath	**un baño** *(oon 'bah-noyh)*
a collar	**un collar** *(oon koh-'yahr)*
a haircut	**un corte de pelo** *(oon 'kohr-teh deh 'peh-loh)*
a leash	**una traílla** *('oo-nah trah-'ee-yah)*

a mate	**una pareja** *('oo-nah pah-'reh-hah)*
a vet	**un veterinario** *(oon beh-teh-ree-'nah-ree·oh)*
exercise	**ejercicio** *(eh-hehr-'see-see·oh)*
food at _____	**comida a las __,** *(koh-'mee-dah ah lahs __)*
fresh air	**el aire fresco** *(ehl 'ah·ee-reh 'frehs-koh)*
special care	**cuidado especial** *(kwee-'dah-doh eh-speh-see-'ahl)*

 MÁS AYUDA

Here are some special terms for bird care:

It's the...	**Es...** *(ehs)*
bird bath	**la bañera de pájaros** *(lah bah-'nyeh-rah deh 'pah-hah-rohs)*
bird cage	**la jaula de pájaros** *(lah 'hah·oo-lah deh 'pah-hah-rohs)*
bird dropping	**el excremento de pájaros** *(ehl ehks-kreh-'mehn-toh deh 'pah-hah-rohs)*
bird feeder	**el alimentador de pájaros** *(ehl ah-lee-mehn-tah-'dohr deh 'pah-hah-rohs)*
bird nest	**el nido de pájaros** *(ehl 'nee-doh deh 'pah-hah-rohs)*

 REPASEMOS

Match each animal with its appropriate home:

el caballo *(ehl kah-'bah-yoh)*   **el acuario** *(ehl ah-'kwah-ree·oh)*
el pájaro *(ehl 'pah-hah-roh)*   **la jaula** *(lah 'hah·oo-lah)*
el pez *(ehl pehs)*   **el establo** *(ehl eh-'stah-bloh)*

 TEMAS CULTURALES

People raised in rural areas often have a unique appreciation of domestic animals. It's possible that your employee knows a great deal about your particular pet, and can offer helpful suggestions concerning feeding habits, breeding, and general care. Listen to him/her.

HANDYMAN'S HELPERS
Ayuda para los ayudantes
(ah-'yoo-dah 'pah-rah lohs ah-yoo-'dahn-tehs)
Need something built or rebuilt around the house? Why not contact a Spanish-speaking construction crew and hammer away at these:

I need the...	**Necesito...** *(neh-seh-'see-toh)*
Bring the...	**Traiga...** *('trah·ee-gah)*
blade	**la cuchilla** *(lah koo-'chee-yah)*
bolt	**el perno** *(ehl 'pehr-noh)*
chain	**la cadena** *(lah kah-'deh-nah)*
chisel	**el cincel** *(ehl seen-'sehl)*
clamp	**la prensa de sujetar** *(lah 'prehn-sah deh soo-heh-'tahr)*
compressor	**el compresor de aire** *(ehl kohm-preh-'sohr deh 'ah·ee-reh)*
drill	**el taladro** *(ehl tah-'lah-droh)*
electric cord	**el cordón eléctrico** *(ehl kohr-'dohn eh-'lehk-tree-koh)*
glue	**el pegamento** *(ehl peh-gah-'mehn-toh)*
hacksaw	**la sierra para cortar metal** *(lah see-'eh-rrah 'pah-rah kohr-'tahr meh-'tahl)*
hammer	**el martillo** *(ehl mahr-'tee-yoh)*
jack	**el gato** *(ehl 'gah-toh)*
lacquer	**la laca** *(lah 'lah-kah)*
ladder	**la escalera** *(lah eh-skah-'leh-rah)*
level	**el nivel** *(ehl nee-'behl)*
measuring tape	**la cinta para medir** *(lah 'seen-tah 'pah-rah meh-'deer)*
nail	**el clavo** *(ehl 'klah-boh)*
nut	**la tuerca** *(lah 'twehr-kah)*
paint brush	**la brocha de pintar** *(lah 'broh-chah deh peen-'tahr)*
paint	**la pintura** *(lah peen-'too-rah)*
plan	**el plano** *(ehl 'plah-noh)*
plane	**el cepillo** *(ehl seh-'pee-yoh)*
pliers	**las pinzas** *(lahs 'peen-sahs)*
ramp	**la rampa** *(lah 'rahm-pah)*

safety glasses	**los lentes de seguridad** *(lohs 'lehn-tehs deh seh-goo-ree-'dahd)*
sandpaper	**el papel de lija** *(ehl pah-'pehl deh 'lee-hah)*
saw	**el serrucho** *(ehl seh-'rroo-choh)*
scaffold	**el andamio** *(ehl ahn-'dah-mee·oh)*
scraper	**el raspador** *(ehl rah-spah-'dohr)*
screw	**el tornillo** *(ehl tohr-'nee-yoh)*
screwdriver	**el desarmador** *(ehl dehs-ahr-mah-'dohr)*
shovel	**la pala** *(lah 'pah-lah)*
staple	**la grapa** *(lah 'grah-pah)*
tape	**la cinta** *(lah 'seen-tah)*
toolbox	**la caja de herramientas** *(lah 'kah-hah deh eh-rrah-mee-'ehn-tahs)*
trowel	**la llana** *(lah 'yah-nah)*
wire	**el alambre** *(ehl ah-'lahm-breh)*
wrench	**la llave inglesa** *(lah 'yah-beh een-'gleh-sah)*

¡ Yo preparo sopa de clavos y tuercas!

Let's install the...	**Vamos a instalar...** *('bah-mohs ah een-stah-'lahr)*
block	**el bloque** *(ehl 'bloh-keh)*
brace	**el grapón** *(ehl grah-'pohn)*
duct	**el conducto** *(ehl kohn-'dook-toh)*
footing	**el pie** *(ehl 'pee-eh)*
foundation	**la fundación** *(lah foon-dah-see·'ohn)*
frame	**la armadura** *(lah ahr-mah-'doo-rah)*
hinges	**las bisagras** *(lahs bee-'sah-grahs)*
gutters	**los canales** *(lohs kah-'nah-lehs)*

insulation	**la aislamiento** *(ehl ah-ees-lah-mee-'ehn-toh)*
joint	**la unión** *(lah oo-nee-'ohn)*
rafter	**la viga** *(lah 'bee-gah)*
railing	**la baranda** *(lah bah-'rahn-dah)*
shingles	**las pizarras** *(lahs pee-'sah-rrahs)*
stud	**el poste** *(ehl 'poh-steh)*
trim	**la moldura** *(lah mohl-'doo-rah)*
It goes in the...	**Va en...** *(bah ehn)*
corner	**la esquina** *(lah eh-'skee-nah)*
edge	**el borde** *(ehl 'bohr-deh)*
end	**la punta** *(lah 'poon-tah)*
front	**el frente** *(ehl 'frehn-teh)*
middle	**el medio** *(ehl 'meh-dee-oh)*
opening	**la abertura** *(lah ah-behr-'too-rah)*

 MÁS AYUDA

Are these secured?

deadbolt	**el pestillo** *(ehl peh-'stee-yoh)*
padlock	**el candado** *(ehl kahn-'dah-doh)*
lock	**la cerradura** *(lah seh-rrah-'doo-rah)*
latch	**el cerrojo** *(ehl seh-'rroh-hoh)*
key	**la llave** *(lah 'yah-beh)*
chain	**la cadena** *(lah kah-'deh-nah)*

MORE MATERIALS
Más materiales (mahs mah-teh-ree-'ah-lehs)

Please buy...	**Favor de comprar...** *(fah-'bohr deh kohm-'prahr)*
asphalt	el **asfalto** *(ehl ahs-'fahl-toh)*
brass	el **latón** *(ehl lah-'tohn)*
brick	el **ladrillo** *(ehl lah-'dree-yoh)*
bronze	el **bronce** *(ehl 'brohn-seh)*
cement	el **cemento** *(ehl seh-'mehn-toh)*
clay	la **arcilla** *(lah ahr-'see-yah)*
glass	el **vidrio** *(ehl 'bee-dree·oh)*
gravel	la **grava** *(lah 'grah-bah)*
iron	el **hierro** *(ehl 'yeh-rroh)*
linoleum	el **linóleo** *(ehl lee-'noh-leh-oh)*
lumber	la **madera** *(lah mah-'deh-rah)*
marble	el **mármol** *(ehl 'mahr-mohl)*
mortar	el **mortero** *(ehl-mohr-'teh-roh)*
pavement	el **pavimento** *(ehl pah-bee-'mehn-toh)*
pipe	el **tubo** *(ehl 'too-boh)*
plaster	el **yeso** *(ehl 'yeh-soh)*
plastic	el **plástico** *(ehl 'plah-stee-koh)*
plywood	la **madera terciada** *(lah mah-'deh-rah ter-see-'ah-dah)*
putty	la **masilla** *(lah mah-'see-yah)*
screen	el **mosquitero** *(ehl moh-skee-'teh-roh)*
slab	la **losa de cemento** *(lah 'loh-sah deh seh-'mehn-toh)*
steel	el **acero** *(ehl ah-'seh-roh)*
stone	la **piedra** *(lah pee-'eh-drah)*
stucco	el **estuco** *(ehl eh-'stoo-koh)*
tar	la **brea** *(lah 'breh-ah)*
tile	la **baldosa** *(lah bahl-'doh-sah)*
wallpaper	el **empapelado** *(ehl ehm-pah-peh-'lah-doh)*
wire mesh	la **malla de acero** *(lah 'mah-yah deh ah-'seh-roh)*
It's...	**Está...** *(eh-'stah)*
level	**llano** *('yah-noh)*

parallel	**paralelo** *(pah-rah-'leh-loh)*
straight	**derecho** *(deh-'reh-choh)*
uneven	**desigual** *(dehs-ee-'gwahl)*
	Es... *(ehs)*
the angle	**el ángulo** *(ehl 'ahn-goo-loh)*
the circle	**el círculo** *(ehl 'seer-koo-loh)*
the groove	**la muesca** *(lah moo-'ehs-kah)*
the line	**la línea** *(lah 'lee-neh-ah)*
the point	**la punta** *(lah 'poon-tah)*
the square	**el cuadro** *(ehl 'kwah-droh)*
the stripe	**el rayo** *(ehl 'rah-yoh)*
the triangle	**el triángulo** *(ehl tree-'ahn-goo-loh)*
Call the...	**Llame a...** *('yah-meh ah)*
carpenter	**el carpintero** *(ehl kahr-peen-'teh-roh)*
contractor	**el contratista** *(ehl kohn-trah-'tees-tah)*
electrician	**el electricista** *(ehl eh-lehk-tree-'sees-tah)*
laborer	**el trabajador** *(ehl trah-bah-hah-'dohr)*
painter	**el pintor** *(ehl peen-'tohr)*
plumber	**el plomero** *(ehl ploh-'meh-roh)*
roofer	**el tejador** *(ehl teh-hah-'dohr)*
stonemason	**el albañil** *(ehl ahl-bah-'nyeel)*

 MÁS AYUDA

Bear in mind that most construction work requires knowledge of simple measurements. Do you recall any of these?

centimeter	**el centímetro** *(ehl sehn-'tee-meh-troh)*
foot	**el pie** *(ehl 'pee-eh)*
inch	**la pulgada** *(lah pool-'gah-dah)*
meter	**el metro** *(ehl 'meh-troh)*
yard	**la yarda** *(lah 'yahr-dah)*

The board measures two inches by four inches.

La tabla mide dos pulgadas por cuatro pulgadas *(lah 'tah-blah 'mee-deh dohs pool-'gah-dahs pohr 'kwah-troh pool-gah-dahs)*

REPASEMOS

Say these in Spanish: 2" x 4", 4" x 4", 2" x 12"

- Match each tool...
  el pegamento *(ehl peh-gah-'mehn-toh)*
  la llana *(lah 'yah-nah)*
  el papel de lija *(ehl pah-'pehl deh 'lee-hah)*

...with the appropriate material:

  el empapelado *(ehl ehm-pah-peh-'lah-doh)*
  la madera *(lah mah-'deh-rah)*
  el cemento *(ehl seh-'mehn-toh)*

 ¡EL SUPERESPAÑOL!

A fast effective way to tell someone in Spanish that an activity was "just completed" is to add the *base verb* infinitives to the following forms of the phrase,

To just finish	**Acabar de** *(ah-kah-'bahr deh)*
I just finished...	**Acabo de...** *(ah-'kah-boh deh)*
I just finished sweeping.	**Acabo de barrer** *(ah-'kah-boh deh bah-'rrehr)*
You, He, She just finished...	**Acaba de...** *(ah-'kah-bah deh)*
He just finished painting.	**Acaba de pintar** *(ah-'kah-bah deh peen-'tahr)*
They, You (plural) just finished...	**Acaban de...** *(ah-'kah-bahn deh)*
They just finished talking.	**Acaban de hablar** *(ah-'kah-bahn deh ah-'blahr)*
We just finished...	**Acabamos de...** *(ah-kah-'bah-mohs deh)*
We just finished eating.	**Acabamos de comer** *(ah-kah-'bah-mohs deh koh-'mehr)*

La Niña acabó de comer.

By the way, the verb **acabar** means "to finish," and can be used as a regular action word:

I'm finishing now.	**Estoy acabando ahorita** *(eh-'stoh-ee ah-kah-'bahn-doh ah·oh-'ree-tah)*
I finish at five.	**Acabo a las cinco** *(ah-'kah-boh ah lahs 'seen-koh)*
I was finishing.	**Estaba acabando** *(eh-'stah-bah ah-kah-'bahn-doh)*
I finished with the job.	**Acabé con el trabajo** *(ah-kah-'beh kohn ehl trah-'bah-hoh)*

 ¡MÁS ACCIÓN!

Study this powerful two-part verb pattern. It's extremely important in household conversations because if refers to actions that have already taken place. It's a *past action* pattern that is used frequently in everyday communication, so pay close attention to each example. Here's how the words go together:

The first part consists of forms of the verb **haber** *(ah-'behr)*.

The second part consists of the *past participle* of the action word. Both parts must be used together.

I've	**He**	gone	**ido** *('ee-doh)*
		eaten	**comido** *(koh-'mee-doh)*
you've, she's, he's	**Ha**	cooked	**cocinado** *(koh-see-'nah-doh)*
		cleaned	**limpiado** *(leem-pee-'ah-doh)*

199

they've, you've (plural)	**Han**	worked	**trabajado** *(trah-bah-'hah-doh)*
		driven	**manejado** *(mah-neh-'hah-doh)*
we've	**Hemos**	painted	**pintado** *(peen-'tah-doh)*

I've cooked breakfast many times.	**He cocinado el desayuno muchas veces** *(eh koh-see-'nah-doh ehl deh-sah-'yoo-noh 'moo-chahs 'beh-sehs)*
She's driven a truck.	**Ella ha manejado un camión** *('eh-yah ah mah-neh-'hah-doh oon kah-mee-'ohn)*
We've cleaned houses before.	**Hemos limpiado casas antes** *('eh-mohs leem-pee-'ah-doh 'kah-sahs 'ahn-tehs)*

To learn more about *past participle* verb forms, consider taking a beginning Spanish class. This two-part verb tense can be very useful.

 REPASEMOS

Read this story and then translate:

Estoy trabajando en el jardín del Sr. Jackson *(eh-'stoh-ee trah-bah-'hahn-doh ehn ehl hahr-'deen del seh-'nyohr Jackson)*. **Trabajo todos los sábados aquí** *(trah-'bah-hoh 'toh-dohs lohs 'sah-bah-dohs ah-'kee)*. **Estamos construyendo una cerca de madera** *(eh-'stah-mohs kohn-stroo-'yehn-doh 'oo-nah 'sehr-kah deh mah-'deh-rah)*. **Acabo de poner los postes** *(ah-'kah-boh deh poh-'nehr lohs poh-'stehs)*. **Hemos trabajado todo el día aquí** *('eh-mohs trah-bah-'hah-doh 'toh-doh ehl 'dee-ah ah-'kee)*.

 PALABRAS CLAVES

You can't get any yardwork done if the weather's bad. When there's a conversation about the weather, listen for consistent patterns. These words and phrases will help:

What's the weather like?	**¿Cómo está el tiempo?** *('koh-moh eh-'stah ehl tee-'ehm-poh)*
It's...	**Hace...** *('ah-seh)*
cold	**frío** *('free-oh)*
hot	**calor** *(kah-'lohr)*
nice weather	**buen tiempo** *('bwehn tee-'ehm-poh)*

sunny	**sol** *(sohl)*
windy	**viento** *(bee-'ehn-toh)*
It's...	**Está...** *(eh-'stah)*
clear	**despejado** *(dehs-peh-'hah-doh)*
cloudy	**nublado** *(noo-'blah-doh)*
cool	**fresco** *('frehs-koh)*
drizzling	**lloviznando** *(yoh-bees-'nahn-doh)*
freezing	**helado** *(eh-'lah-doh)*
raining	**lloviendo** *(yoh-bee-'ehn-doh)*
snowing	**nevando** *(neh-'bahn-doh)*
stormy	**tempestuoso** *(tehm-peh-stoo-'oh-soh)*
I don't like...	**No me gusta...** *(noh meh 'goo-stah)*
frost	**la escarcha** *(lah eh-'skahr-chah)*
hail	**el granizo** *(ehl grah-'nee-soh)*
lightening	**el relámpago** *(ehl reh-'lahm-pah-goh)*
rain	**la lluvia** *(lah 'yoo-bee-ah)*
snow	**la nieve** *(lah nee-'eh-beh)*
thunder	**el trueno** *(ehl troo-'eh-noh)*

 REPASEMOS

Answer these questions:

¿Dónde vive? *('dohn-deh 'bee-beh)*

_____

¿Cuándo hace calor allí? *('kwahn-doh 'ah-seh kah-'lohr ah-'yee)*

_____

¿Cómo está el tiempo hoy? *('koh-moh eh-'stah ehl tee-'ehm-poh 'oh-ee)*

_____

CHAPTER SEVEN   Capítulo Siete
(kah-'pee-too-loh see-'eh-teh)

ERRANDS
Los encargos (lohs ehn-'kahr-gohs)

THERE'S SO MUCH TO DO!
¡Hay tanto que hacer! *('ah·ee 'tahn-toh keh ah-'sehr)*
Although most people need extra help in the areas of housecleaning, cooking, childcare, and yardwork, it's not uncommon for many to need help, to seek assistance in running daily errands. Finding a responsible assistant to take over these routine tasks isn't always easy, but when you do, life can become a lot less stressful.

If the person you hire speaks only Spanish, take as much time as you need to hand out instructions. Since most errands require travel, money, and some interaction with others, make sure that your messages are clear and that everyone knows what they are supposed to do.

ALL AROUND THE TOWN!
Por Toda la Ciudad *(pohr 'toh-dah lah see-oo-'dahd)*
Regardless of the size of your community, there are certain words that must be used to explain life in your neighborhood and beyond. Let's begin by practicing those items that describe what most of our cities look like:

alley	**el callejón** *(ehl kah-yeh-'hohn)*
apartment building	**el edificio de departamentos** *(ehl eh-dee-'fee-see·oh deh deh-pahr-tah-'mehn-tohs)*
avenue	**la avenida** *(lah ah-beh-'nee-dah)*
bridge	**el puente** *(ehl 'pwehn-teh)*
building	**el edificio** *(ehl eh-dee-'fee-see·oh)*
bus stop	**la parada de autobús** *(lah pah-'rah-dah deh aw-toh-'boos)*
city block	**la cuadra** *(lah 'kwah-drah)*
community	**la comunidad** *(lah koh-moo-nee-'dahd)*

corner	la **esquina** *(lah eh-'skee-nah)*
crosswalk	el **cruce de peatones** *(ehl 'kroo-seh deh peh-ah-'toh-nehs)*
downtown	el **centro** *(ehl 'sehn-troh)*
elevator	el **elevador** *(ehl eh-leh-bah-'dohr)*
entrance	la **entrada** *(lah ehn-'trah-dah)*
escalator	la **escalera mecánica** *(lah ehs-kah-'leh-rah meh-'kah-nee-kah)*
exit	la **salida** *(lah sah-'lee-dah)*
fence	la **cerca** *(lah 'sehr-kah)*
fountain	la **fuente** *(lah 'fwehn-teh)*
highway	la **carretera** *(lah kah-rreh-'teh-rah)*
mailbox	el **buzón** *(ehl boo-'sohn)*
neighborhood	el **barrio** *(ehl 'bah-rree-oh)*
outskirts	las **afueras** *(lahs ah-'fweh-rahs)*
parking lot	el **estacionamiento** *(ehl eh-stah-see-oh-nah-mee-'ehn-toh)*
pool	la **piscina** *(lah pee-'see-nah)*
restroom	el **excusado** *(ehl ehks-koo-'sah-doh)*
road	el **camino** *(ehl kah-'mee-noh)*
shed	el **cobertizo** *(ehl koh-behr-'tee-soh)*
sidewalk	la **acera** *(lah ah-'seh-rah)*
sign	el **anuncio** *(ehl ah-'noon-see-oh)*
skyscraper	el **rascacielos** *(ehl rah-skah-see-'eh-lohs)*
stairs	las **escaleras** *(lahs eh-skah-'leh-rahs)*
statue	la **estatua** *(lah eh-'stah-too-ah)*
stop sign	el **señal de alto** *(ehl seh-'nyahl deh 'ahl-toh)*
street	la **calle** *(lah 'kah-yeh)*
traffic	el **tráfico** *(ehl 'trah-fee-koh)*
traffic signal	el **semáforo** *(ehl seh-'mah-foh-roh)*
tunnel	el **túnel** *(ehl 'too-nehl)*

Yo he pintado casas, puentes, estatuas y túneles, pero no he pintado labios.

PLACES AND SITES
Lugares y sitios (loo-'gah-rehs ee 'see-tee·ohs)
Now let's identify some of the places you or your help might visit from time to time:

Go to the...   **Vaya a...** *('bah-yah ah)*

airport	**el aeropuerto** *(ehl ah·eh-roh-'pwehr-toh)*
bank	**el banco** *(ehl 'bahn-koh)*
bar	**el bar** *(ehl 'bahr)*
beauty salon	**el salón de belleza** *(ehl sah-'lohn deh beh-'yeh-sah)*
campgrounds	**el campamento** *(ehl kahm-pah-'mehn-toh)*
cemetery	**el cementerio** *(ehl seh-mehn-'teh-ree·oh)*
church	**la iglesia** *(lah ee-'gleh-see·ah)*
circus	**el circo** *(ehl 'seer-koh)*
city hall	**el municipio** *(ehl moo-nee-'see-pee·oh)*
courthouse	**la corte** *(lah 'kohr-teh)*
department store	**el almacén** *(ehl ahl-mah-'sehn)*
factory	**la fábrica** *(lah 'fah-bree-kah)*
fire department	**el departamento de bomberos** *(ehl deh-pahr-tah-'mehn-toh deh bohm-'beh-rohs)*
florist	**la florería** *(lah floh-reh-'ree-ah)*
gas station	**la gasolinera** *(lah gah-soh-lee-'neh-rah)*
hospital	**el hospital** *(ehl oh-spee-'tahl)*
jail	**la cárcel** *(lah 'kahr-sehl)*
library	**la biblioteca** *(lah beeb-lee-oh-'teh-kah)*
movie theater	**el cine** *(ehl 'see-neh)*
museum	**el museo** *(ehl moo-'seh-oh)*
office	**la oficina** *(lah oh-fee-'see-nah)*
park	**el parque** *(ehl 'pahr-keh)*
pharmacy	**la farmacia** *(lah fahr-'mah-see·ah)*
police station	**la estación de policía** *(lah eh-stah-see-'ohn deh poh-lee-'see-ah)*
post office	**el correo** *(ehl koh-'rreh-oh)*
restaurant	**el restaurante** *(ehl reh-stah·oo-'rahn-teh)*
school	**la escuela** *(lah eh-'skweh-lah)*
store	**la tienda** *(lah tee-'ehn-dah)*

supermarket	**el supermercado** *(ehl soo-pehr-mehr-'kah-doh)*
zoo	**el zoológico** *(ehl soh-oh-'loh-hee-koh)*

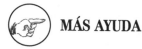

MÁS AYUDA

The names for businesses all over town follow a similar pattern in the Spanish language. They end in the letters "**ería**." This is just a sample:

bakery	**la panadería** *('lah pah-nah-deh-'ree-ah)*
barber shop	**la peluquería** *(lah peh-loo-keh-'ree-ah)*
book store	**la librería** *(lah lee-breh-'ree-ah)*
butcher shop	**la carnicería** *(lah kahr-nee-seh-'ree-ah)*
laundromat	**la lavandería** *(lah lah-bahn-deh-'ree-ah)*
shoe store	**la zapatería** *(lah sah-pah-teh-'ree-ah)*

TEMAS CULTURALES

Spanglish in the city!

el hotel *(ehl oh-'tehl)*
el motel *(ehl moh-'tehl)*
la cafetería *(lah kah-feh-teh-'ree-ah)*

TRANSPORTATION

El transporte (ehl trahns-'pohr-teh)

If you're sending anyone into the city, it's a good idea to discuss your concerns about their means of transportation. Open up with a few of these:

Go by...	**Vaya en...** *('bah-yah ehn)*
bicycle	**bicicleta** *(lbee-see-'kleh-tah)*
boat	**barco** *('bahr-koh)*
bus	**autobús** *(ow-boh-'boos)*
car	**carro** *('kah-rroh)*
foot	**pie** *('pee-eh)*
helicopter	**helicóptero** *(eh-lee-'kohp-teh-roh)*
motorcycle	**motocicleta** *(lmoh-toh-see-'kleh-tah)*
plane	**avión** *(ah-bee-'ohn)*
subway	**metro** *('meh-troh)*

taxi	**taxi** *(e'tahk-see)*
train	**tren** *(trehn)*
truck	**camión** *(kah-mee-'ohn)*

 MÁS AYUDA

Whether it's for travel, fishing, or occasional recreation, lots of people own a boat. The trouble is, boats need to be cleaned and maintained, which might require the services of outside help.

Do you own any of these? Learn how to say them:

canoe	**la canoa** *(lah kah-'noh-ah)*
rowboat	**el bote de remos** *(ehl 'boh-teh deh 'reh-mohs)*
sailboat	**el velero** *(ehl beh-'leh-roh)*
speedboat	**la lancha de motor** *(lah 'lahn-chah deh moh-'tohr)*
yacht	**el yate** *(ehl 'yah-teh)*

 REPASEMOS

• Match the words that are similar in meaning:

la comunidad *(lah koh-moo-nee-'dahd)*   **el rascacielos** *(ehl rah-skah-see-'eh-lohs)*

la calle *('kah-yeh)*   **el barrio** *(ehl 'bah-ree·oh)*

el edificio *(ehl eh-dee-'fee-see·oh)*   **el camino** *(ehl kah-'mee-noh)*

• Answer these questions with either **sí** or **no**:

¿Hay una escuela cerca de su casa? *('ah-ee 'oo-nah eh-'skweh-lah' sehr-kah deh soo 'kah-sah)* _____

¿Tiene usted una bicicleta? *(tee-'eh-neh oo-'stehd 'oo-nah bee-see-'kleh-tah)* _____

206

¿Quiere visitar un museo? *(kee-'eh-reh bee-see-'tahr oon moo-'seh-oh)* _____

¿Tiene que ir a una oficina mañana? *(tee-'eh-neh keh eer ah 'oo-nah oh-fee-'see-nah mah-'nyah-nah)* _____

 PALABRAS CLAVES

No one should be without insurance coverage. If you have anyone on the street working for you, check up on the proper protection:

Do you have insurance?	**¿Tiene seguro?** *(tee-'eh-neh seh-'goo-roh)*
What kind?	**¿Qué tipo?** *(keh 'tee-poh)*
Insurance for...	**El seguro de...** *(ehl seh-'goo-roh deh)*
accidents	**accidentes** *(ahk-see-'dehn-tehs)*
automobile	**automóvil** *(ow-toh-'moh-beel)*
disability	**incapacidad** *(een-kah-pah-see-'dahd)*
family	**familia** *(fah-'mee-lee·ah)*
health	**salud** *(sah-'lood)*
hospital	**hospital** *(oh-spee-'tahl)*
life	**vida** *('bee-dah)*
medical	**médico** *('meh-dee-koh)*
personal	**personal** *(pehr-soh-'nahl)*

 ¡HÁGALO, POR FAVOR!

Once you know where you are going and how you're going to get there, the next step is to figure out what you will do when you arrive. The following list of commands will guide your helper through a variety of outside errands, chores, and responsibilities. Be sure to combine them with the vocabulary that was just presented, or any of the other Spanish you already know. And note how great they are all by themselves!

Bring it	**Tráigalo** *('trah·ee-gah-loh)*
Buy it	**Cómprelo** *('kohm-preh-loh)*
Charge it	**Cárguelo** *('kahr-geh-loh)*
Choose it	**Escójalo** *(eh-'skoh-hah-loh)*
Deliver it	**Entréguelo** *(ehn-'treh-geh-loh)*
Do it	**Hágalo** *('ah-gah-loh)*
Exchange it	**Cámbielo** *('kahm-bee-eh-loh)*

Get it	**Consígalo** *(kohn-'see-gah-loh)*
Look for it	**Búsquelo** *('boo-skeh-loh)*
Park it	**Estaciónelo** *(eh-stah-see-'oh-neh-loh)*
Pay it	**Páguelo** *('pah-geh-loh)*
Pick it up	**Recójalo** *(reh-'koh-hah-loh)*
Put it	**Póngalo** *('pohn-gah-loh)*
Rent it	**Alquílelo** *(ahl-'kee-leh-loh)*
Return it	**Regréselo** *(reh-'greh-seh-loh)*
Sell it	**Véndalo** *('behn-dah-loh)*
Send it	**Mándelo** *('mahn-deh-loh)*
Sign it	**Fírmelo** *('feer-meh-loh)*
Take it	**Llévelo** *('yeh-beh-loh)*

 ## MÁS AYUDA

And as you know, the **lo** changes to **la** when the object refers to the feminine:

I need the chair. Bring it here, please!
Necesito la silla *(neh-seh-'see-toh lah 'see-yah)* **¡Tráigala, por favor!** *('trah·ee-gah-lah, pohr fah-'bohr)*.

 ## TEMAS CULTURALES

Commands are practical and easy to use, but try not to overdo it. Those employers who tend to be overbearing have problems earning respect. Try to give your orders sparingly and always add, **por favor** *(pohr fah-'bohr)* (please).

LET'S GO SHOPPING!
¡Vamos de compras! *('bah-mohs deh 'kohm-prahs)*
Everyone has to shop, but once in a while, there just isn't enough time to purchase all that you need.

Many homes and businesses have established relationships with Spanish-speaking helpers, housekeepers, or babysitters, who are frequently entrusted to handle such responsibilities.

Take extra time to practice and review the terms and phrases below.
Start off by discussing the finances:

Take the...	Lleve... *('yeh-beh)*
bill	**la cuenta** *(lah 'kwehn-tah)*
bills	**los billetes** *(lohs bee-'yeh-tehs)*
change	**el cambio** *(ehl 'kahm-bee·oh)*
check	**el cheque** *(ehl 'cheh-keh)*
coins	**las monedas** *(lahs moh-'neh-dahs)*
credit card	**la tarjeta de crédito** *(lah tahr-'heh-tah deh 'kreh-dee-toh)*
invoice	**la factura** *(lah fahk-'too-rah)*
money	**el dinero** *(ehl dee-'neh-roh)*
order	**el orden** *(ehl 'ohr-dehn)*
payment	**el pago** *(ehl 'pah-goh)*
receipt	**el recibo** *(ehl reh-'see-boh)*
tip	**la propina** *(lah proh-'pee-nah)*

Here is (are) the...

bargain	**la ganga** *(lah 'gahn-gah)*
billfold	**la billetera** *(lah bee-yeh-'teh-rah)*
checkbook	**la chequera** *(lah cheh-'keh-rah)*
coupon	**el cupón** *(ehl koo-'pohn)*
directions	**las direcciones** *(lahs dee-rehk-see-'oh-nehs)*
discount	**el descuento** *(ehl dehs-'kwehn-toh)*
label	**la etiqueta** *(lah eh-tee-'keh-tah)*
map	**el mapa** *(ehl 'mah-pah)*
offer	**la oferta** *(lah oh-'fehr-tah)*

price	**el precio** *(ehl 'preh-see·oh)*
purse	**la bolsa** *(lah 'bohl-sah)*
sale	**la venta** *(lah 'behn-tah)*
shopping list	**la lista de compras** *(lah 'lee-stah deh 'kohm-prahs)*
ticket	**el boleto** *(ehl boh-'leh-toh)*

 ## TEMAS CULTURALES

To truly get a feel for communication in Spanish, find time to observe a group of Hispanics in public or at a social gathering. Facial expressions, touch, changes in tone, and hand signals are a few of the many nonverbal differences between the Latin American and U.S. cultures.

 ## MÁS AYUDA

• Make efforts to learn as many shopping phrases as you can. Not only will your ability to give instructions improve, but you will have fewer problems wherever you shop in a Spanish-speaking country.

Does it fit?	**¿Le queda bien?** *(leh 'keh-dah bee-'ehn)*
Is it free?	**¿Es gratis?** *(ehs 'grah-tees)*
Is it included?	**¿Está incluido?** *(eh-'stah een-kloo-'ee-doh)*
Is it "to go?"	**¿Es para llevar?** *(ehs 'pah-rah yeh-'bahr)*
Is that all?	**¿Es todo?** *(ehs 'toh-doh)*
Something else?	**¿Algo más?** *('ahl-goh mahs)*
What brand is it?	**¿Qué marca es?** *(keh 'mahr-kah ehs)*
Speak with the...	**Hable con...** *('ah-bleh kohn)*
boss	**el jefe** *(ehl 'heh-feh)*
cashier	**el cajero** *(ehl kah-'heh-roh)*
clerk	**el cliente** *(ehl klee-'ehn-teh)*
manager	**el gerente** *(ehl heh-'rehn-teh)*
owner	**el dueño** *(ehl 'dweh-nyoh)*
salesperson	**el vendedor** *(ehl behn-deh-'dohr)*
supervisor	**el supervisor** *(ehl soo-pehr-bee-'sohr)*

REPASEMOS

Match the command with the related vocabulary word:

Cárguelo *('kahr-geh-loh)*   la venta *(lah 'behn-tah)*
Búsquelo *('boo-skeh-loh)*   la orden *(lah ohr-'dehn)*
Entréguelo *(ehn-'treh-geh-loh)* la tarjeta de crédito *(lah tahr-'heh-tah deh 'kreh-dee-toh)*

Translate:

¿Dónde está el dueño, el gerente, y el cajero? *('dohn-deh eh-'stah ehl 'dweh-nyoh, ehl heh-'rehn-teh ee ehl kah-heh-roh)*

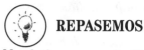 **TEMAS CULTURALES**

Did your employee just move to this country? Are they a bit confused about our language and culture? When you find the time, share a few insights on U.S. customs toward tipping, dress, dating, holidays, and social skills. Make them feel welcome by respecting their perspective, and watch your relationship grow!

MORE IMPORTANT WORDS
Más palabras importantes
(mahs pah-'lah-brahs eem-pohr-'tahn-tehs)

Your shopping assignment would be incomplete without these Spanish terms that express the quantity of items you need purchased. Although we discussed most of these measurements in previous chapters, the following selection can be particularly helpful in the marketplace:

I want a...	Quiero... *(kee-'eh-roh)*
bag	una bolsa *('oo-nah 'bohl-sah)*
bottle	una botella *('oo-nah boh-'teh-yah)*
box	una caja *('oo-nah 'kah-hah)*
case	un cajón *(oon kah-'hohn)*
dozen	una docena *('oo-nah doh-'seh-nah)*
package	un paquete *(oon pah-'keh-teh)*
pair	un par *(oon pahr)*

six-pack	**una caja de seis** *('oo-nah 'kah-hah deh 'seh-ees)*
ton	**una tonelada** *('oo-nah toh-neh-'lah-dah)*
one fifth	**un quinto** *(oon 'keen-toh)*
one fourth	**un cuarto** *(oon 'kwahr-toh)*
one half	**una mitad** *('oo-nah mee-'tahd)*
one third	**un tercio** *(oon 'tehr-see-oh)*

Discuss each detail with your Spanish-speaking helper. One mistake could lead to a lot of frustration!

How much...?	**¿Cuánto...?** *('kwahn-toh)*
did you buy?	**compró?** *(kohm-'proh)*
did you save?	**ahorró?** *(ah-oh-'rroh)*
did you spend?	**gastó?** *(gah-'stoh)*
does it cost?	**cuesta?** *('kweh-stah)*
is it worth?	**vale?** *('bah-leh)*
is it?	**es?** *(ehs)*

What's the...?	**¿Cuál es...?** *(kwahl ehs)*
amount	**la cantidad** *(lah kahn-tee-'dahd)*
height	**la altura** *(lah ahl-'too-rah)*
length	**el largo** *(ehl 'lahr-goh)*
measurement	**la medida** *(lah meh-'dee-dah)*
number	**el número** *(ehl 'noo-meh-roh)*
percent	**por ciento** *(pohr see-'ehn-toh)*
shape	**la forma** *(lah 'fohr-mah)*

size	el tamaño *(ehl tah-'mahn-yoh)*
weight	el peso *(ehl 'peh-soh)*
width	el ancho *(ehl 'ahn-choh)*
It's...	Es... *(ehs)*
small	chico *('chee-koh)*
medium	mediano *(meh-dee-'ah-noh)*
large	grande *('grahn-deh)*
X-large	extragrande *('ehks-trah-grahn-deh)*

 TEMAS CULTURALES

• What do you know about the metric system?

5/8 mi.	=	un kilómetro *(oon kee-'loh-meh-troh)*
2.2 lbs.	=	un kilogramo *(oon kee-loh-'grah-moh)*
32° F	=	0° C

• Does everyone understand U.S. currency? Go over the following vocabulary with your help:

cent	el centavo *(ehl sehn-'tah-boh)*
dime	diez centavos *(dee-'ehs sehn-'tah-bohs)*
dollar	el dólar *(ehl 'doh-lahr)*
nickle	cinco centavos *('seen-koh sehn-'tah-bohs)*
penny	un centavo *(oon sehn-'tah-boh)*
quarter	veinticinco centavos *(beh·een-tee-'seen-koh sehn-'tah-bohs)*

DON'T FORGET!
¡No se olvide! *(noh seh ohl-'bee-deh)*
It would be impossible to list everything you'll find at the local supermarket or department store in a single Spanish guidebook. Therefore, the best approach to preparing a shopping list is to divide all miscellaneous items into helpful categories.

Toiletries
Cosas para el baño *('koh-sahs 'pah-rah ehl 'bah-nyoh)*

| blow dryer | la secadora de pelo *(lah seh-kah-'doh-rah deh 'peh-loh)* |
| cologne | la colonia *(lah koh-'loh-nee·ah)* |

comb	**el peine** *(ehl 'peh·ee·neh)*
conditioner	**el acondicionador** *(ehl ah-kohn-dee-see·oh-nah-'dohr)*
cosmetics	**los cosméticos** *(lohs kohs-'meh-tee-kohs)*
cotton	**el algodón** *(ehl ahl-goh-'dohn)*
cream	**la crema** *(lah 'kreh-mah)*
deodorant	**el desodorante** *(ehl dehs-oh-doh-'rahn-teh)*
feminine napkins	**los paños femeninos** *(lohs 'pah-nyohs feh-meh-'nee-nohs)*
hairbrush	**el cepillo de pelo** *(ehl seh-'pee-yoh deh 'peh-loh)*
hairpin	**la horquilla** *(lah ohr-'kee-yah)*
hairspray	**la laca** *(lah 'lah-kah)*
make-up	**el maquillaje** *(ehl mah-kee-'yah-heh)*
nail file	**la lima de uñas** *(lah 'lee-mah deh 'oo-nyahs)*
nail polish	**la pintura de uñas** *(lah peen-'too-rah deh 'oo-nyahs)*
perfume	**el perfume** *(ehl pehr-'foo-meh)*
razor blade	**la hoja de afeitar** *(lah 'oh-hah deh ah-fee·ee-'tahr)*
scissors	**las tijeras** *(lahs tee-'heh-rahs)*
shampoo	**el champú** *(ehl chahm-'poo)*
shaver	**la afeitadora** *(lah ah-feh·ee-tah-'doh-rah)*
suntan lotion	**el bronceador** *(ehl brohn-seh-ah-'dohr)*
toilet paper	**el papel higiénico** *(ehl pah-'pehl ee-hee-'eh-nee-koh)*
toothbrush	**el cepillo de dientes** *(ehl seh-'pee-yoh deh dee-'ehn-tehs)*

¡Este papel higiénico es muy grande y éste es muy chico!

| toothpaste | la pasta de dientes *(lah 'pah-stah deh dee-'ehn-tehs)* |
| tweezers | las pinzas *(lahs 'peen-sahs)* |

Family Jewelry
Las joyas de la familia (lahs 'hoh-yahs deh lah fah-'mee-lee·ah)

Look for the...	Busque... *('boo-skeh)*
bracelet	el brazalete *(ehl brah-sah-'leh-teh)*
broach	el broche *(ehl 'broh-cheh)*
chain	la cadena *(luh kuh-'deh-nuh)*
cufflinks	los gemelos *(lohs heh-'meh-lohs)*
earring	el arete *(ehl ah-'reh-teh)*
necklace	el collar *(ehl koh-'yahr)*
ring	el anillo *(ehl ah-'nee-yoh)*
watch	el reloj de pulsera *(ehl reh-'loh deh pool-'seh-rah)*

Everything else
El resto (ehl 'reh-stoh)

Here are some miscellaneous items you may want to buy:

I need (the)...	Necesito... *(neh-seh-'see-toh)*
batteries	las pilas *(lahs 'pee-lahs)*
book	el libro *(ehl 'lee-broh)*
cigarettes	los cigarillos *(lohs see-gah-'ree-yohs)*
combination lock	el candado *(ehl kahn-'dah-doh)*
envelopes	los sobres *(lohs 'soh-brehs)*
gas	la gasolina *(lah gah-soh-'lee-nah)*
gift	el regalo *(ehl reh-'gah-loh)*
greeting cards	las tarjetas de saludo *(lahs tahr-'heh-tahs deh sah-'loo-doh)*
handkerchief	el pañuelo *(ehl pah-nyoo-'eh-loh)*
light bulbs	los focos *(lohs 'foh-kohs)*
luggage	el equipaje *(ehl eh-kee-'pah-heh)*
magazines	las revistas *(lahs reh-'bee-stahs)*
matches	los fósforos *(lohs 'fohs-foh-rohs)*
medicine	la medicina *(lah meh-dee-'see-nah)*
needle	la aguja *(lah ah-'goo-hah)*
newspapers	los periódicos *(lohs peh-ree-'oh-dee-kohs)*
notebook	el cuaderno *(ehl kwah-'dehr-noh)*

oil	**el aceite** *(ehl ah-'seh-ee-teh)*
paper	**el papel** *(ehl pah-'pehl)*
pen	**la pluma** *(lah 'ploo-mah)*
pencil	**el lápiz** *(ehl 'lah-pees)*
pin	**el alfiler** *(ehl ahl-fee-'lehr)*
postcard	**la tarjeta postal** *(lah tahr-'heh-tah poh-'stahl)*
roll of film	**el rollo de foto** *(ehl 'roh-yoh deh 'foh-toh)*
stamps	**las estampillas** *(lahs eh-stahm-'pee-yahs)*
sunglasses	**los lentes de sol** *(lohs 'lehn-tehs deh sohl)*
tape	**la cinta** *(lah 'seen-tah)*
thread	**el hilo** *(ehl 'ee-loh)*
tools	**las herramientas** *(lahs eh-rrah-mee-'ehn-tahs)*
umbrella	**la sombrilla** *(lah sohm-'bree-yah)*

 ## MÁS AYUDA

Obviously, when you think of shopping, food comes to mind. Go back to Chapter Five and add those words to the line below:

Go to the market and buy...
Vaya al mercado y compre... *('bah-yah ahl mehr-'kah-doh ee 'kohm-preh)*

 ## REPASEMOS

Translate:
Compre la pasta de dientes, el peine, los lentes del sol, el periódico, los fósforos, y las estampillas *('kohm-preh lah 'pah-stah deh dee-'ehn-tehs, ehl 'peh-ee-neh, lohs 'lehn-tehs dehl sohl, ehl peh-ree-'oh-dee-koh, lohs 'fohs-foh-rohs, ee lahs eh-stahm-'pee-yahs)*

DO ME A FAVOR!
Hágame un favor ('ah-gah-meh oon fah-'bohr)

Are you able to formulate your own requests in Spanish? When you need things done around town, keep your explanations brief:

| Please remind me of (the)... | **Por favor, recuérde me de...** *(pohr fah-'bohr, reh-'kwehr-deh-meh deh)* |
| appointment | **la cita** *(lah 'see-tah)* |

conference	**la conferencia** *(lah kohn-feh-'rehn-see·ah)*
flight	**el vuelo** *(ehl 'bweh-loh)*
meeting	**la reunión** *(lah reh-oo-nee-'ohn)*
party	**la fiesta** *(lah fee-'eh-stah)*
picnic	**la comida campestre** *(lah koh-'mee-dah kahm-'pehs-treh)*
trip	**el viaje** *(ehl bee-'ah-heh)*
wedding	**la boda** *(lah 'boh-dah)*

Hágame el favor de ir a la tienda y comprar un collar de diamantes.

Please...	**Favor de...** *(fah-'bohr deh)*
buy cigarettes	**comprar cigarillos** *(kohm-'prahr see-gah-'ree-yohs)*
change the oil	**cambiar el aceite** *(kahm-bee-'ahr ehl ah-'seh·ee-teh)*
go to the store	**ir a la tienda** *(eer ah lah tee-'ehn-dah)*
pick them up	**recogerlos** *(reh-koh-'hehr-lohs)*
rent a video	**alquilar un vídeo** *(ahl-kee-'lahr oon 'bee-deh-oh)*
send it by mail	**mandarlo por correo** *(mahn-'dahr-loh pohr koh-'reh-oh)*
stop at the cleaners	**parar en la tintorería** *('pah-rahr ehn lah teen-toh-reh-'ree-ah)*
take the kids to school	**llevar a los niños a la escuela** *(yeh-'bahr ah lohs 'nee-nyohs ah lah eh-'skweh-lah)*
walk the dog	**caminar el perro** *(kah-mee-'nahr ehl 'peh-rroh)*

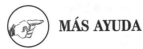

MÁS AYUDA

Keep in mind that not every errand can be handled downtown. In many areas, it's possible you'll need to visit one of these:

barn	**la granja** *(lah 'grahn-hah)*
barnyard	**el corral** *(ehl koh-'rrahl)*
dairy	**la lechería** *(lah leh-cheh-'ree-ah)*
farm	**la finca** *(lah 'feen-kah)*
ranch	**el rancho** *(ehl 'rahn-choh)*
stable	**el establo** *(ehl eh-'stah-bloh)*

TEMAS CULTURALES

The more trust that builds between you and your employee, the more comfortable you will feel around each other. Since hugging is a common form of greeting between friends, don't panic if someone leans forward to embrace you! Healthy touch is an active part of many cultures, and in Latin America, **cariño** *(kah-'ree-nyoh)* (affection) is openly displayed between friends and co-workers.

¡MÁS ACCIÓN!

So far we have discovered that in order to converse about activities in the present and the past tenses, it was necessary to change the ending of the basic action verb. For example:

To work	**Trabajar** *(trah-bah-'hahr)*
I'm working.	**Estoy trabajando** *(eh-'stoh-ee trah-bah-'hahn-doh)*
I work.	**Trabajo** *(trah-'bah-hoh)*
I worked.	**Trabajé** *(trah-bah-'heh)*

However, to refer to future actions, that is, those activities that you *will* do, it is necessary to add sounds to the end of the base verb instead.

I will work	**Trabajar é** *(trah-bah-hah-'reh)*
You, He, She will work	**Trabajar á** *(trah-bah-hah-'rah)*
You (plural), they will work	**Trabajar án** *(trah-bah-hah-'rahn)*

218

| We will work | **Trabajar emos** *(trah-bah-hah-'reh-mohs)* |

The same patterns hold true for the **er** and **ir** verbs as well:

to eat **(comer)**	I'll eat. **Comeré** *(koh-meh-'reh)*
to live **(vivir)**	He'll live. **Vivirá** *(bee-bee-'rah)*
to serve **(servir)**	They'll serve. **Servirán** *(sehr-bee-'rahn)*
to run **(correr)**	We'll run. **Correremos** *(koh-rreh-'reh-mohs)*

 ¡EL SUPERESPAÑOL!

As luck would have it, there's still another way in Spanish to discuss what's going to happen in the future. It's the same form used to talk about where you are going. These are the basic forms of the verb "to go" (**ir**):

I'm going to...	**Voy a...** *('boh-ee ah)*
You're, He's, She's going to...	**Va a...** *('bah ah)*
You (plural) are, They're going to...	**Van a...** *(bahn ah)*
We're going to...	**Vamos a...** *('bah-mohs ah)*

Here's how they work. Notice how these statements refer to <u>future actions</u>.

I'm going to the bathroom.	**Voy al baño** *('boh-ee ahl 'bah-nyoh)*
I'm going to clean.	**Voy a limpiar** *(boh-ee ah leem-pee-'ahr)*
She's going to church.	**Va a la iglesia** *(bah ah lah ee-'gleh-see·ah)*
She's going to pray.	**Va a rezar** *(bah ah reh-'sahr)*
They're going to the park.	**Van al parque** *(bahn ahl 'pahr-keh)*
They're going to play.	**Van a jugar** *(bahn ah hoo-'gahr)*
We're going to the kitchen.	**Vamos a la cocina** *('bah-mohs ah lah koh-'see-nah)*
We're going to cook.	**Vamos a cocinar** *('bah-mohs ah koh-see-'nahr)*

Use this new verb form whenever you head out the door:

I'll be at this number.	**Voy a estar en este número** *('boh-ee ah eh-'stahr ehn 'eh-steh 'noo-meh-roh)*
I'll be at this address.	**Voy a estar en esta dirección** *('boh-ee ah eh-'stahr ehn 'eh-stah dee-rehk-see·'ohn)*
I'll be back soon.	**Voy a regresar pronto** *('boh-ee ah reh-greh-'sahr 'prohn-toh)*
I won't be late.	**No voy a llegar tarde** *(noh 'boh-ee ah yeh-'gahr 'tahr-deh)*
I will call if there is a problem.	**Voy a llamar si hay un problema** *('boh-ee ah yah-'mahr see 'ah·ee oon proh-'bleh-mah)*

La señora dice que no está aquí.

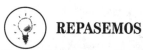 **REPASEMOS**

Follow the pattern of the first two sentences:

I will walk.	**Caminaré** *(kah-mee-nah-'reh)*
I'm going to walk.	**Voy a caminar** *('boh·ee ah kah-mee-'nahr)*
I will cook.	Cocinaré
I'm going to cook.	Voy a cocinar
I will clean.	limpiare
I'm going to clean.	Voy a limpiar

THE LAST WORD

If by chance your Spanish-speaking assistant is unfamiliar with English signs and signals, you may want to review some of the key words that are posted on our roadways. And don't forget, these terms are great to know when traveling in a foreign country!

Closed	**CERRADO** *(seh-'rrah-doh)*
Danger	**PELIGRO** *(peh-'lee-groh)*
Detour	**DESVIACIÓN** *(dehs-bee-ah-see·'ohn)*
Do Not Cross	**NO CRUZAR** *(noh kroo-'sahr)*
Emergency	**EMERGENCIA** *(eh-mehr-'hehn-see·ah)*
Entrance	**ENTRADA** *(ehn-'trah-dah)*
Exit	**SALIDA** *(sah-'lee-dah)*
For Rent	**SE ALQUILA** *(seh ahl-'kee-lah)*
For Sale	**SE VENDE** *(seh 'behn-deh)*
No Entrance	**PASO PROHIBIDO** *('pah-soh proh-ee-'bee-doh)*
No Passing	**NO PASAR** *(noh pah-'sahr)*
No Smoking	**NO FUMAR** *(noh foo-'mahr)*
One Way	**CIRCULACIÓN** *(seer-koo-lah-see·'ohn)*
Open	**ABIERTO** *(ah-bee-'ehr-toh)*
Out of Order	**DESCOMPUESTO** *(dehs-kohm-'pweh-stoh)*
Parking	**ESTACIONAMIENTO** *(eh-stah-see·oh-nah-mee-'ehn-toh)*
Pedestrian Crossing	**PASO DE PEATONES** *('pah-soh deh peh-ah-'toh-nehs)*
Pull	**JALE** *('hah-leh)*
Push	**EMPUJE** *(ehm-'poo-heh)*

Railroad Crossing	**CRUCE DE VÍAS** *('kroo-seh deh 'bee-ahs)*
Red Cross	**CRUZ ROJA** *('kroos 'roh-hah)*
Restrooms	**SANITARIOS** *(sah-nee-'tah-ree·ohs)*
Slow	**DESPACIO** *(deh-'spah-see·oh)*
Speed Limit	**LÍMITE DE VELOCIDAD** *('lee-mee-teh deh beh-loh-see-'dahd)*
Stop	**ALTO** *('ahl-toh)*
Traffic Circle	**GLORIETA** *(gloh-ree-'eh-tah)*
Yield	**CEDA EL PASO** *('seh-dah ehl 'pah-soh)*

 REPASEMOS

Connect the opposites:

abierto *(ah-bee-'ehr-toh)*	**salida** *(sah-'lee-dah)*
entrada *(ehn-'trah-dah)*	**empuje** *(ehm-'poo-heh)*
jale *('hah-leh)*	**cerrado** *(seh-'rrah-doh)*

DO YOU SPEAK ENGLISH?
¿Habla inglés? *('ah-blah een-'glehs)*

Putting all this time and energy into learning Spanish is really only half the battle. The truth is, household life would be a whole lot easier if everyone spoke English. Check out these suggestions on how you can help your Spanish-speaking employees pick up the language quickly:

• Keep the radio or TV on. The more exposure to English they have, the faster they'll pick it up.

• Continue to write brief notes in English. They'll soon be recognizing key words and phrases.

• Don't over-stress pronunciation or grammar skills. Those skills will repair themselves as more English is spoken.

• Try children's stories, games, songs, and puzzles. The more fun and relaxed people are, the faster they learn.

• Giving instructions to people is a tremendous teaching technique. The person hears the action word and the object at the same time. This "hands-on" experience with language seems to accelerate the English acquisition process.

- Exchange lots of questions and answers. By focusing on the primary question words, beginners learn practical ways to speak survival English.

- Regular exchanges of friendly greetings, courteous remarks, and ordinary expressions encourage non-English speakers to participate in conversations and speak up on their own.

- Repetition of any English word helps people remember it. For any key vocabulary item, say it clearly more than once, and if you like, have them repeat it back to you.

- Have a Spanish–English dictionary nearby in case one of you is stuck for a word.

- Make sure your employees can properly pronounce your name, address, and phone number in English. You never know when they'll be needed!

ENGLISH-SPANISH VOCABULARY

Please note that the gender of nouns is indicated by either **el** or **la**. The gender of adjectives and pronouns shown here is always masculine. To switch the gender to feminine, change the ending to **a** (americano=americana, solo=sola, mucho = mucha).

a un (m.), una (f.) *(oon, 'oo-nah)*
a little poco *(oon 'poh-koh)*
a lot mucho (sing.), muchos (pl.) *('moo-choh, 'moo-chohs)*
A.M. de la mañana *(deh luh mah-'nyah-nah)*
above encima *(ehn-'see-mah)*
accident accidente, el *(ehl ahk-see-'dehn-teh)*
accompany (to) acompañar *(ah-kohm-pah-'nyahr)*
acid ácido, el *(ehl 'ah-see-doh)*
acrylic acrílico *(ah-'kree-lee-koh)*
add (to) añadir *(ah-nyah-'deer)*
address dirección, la *(lah dee-rehk-see-'ohn)*
afterward después *(deh-'spwehs)*
again otra vez *('oh-trah behs)*
age edad, la *(lah eh-'dahd)*
agency agencia, la *(lah ah-'hehn-see-ah)*
ago hace *('ah-seh)*
air aire, el *(ehl 'ah-ee reh)*
air conditioner acondicionador de aire, el *(ehl ah-kohn-dee-see-oh-nah-'dohr deh 'ah-ee-reh)*
airplane avión, el *(ehl ah-bee-'ohn)*
airport aeropuerto, el *(ehl ah-eh-roh-'pwehr-toh)*
alarm alarma, la *(lah ah-'lahr-mah)*
algae alga, el *(ehl 'ahl-gah)*
allergy alergia, la *(lah ah-'lehr-hee-ah)*
alley callejón, el *(ehl kah-yeh-'hohn)*
alone solo *('soh-loh)*
already ya *(yah)*
also también *(tahm-bee-'ehn)*
always siempre *(see-'ehm-preh)*
ambitious ambicioso *(ahm-bee-see-'oh-soh)*
ambulance ambulancia, la *(lah ahm-boo-'lahn-see-ah)*
American americano *(ah-meh-ree-'kah-noh)*
ammonia amoníaco, el *(ehl ah-moh-'nee-ah-koh)*
amount cantidad, la *(lah kahn-tee-'dahd)*
and y *(ee)*

angle ángulo, el *(ehl 'ahn-goo-loh)*
angry enojado *(eh-noh-'hah-doh)*
animal animal, el *(ehl ah-nee-'mahl)*
anniversary aniversario, el *(ehl ah-nee-behr-'sah-ree-oh)*
ankle tobillo, el *(ehl toh-'bee-yoh)*
answer respuesta (la) *(lah reh-'spweh-stah)*
answer (to) contestar *(kohn-teh-'stahr)*
ant hormiga, la *(lah ohr-'mee-gah)*
antique antigüedad, la *(lah ahn-tee-gweh-'dahd)*
anyone cualquier persona *(kwahl-kee-'ehr pehr-'soh-nah)*
anything cualquier cosa *(kwahl-kee-'ehr 'koh-sah)*
anywhere cualquier sitio *(kwahl-kee-'ehr 'see-tee-oh)*
apartment apartamento, el *(ehl ah-pahr-tah 'mehn-toh)*
apple manzana, la *(lah mahn-'sah-nah)*
appliance aparato, el *(ehl ah-pah-'rah-toh)*
application solicitud, la *(lah soh-lee-see-'tood)*
apply (to) aplicar *(ah-plee-'kahr)*
appointment cita, la *(lah 'see-tah)*
apricot albaricoque, el *(ehl ahl-bah-ree-'koh-keh)*
April abril *(ah-'breel)*
apron delantal, el *(ehl deh-lahn-'tahl)*
aquarium acuario, el *(ehl ah-'kwah-ree-oh)*
architect arquitecto, el *(ehl ahr-kee-'tehk-toh)*
arm brazo, el *(ehl 'brah-soh)*
armchair sillón, el *(ehl see-'yohn)*
armoire armario, el *(ehl ahr-'mah-ree-oh)*
arrange (to) arreglar *(ah-rreh-'glahr)*
arrive (to) llegar *(yeh-'gahr)*
art arte, el *(ehl 'ahr-teh)*
artichoke alcachofa, la *(lah ahl-kah-'choh-fah)*
artist artista, el *(ehl ahr-'tees-tah)*
ash ceniza, la *(lah seh-'nee-sah)*
ashtray cenicero, el *(ehl seh-nee-'seh-roh)*

ask (to) preguntar *(preh-goon-'tahr)*
ask for (to) pedir *(peh-'deer)*
asparagus espárrago, el *(ehl eh-'spah-rrah-goh)*
asphalt asfalto, el *(ehl ahs-'fahl-toh)*
aspirin aspirina, la *(lah ah-spee-'ree-nah)*
assistant asistente, el or la *(ehl or lah ah-sees-'tehn-teh)*
at en *(ehn)*
at first al principio *(ahl preen-'see-pee-oh)*
attend (to) asistir *(ah-sees-'teer)*
attendance asistencia, la *(lah ah-sees-'tehn-see-ah)*
attic desván, el *(ehl dehs-'bahn)*
August agosto *(ah-'goh-stoh)*
aunt tía, la *(lah 'tee-ah)*
automatic automático *(ow-toh-'mah-tee-koh)*
autumn otoño, el *(ehl oh-'toh-nyoh)*
available disponible *(dee-spoh-'nee-bleh)*
avenue avenida, la *(lah ah-beh-'nee-dah)*
avocado aguacate, el *(ehl ah-gwah-'kah-teh)*
avoid (to) evitar *(eh-bee-'tahr)*
ax hacha, el *(ehl 'ah-chah)*
azalea azalea, la *(lah ah-sah-'leh-ah)*
baby bebé, el *(ehl beh-'beh)*
babysitter niñero, el *(ehl nee-'nyeh-roh)*
back espalda, la *(lah eh-'spahl-dah)*
backyard patio, el *(ehl 'pah-tee-oh)*
bacon tocino, el *(ehl toh-'see-noh)*
bad malo *('mah-loh)*
bag bolsa, la *(lah 'bohl-sah)*
bake (to) hornear *(hohr-neh-'ahr)*
bakery panadería, la *(lah pah-nah-deh-'ree-ah)*
baking powder polvo de hornear *(ehl 'pohl-boh deh ohr-neh-'ahr)*
baking soda bicarbonato de soda, el *(ehl bee-kahr-boh-'nah-toh deh 'soh-dah)*
bald calvo *('kahl-boh)*
ball pelota, la *(lah peh-'loh-tah)*
balloon globo, el *(ehl 'gloh-boh)*
banana plátano, el *(ehl 'plah-tah-noh)*
bandage vendaje, el *(ehl behn-'dah-heh)*
Band-Aid® curita, la *(lah coo-'ree-tah)*
bannister baranda, la *(lah bah-'rahn-dah)*
bank banco, el *(ehl 'bahn-koh)*
bar bar, el *(ehl bahr)*
barbecue barbacoa, la *(lah bahr-bah-'koh-ah)*
barbecue (to) asar a la parrilla *(ah-'sahr ah lah pah-'rree-yah)*
barber shop peluquería, la *(lah peh-loo-keh-'ree-ah)*

bargain ganga, la *(lah 'gahn-gah)*
bark (to) ladrar *(lah-'drahr)*
bartender cantinero, el *(ehl kahn-tee-'neh-roh)*
baseball béisbol, el *(ehl 'beh-ees-bohl)*
basement sótano, el *(ehl 'soh-tah-noh)*
basket canasta, la *(lah kah-'nah-stah)*
basketball básquetbol, el *(ehl 'bah-skeht-bohl)*
bassinet bacinete, el *(ehl bah-see-'neh-teh)*
bath baño, el *(ehl 'bah-nyoh)*
bathe (to) bañarse *(bah-'nyahr-seh)*
bathing suit traje de baño, el *(ehl 'trah-heh deh 'bah-nyoh)*
bathrobe bata, la *(lah 'bah-tah)*
bathroom cuarto de baño, el *(ehl 'kwahr-toh deh 'bah-nyoh)*
bathtub tina de baño, la *(lah 'tee-nah deh 'bah-nyoh)*
battery pila, la *(lah 'pee-lah)*
be (to) estar, ser *(eh-'stahr, sehr)*
be able to (to) poder *(poh-'dehr)*
be careful (to) tener cuidado *(teh-'nehr kwee-'dah-doh)*
beach playa, la *(lah 'plah-yah)*
bean frijol, el *(ehl free-'hohl)*
bear oso, el *(ehl 'oh-soh)*
beat (to) batir *(bah-'teer)*
beauty salon salón de belleza, el *(ehl sah-'lohn deh beh-'yeh-sah)*
beaver castor, el *(ehl kah-'stohr)*
because porque *('pohr-keh)*
bed cama, la *(lah 'kah-mah)*
bedroom dormitorio, la *(lah dohr-mee-'toh-ree-oh)*
bee abeja, la *(lah ah-'beh-hah)*
beer cerveza, la *(lah sehr-'beh-sah)*
beet remolacha, la *(lah reh-moh-'lah-chah)*
before antes *('ahn-tehs)*
begin (to) empezar *(ehm-peh-'sahr)*
behave (to) comportarse *(kohm-pohr-'tahr-seh)*
behind detrás *(deh-'trahs)*
belch eructo, el *(ehl eh-'rook-toh)*
bellhop botones, el *(ehl boh-'toh-nehs)*
bend (to) doblar *(doh-'blahr)*
benefit beneficio, el *(ehl beh-neh-'fee-see-oh)*
between entre *('ehn-treh)*
bib biberón, el *(ehl bee-beh-'rohn)*
bicycle bicicleta, la *(lah bee-see-'kleh-tah)*
big grande *('grahn-deh)*
bill cuenta, la *(lah 'kwehn-tah)*
billfold billetera, la *(lah bee-yeh-'teh-rah)*
birch abedul, el *(ehl ah-beh-'dool)*

bird pájaro, el *(ehl 'pah-hah-roh)*
birth nacimiento, el *(ehl nah-see-mee-'ehn-toh)*
birthday cumpleaños, el *(ehl koom-pleh-'ah-nyohs)*
bite mordedura, la *(lah mohr-deh-'doo-rah)*
bite (to) morder *(mohr-'dehr)*
bitter amargo *(ah-'mahr-goh)*
black negro *('neh-groh)*
blackberry mora, la *(lah 'moh-rah)*
bladder vejiga, la *(lah beh-'hee-gah)*
blanket frazada, la *(lah frah-'sah-dah)*
bleach blanqueador, el *(ehl blahn-keh-ah-'dohr)*
bleach (to) blanquear *(blahn-keh-'ahr)*
bleed (to) sangrar *(sahn-'grahr)*
blend (to) licuar *(lee-koo-'ahr)*
blender licuadora, la *(lah lee-kwah-'doh-rah)*
blinds persianas, las *(lahs pehr-see-'ah-nahs)*
blister ampolla, la *(lah ahm-'poh-yah)*
block bloque, el *(ehl 'bloh-keh)*
blond rubio *('roo-bee-oh)*
blood sangre, la *(lah 'sahn-greh)*
blouse blusa, la *(lah 'bloo-sah)*
blue azul *(ah-'sool)*
blueberry mora azul, la *(lah 'moh-rah ah-'sool)*
board tabla, la *(la 'tah-blah)*
boat bote, el *(ehl 'boh-teh)*
boating paseo en bote, el *(ehl pah-'seh-oh ehn 'boh-teh)*
body cuerpo, el *(ehl 'kwehr-poh)*
boil (to) hervir *(ehr-'beer)*
bolt perno, el *(ehl 'perh-noh)*
bone hueso, el *(ehl 'weh-soh)*
book libro, el *(ehl 'lee-broh)*
bookshelf librero, el *(ehl lee-'breh-roh)*
boot bota, la *(lah 'boh-tah)*
bored aburrido *(ah-boo-'rree-doh)*
boss jefe, el *(ehl 'heh-feh)*
bottle botella, la *(lah boh-'teh-yah)*
bottom fondo, el *(ehl 'fohn-doh)*
bowl plato hondo, el *(ehl 'plah-toh 'ohn-doh)*
bowling boliche, el *(ehl boh-'lee-cheh)*
box caja, la *(lah 'kah-hah)*
boxing boxeo, el *(ehl bohk-'seh-oh)*
boy niño, el *(ehl 'nee-nyoh)*
boyfriend novio, el *(ehl 'noh-bee-oh)*
bracelet brazalete, el *(ehl brah-sah-'leh-teh)*
brain cerebro, el *(ehl seh-'reh-broh)*
brake freno, el *(ehl 'freh-noh)*

branch rama, la *(lah 'rah-mah)*
brand marca, la *(lah 'mahr-kah)*
brass latón, el *(ehl lah-tohn)*
brassiere sostén, el *(ehl soh-'stehn)*
brave valiente *(bah-lee-'ehn-teh)*
bread pan (el) *(ehl pahn)*
break (to) quebrar *(keh-'brahr)*, romper *(rohm-'pehr)*
breakfast desayuno, el *(ehl deh-sah-'yoo-noh)*
breathe (to) respirar *(reh-spee-'rahr)*
brick ladrillo, el *(ehl lah-'dree-yoh)*
bridge puente, el *(ehl 'pwehn-teh)*
bright brillante *(hree 'yuhn-teh)*
bring (to) traer *(trah-'ehr)*
broach broche, el *(ehl 'broh-cheh)*
broil (to) asar *(ah-'sahr)*
broken roto *('roh-toh)*, quebrado *(kweh-'brah-doh)*
bronze bronce, el *(ehl 'brohn-seh)*
broom escoba, la *(lah eh-'skoh-bah)*
broth caldo, el *(ehl 'kahl-doh)*
brother hermano, el *(ehl ehr-'mah-noh)*
brother-in-law cuñado, el *(ehl koo-'nyah-doh)*
brown café *(kah-'feh)*
brown (to) dorar *(doh 'rahr)*
bruise contusión, la *(lah kohn-too-see-'ohn)*
brush cepillo, el *(ehl seh-'pee-yoh)*
brush (to) cepillar *(seh-pee-'yahr)*
bucket balde, el *(ehl 'bahl-deh)*
buckle hebilla, la *(lah eh-'bee-yah)*
bud botón, el *(ehl boh-'tohn)*
bug insecto, el *(ehl een-'sehk-toh)*
build (to) construir *(kohn-stroo-'eer)*
building edificio, el *(ehl eh-dee-'fee-see-oh)*
bumper parachoques, el *(ehl pah-rah-'choh-kehs)*
burn quemadura, la *(lah keh-mah-'doo-rah)*
burn (to) quemar *(keh-'mahr)*
bus autobús, el *(ehl ow-toh-'boos)*
bus stop parada de autobús, la *(lah pah-'rah-dah deh ow-toh-'boos)*
busboy ayudante de camarero, el *(ehl ah-yoo-'dahn-teh deh kah-mah-'reh-roh)*
bush arbusto, el *(ehl ahr-'boo-stoh)*
business negocio, el *(ehl neh-'goh-see-oh)*
busy ocupado *(oh-koo-'pah-doh)*
but pero *('peh-roh)*
butcher carnicero, el *(ehl kahr-nee-'seh-roh)*
butter mantequilla, la *(lah mahn-teh-'kee-yah)*
butterfly mariposa, la *(lah mah-ree-'poh-sah)*

button botón, el *(ehl boh-'tohn)*
buttock nalga, la *(lah 'nahl-gah)*
cabbage repollo, el *(ehl reh-'poh-yoh)*
cabinet gabinete, el *(ehl gah-bee-'neh-teh)*
cage jaula, la *(lah 'hah-oo-lah)*
cake torta, la *(lah 'tohr-tah)*
calculator calculadora, la *(lah kahl-koo-lah-'doh-rah)*
call (to) llamar *(yah-'mahr)*
calm down (to) calmarse *(kahl-'mahr-seh)*
campgrounds campamento, el *(ehl kahm-pah-'mehn-toh)*
can lata, la *(lah 'lah-tah)*
can opener abrelatas, el *(ehl ah-breh-'lah-tahs)*
canary canario, el *(ehl kah-'nah-ree-oh)*
cancel (to) cancelar *(kah-seh-'lahr)*
candle vela, la *(lah 'beh-lah)*
candy dulces, los *(lohs 'dool-sehs)*
cane bastón, el *(ehl bah-'stohn)*
canoe canoa, la *(lah kah-'noh-ah)*
cantaloupe melón, el *(ehl meh-'lohn)*
cap gorra, la *(lah 'goh-rrah)*
capsule cápsula, la *(lah 'kahp-soo-lah)*
car carro, el *(ehl 'kah-rroh)*
card tarjeta, la *(lah tahr-'heh-tah)*
cardboard cartón, el *(ehl kahr-'tohn)*
care for (to) cuidar *(kwee-'dahr)*
career carrera, la *(lah kah-'rreh-rah)*
carpenter carpintero, el *(ehl kahr-peen-'teh-roh)*
carrot zanahoria, la *(lah sah-nah-'oh-ree·ah)*
carry (to) llevar *(yeh-'bahr)*
cartoons dibujos animados, los *(lohs dee-'boo-hohs ah-nee-'mah-dohs)*
case estuche, el *(ehl eh-'stoo-cheh)*
cash register registradora, la *(lah reh-hee-strah-'doh-rah)*
cashier cajero, el *(ehl kah-'heh-roh)*
cat gato, el *(ehl 'gah-toh)*
catch (to) coger *(koh-'hehr)*
Catholic católico *(kah-'toh-lee-koh)*
cauliflower coliflor, el *(ehl koh-lee-'flohr)*
cause (to) causar *('kah·oo-'sahr)*
cedar cedro, el *(ehl 'seh-droh)*
ceiling techo, el *(ehl 'teh-choh)*
celebrate (to) celebrar *(seh-leh-'brahr)*
celery apio, el *(ehl 'ah-pee·oh)*
cement cemento, el *(ehl seh-'mehn-toh)*
cemetery cementerio, el *(ehl seh-mehn-'teh-ree·oh)*
cent centavo, el *(ehl seh-'tah-boh)*

centimeter centímetro, el *(ehl sehn-'tee-meh-troh)*
chain cadena, la *(lah kah-'deh-nah)*
chainsaw motosierra, la *(lah moh-toh-see-'eh-rah)*
chair silla, la *(lah 'see-yah)*
change cambio, el *(ehl 'kahm-bee-oh)*
change (to) cambiar *(kahm-bee-'ahr)*
changing table mesa para cambiar de pañales, la *(lah 'meh-sah 'pah-rah kahm-bee-'ahr deh pah-'nyah-lehs)*
channel canal, el *(ehl kah-'nahl)*
chat (to) charlar *(chahr-'lahr)*
cheap barato *(bah-'rah-toh)*
check cheque, el *(ehl 'cheh-keh)*
check on (to) comprobar *(kohm-proh-'bahr)*
checkbook chequera, la *(lah cheh-'keh-rah)*
checkers juego de damas, el *(ehl hoo-'eh-goh deh 'dah-mahs)*
cheek mejilla, la *(lah meh-'hee-yah)*
cheese queso, el *(ehl 'keh-soh)*
  cottage cheese requesón, el *(ehl reh-keh-'sohn)*
  cream cheese queso crema, el *(ehl 'keh-soh 'kreh-mah)*
  Parmesan cheese queso parmesano, el *(ehl 'keh-soh pahr-meh-'sah-noh)*
chemical producto químico, el *(ehl proh-'dook-toh 'kee-mee-koh)*
cherry cereza, la *(lah seh-'reh-sah)*
chess ajedrez, el *(ehl ah-heh-'drehs)*
chest (body) pecho, el *(ehl 'peh-choh)*
chest (box) baúl, el *(ehl bah-'ool)*
chicken gallina, la *(lah gah-'yee-nah)*
chill escalofrío, el *(ehl eh-skah-loh-'free-oh)*
chimney chimenea, la *(lah chee-meh-'neh-ah)*
chin barbilla, la *(lah bahr-'bee-lah)*
china porcelana, la *(lah pohr-seh-'lah-nah)*
chinaware vajilla de porcelana, la *(lah bah-'hee-yah deh pohr-seh-'lah-nah)*
chisel cincel, el *(ehl seen-'sehl)*
chlorine cloro, el *(ehl 'kloh-roh)*
chocolate chocolate, el *(ehl choh-koh-'lah-teh)*
choose (to) escoger *(eh-skoh-'hehr)*
chop chuleta, la *(lah choo-'leh-tah)*
chop (to) picar *(pee-'kahr)*
chore tarea, la *(lah tah-'reh-ah)*
church iglesia, la *(lah ee-'gleh-see-ah)*
cigar puro, el *(ehl 'poo-roh)*
cigarette cigarrillo, el *(ehl see-gah-'rree-yoh)*
cinnamon canela, la *(lah kah-'neh-lah)*

circle   círculo, el *(ehl 'seer-koo-loh)*
circus   circo, el *(ehl 'seer-koh)*
citizen   ciudadano, el *(ehl see-oo-dah-'dah-noh)*
city   ciudad, la *(lah see-oo-'dahd)*
city block   cuadra, la *(lah 'kwah-drah)*
city hall   municipio, el *(ehl moo-nee-'see-pee-oh)*
clam   almeja, la *(lah ahl-'meh-hah)*
clarinet   clarinete, el *(ehl klah-ree-'neh-teh)*
class   clase, la *(lah 'klah-seh)*
clean   limpio *('leem-pee-oh)*
clean (to)   limpiar *(leem-pee-'ahr)*
cleaners   tintorería, la *(lah teen-toh-reh-'ree-ah)*
cleanser   limpiadora, la *(lah leem-pee-ah-'doh-rah)*
clear   despejado *(deh-speh-'hah-doh)*
clerk   dependiente, el *(ehl deh-pehn-dee-'ehn-teh)*
client   cliente, el *(ehl klee-'ehn-teh)*
climb (to)   subir *(soo-'beer)*
clinic   clínica, la *(lah 'klee-nee-kah)*
clock   reloj, el *(ehl reh-'loh)*
close   cerca de *('sehr-kah deh)*
close (to)   cerrar *(seh-'rrahr)*
closet   ropero, el *(ehl roh-'peh-roh)*
cloth   tela, la *(lah 'teh-lah)*
clothing   ropa, la *(lah 'roh-pah)*
cloud   nube, la *(lah 'noo-beh)*
co-worker   compañero, el *(ehl kohm-pah-'nyeh-roh)*
coat   saco, el *(ehl 'sah-koh)*
cocktail   coctel, el *(ehl kohk-'tehl)*
coconut   coco, el *(ehl 'koh-koh)*
coffee   café, el *(ehl kah-'feh)*
coin   moneda, la *(lah moh-'neh-dah)*
cold   frío *('free-oh)*
cold (illness)   resfriado, el *(ehl rehs-free-'ah-doh)*
colic   cólico, el *(ehl 'koh-lee-koh)*
cologne   colonia, la *(lah koh-'loh-nee-ah)*
color   color, el *(ehl koh-'lohr)*
comb   peine, el *(ehl 'peh-ee-neh)*
come (to)   venir *(beh-'neer)*
comfortable   cómodo *('koh-moh-doh)*
community   comunidad, la *(lah koh-moo-nee-'dahd)*
complete   completo *(kohm-'pleh-toh)*
computer   computadora, la *(lah kohm-poo-tah-'doh-rah)*
condiment   condimento, el *(ehl kohn-dee-'mehn-toh)*

conditioner   acondicionador, el *(ehl ah-kohn-dee-see-oh-nah-'dohr)*
condominium   condominio, el *(ehl kohn-doh-'mee-nee-oh)*
congratulations   felicitaciones *(feh-lee-see-tah-see-'oh-nehs)*
constipation   estreñimiento, el *(ehl eh-streh-nyee-mee-'ehn-toh)*
contact lenses   lentes de contacto, los *(lohs 'lehn-tehs deh kohn-'tahk-toh)*
contaminated   contaminado *(kohn-tah-mee-'nah-doh)*
contract   contrato, el *(ehl kohn-'trah-toh)*
contractor   contratista, el *(ehl kohn-trah-'tee-stah)*
cook   cocinero, el *(ehl koh-see-'neh-roh)*
cook (to)   cocinar *(koh-see-'nahr)*
cookie   galleta, la *(lah gah-'yeh-tah)*
cool   fresco *('freh-skoh)*
copier   copiadora, la *(lah koh-pee-ah-'doh-rah)*
copper   cobre, el *(ehl 'koh-breh)*
cord   cordón, el *(ehl kohr-'dohn)*
corn   maíz, el *(ehl mah-'ees)*
cornstarch   almidón de maíz, el *(ehl ahl-mee-'dohn deh mah-'ees)*, maicena *(mah-ee-'seh-nah)*
corner   esquina, la *(lah eh-'skee-nah)*
correct   correcto *(koh-'rrehk-toh)*
correct (to)   corregir *(koh-rreh-'heer)*
cosmetics   cosméticos, los *(lohs kohs-'meh-tee-kohs)*
costume   disfraz, el *(ehl dees-'frahs)*
cotton   algodón, el *(ehl ahl-goh-'dohn)*
cough   tos, la *(lah tohs)*
counselor   consejero, el *(ehl kohn-seh-'heh-roh)*
count (to)   contar *(kohn-'tahr)*
counter   mostrador, el *(ehl moh-strah-'dohr)*
country   país, el *(ehl pah-'ees)*
county   condado, el *(ehl kohn-'dah-doh)*
couple   pareja, la *(lah pah-'reh-hah)*
coupon   cupón, el *(ehl koo-'pohn)*
court   cancha, la *(lah 'kahn-chah)*
courtesy   cortesía, la *(lah kohr-teh-'see-ah)*
courthouse   corte, la *(lah 'kohr-teh)*
cousin   primo, el *(ehl 'pree-moh)*
cover   tapa, la *(lah 'tah-pah)*
cover (to)   cubrir *(koo-'breer)*
cow   vaca, la *(lah 'bah-kah)*
CPR   respiración artificial, la *(lah reh-spee-rah-see-'ohn ahr-tee-fee-see-'ahl)*
crab   cangrejo, el *(ehl kahn-'greh-hoh)*
crack   grieta, la *(lah gree-'eh-tah)*

cracker galleta salada, la *(lah gah-'yeh-tah sah-'lah-dah)*
crawl (to) gatear *(gah-teh-'ahr)*
cream crema, la *(lah 'kreh-mah)*
creamer cremera, la *(lah kreh-'meh-rah)*
credit card tarjeta de crédito, la *(lah tahr-'heh-tah deh 'kreh-dee-toh)*
crib cuna, la *(lah 'koo-nah)*
cricket grillo, el *(ehl 'gree-yoh)*
crime crimen, el *(ehl 'kree-mehn)*
crop cosecha, la *(lah koh-'seh-chah)*
crosswalk cruce de peatones, el *(ehl 'kroo-seh deh peh-ah-'toh-nehs)*
crow cuervo, el *(ehl 'kwehr-boh)*
crumbs migas, las *(lahs 'mee-gahs)*
crush (to) machacar *(mah-chah-'kahr)*
crushed machacado *(mah-chah-'kah-doh)*
crutches muletas, las *(lahs moo-'leh-tahs)*
cry (to) llorar *(yoh-'rahr)*
cucumber pepino, el *(ehl peh-'pee-noh)*
cuff puño, el *(ehl 'poo-nyoh)*
cuff links gemelos, los *(lohs heh-'meh-lohs)*
cultivate (to) cultivar *(kool-tee-'bahr)*
cup taza, la *(lah 'tah-sah)*
curtains cortinas, las *(lahs kohr-'tee-nahs)*
cushion cojín, el *(ehl koh-'heen)*
custodian guardián, el *(ehl gwahr-dee-'ahn)*
cut cortada, la *(lah kohr-'tah-dah)*
cut (to) cortar *(kohr-'tahr)*
cute precioso *(preh-see-'oh-soh)*
cycle ciclo, el *(ehl 'see-kloh)*
daily diario *(dee-'ah-ree-oh)*
dairy lechería, la *(lah leh-cheh-'ree-ah)*
daisy margarita, la *(lah mahr-gah-'ree-tah)*
damage daño, el *(ehl 'dah-nyoh)*
damp húmedo *('oo-meh-doh)*
dance baile, el *(ehl 'bah-ee-leh)*
dance (to) bailar *(bah-ee-'lahr)*
dandelion diente de león, el *(ehl dee-'ehn-teh deh leh-'ohn)*
danger peligro, el *(ehl peh-'lee-groh)*
dangerous peligroso *(peh-lee-'groh-soh)*
dark oscuro *(oh-'skoo-roh)*
dashboard tablero, el *(ehl tah-'bleh-roh)*
date fecha, la *(lah 'feh-chah)*
daughter hija, la *(lah 'ee-hah)*
daughter-in-law nuera, la *(lah noo-'eh-rah)*
dawn madrugada, la *(lah mah-droo-'gah-dah)*
day día, el *(ehl 'dee-ah)*
deadbolt pestillo, el *(ehl peh-'stee-yoh)*
death muerte, la *(lah 'mwehr-teh)*
December diciembre *(dee-see-'ehm-breh)*

deck terraza, la *(lah teh-'rrah-sah)*
decorate (to) decorar *(deh-koh-'rahr)*
deep profundo *(proh-'foon-doh)*
deer venado, el *(ehl beh-'nah-doh)*
defrost (to) descongelar *(dehs-kohn-heh-'lahr)*
delicate delicado *(deh-lee-'kah-doh)*
delicious delicioso *(deh-lee-see-'oh-soh)*
dentist dentista, el or la *(ehl or lah dehn-'tees-tah)*
deodorant desodorante, el *(ehl dehs-oh-doh-'rahn-teh)*
department store almacén, el *(ehl ahl-mah-'sehn)*
describe (to) describir *(deh-skree-'beer)*
desert desierto, el *(ehl deh-see-'ehr-toh)*
desire (to) desear *(deh-seh-'ahr)*
desk escritorio, el *(ehl eh-skree-'toh-ree-oh)*
dessert postre, el *(ehl 'poh-streh)*
detergent detergente, el *(ehl deh-tehr-'hehn-teh)*
develop (to) desarollar *(dehs-ah-roh-'yahr)*
dial marcador, el *(ehl mahr-kah-'dohr)*
dial (to) marcar *(mahr-'kahr)*
diamond diamante, el *(ehl dee-ah-'mahn-teh)*
diaper pañal, el *(ehl pah-'nyahl)*
difficult difícil *(dee-'fee-seel)*
dig (to) excavar *(ehks-kah-'bahr)*
dining room comedor, el *(ehl koh-meh-'dohr)*
dinner cena, la *(lah 'seh-nah)*
diploma título, el *(ehl 'tee-too-loh)*
direction dirección, la *(lah dee-rehk-see-'ohn)*
dirt tierra, la *(lah tee-'eh-rrah)*
dirty sucio *('soo-see-oh)*
disability incapacidad, la *(lah een-kah-pah-see-'dahd)*
disaster desastre, el *(ehl deh-'sah-streh*
discount descuento, el *(ehl dehs-'kwehn-toh)*
discover (to) descubrir *(deh-skoo-'breer)*
discuss (to) discutir *(dee-skoo-'teer)*
disease enfermedad, la *(lah ehn-fehr-meh-'dahd)*
dish plato, el *(ehl 'plah-toh)*
dish washer lavador de platos, el *(ehl lah-bah-'dohr deh 'plah-tohs)*
dishwasher lavaplatos, el *(ehl lah-bah-'plah-tohs)*
dishwashing detergent jabón para los platos, el *(ehl hah-'bohn 'pah-rah lohs 'plah-tohs)*

disinfect (to)   desinfectar *(dehs-een-fehk-'tahr)*
disinfectant   desinfectante, el *(ehl dehs-een-fehk-'tahn-teh)*
disposable   desechable *(dee-seh-'chah-bleh)*
dissolve (to)   disolver *(dee-sohl-'behr)*
ditch   zanja, la *(lah 'sahn-hah)*
divide (to)   dividir *(dee-bee-'deer)*
diving board   trampolín, el *(ehl trahm-poh-'leen)*
divorce   divorcio, el *(ehl dee-'bohr-see-oh)*
do (to)   hacer *(ah-'sehr)*
doctor   doctor, el *(ehl dohk-'tohr)*
dog   perro, el *(ehl 'peh-rroh)*
doll   muñeca, la *(lah moo-'nyeh-kah)*
dollar   dólar, el *(ehl 'doh-lahr)*
don't   no *(noh)*
door   puerta, la *(lah 'pwehr-tah)*
doorbell   timbre, el *(ehl 'teem-breh)*
doorman   portero, el *(ehl pohr-'teh-roh)*
double   doble *('doh-bleh)*
dough   masa, la *(lah 'mah-sah)*
down   abajo *(ah-'bah-hoh)*
downtown   centro, el *(ehl 'sehn-troh)*
dozen   docena, la *(lah doh-'seh-nah)*
drain   desaguadero, el *(ehl dehs-ah-gwah-'deh-roh)*
drain (to)   desaguar *(dehs-ah-'gwahr)*
drainage   drenaje, el *(ehl dreh-'nah-heh)*
draperies   colgaduras, los *(lohs kohl-gah-'doo-rahs)*
draw (to)   dibujar *(dee-boo-'hahr)*
drawer   cajón, el *(ehl kah-'hohn)*
dream (to)   soñar *(soh-'nyahr)*
dresser   tocador, el *(ehl toh-kah-'dohr)*
drill   taladro, el *(ehl tah-'lah-droh)*
drill (to)   taladrar *(tah-lah-'drahr)*
drink   bebida, la *(lah beh-'bee-dah)*
drink (to)   beber, tomar *(beh-'behr, toh-'mahr)*
drip (to)   chorrear *(choh-rreh-'ahr)*
drive (to)   manejar *(mah-neh-'hahr)*
driver   chofer, el *(ehl choh-'fehr)*
driveway   entrada para carros, la *(lah ehn-'trah-dah 'pah-rah 'kah-rrohs)*
drop   gota, la *(lah 'goh-tah)*
drug   droga, la *(lah 'droh-gah)*
drum   tambor, el *(ehl tahm-'bohr)*
dry   seco *('seh-koh)*
dry (to)   secar *(seh-'kahr)*
dryer   secadora, la *(lah seh-kah-'doh-rah)*
duck   pato, el *(ehl 'pah-toh)*
duct   conducto, el *(ehl kohn-'dook-toh)*
dull   romo *('roh-moh)*

dump (to)   tirar *(tee-'rahr)*
duster   plumero, el *(ehl ploo-'meh-roh)*
dusk   anochecer, el *(ehl ah-noh-cheh-'sehr)*
dust   polvo, el *(ehl 'pohl-boh)*
dust (to)   sacudir *(sah-koo-'deer)*
each   cada *('kah-dah)*
ear   oído, el *(ehl oh-'ee-doh)*
early   temprano *(tehm-'prah-noh)*
earn (to)   ganar *(gah-'nahr)*
earring   arete, el *(ehl ah-'reh-teh)*
earthquake   terremoto, el *(ehl teh-rreh-'moh-toh)*
east   este *('eh-steh)*
easy   fácil *('fah-seel)*
eat (to)   comer *(koh-'mehr)*
edge   borde, el *(ehl 'bohr-deh)*
egg   huevo, el *(ehl 'weh-boh)*
eight   ocho *('oh-choh)*
eighteen   dieciocho *(dee-ehs-ee-'oh-choh)*
eighth   octavo *('ohk-'tah-boh)*
eighty   ochenta *(oh-'chehn-tah)*
elbow   codo, el *(ehl 'koh-doh)*
electric   eléctrico *(eh-'lehk-tree-koh)*
electrician   electricista, el *(ehl eh-lehk-tree-'sees-tah)*
elephant   elefante, el *(ehl eh-leh-'fahn-teh)*
elevator   elevador, el *(ehl eh-leh-bah-'dohr)*
eleven   once *('ohn-seh)*
elm   olmo, el *(ehl 'ohl-moh)*
embroidery   bordado, el *(ehl bohr-'dah-doh)*
emerald   esmeralda, la *(lah ehs-meh-'rahl-dah)*
employ (to)   emplear *(ehm-pleh-'ahr)*
empty   vacío *(bah-'see-oh)*
empty (to)   vaciar *(bah-see-'ahr)*
end   punta, la *(lah 'poon-tah)*
engagement   cita, la *(lah 'see-tah)*
engine   motor, el *(ehl moh-'tohr)*
engineer   ingeniero, el *(ehl een-heh-nee-'eh-roh)*
English   inglés, el *(ehl een-'glehs)*
enjoy (to)   disfrutar *(dees-froo-'tahr)*
enough   bastante *(bah-'stahn-teh)*
enter (to)   entrar *(ehn-'trahr)*
entrance   entrada, la *(lah ehn-'trah-dah)*
envelope   sobre, el *(ehl 'soh-breh)*
equipment   equipo, el *(ehl eh-'kee-poh)*
erase (to)   borrar *(boh-'rrahr)*
errand   encargo, el *(ehl ehn-'kahr-goh)*
escalator   escala mecánica, la *(lah eh-'skah-lah meh-'kah-nee-kah)*
everybody   todo el mundo *('toh-doh ehl 'moon-doh)*
everything   todo *('toh-doh)*

everywhere   por todas partes *(pohr 'toh-dahs 'pahr-tehs)*

excellent   excelente *(ehk-seh-'lehn-teh)*

excited   excitado *(ehk-see-'tah-doh)*

exercise   ejercicio, el *(ehl eh-hehr-'see-see-oh)*

exit   salida, la *(lah sah-'lee-dah)*

expensive   caro *('kah-roh)*

experience   experiencia, la *(lah ehks-peh-ree-'ehn-see·ah)*

explain (to)   explicar *(ehks-plee-'kahr)*

exterminator   exterminador, el *(ehl ehks-tehr-mee-nah-'dohr)*

eye   ojo, el *(ehl 'oh-hoh)*

fabric softener   suavizador, el *(ehl swah-bee-sah-'dohr)*

face   cara, la *(lah 'kah-rah)*

factory   fábrica, la *(lah 'fah-bree-kah)*

fall (to)   caer *(cah-'ehr)*

family   familia, la *(lah fah-'mee-lee·ah)*

famous   famoso *(fah-'moh-soh)*

far   lejos *('leh-hohs)*

farmer   campesino, el *(ehl kahm-peh-'see-noh)*

fast   rápido *('rah-pee-doh)*

fasten (to)   amarrar *(ah-mah-'rrahr)*

fat   gordo *('gohr-doh)*

father   padre, el *(ehl 'pah-dreh)*

father-in-law   suegro, el *(ehl 'sweh-groh)*

faucet   grifo, el *(ehl 'gree-foh)*

fault   culpa, la *(lah 'kool-pah)*

favor   favor, el *(ehl fah-'bohr)*

fear   miedo, el *(ehl mee-'eh-doh)*

February   febrero *(feh-'breh-roh)*

feed (to)   alimentar *(ah-lee-mehn-'tahr)*

fence   cerca, la *(lah 'sehr-kah)*

fern   helecho, el *(ehl eh-'leh-choh)*

fertilize (to)   fertilizar *(ferh-tee-lee-'sahr)*

fertilizer   abono, el *(ehl ah-'boh-noh)*

fever   fiebre, la *(lah fee-'eh-breh)*

few   pocos *('poh-kohs)*

field   campo, el *(ehl 'kahm-poh)*

fifteen   quince *('keen-seh)*

fifty   cincuenta *(seen-'kwehn-tah)*

fig   higo, el *(ehl 'ee-goh)*

fight (to)   pelear *(peh-leh-'ahr)*

file   lima, la *(lah 'lee-mah)*

file (to)   limar *(lee-'mahr)*

fill (to)   llenar *(yeh-'nahr)*

film   película, la *(lah peh-'lee-koo-lah)*

filter   filtro, el *(ehl 'feel-troh)*

find (to)   encontrar *(ehn-kohn-'trahr)*

fine   bien *('bee-ehn)*

finger   dedo, el *(ehl 'deh-doh)*

fingernail   uña, la *(lah 'oo-nyah)*

finish (to)   terminar *(tehr-mee-'nahr)*

fire   fuego, el *(el 'fweh-goh)*

fire (to)   despedir *(dehs-peh-'deer)*

fire fighter   bombero, el *(ehl bohm-'beh-roh)*

fireplace   fogón, el *(ehl foh-'gohn)*

fireworks   fuegos artificiales, los *(lohs 'fweh-gohs ahr-tee-fee-see-'ah-lehs)*

first   primero *(pree-meh-roh)*

first aid   primeros auxilios, los *(lohs pree-'meh-rohs aw·ook-'see-lee-ohs)*

fish   pescado, el *(ehl peh-'skah-doh)*

fish (to)   pescar *(pehs-'kahr)*

fishes   peces, los *(lohs 'peh-sehs)*

five   cinco *('seen-koh)*

fix (to)   reparar *(reh-pah-'rahr)*

fixture   instalación, la *(lah een-stah-lah-see·'ohn)*

flame   llama, la *(lah 'yah-mah)*

flashlight   linterna, la *(lah leen-'tehr-nah)*

flea   pulga, la *(lah 'pool-gah)*

flight   vuelo, el *(ehl 'bweh-loh)*

flood   inundación, la *(lah een-oon-dah-see·'ohn)*

floor   piso, el *(ehl 'pee-soh)*

floor tile   baldosa, la *(lah bahl-'doh-sah)*

florist   florista, el *(ehl floh-'rees-tah)*

flour   harina, la *(lah ah-'ree-nah)*

flower   flor, la *(lah flohr)*

flu (cold)   resfriado, el *(ehl rehs-free-'ah-doh)*

fly   mosca, la *(lah 'mohs-kah)*

fly (to)   volar *(boh-'lahr)*

fold   doblar *(doh-'blahr)*

foliage   follaje, el *(ehl foh-'yah-heh)*

follow (to)   seguir *(seh-'geer)*

food   comida, la *(lah koh-'mee-dah)*

foot   pie, el *(ehl 'pee-eh)*

football   fútbol americano *(ehl 'foot-bohl ah-meh-ree-'kah-noh)*

for   para, por *('pah-rah, pohr)*

forest   bosque, el *(ehl 'boh-skeh)*

forget   olvidar *(ohl-bee-'dahr)*

fork   tenedor, el *(ehl teh-neh-'dohr)*

form   forma, la *(lah 'fohr-mah)*

forsythia   forsitia, la *(lah fohr-'see-tee·ah)*

forty   cuarenta *(kwah-'rehn-tah)*

forward   adelante *(ah-deh-'lahn-teh)*

fountain   fuente, la *(lah 'fwehn-teh)*

four   cuatro *('kwah-troh)*

fourteen   catorce *(kah-'tohr-seh)*

fourth   cuarto *('kwahr-toh)*

fox   zorro, el *(ehl 'soh-rroh)*

freeze (to)   congelar *(kohn-heh-'lahr)*

freezer congelador, el *(ehl kohn-heh-lah-'dohr)*
fresh fresco *('freh-skoh)*
Friday viernes *(bee-'ehr-nehs)*
frog sapo, el *(ehl 'sah-poh)*
from de *(deh)*
front frente, el *(ehl 'frehn-teh)*
frost escarcha, la *(lah eh-'skahr-chah)*
frostbite congelamiento, el *(ehl kohn-heh-lah-mee-'ehn-toh)*
fruit fruta, la *(lah 'froo-tah)*
fry (to) freír *(freh-'eer)*
frying pan sartén, el *(ehl sahr-'tehn)*
full lleno *('yeh-noh)*
function (to) funcionar *(foon-see-oh-'nahr)*
fungus hongo, el *(ehl 'ohn-goh)*
funnel embudo, el *(ehl ehm-'boo-doh)*
funny curioso *(koo-ree-'oh-soh)*
fur piel, la *(lah pee-'ehl)*
furniture muebles, los *(lohs 'mweh-blehs)*
fuse fusible, el *(ehl foo-'see-bleh)*
fuse box caja de fusibles, la *(lah 'kah-hah deh foo-'see-blehs)*
gallon galón, el *(ehl gah-'lohn)*
game juego, el *(ehl hoo-'eh-goh)*
garage garaje, el *(ehl gah-'rah-heh)*
garbage basura, la *(lah bah-'soo-rah)*
garbage disposal desechador, el *(ehl dehs-eh-chah-'dohr)*
garden jardín, el *(ehl hahr-'deen)*
gardener jardinero, el *(ehl hahr-dee-'neh-roh)*
garlic ajo, el *(ehl 'ah-hoh)*
gas gasolina, la *(lah gah-soh-'lee-nah)*
gate portón, el *(ehl pohr-'tohn)*
gentle delicado *(deh-lee-'kah-doh)*
gift regalo, el *(ehl reh-'gah-loh)*
gin ginebra, la *(lah hee-'neh-brah)*
giraffe jirafa, la *(lah hee-'rah-fah)*
girdle faja, la *(lah 'fah-hah)*
girl niña, la *(lah 'nee-nyah)*
girlfriend novia, la *(lah 'noh-bee-ah)*
give (to) dar *(dahr)*
glass vidrio, el *(ehl 'bee-dree-oh)*
glass (drinking) vaso, el *(ehl 'bah-soh)*
glasses lentes, los *(lohs 'lehn-tehs)*
glove guante, el *(ehl 'gwahn-teh)*
glue pegamento, el *(ehl peh-gah-'mehn-toh)*
glue (to) pegar *(peh-'gahr)*
go (to) ir *(eer)*
go to bed (to) acostarse *(ah-koh-'stahr-seh)*
goat chivo, el *(ehl 'chee-boh)*
God Dios *('dee-ohs)*
godchild ahijado, el *(ehl ah-ee-'hah-doh)*

godfather compadre, el *(ehl kohm-'pah-dreh)*
godmother comadre, la *(lah koh-'mah-dreh)*
gold oro, el *(ehl 'oh-roh)*
golf golf, el *(ehl gohlf)*
golf course campo de golf, el *(ehl 'kahm-poh deh gohlf)*
good bueno *('bweh-noh)*
good-bye adiós *(ah-dee-'ohs)*
grain grano, el *(ehl 'grah-noh)*
granddaughter nieta, la *(lah nee-'eh-tah)*
grandfather abuelo, el *(ehl ah-'bweh-loh)*
grandmother abuela, la *(lah ah-'bweh-lah)*
grandson nieto, el *(ehl nee-'eh-toh)*
grape uva, la *(lah 'oo-bah)*
grapefruit toronja, la *(lah toh-'rohn-hah)*
grass la hierba, el pasto *(lah 'yehr-bah, ehl 'pah-stoh)*
grasshopper saltamontes, el *(ehl sahl-tah-'mohn-tehs)*
grate (to) rallar *(rah-'yahr)*
gravel grava, la *(lah 'grah-bah)*
gray gris *(grees)*
grease grasa, la *(lah 'grah-sah)*
green verde *('behr-deh)*
grill parrilla, la *(lah pah-'rree-yah)*
grill (to) asar *(ah-'sahr)*
grind (to) moler *(moh-'lehr)*
groceries comestibles, los *(lohs koh-meh-'stee-blehs)*
grove arboleda, la *(lah ahr-boh-'leh-dah)*
grow (to) crecer *(kreh-'sehr)*
guess (to) adivinar *(ah-dee-bee-'nahr)*
guest huésped, el *(ehl 'wehs-pehd)*
guide guía, el *(ehl 'gee-ah)*
guitar guitarra, la *(lah gee-'tah-rrah)*
gum (chewing) chicle, el *(ehl 'chee-kleh)*
gums encías, las *(lahs ehn-'see-ahs)*
gymnasium gimnasio, el *(ehl heem-'nah-see-oh)*
hair pelo, el *(ehl 'peh-loh)*
hair dryer secador de pelo, el *(ehl seh-kah-'dohr deh 'peh-loh)*
half mitad, la *(lah mee-'tahd)*
hallway pasillo, el *(ehl pah-'see-yoh)*
ham jamón, el *(ehl hah-'mohn)*
hamburger hamburguesa, la *(lah ahm-boor-'geh-sah)*
hammer martillo, el *(ehl mahr-'tee-yoh)*
hammock hamaca, la *(lah ah-'mah-kah)*
hand mano, la *(lah 'mah-noh)*
handkerchief pañuelo, el *(ehl pah-nyoo-'eh-loh)*
handle tirador, el *(ehl tee-rah-'dohr)*

handsome guapo *('gwah-poh)*
hang (to) colgar *(kohl-'gahr)*
hanger gancho, el *(ehl 'gahn-choh)*
happy contento *(kohn-'tehn-toh)*
Happy Birthday! ¡Feliz cumpleaños! *(feh-'lees koom-pleh-'ah-nyohs)*
Happy Easter! ¡Felices Pascuas! *(feh-'lee-sehs 'pah-skwahs)*
Happy New Year! ¡Feliz Año Nuevo! *(feh-'lees 'ah-nyoh noo-'eh-boh)*
hard duro *('doo-roh)*
hat sombrero, el *(ehl sohm-'breh-roh)*
hate (to) odiar *(oh-dee-'ahr)*
have (to) tener *(teh-'nehr)*, haber *(ah-'behr)*
have to (to) tener que *(teh-'nehr keh)*
hawk halcón, el *(ehl ahl-'kohn)*
hay heno, el *(ehl 'eh-noh)*
he él *(ehl)*
head cabeza, la *(lah kah-'beh-sah)*
health salud, la *(lah sah-'lood)*
health insurance card tarjeta de salud, la *(lah tahr-'heh-tah deh sah-'lood)*
hear (to) oír *(oh-'eer)*
heart corazón, el *(ehl koh-rah-'sohn)*
heat calor, el *(ehl kah-'lohr)*
heat (to) calentar *(kah-lehn-'tahr)*
heater calentador, el *(ehl kah-lehn-tah-'dohr)*
heating calefacción, la *(lah kah-leh-fahk-see-'ohn)*
heavy pesado *(peh-'sah-doh)*
height altura *(ahl-'too-rah)*
helicopter helicóptero, el *(ehl eh-lee-'kohp-teh-roh)*
helmet casco, el *(ehl 'kah-skoh)*
help ayuda, la *(lah ah-'yoo-dah)*
help (to) ayudar *(ah-yoo-'dahr)*
her su *(soo)*
here aquí *(ah-'kee)*
hi hola *('oh-lah)*
hide (to) esconder *(eh-skohn-'dehr)*
high alto *('ahl-toh)*
highway carretera, la *(lah kah-rreh-'teh-rah)*
hill cerro, el *(ehl 'seh-rroh)*
hip cadera, la *(lah kah-'deh-rah)*
hire (to) contratar *(kohn-trah-'tahr)*
his su *(soo)*
hit (to) golpear *(gohl-peh-'ahr)*
hoe azadón, el *(ehl ah-sah-'dohn)*
hole hoyo, el *(ehl 'oh-yoh)*
holiday día de fiesta, el *(ehl 'dee-ah deh fee-'eh-stah)*

honey miel, la *(lah mee-'ehl)*
hornet avispa, la *(lah ah-'vees-pah)*
horse caballo, el *(ehl kah-'bah-yoh)*
horseback riding equitación, la *(lah eh-kee-tah-see-'ohn)*
hose manguera, la *(lah mahn-'geh-rah)*
hospital hospital, el *(ehl oh-spee-'tahl)*
hot caliente *(kah-lee-'ehn-teh)*
hot pepper chile, el *(ehl 'chee-leh)*
hot water heater calentador para el agua, *(ehl kah-'lehn-tah-dohr 'pah-rah ehl 'ah-gwah)*
house casa, la *(lah 'kah-sah)*
how cómo *('koh-moh)*
how many cuántos *('kwahn-tohs)*
how much cuánto *('kwahn-toh)*
hug abrazo, el *(ehl ah-'brah-soh)*
hug (to) abrazar *(ah-brah-'sahr)*
hunger hambre, el *(ehl 'ahm-breh)*
hunt (to) cazar *(kah-'sahr)*
hurricane huracán, el *(ehl oo-rah-'kahn)*
hurry (to) apurarse *(ah-poo-'rahr-seh)*
hurt (to) herir *(eh-'reer)*
husband esposo, el *(ehl eh-'spoh-soh)*
I yo *(yoh)*
ice hielo, el *(ehl 'yeh-loh)*
ice cream helado, el *(ehl eh-'lah-doh)*
if si *(see)*
ignite (to) prender *(prehn-'dehr)*
imaginative imaginativo *(ee-mah-hee-nah-'tee-boh)*
important importante *(eem-pohr-'tahn-teh)*
in en *(ehn)*
inch pulgada, la *(lah pool-'gah-dah)*
include (to) incluir *(een-kloo-'eer)*
indigestion indigestión, la *(lah een-dee-hehs-tee-'ohn)*
information información, la *(lah een-fohr-mah-see-'ohn)*
injury herida, la *(lah eh-'ree-dah)*
insert (to) meter *(meh-'tehr)*
inside adentro *(ah-'dehn-troh)*
inspect (to) inspeccionar *(een-spehk-see-oh-'nahr)*
install (to) instalar *(een-stah-'lahr)*
instruction instrucción, la *(lah een-strook-see-'ohn)*
instrument instrumento, el *(ehl een-stroo-'mehn-toh)*
insulation aislamiento, el *(ehl ah-ees-lah-mee-'ehn-toh)*
insurance seguro, el *(ehl seh-'goo-roh)*
intelligent inteligente *(een-teh-lee-'hehn-teh)*

interesting interesante *(een-teh-reh-'sahn-teh)*
interpret (to) interpretar *(een-tehr-preh-'tahr)*
interview entrevista, la *(lah ehn-treh-'bee-stah)*
invoice factura, la *(lah fahk-'too-rah)*
iodine yodo, el *(ehl 'yoh-doh)*
iron plancha, la *(lah 'plahn-chah)*
iron (to) planchar *(plahn-'chahr)*
irrigation irrigación, la *(lah ee-ree-gah-see-'ohn)*
ivy hiedra, la *(lah 'yeh-dra)*
jacket chaqueta, la *(lah chah-'keh-tah)*
jail cárcel, la *(lah 'kahr-sehl)*
janitor conserje, el *(ehl kohn-'sehr-heh)*
January enero *(eh-'neh-roh)*
Japanese japonés *(hah-poh-'nehs)*
jar frasco, el *(ehl 'frah-skoh)*
jello gelatina, la *(lah heh-lah-'tee-nah)*
jewelry joyas, las *(lahs 'hoh-yahs)*
job trabajo, el *(ehl trah-'bah-hoh)*
join (to) juntar *(hoon-'tahr)*
joint unión, la *(lah oo-nee-'ohn)*
joke chiste, el *(ehl 'chee-steh)*
juice jugo, el *(ehl 'hoo-goh)*
July julio *('hoo-lee-oh)*
June junio *('hoo-nee-oh)*
jungle selva, la *(lah 'sehl-bah)*
just apenas *(ah-'peh-nahs)*
keep (to) guardar *(gwahr-'dahr)*
key llave, la *(lah 'yah-beh)*
kick (to) patear *(pah-teh-'ahr)*
kill (to) matar *(mah-'tahr)*
kind (type of) tipo, el *(ehl 'tee-poh)*
kind (nice) bondadoso *(bohn-dah-'doh-soh)*
kiss beso, el *(ehl 'beh-soh)*
kiss (to) besar *(beh-'sahr)*
kitchen cocina, la *(lah koh-'see-nah)*
kite cometa, la *(lah koh-'meh-tah)*
knee rodilla, la *(lah roh-'dee-yah)*
knife cuchillo, el *(ehl koo-'chee-yoh)*
knit (to) tejer *(teh-'hehr)*
knob perilla, la *(lah peh-'ree-yah)*
knot nudo, el *(ehl 'noo-doh)*
know someone (to) conocer a alguien *(koh-noh-'sehr ah 'ahl-hee-ehn)*
know something (to) saber *(sah-'behr)*
label etiqueta, la *(lah eh-tee-'keh-tah)*
laborer obrero, el *(ehl oh-'breh-roh)*
lace encaje, el *(ehl ehn-'kah-heh)*
lacrosse lacrosse, el *(ehl lah-'kroh-sseh)*
ladder escalera, la *(lah eh-skah-'leh-rah)*
ladle cucharón, el *(ehl koo-chah-'rohn)*

lake lago, el *(ehl 'lah-goh)*
lamb cordero, el *(ehl kohr-'deh-roh)*
lampshade pantalla, la *(lah pahn-'tah-yah)*
land terreno, el *(ehl teh-'rreh-noh)*
language lenguaje, el *(ehl lehn-'gwah-heh)*
lard manteca, la *(lah mahn-'teh-kah)*
latch cerrojo, el *(ehl seh-'rroh-hoh)*
late tarde *('tahr-deh)*
later luego *(loo-'eh-goh)*
laugh (to) reír *(reh-'eer)*
laundromat lavandería, la *(lah lah-bahn-deh-'ree-ah)*
laundry ropa sucia, la *(lah 'roh-pah 'soo-see-ah)*
lawn césped, el *(ehl 'seh-spehd)*
lawn mower segadora, la *(lah seh-gah-'doh-rah)*
lawyer abogado, el *(ehl ah-boh-'gah-doh)*
lazy perezoso *(peh-reh-'soh-soh)*
leaf hoja, la *(lah 'oh-hah)*
learn aprender *(ah-prehn-'dehr)*
leash traílla, la *(lah trah-'ee-yah)*
leather cuero, el *(ehl 'kweh-roh)*
leave (to) salir *(sah-'leer)*
left izquierda *(ees-kee-'ehr-dah)*
leg pierna, la *(lah pee-'ehr-nah)*
lemon limón, el *(ehl lee-'mohn)*
lemonade limonada, la *(lah lee-moh-'nah-dah)*
lend (to) prestar *(preh-'stahr)*
length largo, el *(ehl 'lahr-goh)*
less menos *('meh-nohs)*
lettuce lechuga, la *(lah leh-'choo-gah)*
level nivel, el *(ehl nee-'behl)*
librarian bibliotecario, el *(ehl bee-blee-oh-teh-'kah-ree-oh)*
library biblioteca, la *(lah bee-blee-oh-'teh-kah)*
license licencia, la *(lah lee-'sehn-see-ah)*
lie (to) mentir *(mehn-'teer)*
life vida, la *(lah 'bee-dah)*
lift (to) levantar *(leh-bahn-'tahr)*
light luz, la *(lah loos)*
lightning relámpago, el *(ehl reh-'lahm-pah-goh)*
like (to) gustar *(goh-'stahr)*
lime lima, la *(lah 'lee-mah)*
line línea, la *(lah 'lee-neh-ah)*
linen lino, el *(ehl 'lee-noh)*
linoleum linóleo, el *(ehl lee-'noh-leh-oh)*
lint hilas, las *(lahs 'ee-lahs)*
lip labio, el *(ehl 'lah-bee-oh)*
liquid líquido, el *(ehl 'lee-kee-doh)*
liquor licor, el *(ehl lee-'kohr)*

list   lista, la *(lah 'lee-stah)*
listen (to)   escuchar *(eh-skoo-'chahr)*
liver   hígado, el *(ehl 'ee-gah-doh)*
living room   sala, la *(lah 'sah-lah)*
lizard   lagarto, el *(ehl lah-'gahr-toh)*
load   carga, la *(lah 'kahr-gah)*
load (to)   cargar *(kahr-'gahr)*
lobby   vestíbulo, el *(ehl beh-'stee-boo-loh)*
lobster   langosta, la *(lah lahn-'goh-stah)*
lock   cerradura, la *(lah seh-rrah-'doo-rah)*
lock (to)   cerrar con llave *(seh-'rrahr kohn 'yah-beh)*
long   largo *('lahr-goh)*
look at (to)   mirar *(mee-'rahr)*
look for (to)   buscar *(boo-'skahr)*
loose   flojo *('floh-hoh)*
lose (to)   perder *(pehr-'dehr)*
lost   perdido *(pehr-'dee-doh)*
love   amor, el *(ehl ah-'mohr)*
love (to)   amar *(ah-'mahr)*
lovely   lindo *('leen-doh)*
low   bajo *('bah-hoh)*
lower (to)   bajar *(bah-'hahr)*
luggage   equipaje, el *(ehl eh-kee-'pah-heh)*
lumber   madera, la *(lah mah-'deh-rah)*
lunch   almuerzo, el *(ehl ahl-moo-'ehr-soh)*
lung   pulmón, el *(ehl pool-'mohn)*
machine   máquina, la *(lah 'mah-kee-nah)*
magazine   revista, la *(lah reh-'bee-stah)*
maid   criada, la *(lah kree-'ah-dah)*
mail   correo, el *(ehl koh-'rreh-oh)*
mail carrier   cartero, el *(ehl kahr-'teh-roh)*
mailbox   buzón, el *(ehl boo-'sohn)*
maintain (to)   mantener *(mahn-tehn-'nehr)*
make the bed (to)   tender la cama *(tehn-'dehr lah 'kah-mah)*
make, do (to)   hacer *(ah-'sehr)*
make-up   maquillaje, el *(ehl mah-kee-'yah-heh)*
man   hombre, el *(ehl 'ohm-breh)*
manager   gerente, el *(ehl heh-'rehn-teh)*
many   muchos *('moo-chohs)*
map   mapa, el *(ehl 'mah-pah)*
marble   mármol, el *(ehl 'mahr-mohl)*
March   marzo *('mahr-soh)*
margarine   margarina, la *(lah mahr-gah-'ree-nah)*
marinate (to)   marinar *(mah-ree-'nahr)*
mark (to)   marcar *(mahr-'kahr)*
marry (to)   casarse *(kah-'sahr-seh)*
match   fósforo, el *(ehl 'fohs-foh-roh)*
mattress   colchón, el *(ehl kohl-'chohn)*
mature   maduro *(mah-'doo-roh)*
May   mayo *('mah-yoh)*

maybe   quizás *(kee-'sahs)*
mayonnaise   mayonesa, la *(lah mah-yoh-'neh-sah)*
meals   comidas, las *(lahs koh-'mee-dahs)*
measure (to)   medir *(meh-'deer)*
meat   carne, la *(lah 'kahr-neh)*
meatball   albóndiga, la *(lah ahl-'bohn-dee-gah)*
mechanic   mecánico, el *(ehl meh-'kah-nee-koh)*
medicine   medicina, la *(lah meh-dee-'see-nah)*
medium   mediano *(meh-dee-'ah-noh)*
meet (to)   encontrar *(ehn-kohn-'trahr)*
meeting   conferencia, la *(lah kohn-feh-'rehn-see-ah)*
melt (to)   derretir *(deh-rreh-'teer)*
mend (to)   remendar *(reh-mehn-'dahr)*
Merry Christmas!   ¡Feliz Navidad! *(feh-'lees nah-bee-'dahd)*
message   mensaje, el *(ehl mehn-'sah-heh)*
metal   metal, el *(ehl meh-'tahl)*
meter   medidor, el *(ehl meh-dee-'dohr)*
microwave   microondas, el *(ehl mee-kroh-'ohn-dahs)*
middle   medio, el *(ehl 'meh-dee-oh)*
mildew   moho, el *(ehl 'moh-oh)*
mile   milla, la *(lah 'mee-yah)*
milk   leche, la *(lah 'leh-cheh)*
million   millón, el *(ehl mee-'yohn)*
mine   mío *('mee-oh)*
mint   menta, la *(lah 'mehn-tah)*
mirror   espejo, el *(ehl eh-'speh-hoh)*
miscellaneous   misceláneo *(mee-seh-'lah-neh-oh)*
Miss   señorita *(seh-nyoh-'ree-tah)*
mix (to)   mezclar *(mehs-'klahr)*
mixer   batidora, la *(lah bah-tee-'doh-rah)*
model   modelo, el *(ehl moh-'deh-loh)*
moist   húmedo *('oo-meh-doh)*
mold   molde, el *(ehl 'mohl-deh)*
mole   topo, el *(ehl 'toh-poh)*
Monday   lunes *('loo-nehs)*
money   dinero, el *(ehl dee-'neh-roh)*
monkey   mono, el *(ehl 'moh-noh)*
month   mes, el *(ehl mehs)*
moon   luna, la *(lah 'loo-nah)*
moose   alce, el *(ehl 'ahl-seh)*
mop   trapeador, el *(ehl trah-peh-ah-'dohr)*
mop (to)   trapear *(trah-peh-'ahr)*
more   más *(mahs)*
mosquito   zancudo, el *(ehl sahn-'kooh-doh)*
moth   polilla, la *(lah poh-'lee-yah)*
mother   madre, la *(lah 'mah-dreh)*

mother-in-law suegra, la *(lah 'sweh-grah)*

motorcycle motocicleta, la *(lah moh-toh-see-'kleh-tah)*

mountain montaña, la *(lah mohn-'tah-nyah)*

mouse ratón, el *(ehl rah-'tohn)*

mouth boca, la *(lah 'boh-kah)*

move (to) mover *(moh-'behr)*

movie theater cine, el *(ehl 'see-neh)*

mow (to) cortar el pasto *(kohr-'tahr ehl 'pah-stoh)*

Mr. señor *(seh-'nyohr)*

Mrs. señora *(seh-'nyoh-rah)*

much mucho *('moo-choh)*

mud lodo, el *(ehl 'loh-doh)*

muffler silenciador, el *(ehl see-lehn-see-ah-'dohr)*

museum museo, el *(ehl moo-'seh-oh)*

mushroom champiñón, el *(ehl chahm-pee-'nyohn)*

music música, la *(lah 'moo-see-kah)*

musician músico, el *(ehl 'moo-see-koh)*

mustard mostaza, la *(lah moh-'stah-sah)*

my mi *(mee)*

nail clavo, el *(ehl 'klah-boh)*

name nombre, el *(ehl 'nohm-breh)*

nap siesta, la *(lah see-'eh-stah)*

napkin servilleta, la *(lah sehr-bee-'yeh-tah)*

narrow estrecho *(eh-'streh-choh)*

nationality nacionalidad, la *(lah nah-see-oh-nah-lee-'dahd)*

navel ombligo, el *(ehl ohm-'blee-goh)*

near cerca *('sehr-kah)*

neck cuello, el *(ehl 'kweh-yoh)*

necklace collar, el *(ehl koh-'yahr)*

nectarine nectarina, la *(lah nehk-tah-'ree-nah)*

need (to) necesitar *(neh-seh-see-'tahr)*

needle aguja, la *(lah ah-'goo-hah)*

neighbor vecino, el *(ehl beh-'see-noh)*

neighborhood barrio, el *(ehl 'bah-rree-oh)*

nephew sobrino, el *(ehl soh-'bree-noh)*

nervioso nervioso *(nehr-bee-'oh-soh)*

nest nido, el *(ehl 'nee-doh)*

never nunca *('noon-kah)*

new nuevo *(noo-'eh-boh)*

newspaper periódico, el *(ehl peh-ree-'oh-dee-koh)*

next to al lado *(ahl 'lah-doh)*

nice simpático *(seem-'pah-tee-koh)*

niece sobrina, la *(lah soh-'bree-nah)*

nightmare pesadilla, la *(lah peh-sah-'dee-yah)*

nightstand mesa de noche, la *(lah 'meh-sah deh 'noh-cheh)*

nine nueve *(noo-'eh-beh)*

nineteen diecinueve *(dee-ehs-ee-noo-'eh-beh)*

ninety noventa *(noh-'behn-tah)*

ninth noveno *(noh-'beh-noh)*

no one nadie *('nah-dee-eh)*

noise ruido, el *(ehl roo-'ee-doh)*

none ninguno *(neen-'goo-noh)*

noodle fideo, el *(ehl fee-'deh-oh)*

north norte *('nohr-teh)*

nose nariz, la *(lah nah-'rees)*

notebook cuaderno, el *(ehl kwah-'dehr-noh)*

nothing nada *('nah-dah)*

November noviembre *(noh-bee-'ehm-breh)*

nowadays ahora *(ah-'oh-rah)*

nozzle tobera, la *(lah toh-'beh-rah)*

number número, el *(ehl 'noo-meh-roh)*

nurse enfermero, el *(ehl ehn-fehr-'meh-roh)*

nurse (to) amamantar *(ah-mah-mahn-'tahr)*

nursery (children) guardería, la *(lah gwahr-deh-'ree-ah)*

nursery (plants) criadero, el *(ehl kree-ah-'deh-roh)*

nut (bolt) tuerca, la *(lah too-'ehr-kah)*

nut (food) nuez, la *(lah noo-'ehs)*

oak roble, el *(ehl 'roh-bleh)*

obey (to) obedecer *(oh-beh-deh-'sehr)*

obstruct (to) obstruir *(ohb-stroo-'eer)*

October octubre *(ohk-'too-breh)*

odor olor, el *(ehl oh-'lohr)*

of de *(deh)*

offer oferta, la *(lah oh-'fehr-tah)*

office oficina, la *(lah oh-fee-'see-nah)*

oil aceite, el *(ehl ah-'seh-ee-teh)*

old viejo *(bee-'eh-hoh)*

older mayor *(mah-'yohr)*

olive aceituna, la *(lah ah-seh-ee-'too-nah)*

on en *(ehn)*

once una vez *('oo-nah behs)*

one uno *('oo-noh)*

one hundred cien *('see-ehn)*

onion cebolla, la *(lah seh-'boh-yah)*

only solamente *(soh-lah-'mehn-teh)*

onyx ónix, el *(ehl 'oh-neeks)*

opal ópalo, el *(ehl 'oh-pah-loh)*

open (to) abrir *(ah-'breer)*

operate (to) operar *(oh-peh-'rahr)*

operator operadora, la *(lah oh-peh-rah-'doh-rah)*

opportunity oportunidad, la *(lah oh-pohr-too-nee-'dahd)*

or o *(oh)*

orange (color) anaranjado *(ah-nah-rahn-'hah-doh)*
orange (fruit) naranja, la *(lah nah-'rahn-hah)*
orchard huerta, la *(lah 'wehr-tah)*
order orden, la *(lah 'ohr-dehn)*
order (to) ordenar *(ohr-deh-'nahr)*
organize (to) organizar *(ohr-gah-nee-'sahr)*
ounce onza, la *(lah 'ohn-sah)*
our nuestra *(noo-'eh-strah)*
outdoors afueras, las *(lahs ah-'fweh-rahs)*
outlet enchufe, el *(ehl ehn-'choo-feh)*
outside afuera *(ah-'fweh-rah)*
overcoat abrigo, el *(ehl ah-'bree-goh)*
owe (to) deber *(deh-'behr)*
owl búho, el *(ehl 'boo-oh)*
owner dueño, el *(ehl 'dweh-nyoh)*
P.M. de la tarde *(deh lah 'tahr-deh)*
pacifier chupete, el *(ehl choo-'peh-teh)*
package paquete, el *(ehl pah-'keh-teh)*
padlock candado, el *(ehl kahn-'dah-doh)*
pain dolor, el *(ehl doh-'lohr)*
paint pintura, la *(lah peen-'too-rah)*
paint (to) pintar *(peen-'tahr)*
painting cuadro, el *(ehl 'kwah-droh)*
pair par, el *(ehl pahr)*
pajamas pijama, el *(ehl pee-'hah-mah)*
palm palmera, la *(lah pahl-'meh-rah)*
panties bragas, las *(lahs 'brah-gahs)*, calzones, los *(lohs kahl-'soh-nehs)*
pants pantalones, los *(lohs pahn-tah-'loh-nehs)*
paper papel, el *(ehl pah-'pehl)*
parade desfile, el *(ehl dehs-'fee-leh)*
parakeet perico, el *(ehl peh-'ree-koh)*
parallel paralelo *(ehl pah-rah-'leh-loh)*
paramedic paramédico, el *(ehl pah-rah-'meh-dee-koh)*
parents padres, los *(lohs 'pah-drehs)*
park parque, el *(ehl 'pahr-keh)*
park (to) estacionar *(eh-stah-see-oh-'nahr)*
parking lot estacionamiento, el *(ehl eh-stah-see-oh-nah-mee-'ehn-toh)*
parsley perejil, el *(ehl peh-reh-'heel)*
part parte, la *(lah 'pahr-teh)*
party fiesta, la *(lah fee-'eh-stah)*
paste pasta, la *(lah 'pah-stah)*
path camino, el *(ehl kah-'mee-noh)*
patient paciente, el *(ehl pah-see-'ehn-teh)*
pattern patrón, el *(ehl pah-'trohn)*
pay (to) pagar *(pah-'gahr)*
payment pago, el *(ehl 'pah-goh)*
pea arvejita, la *(lah ahr-beh-'hee-tah)*
peach durazno, el *(ehl doo-'rahs-noh)*

peanut butter crema de maní, la *(lah 'kreh-mah deh mah-'nee)*
pear pera, la *(lah 'peh-rah)*
pearl perla, la *(lah 'pehr-lah)*
pediatrician pediatra, el *(ehl peh-dee-'ah-trah)*
peel (to) pelar *(peh-'lahr)*
pen pluma, la *(lah 'ploo-mah)*
pencil lápiz, el *(ehl 'lah-pees)*
penicillin penicilina, la *(lah peh-nee-see-'lee-nah)*
penis pene, el *(ehl 'peh-neh)*
people gente, la *(lah 'hehn-teh)*
pepper pimienta, la *(lah pee-mee-'ehn-tah)*
percent por ciento *(pohr see-'ehn-toh)*
perfume perfume, el *(ehl pehr-'foo-meh)*
permanent press planchado permanente *(plahn-'chah-doh pehr-mah-'nehn-teh)*
permission permiso, el *(ehl pehr-'mee-soh)*
permit (to) permitir *(pehr-mee-'teer)*
person persona, la *(lah pehr-'soh-nah)*
pet mascota, la *(lah mah-'skoh-tah)*
pharmacist farmacéutico, el *(ehl fahr-mah-'seh-oo-tee-koh)*
pharmacy farmacia, la *(lah fahr-'mah-see-ah)*
photograph foto, la *(lah 'foh-toh)*
pickax pico, el *(ehl 'pee-koh)*
pick (to) recoger *(reh-koh-'hehr)*
pickle encurtido, el *(ehl ehn-koor-'tee-doh)*
picnic comida compestre, la *(lah koh-'mee-dah kahm-'pehs-treh)*
pie pastel, el *(ehl pah-'stehl)*
piece pedazo, el *(ehl peh-'dah-soh)*
pig puerco, el *(ehl 'pwehr-koh)*
pile montón *(ehl mohn-'tohn)*
pill píldora, la *(lah 'peel-doh-rah)*
pillow almohada, la *(lah ahl-moh-'ah-dah)*
pillowcase funda, la *(lah 'foon-dah)*
pilot piloto, el *(ehl pee-'loh-toh)*
pin alfiler, el *(ehl ahl-fee-'lehr)*
pine pino, el *(ehl 'pee-noh)*
pineapple piña, la *(lah 'pee-nyah)*
pint pinta, la *(lah 'peen-tah)*
pipe tubo, el *(ehl 'too-boh)*
pitcher cántaro, el *(ehl 'kahn-tah-roh)*
pitchfork horquilla, la *(lah ohr-'kee-yah)*
place lugar, el *(ehl loo-'gahr)*
plan plano, el *(ehl 'plah-noh)*
plan (to) planear *(plah-neh-'ahr)*
plant planta, la *(lah 'plahn-tah)*
plant (to) plantar *(plahn-'tahr)*
plaster yeso, el *(ehl 'yeh-soh)*
plastic plástico, el *(ehl 'plah-stee-koh)*

plate plato, el *(ehl 'plah-toh)*

play (to) jugar *(hoo-'gahr)*

playground campo de recreo, el *(ehl 'kahm-poh deh reh-'kreh-oh)*

please por favor *(pohr fah-'bohr)*

pliers pinzas, las *(lahs 'peen-sahs)*

plug (to) tapar *(tah-'pahr)*

plug in (to) enchufar *(ehn-choo-'fahr)*

plum ciruela, la *(lah see-roo-'eh-lah)*

plumber plomero, el *(ehl ploh-'meh-roh)*

plumbing tubería, la *(lah too-beh-'ree-ah)*

pocket bolsillo, el *(ehl bohl-'see-yoh)*

point (to) señalar *(seh-nyah-'lahr)*

poison veneno, el *(ehl beh-'neh-noh)*

police policía, la *(lah poh-lee-'see-ah)*

polish lustre, el *(ehl 'loo-streh)*

polish (to) lustrar *(loos-'trar)*

pond charca, la *(lah 'chahr-kah)*

pony caballito, el *(ehl kah-bah-'yee-toh)*

pool piscina, la *(lah pee-'see-nah)*

poor pobre *('poh-breh)*

porch portal, el *(ehl pohr-'tahl)*

porcupine puercoespín, el *(ehl 'pwehr-koh-eh-'speen)*

pork cerdo, el *(ehl 'sehr-doh)*

portrait retrato, el *(ehl reh-'trah-toh)*

position puesto, el *(ehl 'pweh-stoh)*

post poste, el *(ehl 'poh-steh)*

post office correo, el *(ehl koh-'rreh-oh)*

postcard tarjeta postal, la *(lah tahr-'heh-tah poh-'stahl)*

pot (cooking) olla, la *(lah 'oh-yah)*

pot (plant) maceta, la *(lah mah-'seh-tah)*

potato papa, la *(lah 'pah-pah)*

pottery alfarería, la *(lah ahl-fahr-reh-'ree-ah)*

pound libra, la *(lah 'lee-brah)*

pour (to) servir *(sehr-'beer)*

powder polvo, el *(ehl 'pohl-boh)*

power poder, el *(ehl poh-'dehr)*

practice práctica, la *(lah 'prahk-tee-kah)*

practice (to) practicar *(prahk-tee-'kahr)*

pre-cooked pre-cocido *(preh-koh-'see-doh)*

prefer (to) preferir *(preh-feh-'reer)*

pregnant embarazada *(ehm-bah-rah-'sah-dah)*

prepare (to) preparar *(preh-pah-'rahr)*

prescription receta, la *(lah reh-'seh-tah)*

press (to) apretar, oprimir *(ah-preh-'tahr, oh-pree-'meer)*

pretty bonito *(boh-'nee-toh)*

prevent (to) prevenir *(preh-beh-'neer)*

price precio, el *(ehl 'preh-see-oh)*

priest cura, el *(ehl 'koo-rah)*

private privado *(pree-'bah-doh)*

privilege privilegio, el *(ehl pree-bee-'leh-hee-oh)*

problem problema, el *(ehl proh-'bleh-mah)*

procedure procedimiento, el *(ehl proh-seh-dee-mee-'ehn-toh)*

prohibit (to) prohibir *(proh-ee-'beer)*

promise (to) prometer *(proh-meh-'tehr)*

prompt (to) incitar a hacer *(een-see-'tahr ah ah-'sehr)*

pronounce (to) pronunciar *(proh-noon-see-'ahr)*

prune (to) podar *(poh-'dahr)*

pull (to) jalar *(hah-'lahr)*

pudding pudín, el *(ehl poo-'deen)*

pump bomba, la *(lah 'bohm-bah)*

pumpkin calabaza, la *(lah kah-lah-'bah-sah)*

punish (to) castigar *(kah-stee-'gahr)*

punishment castigo, el *(ehl kah-'stee-goh)*

purify (to) purificar *(poo-ree-fee-'kahr)*

purple morado *(moh-'rah-doh)*

purse bolsa, la *(lah 'bohl-sah)*

push (to) empujar *(ehm-poo-'hahr)*

put (to) poner *(poh-'nehr)*

quart cuarta, la *(lah 'kwahr-tah)*

question pregunta, la *(lah preh-'goon-tah)*

quiet quieto *(kee-'eh-toh)*

quilt colcha, la *(lah 'kohl-chah)*

quit (to) renunciar *(reh-noon-see-'ahr)*

rabbit conejo, el *(ehl koh-'neh-hoh)*

race raza, la *(lah 'rah-sah)*

rack estilador, el *(ehl eh-stee-lah-'dohr)*

racoon mapache, el *(ehl mah-'pah-cheh)*

radio radio, el *(ehl 'rah-dee-oh)*

radish rábano, el *(ehl 'rah-bah-noh)*

rag trapo, el *(ehl 'trah-poh)*

railing baranda, la *(lah bah-'rahn-dah)*

rain lluvia, la *(lah 'yoo-bee-ah)*

raincoat impermeable, el *(ehl eem-pehr-meh-'ah-bleh)*

raisin pasa, la *(lah 'pah-sah)*

rake rastrillo, el *(ehl rah-'stree-yoh)*

rake (to) rastrillar *(rah-stree-'yahr)*

rape violación, la *(lah bee-oh-lah-see-'ohn)*

rape (to) violar *(bee-oh-'lahr)*

rash erupción, la *(lah eh-roo—see-'ohn)*

rat rata, la *(lah 'rah-tah)*

raw crudo *('kroo-doh)*

razor navaja, la *(lah nah-'bah-hah)*

read (to) leer *(leh-'ehr)*

ready listo *('lee-stoh)*

rear atrás *(ah-'trahs)*

receipt recibo, el *(ehl reh-'see-boh)*

receive (to) recibir *(reh-see-'beer)*

239

receptionist recepcionista, el or la *(ehl or lah reh-sehp-see-oh-'nee-stah)*

recognize (to) reconocer *(reh-koh-noh-'sehr)*

recommend (to) recomendar *(reh-koh-mehn-'dahr)*

red rojo *('roh-hoh)*

red-headed pelirrojo *(peh-lee-'rroh-hoh)*

refer (to) referir *(reh-feh-'reer)*

references referencias, las *(lahs reh-feh-'rehn-see·ahs)*

relationship relación, la *(lah reh-lah-see-'ohn)*

relative pariente, el *(ehl pah-ree-'ehn-teh)*

religion religión, la *(lah reh-lee-hee-'ohn)*

relocate (to) mudarse *(moo-'dahr-seh)*

remedy remedio, el *(ehl reh-'meh-dee-oh)*

remember (to) recordar *(reh-kohr-'dahr)*

remove (to) quitar *(kee-'tahr)*

renovate (to) renovar *(reh-noh-'bahr)*

repair (to) reparar *(reh-pah-'rahr)*

repeat (to) repetir *(reh-peh-'teer)*

replace (to) reemplazar *(reh-ehm-plah-'sahr)*

respect (to) respetar *(reh-speh-'tahr)*

rest descanso, el *(ehl deh-'skahn-soh)*

rest (to) descansar *(deh-skahn-'sahr)*

restaurant restaurante, el *(ehl reh-stah·oo-'rahn-teh)*

restroom servicio, el *(ehl sehr-'bee-see·oh)*

retire (to) retirar *(reh-tee-'rahr)*

return (to) devolver, volver *(deh-bohl-'behr, bohl-'behr)*

rhododendron rododendro, el *(ehl roh-doh-'dehn-droh)*

rib costilla, la *(lah koh-'stee-yah)*

rice arroz, el *(ehl ah-'rrohs)*

rich rico *('ree-koh)*

ride (to) montar *(mohn-'tahr)*

right derecha *(deh-'reh-chah)*

ring anillo, el *(ehl ah-'nee-yoh)*

rinse (to) enjuagar *(ehn-hoo·ah-'gahr)*

ripe maduro *(mah-'doo-roh)*

river río, el *(ehl 'ree-oh)*

road camino, el *(ehl kah-'mee-noh)*

roast (to) asar *(ah-'sahr)*

roasting pan asador, el *(ehl ah-sah-'dohr)*

robbery robo, el *(ehl 'roh-boh)*

robin petirrojo, el *(ehl peh-tee-'rroh-hoh)*

rock piedra, la *(lah pee-'eh-drah)*

roll panecillo, el *(ehl pah-neh-'see-yoh)*

roll (to) enrollar *(ehn-roh-'yahr)*

roof tejado, el *(ehl teh-'hah-doh)*

roofer techador, el *(ehl teh-chah-'dohr)*

root raíz, la *(lah rah-'ees)*

rope soga, la *(lah 'soh-gah)*

rose rosa, la *(lah 'roh-sah)*

rotten podrido *(poh-'dree-doh)*

rough áspero *('ahs-peh-roh)*

rub (to) frotar *(froh-'tahr)*

rubber goma, la *(lah 'goh-mah*

rug alfombra, la *(lah ahl-'fohm-brah)*

rule regla, la *(lah 'reh-glah)*

run (to) correr *(koh-'rrehr)*

rust herrumbre, la *(lah eh-'rroom-breh)*

rusty herrumbroso *(eh-rroom-'broh-soh)*

rye centeno, el *(ehl sehn-'teh-noh)*

sad triste *('tree-steh)*

safety seguridad, la *(lah seh-goo-ree-'dahd)*

sail (to) navegar *(nah-beh-'gahr)*

salad ensalada, la *(lah ehn-sah-'lah-dah)*

salary sueldo, el *(ehl 'swehl-doh)*

sale venta, la *(lah 'behn-tah)*

salesman vendedor, el *(ehl behn-deh-'dohr)*

saleswoman vendedora, la *(lah behn-deh-'doh-rah)*

salmon salmón, el *(ehl sahl-'mohn)*

salt sal, la *(lah sahl)*

same mismo *('mees-moh)*

sand arena, la *(lah ah-'reh-nah)*

sandal sandalia, la *(lah sahn-'dah-lee·ah)*

sandpaper papel de lija,el *(ehl pah-'pehl deh 'lee-hah)*

Saturday sábado *('sah-bah-doh)*

sauce salsa, la *(lah 'sahl-sah)*

sausage salchicha, la *(lah sahl-'chee-chah)*

sauté (to) saltear *(sahl-teh-'ahr)*

save (to) ahorrar *(ah-oh-'rrahr)*

saw serrucho, el *(ehl seh-'rroo-choh)*

scale báscula, la *(lah 'bah-skoo-lah)*

scarf bufanda, la *(lah boo-'fahn-dah)*

schedule horario, el *(ehl oh-'rah-ree·oh)*

school escuela, la *(lah eh-'skweh-lah)*

scissors tijeras, las *(lahs tee-'heh-rahs)*

scold (to) regañar *(reh-gah-'nyahr)*

scorpion alacrán, el *(ehl ah-lah-'krahn)*

scrape rasguño, el *(ehl rahs-'goo-nyoh)*

scrape (to) raspar *(rah-'spahr)*

scraper raspador, el *(ehl rah-spah-'dohr)*

scratch rasguño, el *(ehl rahs-'goo-nyoh)*

scratch (to) rasguñar *(rahs-goo-'nyahr)*

screen mosquitero, el *(ehl moh-skee-'teh-roh)*

screw tornillo, el *(ehl tohr-'nee-yoh)*

screwdriver atornillador, el *(ehl ah-tohr-nee-yah-'dohr)*

scrub (to) fregar *(freh-'gahr)*

sea mar, el *(ehl 'mahr)*

seafood marisco, el *(ehl mah-'rees-koh)*
seamstress costurera, la *(lah koh-stoo-'reh-rah)*
seat asiento, el *(ehl ah-see-'ehn-toh)*
second segundo *(seh-'goon-doh)*
secretary secretario, el *(ehl seh-kreh-'tah-ree·oh)*
seed semilla, la *(lah seh-'mee-yah)*
seed (to) sembrar *(sehm-'brahr)*
seizure convulsión, la *(lah kohn-bool-see·'ohn)*
sell (to) vender *(behn-'dehr)*
separate (to) separar *(seh-pah-'rahr)*
September septiembre *(sehp-tee-'ehm-breh)*
servant criado, el *(ehl kree-'ah-doh)*
serve (to) servir *(sehr-'beer)*
seven siete *(see-'eh-teh)*
seventeen diecisiete *(dee-ehs-ee-see-'eh-teh)*
seventh séptimo *('sehp-tee-moh)*
seventy setenta *(seh-'tehn-tah)*
sew (to) coser *(koh-'sehr)*
sewing machine máquina de coser, la *(lah 'mah-kee-nah deh koh-'sehr)*
sewage desagüe, el *(ehl dehs-'ah-gweh)*
sex sexo, el *(ehl 'sehk-soh)*
shade sombra, la *(lah 'sohm-brah)*
shake batido, el *(ehl bah-'tee-doh)*
shake (to) agitar *(ah-hee-'tahr)*
shampoo champú, el *(ehl chahm-'poo)*
shape forma, la *(lah 'fohr-mah)*
shape (to) formar *(fohr-'mahr)*
share (to) repartir *(reh-pahr-'teer)*
sharp agudo *(ah-'goo-doh)*
shave (to) afeitar *(ah-feh·ee-'tahr)*
she ella *('eh-yah)*
shed cobertizo, el *(ehl koh-behr-'tee-soh)*
sheep oveja, la *(lah oh-'beh-hah)*
sheet sábana, la *(lah 'sah-bah-nah)*
sheets (to change) cambiar las sábanas *(kahm-bee-'ahr lahs 'sah-bah-nahs)*
shelf repisa, la *(lah reh-'pee-sah)*
shirt camisa, la *(lah kah-'mee-sah)*
shoe zapato, el *(ehl sah-'pah-toh)*
shopping compras, las *(lahs 'kohm-prahs)*
shopping (to go ...) ir de compras *(eer deh 'kohm-prahs)*
short (in height) bajo *('bah-hoh)*
short (in length) corto *('kohr-toh)*
shorts calzoncillos, los *(lohs kahl-sohn-'see-yohs)*
shoulder hombro, el *(ehl 'ohm-broh)*
shout (to) gritar *(gree-'tahr)*
shovel pala, la *(lah 'pah-lah)*
show mostrar *(moh-'strahr)*

showroom salón de demostraciones, el *(ehl sah-'lohn deh deh-moh-strah-see·'ohn-nehs)*
shower ducha, la *(lah 'doo-chah)*
shrimp camarón, el *(ehl kah-mah-'rohn)*
sick enfermo *(ehn-'fehr-moh)*
side lado, el *(ehl 'lah-doh)*
sidewalk acera, la *(lah ah-'seh-rah)*
sign anuncio, el *(ehl ah-'noon-see-oh)*
sign (to) firmar *(feer-'mahr)*
silk seda, la *(lah 'seh-dah)*
silver plata, la *(lah 'plah-tah)*
silverware cubiertos, los *(lohs koo-bee-'ehr-tohs)*
sing (to) cantar *(kahn-'tahr)*
single soltero *(sohl-'teh-roh)*
sister hermana, la *(lah ehr-'mah-nah)*
sister-in-law cuñada, la *(lah koo-'nyah-dah)*
sit down (to) sentarse *(sehn-'tahr-seh)*
six seis *('seh·ees)*
sixteen dieciséis *(dee-ehs-ee-'seh·ees)*
sixth sexto *('sehks-toh)*
sixty sesenta *(seh-'sehn-tah)*
size talla, la *(lah 'tah-yah)*
skin piel, la *(lah pee-'ehl)*
skirt falda, la *(lah 'fahl-dah)*
skunk zorrino, el *(ehl soh-'rree-noh)*
sleep (to) dormir *(dohr-'meer)*
sleeve manga, la *(lah 'mahn-gah)*
slice (to) cortar en rodajas *(kohr-'tahr ehn roh-'dah-hahs)*
slipper zapatilla, la *(lah sah-pah-'tee-yah)*
slow lento *('lehn-toh)*
small pequeño *(peh-'keh-nyoh)*
smell (to) oler *(oh-'lehr)*
smile sonrisa, la *(lah sohn-'ree-sah)*
smile (to) sonreír *(sohn-reh-'eer)*
smoke humo, el *(ehl 'oo-moh)*
smoke (to) fumar *(foo-'mahr)*
smooth liso *('lee-soh)*
snack merienda, la *(lah meh-ree-'ehn-dah)*
snail caracol, el *(ehl kah-rah-'kohl)*
snake culebra, la *(lah koo-'leh-brah)*
sneeze estornudo, el *(ehl eh-stohr-'noo-doh)*
snow nieve, la *(lah nee-'eh-beh)*
soak (to) remojar *(reh-moh-'hahr)*
soap jabón, el *(ehl hah-'bohn)*
soccer fútbol, el *(ehl 'foot-bohl)*
social security seguro social, el *(ehl seh-'goo-roh soh-see-'ahl)*
sock calcetín, el *(ehl kahl-seh-'teen)*
sofa sofá, el *(ehl soh-'fah)*
soft suave *('swah-beh)*
soft drink refresco, el *(ehl reh-'freh-skoh)*

soil tierra, la *(lah tee-'eh-rrah)*
soldier soldado, el *(ehl sohl-'dah-doh)*
some algunos *(ahl-'goo-nohs)*
someone alguien *('ahl-gee-ehn)*
something algo *('ahl-goh)*
sometimes a veces *(ah 'beh-sehs)*
son hijo, el *(ehl 'ee-hoh)*
son-in-law yerno, el *(ehl 'yehr-noh)*
song canción, la *(lah kahn-see-'ohn)*
soon pronto *('prohn-toh)*
soup sopa, la *(lah 'soh-pah)*
sour agrio *('ah-gree-oh)*
south sur *(soor)*
spa balneario, el *(ehl bahl-neh-'ah-ree-oh)*
Spanish español, el *(ehl eh-spah-'nyohl)*
spare tire neumático de repuesto, el *(ehl neh-oo-'mah-tee-koh deh reh-'pweh-stoh)*
sparrow gorrión, el *(ehl goh-rree-'ohn)*
speak (to) hablar *(ah-'blahr)*
spend (to) gastar *(gah-'stahr)*
spice especia, la *(lah eh-'speh-see-ah)*
spicy picante *(pee-'kahn-teh)*
spider araña, la *(lah ah-'rah-nyah)*
spill (to) derramarse *(deh-rrah-'mahr-seh)*
spinach espinaca, la *(lah eh-spee-'nah-kah)*
sponge esponja, la *(lah eh-'spohn-hah)*
spoon cuchara, la *(lah koo-'chah-rah)*
sports deportes, los *(lohs deh-'pohr-tehs)*
spray (to) rociar *(roh-see-'ahr)*
spring primavera, la *(lah pree-mah-'beh-rah)*
sprinkler rociadora, la *(lah roh-see-ah-'doh-rah)*
square cuadro, el *(ehl 'kwah-droh)*
squirrel ardilla, la *(lah ahr-'dee-yah)*
stable establo, el *(ehl eh-'stah-bloh)*
stack (to) amontonar *(ah-mohn-toh-'nahr)*
stadium estadio, el *(ehl eh-'stah-dee-oh)*
stain mancha, la *(lah 'mahn-chah)*
stain (to) manchar *(mahn-'chahr)*
stairs escaleras, las *(lahs eh-skah-'leh-rahs)*
stamp estampilla, la *(lah eh-'stahm-'pee-yah)*
stand up (to) enfrentar *(ehn-frehn-'tahr)*
staple grapa, la *(lah 'grah-pah)*
starch almidón, el *(ehl ahl-mee-'dohn)*
start (to) empezar *(ehm-peh-'sahr)*
state estado, el *(ehl eh-'stah-doh)*
statue estatua, la *(lah eh-'stah-too-ah)*
steak bistec, el *(ehl bee-'stehk)*
steal (to) robar *(roh-'bahr)*
steam vapor, el *(ehl bah-'pohr)*
steel acero, el *(ehl ah-'seh-roh)*
steering wheel volante, el *(ehlboh-'lahn-teh)*

stem tallo, el *(ehl 'tah-yoh)*
steps escalones, los *(lohs eh-skah-'loh-nehs)*
stick palo, el *(ehl 'pah-loh)*
stir (to) revolver *(reh-bohl-'behr)*
stocking media, la *(lah 'meh-dee-ah)*
stomach estómago, el *(ehl eh-'stoh-mah-goh)*
stone piedra, la *(lah pee-'eh-drah)*
stonemason albañil, el *(ehl ahl-bah-'nyeel)*
stool banquillo, el *(ehl bahn-'kee-yoh)*
stop (to) parar *(pah-'rahr)*
stop sign señal de alto, la *(lah seh-'nyahl deh 'ahl-toh)*
store tienda, la *(lah tee-'ehn-dah)*
storeroom depósito, el *(ehl deh-'poh-see-toh)*
storm tormenta, la *(lah tohr-'mehn-tah)*
story cuento, el *(ehl 'kwehn-toh)*
stove estufa, la *(lah eh-'stoo-fah)*
straight derecho *(deh-'reh-choh)*
strainer colador, el *(ehl koh-lah-'dohr)*
strange raro *('rah-roh)*
stranger desconocido, el *(ehl dehs-koh-noh-'see-doh)*
strap correa, la *(lah koh-'rreh-ah)*
strawberry fresa, la *(lah 'freh-sah)*
stream arroyo, el *(ehl ah-'rroh-yoh)*
street calle, la *(lah 'kah-yeh)*
stroller cochecillo, el *(ehl koh-cheh-'see-yoh)*
strong fuerte *('fwehr-teh)*
student estudiante, el *(ehl eh-stoo-dee-'ahn-teh)*
subway metro, el *(ehl 'meh-troh)*
sugar azúcar, el *(ehl ah-'soo-kahr)*
suit traje, el *(ehl 'trah-heh)*
summer verano, el *(ehl beh-'rah-noh)*
sun sol, el *(ehl sohl)*
Sunday domingo *(ehl doh-'meen-goh)*
sunglasses lentes de sol, los *(lohs 'lehn-tehs deh sohl)*
sunset puesta del sol, la *(lah 'pweh-stah dehl sohl)*
suntan lotion bronceador, el *(ehl brohn-seh-ah-'dohr)*
supermarket supermercado, el *(ehl soo-pehr-mehr-'kah-doh)*
sure seguro *(seh-'goo-roh)*
surgeon cirujano, el *(ehl see-roo-'hah-noh)*
surprise sorpresa, la *(lah sohr-'preh-sah)*
survive (to) sobrevivir *(soh-breh-bee-'beer)*
swallow (to) tragar *(trah-'gahr)*
swan cisne, el *(ehl 'sees-neh)*
sweater suéter, el *(ehl 'sweh-tehr)*

sweatsuit sudaderas, las *(lahs soo-dah-'deh-rahs)*
sweep (to) barrer *(bah-'rrehr)*
sweet dulce *('dool-seh)*
sweet potato camote, el *(ehl kah-'moh-teh)*
swim (to) nadar *(nah-'dahr)*
switch interruptor, el *(ehl een-teh-rroop-'tohr)*
syrup jarabe, el *(ehl hah-'rah-beh)*
system sistema, el *(ehl see-'steh-mah)*
T-shirt camiseta, la *(lah kah-mee-'seh-tah)*
table mesa, la *(lah 'meh-sah)*
tablecloth mantel, el *(ehl mahn-'tehl)*
tablespoon cucharada, la *(lah koo-chah-'rah-dah)*
tablet tableta, la *(lah tah-'bleh-tah)*
tailor sastre, el *(ehl 'sah-streh)*
take (to) tomar *(toh-'mahr)*
take advantage (to) aprovecharse *(ah-proh-beh-'chahr-seh)*
talcum powder talco, el *(ehl 'tahl-koh)*
tall alto *('ahl-toh)*
tape cinta, la *(lah 'seen-tah)*
tar brea, la *(lah 'breh-ah)*
tea té, el *(ehl teh)*
teach (to) enseñar *(ehn-seh-'nyahr)*
teacher maestro, el *(ehl mah-'eh-stroh)*
teaspoon cucharadita, la *(lah koo-chah-rah-'dee-tah)*
teenager muchacho, el *(ehl moo-'chah-choh)*
telephone teléfono, el *(ehl teh-'leh-foh-noh)*
telephone operator telefonista, la *(lah teh-leh-foh-'nee-stah)*
temperature temperatura, la *(lah tehm-peh-rah-'too-rah)*
ten diez *(dee-'ehs)*
tennis tenis, el *(ehl 'teh-nees)*
tennis shoes zapatillas, las *(lahs sah-pah-'tee-yahs)*
tenth décimo *('deh-see-moh)*
terrace terraza, la *(lah teh-'rrah-sah)*
test examen, el *(ehl ehk-'sah-mehn)*
thanks gracias *('grah-see-ahs)*
that ese *('eh-seh)*
the el (sing.masc.), la (sing.fem.), los (pl.masc.), las (pl. fem.) *(ehl, lah, lohs, lahs)*
their su *(soo)*
then entonces *(ehn-'tohn-sehs)*
there allí *(ah-'yee)*
there is, there are hay *('ah-ee)*
thermometer termómetro, el *(ehl tehr-'moh-meh-troh)*

thermos termo, el *(ehl 'tehr-moh)*
thermostat termostato, el *(ehl tehr-moh-'stah-toh)*
these estos *('eh-stohs)*
they (feminine) ellas *('eh-yahs)*
they (masculine) ellos *('eh-yohs)*
thick grueso *(groo-'eh-soh)*
thief ladrón, el *(ehl lah-'drohn)*
thin delgado *(dehl-'gah-doh)*
thing cosa, la *(lah 'koh-sah)*
think (to) pensar *(pehn-'sahr)*
third tercero *(tehr-'seh-roh)*
thirst sed, la *(lah sehd)*
thirteen trece *('treh-seh)*
thirty treinta *('treh-een-tah)*
this este *('eh-steh)*
those esos *('eh-sohs)*
thousand mil *(meel)*
thread hilo, el *(ehl 'ee-loh)*
three tres *(trehs)*
throat garganta, la *(lah gahr-'gahn-tah)*
throw away (to) tirar *(tee-'rahr)*
thunder trueno, el *(ehl troo-'eh-noh)*
Thursday jueves *(hoo-'eh-behs)*
ticket boleto, el *(ehl boh-'leh-toh)*
tie corbata, la *(lah kohr-'bah-tah)*
tie (to) amarrar *(ah-mah-'rrahr)*
tile loceta, la *(lah loh-'seh-tah)*
time tiempo, el *(ehl tee-'ehm-poh)*
tip propina, la *(lah proh-'pee-nah)*
tire neumático, el *(ehl neh-oo-'mah-tee-koh)*
to a *(ah)*
toast pan tostado, el *(ehl pahn toh-'stah-doh)*
toast (to) tostar *(toh-'stahr)*
toaster tostador, el *(ehl toh-stah-'dohr)*
today hoy *('oh-ee)*
toe dedo del pie, el *(ehl 'deh-doh dehl 'pee-eh)*
toilet excusado, el *(ehl ehk-skoo-'sah-doh)*
toilet paper papel higiénico, el *(ehl pah-'pehl ee-hee-'eh-nee-koh)*
tomato tomate, el *(ehl toh-'mah-teh)*
tomorrow mañana *(mah-'nyah-nah)*
ton tonelada, la *(lah toh-neh-'lah-dah)*
tongue lengua, la *(lah 'lehn-gwah)*
tonight esta noche *('eh-stah 'noh-cheh)*
tool herramienta, la *(lah eh-rrah-mee-'ehn-tah)*
tooth diente, el *(ehl dee-'ehn-teh)*
toothbrush cepillo de dientes, el *(ehl seh-'pee-yoh deh dee-'ehn-tehs)*
toothpaste pasta de dientes, la *(lah 'pah-stah deh dee-'ehn-tehs)*

topaz   topacio, el *(ehl toh-'pah-see·oh)*
torch   antorcha, la *(lah ahn-'tohr-chah)*
torn   rasgado, roto *(rahs-'gah-doh, 'roh-toh)*
touch (to)   tocar *(toh-'kahr)*
tow truck   grúa, la *(lah 'groo-ah)*
toward   hacia *('ah-see-ah)*
towel   toalla, la *(lah toh-'ah-yah)*
toy   juguete, el *(ehl hoo-'geh-teh)*
traffic   tráfico, el *(ehl 'trah-fee-koh)*
traffic signal   semáforo, el *(ehl seh-'mah-foh-roh)*
train   tren, el *(ehl trehn)*
train (to)   entrenar *(ehn-treh-'nahr)*
translate (to)   traducir *(trah-doo-'seer)*
transportation   transporte, el *(ehl trahns-'pohr-teh)*
trash   basura, la *(lah bah-'soo-rah)*
travel (to)   viajar *(bee-ah-'hahr)*
tray   bandeja, la *(lah bahn-'deh-hah)*
tree   árbol, el *(ehl 'ahr-bohl)*
triangle   triángulo, el *(ehl tree-'ahn-goo-loh)*
trip   viaje, el *(ehl bee-'ah-heh)*
truck   camión, el *(ehl kah-mee-'ohn)*
truck driver   camionero, el *(ehl kah-mee-oh-'neh-roh)*
trunk   tronco, el *(ehl 'trohn-koh)*
try (to)   tratar *(trah-'tahr)*
try on (to)   probarse *(proh-'bahr-seh)*
tube   tubo, el *(ehl 'too-boh)*
Tuesday   martes *('mahr-tehs)*
tuna   atún, el *(ehl ah-'toon)*
tunnel   túnel, el *(ehl 'too-nehl)*
turkey   pavo, el *(ehl 'pah-boh)*
turn (to)   voltear *(bohl-teh-'ahr)*
turn off (to)   apagar *(ah-pah-'gahr)*
turn on (to)   prender *(prehn-'dehr)*
turtle   tortuga, la *(lah tohr-'too-gah)*
TV   televisor, el *(ehl teh-leh-bee-'sohr)*
tweezers   pinzas, las *(lahs 'peen-sahs)*
twelve   doce *('doh-seh)*
twenty   veinte *('beh·een-'teh)*
twin   gemelo, el *(ehl heh-'meh-loh)*
two   dos *(dohs)*
typist   mecanógrafa *(lah meh-kah-'noh-grah-fah)*
ugly   feo *('feh-oh)*
umbrella   sombrilla, la *(lah sohm-'bree-yah)*
uncle   tío, el *(ehl 'tee-oh)*
understand (to)   entender *(ehn-tehn-'dehr)*
underwear   ropa interior, la *(lah 'roh-pah een-teh-ree-'ohr)*
uniform   uniforme, el *(ehl oo-nee-'fohr-meh)*
United States   Estados Unidos, los *(lohs eh-'stah-dohs oo-'nee-dohs)*

unload (to)   descargar *(dehs-kahr-'gahr)*
until   hasta *('ah-stah)*
up   arriba *(ah-'rree-bah)*
urine   orina, la *(lah oh-'ree-nah)*
use (to)   usar *(oo-'sahr)*
vacuum (to)   limpiar con aspiradora *(leem-pee-'ahr kohn ah-spee-rah-'doh-rah)*
vacuum cleaner   aspiradora, la *(lah ah-spee-rah-'doh-rah)*
vagina   vagina, la *(lah bah-'hee-nah)*
valley   valle, el *(ehl 'bah-yeh)*
valuable   valioso *(bah-lee-'oh-soh)*
valve   válvula, la *(lah 'bahl-boo-lah)*
vanilla   vainilla, la *(lah bah-ee-'nee-yah)*
vase   florero, el *(ehl floh-'reh-roh)*
veal   ternera, la *(lah tehr-'neh-rah)*
vegetable   vegetal, el *(ehl beh-heh-'tahl)*
vest   chaleco, el *(ehl chah-'leh-koh)*
veterinarian   veterinario, el *(ehl beh-teh-ree-'nah-ree·oh)*
vinegar   vinagre, el *(ehl bee-'nah-greh)*
visitor   visitante, el *(ehl bee-see-'tahn-teh)*
vitamin   vitamina, la *(lah bee-tah-'mee-nah)*
vocabulary   vocabulario, el *(ehl boh-kah-boo-'lah-ree·oh)*
voice   voz, la *(lah bohs)*
volume   volumen, el *(ehl boh-'loo-mehn)*
vomit (to)   vomitar *(boh-mee-'tahr)*
vulgarity   grosería, la *(lah groh-seh-'ree-ah)*
wait (to)   esperar *(eh-speh-'rahr)*
waiter   mesero, el *(ehl meh-'seh-roh)*
wake up (to)   despertar *(dehs-pehr-'tahr)*
walk (to)   caminar *(kah-mee-'nahr)*
wall   pared, la *(lah pah-'rehd)*
wallet   cartera, la *(lah kahr-'teh-rah)*
wallpaper   empapelado, el *(ehl ehm-pah-peh-'lah-doh)*
wall-to-wall carpeting   la alfombra de pared a pared *(lah ahl-'fohm-brah deh pah-'rehd ah pah-'rehd)*
want (to)   querer *(keh-'rehr)*
warehouse   almacén, el *(ehl ahl-mah-'sehn)*
warm   tibio *('tee-bee-oh)*
wash (to)   lavar *(lah-'bahr)*
washcloth   paño, el *(ehl 'pah-nyoh)*
washer   lavadora, la *(lah lah-bah-'doh-rah)*
wasp   avispa, la *(lah ah-'bees-pah)*
waste   desperdicios, los *(lohs dehs-pehr-'dee-see-ohs)*
wastepaper basket   el papelero *(ehl pah-peh-'leh-roh)*
watch   reloj de pulsera, el *(ehl reh-'loh deh pool-'seh-rah)*
watch (to)   mirar *(mee-'rahr)*

water agua, el *(ehl 'ah-gwah)*
water (to) regar *(reh-'gahr)*
wax cera, la *(lah 'seh-rah)*
weak débil *('deh-beel)*
weapon arma, el *(ehl 'ahr-mah)*
wear (to) usar *(oo-'sahr)*
weather tiempo, el *(ehl tee-'ehm-poh)*
wedding boda, la *(lah 'boh-dah)*
Wednesday miércoles *(mee-'ehr-koh-lehs)*
weed mala hierba, la *(lah 'mah-lah 'yehr-bah)*
week semana, la *(lah seh-'mah-nah)*
weekend fin de semana, el *(ehl feen deh seh-'mah-nah)*
weigh (to) pesar *(peh-'sahr)*
weight peso, el *(ehl 'peh-soh)*
welcome bienvenida, la *(lah bee-ehn-beh-'nee-dah)*
well bien *('bee-ehn)*
west oeste *(oh-'eh-steh)*
wet mojado *(moh-'hah-doh)*
what qué *(keh)*
wheelchair silla de ruedas, la *(lah 'see-yah deh roo-'eh-dahs)*
when cuándo *('kwahn-doh)*
where dónde *('dohn-deh)*
which cuál *(kwahl)*
whip (to) batir *(bah-'teer)*
white blanco *('blahn-koh)*
who quién *(kee-'ehn)*
whose de quién *(deh kee-'ehn)*
why por qué *(pohr keh)*
wide ancho *('ahn-choh)*
widow viuda, la *(lah bee-'oo-dah)*
widower viudo, el *(ehl bee-'oo-doh)*
width ancho, el *(ehl 'ahn-choh)*
wife esposa, la *(lah eh-'spoh-sah)*
wind viento, el *(ehl bee-'ehn-toh)*
window ventana, la *(lah behn-'tah-nah)*
wine vino, el *(ehl 'bee-noh)*
winter invierno, el *(ehl een-bee-'ehr-noh)*
wire alambre, el *(ehl ah-'lahm-breh)*
wish (to) desear *(deh-seh-'ahr)*
with con *(kohn)*

within dentro *('dehn-troh)*
without sin *(seen)*
wolf lobo, el *(ehl 'loh-boh)*
woman mujer, la *(lah moo-'hehr)*
wood madera, la *(lah mah-'deh-rah)*
wool lana, la *(lah 'lah-nah)*
word palabra, la *(lah pah-'lah-brah)*
work trabajo, el *(ehl trah-'bah-hoh)*
work (to) trabajar *(trah-bah-'hahr)*
world mundo, el *(ehl 'moon-doh)*
worm gusano, el *(ehl goo-'sah-noh)*
worry (to) preocupar *(preh-oh-koo-'pahr)*
worthless sin valor *(seen bah-'lohr)*
wrap (to) envolver *(ehn-bohl-'behr)*
wren reyezuelo, el *(ehl reh-yeh-soo-'eh-loh)*
wrench llave inglesa, la *(lah 'yah-beh een-'gleh-sah)*
wrist muñeca, la *(lah moo-'nyeh-kah)*
write (to) escribir *(eh-skree-'beer)*
wrong equivocado *(eh-kee-boh-'kah-doh)*
x-rays rayos equis, los *(lohs 'rah-yohs 'eh-kees)*

yard jardín, el *(ehl hahr-'deen)*
yawn bostezo, el *(ehl boh-'steh-soh)*
year año, el *(ehl 'ah-nyoh)*
yell (to) gritar *(gree-'tahr)*
yellow amarillo *(ah-mah-'ree-yoh)*
yes sí *(see)*
yesterday ayer *(ah-'yehr)*
yet todavía *(toh-dah-'bee-ah)*
yolk yema, la *(lah 'yeh-mah)*
you (pl.) ustedes *(oo-'steh-dehs)*
you (sing.) usted *(oo-'stehd)*
young joven *('hoh-behn)*
younger menor *(meh-'nohr)*
your su *(soo)*
zebra cebra, la *(lah 'seh-brah)*
zero cero *('seh-roh)*
zip code zona postal, la *(lah 'soh-nah poh-'stahl)*
zipper cierre, el *(ehl see-'eh-rreh)*
zoo zoológico, el *(ehl soh-oh-'loh-hee-koh)*
zucchini calabacita verde, la *(lah kah-lah-bah-'see-tah 'behr-deh)*

SPANISH-ENGLISH VOCABULARY

Please note that the gender of nouns is indicated by either **el** or **la**. The gender of adjectives or pronouns shown here is always masculine. To switch the gender to feminine, change the ending to **a** (aburrid**o** = aburrid**a**, much**o** = much**a**.

a *(ah)* to
a veces *(ah 'beh-sehs)* sometimes
abajo *(ah-'bah-hoh)* down
abedul, el *(ehl ah-beh-'dool)* birch
abeja, la *(lah ah-'beh-hah)* bee
abogado, el *(ehl ah-boh-'gah-doh)* lawyer
abono, el *(ehl ah-'boh-noh)* fertilizer
abrazar *(ah-brah-'sahr)* hug (to)
abrazo, el *(ehl ah-'brah-soh)* hug
abrelatas, el *(ehl ah-breh-'lah-tahs)* can opener
abrigo, el *(ehl ah-'bree-goh)* overcoat
abril *(ah-'breel)* April
abrir *(ah-'breer)* open (to)
abuela, la *(lah ah-'bweh-lah)* grandmother
abuelo, el *(ehl ah-'bweh-loh)* grandfather
aburrido *(ah-boo-'rree-doh)* bored
accidente, el *(ehl ahk-see-'dehn-teh)* accident
aceite, el *(ehl ah-'seh-ee-teh)* oil
aceituna, la *(lah ah-seh-ee-'too-nah)* olive
acera, la *(lah ah-'seh-rah)* sidewalk
acero, el *(ehl ah-'seh-roh)* steel
ácido, el *(ehl 'ah-see-doh)* acid
acompañar *(ah-kohm-pah-'nyahr)* accompany (to)
acondicionador de aire, el *(ehl ah-kohn-dee-see-oh-nah-'dohr deh 'ah-ee-reh)* air conditioner
acondicionador, el *(ehl ah-kohn-dee-see-oh-nah-'dohr)* conditioner
acostarse *(ah-koh-'stahr-seh)* go to bed (to)
acrílico *(ah-'kree-lee-koh)* acrylic
acuario, el *(ehl ah-'kwah-ree-oh)* aquarium
adelante *(ah-deh-'lahn-teh)* forward
adentro *(ah-'dehn-troh)* inside
adiós *(ah-dee-'ohs)* good-bye
adivinar *(ah-dee-bee-'nahr)* guess (to)
aeropuerto, el *(ehl ah-eh-roh-'pwehr-toh)* airport
afeitar *(ah-feh-ee-'tahr)* shave (to)
afuera *(ah-'fweh-rah)* outside

afueras, las *(lahs ah-'fweh-rahs)* outdoors
agencia, la *(lah ah-'hehn-see-ah)* agency
agitar *(ah-hee-'tahr)* shake (to)
agosto *(ah-'goh-stoh)* August
agrio *('ah-gree-oh)* sour
agua, el *(ehl 'ah-gwah)* water
aguacate, el *(ehl ah-gwah-'kah-teh)* avocado
agudo *(ah-'goo-doh)* sharp
aguja, la *(lah ah-'goo-hah)* needle
ahijado, el *(ehl ah-ee-'hah-doh)* godchild
ahora *(ah-'oh-rah)* nowadays
ahorrar *(ah-oh-'rrahr)* save (to)
aire, el *(ehl 'ah-ee-reh)* air
aislamiento, el *(ehl ah-ees-lah-mee-'ehn-toh)* insulation
ajedrez, el *(ehl ah-heh-'drehs)* chess
ajo, el *(ehl 'ah-hoh)* garlic
al lado *(ahl 'lah-doh)* next to
al principio *(ahl preen-'see-pee-oh)* at first
alambre, el *(ehl ah-'lahm-breh)* wire
alarma, la *(lah ah-'lahr-mah)* alarm
albaricoque, el *(ehl ahl-bah-ree-'koh-keh)* apricot
alcachofa, la *(lah ahl-kah-'choh-fah)* artichoke
alergia, la *(lah ah-'lehr-hee-ah)* allergy
alfarería, la *(lah ahl-fahr-reh-'ree-ah)* pottery
alfiler, el *(ehl ahl-fee-'lehr)* pin
alfombra, la *(lah ahl-'fohm-brah)* rug
alga, el *(ehl 'ahl-gah)* algae
algo *('ahl-goh)* something
algodón, el *(ehl ahl-goh-'dohn)* cotton
alguien *('ahl-gee-ehn)* someone
algunos *(ahl-'goo-nohs)* some
alimentar *(ah-lee-mehn-'tahr)* feed (to)
allí *(ah-'yee)* there
almacén, el *(ehl ahl-mah-'sehn)* warehouse, department store
almeja, la *(lah ahl-'meh-hah)* clam
almidón, el *(ehl ahl-mee-'dohn)* starch

almohada, la *(lah ahl-moh-'ah-dah)* pillow
almuerzo, el *(ehl ahl-moo-'ehr-soh)* lunch
alto *('ahl-toh)* high, tall
altura *(ahl-'too-rah)* height
amamantar *(ah-mah-mahn-'tahr)* nurse
(to)
amar *(ah-'mahr)* love (to)
amargo *(ah-'mahr-goh)* bitter
amarillo *(ah-mah-'ree-yoh)* yellow
amarrar *(ah-mah-'rrahr)* fasten (to), tie (to)
ambicioso *(ahm-bee-see-'oh-soh)* ambitious
ambulancia, la *(lah ahm-boo-'lahn-see-ah)*
ambulance
americano *(ah-meh-ree-'kah-noh)* American
amoníaco, el *(ehl ah-moh-'nee-ah-koh)*
ammonia
amontonar *(ah-mohn-toh-'nahr)* stack (to)
amor, el *(ehl ah-'mohr)* love
ampolla, la *(lah ahm-'poh-yah)* blister
añadir *(ah-nyah-'deer)* add (to)
anaranjado *(ah-nah-rahn-'hah-doh)* orange
(color)
ancho *('ahn-choh)* wide
ancho, el *(ehl 'ahn-choh)* width
ángulo, el *(ehl 'ahn-goo-loh)* angle
anillo, el *(ehl ah-'nee-yoh)* ring
animal, el *(ehl ah-nee-'mahl)* animal
año, el *(ehl 'ah-nyoh)* year
anochecer, el *(ehl ah-noh-cheh-'sehr)* dusk
antes *('ahn-tehs)* before
antigüedad, la *(lah ahn-tee-gweh-'dahd)*
antique
antorcha, la *(lah ahn-'tohr-chah)* torch
anuncio, el *(ehl ah-'noon-see-oh)* sign
apagar *(ah-pah-'gahr)* turn off (to)
aparato, el *(ehl ah-pah-'rah-toh)* appliance
apartamento, el *(ehl ah-pahr-tah-'mehn-toh)*
apartment
apenas *(ah-'peh-nahs)* just
apio, el *(ehl 'ah-pee-oh)* celery
aplicar *(ah-plee-'kahr)* apply (to)
aprender *(ah-prehn-'dehr)* learn
apretar, oprimir *(ah-preh-'tahr, oh-pree-
'meer)* press (to)
aprovecharse *(ah-proh-beh-'chahr-seh)* take
advantage (to)
apurarse *(ah-poo-'rahr-seh)* hurry (to)
aquí *(ah-'kee)* here
araña, la *(lah ah-'rah-nyah)* spider
árbol, el *(ehl 'ahr-bohl)* tree
arboleda, la *(lah ahr-boh-'leh-dah)* grove
arbusto, el *(ehl ahr-'boo-stoh)* bush
ardilla, la *(lah ahr-'dee-yah)* squirrel
arena, la *(lah ah-'reh-nah)* sand

arete, el *(ehl ah-'reh-teh)* earring
arma, el *(ehl 'ahr-mah)* weapon
armario, el *(ehl ahr-'mah-ree-oh)* armoire
arquitecto, el *(ehl ahr-kee-'tehk-toh)*
architect
arreglar *(ah-rreh-'glahr)* arrange (to)
arriba *(ah-'rree-bah)* up
arroyo, el *(ehl ah-'rroh-yoh)* stream
arroz, el *(ehl ah-'rrohs)* rice
arte, el *(ehl 'ahr-teh)* art
artista, el *(ehl ahr-'tee-stah)* artist
arvejita, la *(lah ahr-beh-'hee-tah)* pea
asador, el *(ehl ah-sah-'dohr)* roasting pan
asar *(ah-'sahr)* grill (to), broil (to)
asfalto, el *(ehl ahs-'fahl-toh)* asphalt
asiento, el *(ehl ah-see-'ehn-toh)* seat
asistencia, la *(lah ah-sees-'tehn-see-ah)*
attendance
asistente, el *(ehl ah-sees-'tehn-teh)* assistant
asistir *(ah-sees-'teer)* attend (to)
aspiradora, la *(lah ah-spee-rah-'doh-rah)*
vacuum cleaner
aspiradora, limpiar con *(leem-pee-'ahr kohn
ahs-pee-rah-'doh-rah)* vacuum (to)
aspirina, la *(lah ah-spee-'ree-nah)* aspirin
atornillador, el *(ehl ah-tohr-nee-yah-'dohr)*
screwdriver
atrás *(ah-'trahs)* rear
atún, el *(ehl ah-'toon)* tuna
autobús, el *(ehl ow-toh-'boos)* bus
automático *(ow-toh-'mah-tee-koh)*
automatic
avenida, la *(lah ah-beh-'nee-dah)* avenue
avión, el *(ehl ah-bee-'ohn)* airplane
avispa, la *(lah ah-'vees-pah)* hornet
ayer *(ah-'yehr)* yesterday
ayuda, la *(lah ah-'yoo-dah)* help
ayudante de camarero, el *(ehl ah-yoo-'dahn-
teh deh kah-mah-'reh-roh)* busboy
ayudar *(ah-yoo-'dahr)* help (to)
azadón, el *(ehl ah-sah-'dohn)* hoe
azúcar, el *(ehl ah-'soo-kahr)* sugar
azul *(ah-'sool)* blue
bacinete, el *(ehl bah-see-'neh-teh)* bassinet
bailar *(bah-ee-'lahr)* dance (to)
baile, el *(ehl 'bah-ee-leh)* dance
bajar *(bah-'hahr)* lower (to)
bajo *('bah-hoh)* low, short (in height)
balde, el *(ehl 'bahl-deh)* bucket
baldosa, la *(lah bahl-'doh-sah)* floor tile
balneario, el *(ehl bahl-neh-'ah-ree-oh)* spa
bañarse *(bah-'nyahr-seh)* bathe (to)
banco, el *(ehl 'bahn-koh)* bank
bandeja, la *(lah bahn-'deh-hah)* tray

baño, el *(ehl 'bah-nyoh)* bath
banquillo, el *(ehl bahn-'kee-yoh)* stool
bar, el *(ehl bahr)* bar
baranda, la *(lah bah-'rahn-dah)* railing
barato *(bah-'rah-toh)* cheap
barbacoa, la *(lah bahr-bah-'koh-ah)* barbecue
barbilla, la *(lah bahr-'bee-yah)* chin
barco, el *(ehl 'bahr-koh)* boat
barrer *(bah-'rrehr)* sweep (to)
barrio, el *(ehl 'bah-rree-oh)* neighborhood
báscula, la *(lah 'bah-skoo-lah)* scale
básquetbol *(ehl 'bah-skeht-bohl)* basketball
bastante *(bah-'stahn-teh)* enough
bastón, el *(ehl bah-'stohn)* cane
basura, la *(lah bah-'soo-rah)* garbage
bata, la *(lah 'bah-tah)* bathrobe
batido, el *(ehl bah-'tee-doh)* shake
batidora, la *(lah bah-tee-'doh-rah)* mixer
batir *(bah-'teer)* beat (to), whip (to)
baúl, el *(ehl bah-'ool)* chest (box)
bebé, el *(ehl beh-'beh)* baby
beber, tomar *(beh-'behr, toh-'mahr)* drink (to)
bebida, la *(lah beh-'bee-dah)* drink
béisbol *(ehl 'beh-ees-bohl)* baseball
beneficio, el *(ehl beh-neh-'fee-see-oh)* benefit
besar *(beh-'sahr)* kiss (to)
beso, el *(ehl 'beh-soh)* kiss
biberón, el *(ehl bee-beh-'rohn)* bib
biblioteca, la *(lah bee-blee-oh-'teh-kah)* library
bicarbonato de soda, el *(ehl bee-kahr-boh-'nah-toh deh 'soh-dah)* baking soda
bicicleta, la *(lah bee-see-'kleh-tah)* bicycle
bien *('bee-ehn)* fine, well
bienvenidos *(bee-ehn-beh-'nee-dohs)* welcome
billetera, la *(lah bee-yeh-'teh-rah)* billfold
bistec, el *(ehl bees-'tehk)* steak
blanco *('blahn-koh)* white
blanqueador, el *(ehl blahn-keh-ah-'dohr)* bleach
blanquear *(blahn-keh-'ahr)* bleach (to)
bloque, el *(ehl 'bloh-keh)* block
blusa, la *(lah 'bloo-sah)* blouse
boca, la *(lah 'boh-kah)* mouth
boda, la *(lah 'boh-dah)* wedding
boleto, el *(ehl boh-'leh-toh)* ticket
boliche, el *(ehl boh-'lee-cheh)* bowling
bolsa, la *(lah 'bohl-sah)* bag
bolsa, la *(lah 'bohl-sah)* purse
bolsillo, el *(ehl bohl-'see-yoh)* pocket

bomba, la *(lah 'bohm-bah)* pump
bombero, el *(ehl bohm-'beh-roh)* fire fighter
bonito *(boh-'nee-toh)* pretty
bordado, el *(ehl bohr-'dah-doh)* embroidery
borde, el *(ehl 'bohr-deh)* edge
borrar *(boh-'rrahr)* erase (to)
bosque, el *(ehl 'boh-skeh)* forest
bostezo, el *(ehl boh-'steh-soh)* yawn
bota, la *(lah 'boh-tah)* boot
botella, la *(lah boh-'teh-yah)* bottle
botón, el *(ehl boh-'tohn)* bud, button
botones, el *(ehl boh-'toh-nehs)* bellhop
boxeo, el *(ehl bohk-'seh-oh)* boxing
bragas, las *(lahs 'brah-gahs)* panties
brazalete, el *(ehl brah-sah-'leh-teh)* bracelet
brazo, el *(ehl 'brah-soh)* arm
brea, la *(lah 'breh-ah)* tar
brillante *(bree-'yahn-teh)* bright
broche, el *(ehl 'broh-cheh)* broach
bronce, el *(ehl 'brohn-seh)* bronze
bronceador, el *(ehl brohn-seh-ah-'dohr)* suntan lotion
bueno *('bweh-noh)* good
bufanda, la *(lah boo-'fahn-dah)* scarf
buho, el *(ehl 'boo-oh)* owl
buscar *(boos-'kahr)* look for (to)
buzón, el *(ehl boo-'sohn)* mailbox
caballito, el *(ehl kah-bah-'yee-toh)* pony
caballo, el *(ehl kah-'bah-yoh)* horse
cabeza, la *(lah kah-'beh-sah)* head
cada *('kah-dah)* each
cadena, la *(lah kah-'deh-nah)* chain
cadera, la *(lah kah-'deh-rah)* hip
caer *(cah-'ehr)* fall (to)
café *(kah-'feh)* brown
café el *(ehl kah-'feh)* coffee
caja de fusibles, la *(lah 'kah-hah deh foo-'see-blehs)* fuse box
caja, la *(lah 'kah-hah)* box
cajero, el *(ehl kah-'heh-roh)* cashier
cajón, el *(ehl kah-'hohn)* drawer
calabacita verde, la *(lah kah-lah-bah-'see-tah 'behr-deh)* zucchini
calabaza, la *(lah kah-lah-'bah-sah)* pumpkin
calcetín, el *(ehl kahl-seh-'teen)* sock
calculadora, la *(lah kahl-koo-lah-'doh-rah)* calculator
caldo, el *(ehl 'kahl-doh)* broth
calefacción, la *(lah kah-leh-fahk-see-'ohn)* heating
calentador, el *(ehl kah-lehn-tah-'dohr)* heater

calentador para el agua *(ehl kah-'lehn-tah-dohr 'pah-rah ehl 'ah-gwah)* hot water heater

calentar *(kah-lehn-'tahr)* heat (to)

caliente *(kah-lee-'ehn-teh)* hot

calle, la *(lah 'kah-yeh)* street

callejón, el *(ehl kah-yeh-'hohn)* alley

calmarse *(kahl-'mahr-seh)* calm down (to)

calor, el *(ehl kah-'lohr)* heat

calvo *('kahl-boh)* bald

calzones, los *(lohs kahl-'soh-nehs)* panties

calzoncillos, los *(lohs kahl-sohn-'see-yohs)* shorts

cama, la *(lah 'kah-mah)* bed

camarón, el *(ehl kah-mah-'rohn)* shrimp

cambiar *(kahm-bee-'ahr)* change (to)

cambio, el *(ehl 'kahm-bee-oh)* change

caminar *(kah-mee-'nahr)* walk (to)

camino, el *(ehl kah-'mee-noh)* path, road

camión, el *(ehl kah-mee-'ohn)* truck

camionero, el *(ehl kah-mee-oh-'neh-roh)* truck driver

camisa, la *(lah kah-'mee-sah)* shirt

camiseta, la *(lah kah-mee-'seh-tah)* T-shirt

camote, el *(ehl kah-'moh-teh)* sweet potato

campamento, el *(ehl kahm-pah-'mehn-toh)* campgrounds

campesino, el *(ehl kahm-peh-'see-noh)* farmer

campo de recreo, el *(ehl 'kahm-poh deh reh-'kreh-oh)* playground

campo, el *(ehl 'kahm-poh)* field

canal, el *(ehl kah-'nahl)* channel

canario, el *(ehl kah-'nah-ree-oh)* canary

canasta, la *(lah kah-'nah-stah)* basket

cancelar *(kah-seh-'lahr)* cancel (to)

cancha, la *(lah 'kahn-chah)* court

canción, la *(lah kahn-see-'ohn)* song

candado, el *(ehl kahn-'dah-doh)* padlock

canela, la *(lah kah-'neh-lah)* cinnamon

cangrejo, el *(ehl kahn-'greh-hoh)* crab

canoa, la *(lah kah-'noh-ah)* canoe

cantar *(kahn-'tahr)* sing (to)

cántaro, el *(ehl 'kahn-tah-roh)* pitcher

cantidad, la *(lah kahn-tee-'dahd)* amount

cantinero, el *(ehl kahn-tee-'neh-roh)* bartender

cápsula, la *(lah 'kahp-soo-lah)* capsule

cara, la *(lah 'kah-rah)* face

caracol, el *(ehl kah-rah-'kohl)* snail

cárcel, la *(lah 'kahr-sehl)* jail

carga, la *(lah 'kahr-gah)* load

cargar *(kahr-'gahr)* load (to)

carne, la *(lah 'kahr-neh)* meat

carnicero, el *(ehl kahr-nee-'seh-roh)* butcher

caro *('kah-roh)* expensive

carpintero, el *(ehl kahr-peen-'teh-roh)* carpenter

carrera, la *(lah kah-'rreh-rah)* career

carretera, la *(lah kah-rreh-'teh-rah)* highway

carro, el *(ehl 'kah-rroh)* car

cartera, la *(lah kahr-'teh-rah)* wallet

cartero, el *(ehl kahr-'teh-roh)* mail carrier

cartón, el *(ehl kahr-'tohn)* cardboard

casa, la *(lah 'kah-sah)* house

casarse *(kah-'sahr-seh)* marry (to)

casco, el *(ehl 'kah-skoh)* helmet

castigar *(kah-stee-'gahr)* punish (to)

castigo, el *(ehl kah-'stee-goh)* punishment

castor, el *(ehl kah-'stohr)* beaver

católico *(kah-'toh-lee-koh)* Catholic

catorce *(kah-'tohr-seh)* fourteen

causar *('kah-oo-'sahr)* cause (to)

cazar *(kah-'sahr)* hunt (to)

cebolla, la *(lah seh-'boh-yah)* onion

cebra, la *(lah 'seh-brah)* zebra

cedro, el *(ehl 'seh-droh)* cedar

celebrar *(seh-leh-'brahr)* celebrate (to)

cementerio, el *(ehl seh-mehn-'teh-ree-oh)* cemetery

cemento, el *(ehl seh-'mehn-toh)* cement

cena, la *(lah 'seh-nah)* dinner

cenicero, el *(ehl seh-nee-'seh-roh)* ashtray

ceniza, la *(lah seh-'nee-sah)* ash

centavo, el *(ehl seh-'tah-boh)* cent

centímetro, el *(ehl sehn-'tee-meh-troh)* centimeter

centro, el *(ehl 'sehn-troh)* downtown

cepillar *(seh-pee-'yahr)* brush (to)

cepillo de dientes, el *(ehl seh-'pee-yoh deh dee-'ehn-tehs)* toothbrush

cepillo, el *(ehl seh-'pee-yoh)* brush

cera, la *(lah 'seh-rah)* wax

cerca *('sehr-kah)* near

cerca de *('sehr-kah deh)* close

cerca, la *(lah 'sehr-kah)* fence

cerdo, el *(ehl 'sehr-doh)* pork

cerebro, el *(ehl seh-'reh-broh)* brain

cereza, la *(lah seh-'reh-sah)* cherry

cero *('seh-roh)* zero

cerradura, la *(lah seh-rrah-'doo-rah)* lock

cerrar *(seh-'rrahr)* close (to)

cerrar con llave *(seh-'rrahr kohn 'yah-beh)* lock (to)

cerro, el *(ehl 'seh-rroh)* hill

cerrojo, el *(ehl seh-'rroh-hoh)* latch

cerveza, la *(lah sehr-'beh-sah)* beer
césped, el *(ehl 'seh-spehd)* lawn
chaleco, el *(ehl chah-'leh-koh)* vest
champiñón, el *(ehl chahm-pee-'nyohn)* mushroom
champú, el *(ehl chahm-'poo)* shampoo
chaqueta, la *(lah chah-'keh-tah)* jacket
charca, la *(lah 'chahr-kah)* pond
charlar *(chahr-'lahr)* chat (to)
cheque, el *(ehl 'cheh-keh)* check
chequera, la *(lah cheh-'keh-rah)* checkbook
chicle, el *(ehl 'chee-kleh)* chewing gum
chile, el *(ehl 'chee-leh)* hot pepper
chimenea, la *(lah chee-meh-'neh-ah)* chimney
chiste, el *(ehl 'chee-steh)* joke
chivo, el *(ehl 'chee-boh)* goat
chocolate, el *(ehl choh-koh-'lah-teh)* chocolate
chofer, el *(ehl choh-'fehr)* driver
chorrear *(choh-rreh-'ahr)* drip (to)
chuleta, la *(lah choo-'leh-tah)* chop
chupete, el *(ehl choo-'peh-teh)* pacifier
ciclo, el *(ehl 'see-kloh)* cycle
cien *('see-ehn)* one hundred
cierre, el *(ehl see-'eh-rreh)* zipper
cigarrillo, el *(ehl see-gah-'ree-yoh)* cigarette
cincel, el *(ehl seen-'sehl)* chisel
cinco *('seen-koh)* five
cincuenta *(seen-'kwehn-tah)* fifty
cine, el *(ehl 'see-neh)* movie theater
cinta, la *(lah 'seen-tah)* tape
circo, el *(ehl 'seer-koh)* circus
círculo, el *(ehl 'seer-koo-loh)* circle
ciruela, la *(lah see-roo-'eh-lah)* plum
cisne, el *(ehl 'sees-neh)* swan
cita, la *(lah 'see-tah)* appointment
ciudad, la *(lah see-oo-'dahd)* city
ciudadano, el *(ehl see-oo-dah-'dah-noh)* citizen
clarinete, el *(ehl klah-ree-'neh-teh)* clarinet
clase, la *(lah 'klah-seh)* class
clavo, el *(ehl 'klah-boh)* nail
cliente, el *(ehl klee-'ehn-teh)* client
clínica, la *(lah 'klee-nee-kah)* clinic
cloro, el *(ehl 'kloh-roh)* chlorine
cobertizo, el *(ehl koh-behr-'tee-soh)* shed
cochecillo, el *(ehl koh-cheh-'see-yoh)* stroller
cocina, la *(lah koh-'see-nah)* kitchen
cocinar *(koh-see-'nahr)* cook (to)
cocinero, el *(ehl koh-see-'neh-roh)* cook
coco, el *(ehl 'koh-koh)* coconut
coctel, el *(ehl kohk-'tehl)* cocktail

codo, el *(ehl 'koh-doh)* elbow
coger *(koh-'hehr)* catch (to)
cojín, el *(ehl koh-'heen)* cushion
colador, el *(ehl koh-lah-'dohr)* strainer
colchón, el *(ehl kohl-'chohn)* mattress
colgar *(kohl-'gahr)* hang (to)
cólico *('koh-lee-koh)* colic
coliflor, el *(ehl koh-lee-'flohr)* cauliflower
collar, el *(ehl koh-'yahr)* necklace
colonia, la *(lah koh-'loh-nee-ah)* cologne
color, el *(ehl koh-'lohr)* color
comadre, la *(lah koh-'mah-dreh)* godmother
comedor, el *(ehl koh-meh-'dohr)* dining room
comer *(koh-'mehr)* eat (to)
comestibles, los *(lohs koh-meh-'stee-blehs)* groceries
cometa, la *(lah koh-'meh-tah)* kite
comida, la *(lah koh-'mee-dah)* food
comida campestre, la *(lah koh-'mee-dah kahm-'pehs-treh)* picnic
comidas, las *(lahs koh-'mee-dahs)* meals
cómo *('koh-moh)* how
cómodo *('koh-moh-doh)* comfortable
compadre, el *(ehl kohm-'pah-dreh)* godfather
compañero, el *(ehl kohm-pah-'nyeh-roh)* co-worker
completo *(kohm-'pleh-toh)* complete
comportarse *(kohm-pohr-'tahr-seh)* behave (to)
comprobar *(kohm-proh-'bahr)* check on (to)
compras, las *(lahs 'kohm-prahs)* shopping
computadora, la *(lah kohm-poo-tah-'doh-rah)* computer
comunidad, la *(lah koh-moo-nee-'dahd)* community
con *(kohn)* with
condado, el *(ehl kohn-'dah-doh)* county
condimento, el *(ehl kohn-dee-'mehn-toh)* condiment
condominio, el *(ehl kohn-doh-'mee-nee-oh)* condominium
conducto, el *(ehl kohn-'dook-toh)* duct
conejo, el *(ehl koh-'neh-hoh)* rabbit
conferencia, la *(lah kohn-feh-'rehn-see-ah)* meeting
congelador, el *(ehl kohn-heh-lah-'dohr)* freezer
congelamiento, el *(ehl kohn-heh-lah-mee-'ehn-toh)* frostbite
congelar *(kohn-heh-'lahr)* freeze (to)

conocer *(koh-noh-'sehr)* know someone (to)
consejero, el *(ehl kohn-seh-'heh-roh)* counselor
conserje, el *(ehl kohn-'sehr-heh)* janitor
construir *(kohn-stroo-'eer)* build (to)
contaminado *(kohn-tah-mee-'nah-doh)* contaminated
contar *(kohn-'tahr)* count (to)
contento *(kohn-'tehn-toh)* happy
contestar *(kohn-teh-'stahr)* answer (to)
contratar *(kohn-trah-'tahr)* hire (to)
contratista, el *(ehl kohn-trah-'tees-tah)* contractor
contrato, el *(ehl kohn-'trah-toh)* contract
contusión, la *(lah kohn-too-see-'ohn)* bruise
copiadora, la *(lah koh-pee-ah-'doh-rah)* copier
corazón, el *(ehl koh-rah-'sohn)* heart
corbata, la *(lah kohr-'bah-tah)* tie
cordón, el *(ehl kohr-'dohn)* cord
correa, la *(lah koh-'rreh-ah)* strap
correcto *(koh-'rrehk-toh)* correct
corregir *(koh rreh-'heer)* correct (to)
correo, el *(ehl koh-'rreh-oh)* mail, post office
correr *(koh-'rrehr)* run
cortada, la *(lah kohr-'tah-dah)* cut
cortar *(kohr-'tahr)* cut (to)
cortar el pasto *(kohr-'tahr ehl 'pah-stoh)* mow (to)
corte, la *(lah 'kohr-teh)* courthouse
cortesía, la *(lah kohr-teh-'see-ah)* courtesy
cortinas, las *(lahs kohr-'tee-nahs)* curtains
corto *('kohr-toh)* short (in length)
cosa, la *(lah 'koh-sah)* thing
cosecha, la *(lah koh-'seh-chah)* crop
coser *(koh-'sehr)* sew (to)
cosméticos, los *(lohs kohs-'meh-tee-kohs)* cosmetics
costilla, la *(lah koh-'stee-yah)* rib
crecer *(kreh-'sehr)* grow (to)
crema de maní, la *(lah 'kreh-mah deh mah-'nee)* peanut butter
crema, la *(lah 'kreh-mah)* cream
cremera, la *(lah kreh-'meh-rah)* creamer
criada, la *(lah kree-'ah-dah)* maid
criadero, el *(ehl kree-ah-'deh-roh)* nursery (plants)
criado, el *(ehl kree-'ah-doh)* servant
crimen, el *(ehl 'kree-mehn)* crime
cruce de peatones, el *(ehl 'kroo-seh deh peh-ah-'toh-nehs)* crosswalk
crudo *('kroo-doh)* raw
cuaderno, el *(ehl kwah-'dehr-noh)* notebook

cuadra, la *(lah 'kwah-drah)* city block
cuadro, el *(ehl 'kwah-droh)* painting, square
cuál *(kwahl)* which
cualquier cosa *(kwahl-kee-'ehr 'koh-sah)* anything
cualquier persona *(kwahl-kee-'ehr pehr-'soh-nah)* anyone
cualquier sitio *(kwahl-kee-'ehr 'see-tee-oh)* anywhere
cuándo *('kwahn-doh)* when
cuánto *('kwahn-toh)* how much
cuántos *('kwahn-tohs)* how many
cuarenta *(kwah-'rehn-tah)* forty
cuarta, la *(lah 'kwahr-tah)* quart
cuarto *('kwah-troh)* fourth
cuarto de baño, el *(ehl 'kwahr-toh deh 'bah-nyoh)* bathroom
cuatro *('kwah-troh)* four
cubiertos, los *(lohs koo-bee-'ehr-tohs)* silverware
cubrir *(koo-'breer)* cover (to)
cuchara, la *(lah koo-'chah-rah)* spoon
cucharada, la *(lah koo-chah-'rah-dah)* tablespoon
cucharadita, la *(lah koo-chah-rah-'dee-tah)* teaspoon
cucharón, el *(ehl koo-chah-'rohn)* ladle
cuchillo, el *(ehl koo-'chee-yoh)* knife
cuello, el *(ehl 'kweh-yoh)* neck
cuenta, la *(lah 'kwehn-tah)* bill
cuento, el *(ehl 'kwehn-toh)* story
cuero, el *(ehl 'kweh-roh)* leather
cuerpo, el *(ehl 'kwehr-poh)* body
cuervo, el *(ehl 'kwehr-boh)* crow
cuidar *(kwee-'dahr)* care for (to)
culebra, la *(lah koo-'leh-brah)* snake
culpa, la *(lah 'kool-pah)* fault
cultivar *(kool-tee-'bahr)* cultivate (to)
cuna, la *(lah 'koo-nah)* crib
cuñada, la *(lah koo-'nyah-dah)* sister-in-law
cuñado, el *(ehl koo-'nyah-doh)* brother-in-law
cupón, el *(ehl koo-'pohn)* coupon
cura, el *(ehl 'koo-rah)* priest
curioso *(koo-ree-'oh-soh)* funny
curita, la *(lah koo-'ree-tah)* Band-Aid®
daño, el *(ehl 'dah-nyoh)* damage
dar *(dahr)* give (to)
de *(deh)* from, of
de la mañana *(deh lah mah-'nyah-nah)* A.M.
de la tarde *(deh lah 'tahr-deh)* P.M.
de quién *(deh kee-'ehn)* whose

deber *(deh-'behr)* owe (to)
débil *('deh-beel)* weak
décimo *('deh-see-moh)* tenth
decorar *(deh-koh-'rahr)* decorate (to)
dedo del pie, el *(ehl 'deh-doh dehl 'pee-eh)* toe
dedo, el *(ehl 'deh-doh)* finger
delantal, el *(ehl deh-lahn-'tahl)* apron
delgado *(dehl-'gah-doh)* thin
delicado *(deh-lee-'kah-doh)* gentle
delicioso *(deh-lee-see-'oh-soh)* delicious
dentista, el *(ehl dehn-'tee-stah)* dentist
dentro *('dehn-troh)* within
dependiente, el *(ehl deh-pehn-dee-'ehn-teh)* clerk
deportes, los *(lohs deh-'pohr-tehs)* sports
depósito, el *(ehl deh-'poh-see-toh)* storeroom
derecha *(deh-'reh-chah)* right
derecho *(deh-'reh-choh)* straight
derramarse *(deh-rrah-'mahr-seh)* spill (to)
derretir *(deh-rreh-'teer)* melt (to)
desaguadero, el *(ehl dehs-ah-gwah-'deh-roh)* drain
desaguar *(dehs-ah-'gwahr)* drain (to)
desagüe, el *(ehl dehs-'ah-gweh)* sewage
desarollar *(dehs-ah-roh-'yahr)* develop (to)
desastre, el *(ehl deh-'sah-streh)* disaster
desayuno, el *(ehl deh-sah-'yoo-noh)* breakfast
descansar *(dehs-kahn-'sahr)* rest (to)
descanso, el *(ehl dehs-'kahn-soh)* rest
descargar *(dehs-kahr-'gahr)* unload (to)
descongelar *(dehs-kohn-heh-'lahr)* defrost (to)
desconocido, el *(ehl dehs-koh-noh-'see-doh)* stranger
describir *(dehs-kree-'beer)* describe (to)
descubrir *(dehs-koo-'breer)* discover (to)
descuento, el *(ehl dehs-'kwehn-toh)* discount
desear *(deh-seh-'ahr)* desire (to), wish (to)
desechable *(deh-seh-'chah-bleh)* disposable
desechador, el *(ehl dehs-eh-chah-'dohr)* garbage disposal
desfile, el *(ehl dehs-'fee-leh)* parade
desierto, el *(ehl deh-see-'ehr-toh)* desert
desinfectante, el *(ehl dehs-een-fehk-'tahn-teh)* disinfectant
desinfectar *(dehs-een-fehk-'tahr)* disinfect (to)
desodorante, el *(ehl dehs-oh-doh-'rahn-teh)* deodorant
despedir *(dehs-peh-'deer)* fire (to)

despejado *(dehs-peh-'hah-doh)* clear
desperdicios, los *(lohs dehs-pehr-'dee-see-ohs)* waste
despertarse *(dehs-pehr-'tahr-seh)* wake up (to)
después *(deh-'spwehs)* afterward
desván, el *(ehl dehs-'bahn)* attic
detergente, el *(ehl deh-tehr-'hehn-teh)* detergent
detergente para los platos *(ehl deh-tehr-'hehn-teh 'pah-rah lohs 'plah-tohs)* dishwashing detergent
detrás *(deh-'trahs)* behind
devolver, volver *(deh-bohl-'behr, bohl-'behr)* return (to)
día de fiesta, el *(ehl 'dee-ah deh fee-'eh-stah)* holiday
día, el *(ehl 'dee-ah)* day
diamante, el *(ehl dee-ah-'mahn-teh)* diamond
diario *(dee-'ah-ree-oh)* daily
dibujar *(dee-boo-'hahr)* draw (to)
dibujos animados *(lohs dee-'boo-hohs ah-nee-'mah-dohs)* cartoons
diciembre *(dee-see-'ehm-breh)* December
diecinueve *(dee-ehs-ee-noo-'eh-beh)* nineteen
dieciocho *(dee-ehs-ee-'oh-choh)* eighteen
dieciseis *(dee-ehs-ee-'seh-ees)* sixteen
diecisiete *(dee-ehs-ee-see-'eh-teh)* seventeen
diente, el *(ehl dee-'ehn-teh)* tooth
diez *(dee-'ehs)* ten
difícil *(dee-'fee-seel)* difficult
dinero, el *(ehl dee-'neh-roh)* money
Dios *('dee-ohs)* God
dirección, la *(lah dee-rehk-see-'ohn)* address, direction
discutir *(dees-koo-'teer)* discuss (to)
disfraz, el *(ehl dees-'frahs)* costume
disfrutar *(dees-froo-'tahr)* enjoy (to)
disolver *(dee-sohl-'behr)* dissolve (to)
disponible *(dees-poh-'nee-bleh)* available
dividir *(dee-bee-'deer)* divide (to)
divorcio, el *(ehl dee-'bohr-see-oh)* divorce
doblar *(doh-'blahr)* bend (to), fold
doble *('doh-bleh)* double
doce *('doh-seh)* twelve
docena, la *(lah doh-'seh-nah)* dozen
doctor, el *(ehl dohk-'tohr)* doctor
dólar, el *(ehl 'doh-lahr)* dollar
dolor, el *(ehl doh-'lohr)* pain
domingo *(ehl doh-'meen-goh)* Sunday
dónde *('dohn-deh)* where
dorar *(doh-'rahr)* brown (to)
dormir *(dohr-'meer)* sleep (to)

dormitorio, el *(ehl dohr-mee-'toh-ree-oh)*
bedroom
dos *(dohs)* two
drenaje, el *(ehl dreh-'nah-heh)* drainage
droga, la *(lah 'droh-gah)* drug
ducha, la *(lah 'doo-chah)* shower
dueño, el *(ehl 'dweh-nyoh)* owner
dulce *('dool-seh)* sweet
dulces, los *(lohs 'dool-sehs)* candy
durazno, el *(ehl doo-'rahs-noh)* peach
duro *('doo-roh)* hard
edad, la *(lah eh-'dahd)* age
edificio, el *(ehl eh-dee-'fee-see-oh)* building
ejercicio, el *(ehl eh-hehr-'see-see-oh)*
exercise
el *(ehl)* the (masc.sing.)
él *(ehl)* he
electricista, el *(ehl eh-lehk-tree-'see-stah)*
electrician
eléctrico *(eh-'lehk-tree-koh)* electric
elefante, el *(ehl eh-leh-'fahn-teh)* elephant
elevador, el *(ehl eh-leh-bah-'dohr)* elevator
ella *('eh-yah)* she
ellas *('eh-yahs)* they (feminine)
ellos *('eh-yohs)* they (masculine)
embarazada *(ehm-bah-rah-'sah-dah)*
pregnant
embudo, el *(ehl ehm-'boo-doh)* funnel
empapelado, el *(ehl ehm-pah-peh-'lah-doh)*
wallpaper
empezar *(ehm-peh-'sahr)* begin (to), start (to)
emplear *(ehm-pleh-'ahr)* employ (to)
empujar *(ehm-poo-'hahr)* push (to)
en *(ehn)* at, in, on
encaje, el *(ehl ehn-'kah-heh)* lace
encargo, el *(ehl ehn-'kahr-goh)* errand
enchufar *(ehn-choo-'fahr)* plug in (to)
enchufe, el *(ehl ehn-'choo-feh)* outlet
encías, las *(lahs ehn-'see-ahs)* gums
encima *(ehn-'see-mah)* above
encontrar *(ehn-kohn-'trahr)* find (to),
meet (to)
encurtido, el *(ehl ehn-koor-'tee-doh)* pickle
enero *(eh-'neh-roh)* January
enfermdad, la *(lah ehn-fehr-meh-'dahd)*
disease
enfermero, el *(ehl ehn-fehr-'meh-roh)* nurse
enfermo *(ehn-'fehr-moh)* sick
enjuagar *(ehn-hoo-ah-'gahr)* rinse (to)
enojado *(eh-noh-'hah-doh)* angry
enrollar *(ehn-roh-'yahr)* roll (to)
ensalada, la *(lah ehn-sah-'lah-dah)* salad
enseñar *(ehn-seh-'nyahr)* teach (to)

entender *(ehn-tehn-'dehr)* understand (to)
entonces *(ehn-'tohn-sehs)* then
entrada, la *(lah ehn-'trah-dah)* entrance
entrada para carros, la *(lah ehn-'trah-dah*
'pah-rah 'kah-rrohs) driveway
entrar *(ehn-'trahr)* enter (to)
entre *('ehn-treh)* between
entrenar *(ehn-treh-'nahr)* train (to)
entrevista, la *(lah ehn-treh-'bee-stah)*
interview
envolver *(ehn-bohl-'behr)* wrap (to)
equipaje, el *(ehl eh-kee-'pah-heh)* luggage
equipo, el *(ehl eh-'kee-poh)* equipment
equivocado *(eh-kee-boh-'kah-doh)* wrong
eructo, el *(ehl eh-'rook-toh)* belch
erupción, la *(lah eh-roo-see-'ohn)* rash
escala mecánica, la *(lah eh-'skah-lah meh-*
'kah-nee-kah) escalator
escalera, la *(lah eh-skah-'leh-rah)* ladder
escaleras, las *(lahs eh-skah-'leh-rahs)*
stairs
escalofrío, el *(ehl eh-skah-loh-'free-oh)* chill
escalones, los *(lohs eh-skah-'loh-nehs)* steps
escoba, la *(lah eh-'skoh-bah)* broom
escoger *(ehs-koh-'hehr)* choose (to)
esconder *(eh-skohn-'dehr)* hide (to)
escribir *(eh-skree-'beer)* write (to)
escritorio, el *(ehl eh-skree-'toh-ree-oh)* desk
escuchar *(eh-skoo-'chahr)* listen
escuela, la *(lah eh-'skweh-lah)* school
ese *('eh-seh)* that
esmeralda, la *(lah ehs-meh-'rahl-dah)*
emerald
esos *('eh-sohs)* those
espalda, la *(lah eh-'spahl-dah)* back
español, el *(ehl eh-spah-'nyohl)* Spanish
espárragos, el *(ehl eh-'spah-rrah-gohs)*
asparagus
especia, la *(lah eh-'speh-see-ah)* spice
espejo, el *(ehl eh-'speh-hoh)* mirror
esperar *(eh-speh-'rahr)* wait (to)
espinaca, la *(lah eh-spee-'nah-kah)* spinach
esponja, la *(lah eh-'spohn-hah)* sponge
esposa, la *(lah eh-'spoh-sah)* wife
esposo, el *(ehl eh-'spoh-soh)* husband
esquina, la *(lah eh-'skee-nah)* corner
esta noche *('eh-stah 'noh-cheh)* tonight
establo, el *(ehl eh-'stah-bloh)* stable
estacionamiento, el *(ehl eh-stah-see-oh-nah-*
mee-'ehn-toh) parking lot
estacionar *(eh-stah-see-oh-'nahr)* park (to)
estadio, el *(ehl eh-'stah-dee-oh)* stadium
estado, el *(ehl eh-'stah-doh)* state

Estados Unidos, los *(lohs eh-'stah-dohs oo-'nee-dohs)* United States

estampilla, la *(lah eh-'stahm-'pee-yah)* stamp

estar, ser *(eh-'stahr, sehr)* be (to)

estatua, la *(lah eh-'stah-too-ah)* statue

este *('eh-steh)* east

este *('eh-steh)* this

estilador, el *(ehl eh-stee-lah-'dohr)* rack

estómago, el *(ehl eh-'stoh-mah-goh)* stomach

estornudo, el *(ehl eh-stohr-'noo-doh)* sneeze

estos *('eh-stohs)* these

estrecho *(eh-'streh-choh)* narrow

estreñimiento, el *(ehl eh-streh-nyee-mee-'ehn-toh)* constipation

estuche, el *(ehl eh-'stoo-cheh)* case

estudiante, el *(ehl eh-stoo-dee-'ahn-teh)* student

estufa, la *(lah eh-'stoo-fah)* stove

etiqueta, la *(lah eh-tee-'keh-tah)* label

evitar *(eh-bee-'tahr)* avoid (to)

examen, el *(ehl ehks-'sah-mehn)* test

excavar *(ehks-kah-'bahr)* dig (to)

excelente *(ehk-seh-'lehn-teh)* excellent

excitado *(ehk-see-'tah-doh)* excited

excusado, el *(ehl ehks-koo-'sah-doh)* toilet

experiencia, la *(lah ehks-peh-ree-'ehn-see-ah)* experience

explicar *(ehks-plee-'kahr)* explain (to)

fábrica, la *(lah 'fah-bree-kah)* factory

fácil *('fah-seel)* easy

factura, la *(lah fahk-'too-rah)* invoice

faja, la *(lah 'fah-hah)* girdle

falda, la *(lah 'fahl-dah)* skirt

familia, la *(lah fah-'mee-lee-ah)* family

famoso *(fah-'moh-soh)* famous

farmacéutico, el *(ehl fahr-mah-'seh-oo-tee-koh)* pharmacist

farmacia, la *lah fahr-'mah-see-ah)* pharmacy

favor, el *(ehl fah-'bohr)* favor

febrero *(feh-'breh-roh)* February

fecha, la *(lah 'feh-chah)* date

felicitaciones *(feh-lee-see-tah-see-'oh-nehs)* congratulations

feo *('feh-oh)* ugly

fertilizar *(ferh-tee-lee-'sahr)* fertilize (to)

fideo, el *(ehl fee-'deh-oh)* noodle

fiebre, la *(lah fee-'eh-breh)* fever

fiesta, la *(lah fee-'eh-stah)* party

filtro, el *(ehl 'feel-troh)* filter

fin de semana, el *(ehl feen deh seh-'mah-nah)* weekend

firmar *(feer-'mahr)* sign (to)

flojo *('floh-hoh)* loose

flor, la *(lah flohr)* flower

florero, el *(ehl floh-'reh-roh)* vase

florista, el *(ehl floh-'rees-tah)* florist

fogón, el *(ehl foh-'gohn)* fireplace

follaje, el *(ehl foh-'yah-heh)* foliage

fondo, el *(ehl 'fohn-doh)* bottom, slip

forma, la *(lah 'fohr-mah)* form, shape

formar *(fohr-'mahr)* shape (to)

fósforo, el *(ehl 'fohs-foh-roh)* match

foto, la *(lah 'foh-toh)* photograph

frasco, el *(ehl 'frah-skoh)* jar

frazada, la *(lah frah-'sah-dah)* blanket

fregar *(freh-'gahr)* scrub (to)

freír *(freh-'eer)* fry (to)

freno, el *(ehl 'freh-noh)* brake

frente, el *(ehl 'frehn-teh)* front

fresa, la *(lah 'freh-sah)* strawberry

fresco *('frehs-koh)* cool, fresh

frijol, el *(ehl free-'hohl)* bean

frío *('free-oh)* cold

frotar *(froh-'tahr)* rub (to)

fruta, la *(lah 'froo-tah)* fruit

fuego, el *(el 'fweh-goh)* fire

fuegos artificiales, los *(lohs 'fweh-gohs ahr-tee-fee-see-'ah-lehs)* fireworks

fuente, la *(lah 'fwehn-teh)* fountain

fuerte *('fwehr-teh)* strong

fumar *(foo-'mahr)* smoke (to)

funcionar *(foonk-see-oh-'nahr)* function (to)

funda, la *(lah 'foon-dah)* pillowcase

fusible, el *(ehl foo-'see-bleh)* fuse

fútbol americano *(ehl 'foot-bohl ah-meh-ree-'kah-noh)* football

fútbol, el *(ehl 'foot-bohl)* soccer

gabinete, el *(ehl gah-bee-'neh-teh)* cabinet

galleta, la *(lah gah-'yeh-tah)* cookie

galleta salada, la *(lah gah-'yeh-tah sah-'lah-dah)* cracker

gallina, la *(lah gah-'yee-nah)* chicken

galón, el *(ehl gah-'lohn)* gallon

ganar *(gah-'nahr)* earn (to), win (to)

gancho, el *(ehl 'gahn-choh)* hanger, hook

ganga, la *(lah 'gahn-gah)* bargain

garaje, el *(ehl gah-'rah-heh)* garage

gasolina, la *(lah gah-soh-'lee-nah)* gas

gastar *(gah-'stahr)* spend (to)

gatear *(gah-teh-'ahr)* crawl (to)

gato, el *(ehl 'gah-toh)* cat

gelatina, la *(lah heh-lah-'tee-nah)* jello

gemelo, el *(ehl heh-'meh-loh)* twin, cuff link

gente, la *(lah 'hehn-teh)* people

gerente, el *(ehl heh-'rehn-teh)* manager

gimnasio, el *(ehl heem-'nah-see·oh)* gymnasium

ginebra, la *(lah hee-'neh-brah)* gin

globo, el *(ehl 'gloh-boh)* balloon

golpear *(gohl-peh-'ahr)* hit (to)

goma, la *(lah 'goh-mah)* rubber

gordo *('gohr-doh)* fat

gorra, la *(lah 'goh-rrah)* cap

gorrión, el *(ehl goh-rree-'ohn)* sparrow

gota, la *(lah 'goh-tah)* drop

gracias *('grah-see·ahs)* thanks

grande *('grahn-deh)* big

grano, el *(ehl 'grah-noh)* grain

grapa, la *(lah 'grah-pah)* staple

grasa, la *(lah 'grah-sah)* grease

grava, la *(lah 'grah-bah)* gravel

grieta, la *(lah gree-'eh-tah)* crack

grifo, el *(ehl 'gree-foh)* faucet

grillo, el *(ehl 'gree-yoh)* cricket

gris *(grees)* gray

gritar *(gree-'tahr)* shout (to), yell (to)

grosería, la *(lah groh-seh-'ree·ah)* vulgarity

grúa, la *(lah 'groo-ah)* tow truck

grueso *(groo-'eh-soh)* thick

guante, el *(ehl 'gwahn-teh)* glove

guapo *('gwah-poh)* handsome

guardar *(gwahr-'dahr)* keep (to)

guardería, la *(lah gwahr-deh-'ree-ah)* nursery (children)

guía, el *(ehl 'gee-ah)* guide

guitarra, la *(lah gee-'tah-rrah)* guitar

gusano, el *(ehl goo-'sah-noh)* worm

gustar *(goh-'stahr)* like (to)

haber *(ah-'behr)* have (to)

hablar *(ah-'blahr)* speak (to)

hace *('ah-seh)* ago

hacer *(ah-'sehr)* do (to), make (to)

hacha, el *(ehl 'ah-chah)* ax

hacia *('ah-see·ah)* toward

halcón, el *(ehl ahl-'kohn)* hawk

hamaca, la *(lah ah-'mah-kah)* hammock

hambre, el *(ehl 'ahm-breh)* hunger

hamburguesa, la *(lah ahm-boor-'geh-sah)* hamburger

harina, la *(lah ah-'ree-nah)* flour

hasta *('ah-stah)* until

hay *('ah·ee)* there is, there are

hebilla, la *(lah eh-'bee-yah)* buckle

helado, el *(ehl eh-'lah-doh)* ice cream

helecho, el *(ehl eh-'leh-choh)* fern

helicóptero, el *(ehl eh-lee-'kohp-teh-roh)* helicopter

herida, la *(lah eh-'ree-dah)* injury

herir *(eh-'reer)* hurt (to)

hermana, la *(lah ehr-'mah-nah)* sister

hermano, el *(ehl ehr-'mah-noh)* brother

herramienta, la *(lah eh-rrah-mee-'ehn-tah)* tool

hervir *(ehr-'beer)* boil (to)

hiedra, la *(lah 'yeh-dra)* ivy

hielo, el *(ehl 'yeh-loh)* ice

hierba, la *(lah 'yehr-bah)* grass

hígado, el *(ehl 'ee-gah-doh)* liver

higo, el *(ehl 'ee-goh)* fig

hija, la *(lah 'ee-hah)* daughter

hijo, el *(ehl 'ee-hoh)* son

hilo, el *(ehl 'ee-loh)* thread

hoja, la *(lah 'oh-hah)* leaf

hola *('oh-lah)* hi

hombre, el *(ehl 'ohm-breh)* man

hombro, el *(ehl 'ohm-broh)* shoulder

hongo, el *(ehl 'ohn-goh)* mushroom

horario, el *(ehl oh-'rah-ree·oh)* schedule

hormiga, la *(lah ohr-'mee-gah)* ant

hornear *(hohr-neh-'ahr)* bake (to)

horquilla, la *(lah ohr-'kee-yah)* pitchfork

hospital, el *(ehl oh-spee-'tahl)* hospital

hoy *('oh·ee)* today

hoyo, el *(ehl 'oh-yoh)* hole

huerta, la *(lah 'wehr-tah)* orchard

hueso, el *(ehl 'weh-soh)* bone

huésped, el *(ehl 'weh-spehd)* guest

huevo, el *(ehl 'weh-boh)* egg

huevo duro, el *(ehl 'weh-boh 'doo-roh)* hard-boiled egg

huevo revuelto, el *(ehl 'weh-boh reh-'bwehl-toh)* scrambled egg

húmedo *('oo-meh-doh)* damp, moist

humo, el *(ehl 'oo-moh)* smoke

huracán, el *(ehl oo-rah-'kahn)* hurricane

iglesia, la *(lah ee-'gleh-see·ah)* church

impermeable, el *(ehl eem-pehr-meh-'ah-bleh)* raincoat

importante *(eem-pohr-'tahn-teh)* important

incapacidad, la *(lah een-kah-pah-see-'dahd)* disability

incluir *(een-kloo-'eer)* include (to)

información, la *(lah een-fohr-mah-see-'ohn)* information

ingeniero, el *(ehl een-heh-nee-'eh-roh)* engineer

inglés, el *(ehl een-'glehs)* English

insecto, el *(ehl een-'sehk-toh)* bug

inspeccionar *(een-spehk-see-oh-'nahr)* inspect (to)

instalar *(een-stah-'lahr)* install (to)

instrucción, la *(lah een-strook-see-'ohn)* instruction

instrumento, el *(ehl een-stroo-'mehn-toh)* instrument

inteligente *(een-teh-lee-'hehn-teh)* intelligent

interesante *(een-teh-reh-'sahn-teh)* interesting

interpretar *(een-tehr-preh-'tahr)* interpret (to)

interruptor, el *(ehl een-teh-rroop-'tohr)* switch

inundación, la *(lah een-oon-dah-see-'ohn)* flood

invierno, el *(ehl een-bee-'ehr-noh)* winter

ir *(eer)* go (to)

irrigación, la *(lah ee-ree-gah-see-'ohn)* irrigation

izquierda *(ees-kee-'ehr-dah)* left

jabón, el *(ehl hah-'bohn)* soap

jalar *(hah-'lahr)* pull (to)

jamón, el *(ehl hah-'mohn)* ham

jarabe, el *(ehl hah-'rah-beh)* syrup

jardín, el *(ehl hahr-'deen)* garden, yard

jardinero, el *(ehl hahr-dee-'neh-roh)* gardener

jaula, la *(lah 'hah-oo-lah)* cage

jefe, el *(ehl 'heh-feh)* boss

jirafa, la *(lah hee-'rah-fah)* giraffe

joven *('hoh-behn)* young

joyas, las *(lahs 'hoh-yahs)* jewelry

juego de damas, el *(ehl hoo-'eh-goh deh 'dah-mahs)* checkers

juego, el *(ehl hoo-'eh-goh)* game

jueves *(hoo-'eh-behs)* Thursday

jugar *(hoo-'gahr)* play

jugo, el *(ehl 'hoo-goh)* juice

juguete, el *(ehl hoo-'geh-teh)* toy

julio *('hoo-lee-oh)* July

junio *('hoo-nee-oh)* June

juntar *(hoon-'tahr)* join (to)

la *(lah)* the (sing.fem.)

labio, el *(ehl 'lah-bee-oh)* lip

lado, el *(ehl 'lah-doh)* side

ladrar *(lah-'drahr)* bark (to)

ladrillo, el *(ehl lah-'dree-yoh)* brick

ladrón, el *(ehl lah-'drohn)* thief

lagarto, el *(ehl lah-'gahr-toh)* lizard

lago, el *(ehl 'lah-goh)* lake

lana, la *(lah 'lah-nah)* wool

lápiz, el *(ehl 'lah-pees)* pencil

largo *('lahr-goh)* long

largo, el *(ehl 'lahr-goh)* length

las *(lahs)* the (pl.fem.)

lata, la *(lah 'lah-tah)* can

laton, el *(ehl lah-'tohn)* brass

lavador de platos, el *(ehl lah-bah-'dohr deh 'plah-tohs)* dish washer (person)

lavadora, la *(lah lah-bah-'doh-rah)* clothes washer

lavandería, la *(lah lah-bahn-deh-'ree-ah)* laundromat

lavaplatos, el *(ehl lah-bah-'plah-tohs)* dishwasher (machine)

lavar *(lah-'bahr)* wash (to)

leche, la *(lah 'leh-cheh)* milk

leche condensada, la *(lah 'leh-cheh kohn-'dehn-sah-dah)* condensed milk

leche evaporada, la *(lah 'leh-cheh eh-bah-poh-'rah-dah)* evaporated milk

lechuga, la *(lah leh-'choo-gah)* lettuce

leer *(leh-'ehr)* read (to)

lejos *('leh-hohs)* far

lengua, la *(lah 'lehn-gwah)* tongue

lenguaje, el *(ehl lehn-'gwah-heh)* language

lentes de sol, los *(lohs 'lehn-tehs deh sohl)* sunglasses

lentes, los *(lohs 'lehn-tehs)* glasses

lento *('lehn-toh)* slow

levantar *(leh-bahn-'tahr)* lift (to)

levantarse *(leh-bahn-'tahr-seh)* stand up (to)

libra, la *(lah 'lee-brah)* pound

librero, el *(ehl lee-'breh-roh)* bookshelf

libro, el *(ehl 'lee-broh)* book

licencia, la *(lah lee-'sehn-see-ah)* license

licor, el *(ehl lee-'kohr)* liquor, liqueur

licuadora, la *(lah lee-kwah-'doh-rah)* blender

licuar *(lee-koo-'ahr)* blend (to)

lima, la *(lah 'lee-mah)* file, lime

limar *(lee-'mahr)* file (to)

limón, el *(ehl lee-'mohn)* lemon

limonada, la *(lah lee-moh-'nah-dah)* lemonade

limpiadora, la *(lah leem-pee-ah-'doh-rah)* cleanser

limpiar *(leem-pee-'ahr)* clean (to)

limpio *('leem-pee-oh)* clean

lindo *('leen-doh)* lovely

línea, la *(lah 'lee-neh-ah)* line

lino, el *(ehl 'lee-noh)* linen

linóleo, el *(ehl lee-'noh-leh-oh)* linoleum

linterna, la *(lah leen-'tehr-nah)* flashlight

líquido, el *(ehl 'lee-kee-doh)* liquid

liso *('lee-soh)* smooth

lista, la *(lah 'lee-stah)* list

listo *('lee-stoh)* ready

llama, la *(lah 'yah-mah)* flame

llamar *(yah-'mahr)* call (to)

llave inglesa, la *(lah 'yah-beh een-'gleh-sah)* wrench
llave, la *(lah 'yah-beh)* key
llegar *(yeh-'gahr)* arrive (to)
llenar *(yeh-'nahr)* fill (to)
lleno *('yeh-noh)* full
llevar *(yeh-'bahr)* carry (to)
llorar *(yoh-'rahr)* cry (to)
lluvia, la *(lah 'yoo-bee-ah)* rain
lobo, el *(ehl 'loh-boh)* wolf
loceta, la *(lah loh-'seh-tah)* tile
lodo, el *(ehl 'loh-doh)* mud
los *(lohs)* the (pl.masc.)
luego *(loo-'eh-goh)* later
lugar, el *(ehl loo-'gahr)* place
luna, la *(lah 'loo-nah)* moon
lunes *('loo-nehs)* Monday
lustrar *(loo-'strahr)* polish (to)
lustre, el *(ehl 'loo-streh)* polish
luz, la *(lah loos)* light
maceta, la *(lah mah-'seh-tah)* pot (plant)
machacar *(mah-chah-'kahr)* crush (to)
madera, la *(lah mah-'deh-rah)* lumber, wood
madre, la *(lah 'mah-dreh)* mother
madrugada, la *(lah mah-droo-'gah-dah)* dawn
maduro *(mah-'doo-roh)* mature, ripe
maestro, el *(ehl mah-'eh-stroh)* teacher
maicena, la *(lah mah-ee-'seh-nah)* cornstarch
maíz, el *(ehl mah-'ees)* corn
mala hierba, la *(lah 'mah-lah 'yehr-bah)* weed
malo *('mah-loh)* bad
mañana *(mah-'nyah-nah)* tomorrow
mancha, la *(lah 'mahn-chah)* stain
manchar *(mahn-'chahr)* stain (to)
manejar *(mah-neh-'hahr)* drive (to)
manga, la *(lah 'mahn-gah)* sleeve
manguera, la *(lah mahn-'geh-rah)* hose
mano, la *(lah 'mah-noh)* hand
manteca, la *(lah mahn-'teh-kah)* lard
mantel, el *(ehl mahn-'tehl)* tablecloth
mantener *(mahn-tehn-'nehr)* maintain (to)
mantequilla, la *(lah mahn-teh-'kee-yah)* butter
manzana, la *(lah mahn-'sah-nah)* apple
mapa, el *(ehl 'mah-pah)* map
mapache, el *(ehl mah-'pah-cheh)* raccoon
maquillaje, el *(ehl mah-kee-'yah-heh)* make-up
máquina, la *(lah 'mah-kee-nah)* machine
mar, el *(ehl 'mahr)* sea
marca, la *(lah 'mahr-kah)* brand

marcador, el *(ehl mahr-kah-'dohr)* dial
marcar *(mahr-'kahr)* dial (to), mark (to)
margarina, la *(lah mahr-gah-'ree-nah)* margarine
margarita, la *(lah mahr-gah-'ree-tah)* daisy
marinar *(mah-ree-'nahr)* marinate (to)
mariposa, la *(lah mah-ree-'poh-sah)* butterfly
marisco, el *(ehl mah-'rees-koh)* seafood
mármol, el *(ehl 'mahr-mohl)* marble
martes *('mahr-tehs)* Tuesday
martillo, el *(ehl mahr-'tee-yoh)* hammer
marzo *('mahr-soh)* March
más *(mahs)* more
masa, la *(lah 'mah-sah)* dough
mascota, la *(lah mah-'skoh-tah)* pet
matar *(mah-'tahr)* kill (to)
mayo *('mah-yoh)* May
mayonesa, la *(lah mah-yoh-'neh-sah)* mayonnaise
mayor *(mah-'yohr)* older
mecánico, el *(ehl meh-'kah-nee-koh)* mechanic
media, la *(lah 'meh-dee-ah)* stocking
mediano *(meh-dee-'ah-noh)* medium
medicina, la *(lah meh-dee-'see-nah)* medicine
medidor, el *(ehl meh-dee-'dohr)* meter
medio, el *(ehl 'meh-dee-oh)* middle
medir *(meh-'deer)* measure (to)
mejilla, la *(lah meh-'hee-yah)* cheek
melón, el *(ehl meh-'lohn)* cantaloupe
menor *(meh-'nohr)* younger
menos *('meh-nohs)* less
mensaje, el *(ehl mehn-'sah-heh)* message
menta, la *(lah 'mehn-tah)* mint
mentir *(mehn-'teer)* lie (to)
merienda, la *(lah meh-ree-'ehn-dah)* snack
mes, el *(ehl mehs)* month
mesa de noche, la *(lah 'meh-sah deh 'noh-cheh)* nightstand
mesa, la *(lah 'meh-sah)* table
mesero, el *(ehl meh-'seh-roh)* waiter
metal, el *(ehl meh-'tahl)* metal
meter *(meh-'tehr)* insert (to)
metro, el *(ehl 'meh-troh)* subway
mezclar *(mehs-'klahr)* mix (to)
mi *(mee)* my
microondas, el *(ehl mee-kroh-'ohn-dahs)* microwave
miedo *(ehl mee-'eh-doh)* fear
miel, la *(lah mee-'ehl)* honey
miércoles *(mee-'ehr-koh-lehs)* Wednesday
mil *(meel)* thousand

milla, la *(lah 'mee-yah)* mile
millón *(ehl mee-'yohn)* million
mío *('mee-oh)* mine
mirar *(mee-'rahr)* look at (to), watch (to)
mismo *('mees-moh)* same
mitad, la *(lah mee-'tahd)* half
modelo, el *(ehl moh-'deh-loh)* model
mojado *(moh-'hah-doh)* wet
molde, el *(ehl 'mohl-deh)* mold
moler *(moh-'lehr)* grind (to)
moneda, la *(lah moh-'neh-dah)* coin
mono, el *(ehl 'moh-noh)* monkey
montaña, la *(lah mohn-'tah-nyah)* mountain
montar *(mohn-'tahr)* ride (to)
montón *(ehl mohn-'tohn)* pile
mora azul, la *(lah 'moh-rah ah-'sool)* blueberry
mora, la *(lah 'moh-rah)* blackberry
morado *(moh-'rah-doh)* purple
mordedura, la *(lah mohr-deh-'doo-rah)* bite
morder *(mohr-'dehr)* bite (to)
mosca, la *(lah 'moh-skah)* fly
mosquitero, el *(ehl moh-skee-'teh-roh)* screen
mostaza, la *(lah moh-'stah-sah)* mustard
mostrador, el *(ehl moh-strah-'dohr)* counter
mostrar *(moh-'strahr)* show
motocicleta, la *(lah moh-toh-see-'kleh-tah)* motorcycle
motor, el *(ehl moh-'tohr)* engine
motosierra, la *(lah moh-toh-see-'eh-rrah)* chainsaw
mover *(moh-'behr)* move (to)
muchacho, el *(ehl moo-'chah-choh)* teenager
mucho *('moo-choh)* much
mucho, muchos *('moo-choh, 'moo-chah)* a lot (sing., pl.)
muchos *('moo-chohs)* many
mudarse *(moo-'dahr-seh)* relocate (to)
muebles, los *(lohs 'mweh-blehs)* furniture
muerte, la *(lah 'mwehr-teh)* death
mujer, la *(lah moo-'hehr)* woman
muletas, las *(lahs moo-'leh-tahs)* crutches
mundo, el *(ehl 'moon-doh)* world
muñeca, la *(lah moo-'nyeh-kah)* doll, wrist
municipio, el *(ehl moo-nee-'see-pee-oh)* city hall
museo, el *(ehl moo-'seh-oh)* museum
música, la *(lah 'moo-see-kah)* music
músico, el *(ehl 'moo-see-koh)* musician

nacionalidad, la *(lah nah-see-oh-nah-lee-'dahd)* nationality
nada *('nah-dah)* nothing
nadar *(nah-'dahr)* swim (to)
nadie *('nah-dee-eh)* no one
nalga, la *(lah 'nahl-gah)* buttock
naranja, la *(lah nah-'rahn-hah)* orange (fruit)
nariz, la *(lah nah-'rees)* nose
navaja, la *(lah nah-'bah-hah)* razor
navegar *(nah-beh-'gahr)* sail (to)
necesitar *(neh-seh-see-'tahr)* need (to)
nectarina, la *(lah nehk-tah-'ree-nah)* nectarine
negocio, el *(ehl neh-'goh-see-oh)* business
negro *('neh-groh)* black
nervioso *(nehr-bee-'oh-soh)* nervioso
neumático, el *(ehl neh-oo-'mah-tee-koh)* tire
nido, el *(ehl 'nee-doh)* nest
nieta, la *(lah nee-'eh-tah)* granddaughter
nieto, el *(ehl nee-'eh-toh)* grandson
nieve, la *(lah nee-'eh-beh)* snow
niña, la *(lah 'nee-nyah)* girl
niñero, el *(ehl nee-'nyeh-roh)* babysitter
ninguno *(neen-'goo-noh)* none
niño, el *(ehl 'nee-nyoh)* boy
nivel, el *(ehl nee-'behl)* level
no *(noh)* don't
nombre, el *(ehl 'nohm-breh)* name
norte *('nohr-teh)* north
noveno *(noh-'beh-noh)* ninth
noventa *(noh-'behn-tah)* ninety
novia, la *(lah 'noh-bee-ah)* girlfriend
noviembre *(noh-bee-'ehm-breh)* November
novio, el *(ehl 'noh-bee-oh)* boyfriend
nube, la *(lah 'noo-beh)* cloud
nudo, el *(ehl 'noo-doh)* knot
nuera, la *(lah noo-'eh-rah)* daughter-in-law
nuestra *(noo-'eh-strah)* our
nueve *(noo-'eh-beh)* nine
nuevo *(noo-'eh-boh)* new
nuez, la *(lah noo-'ehs)* nut (food)
número, el *(ehl 'noo-meh-roh)* number
nunca *('noon-kah)* never
o *(oh)* or
obedecer *(oh-beh-deh-'sehr)* obey (to)
obrero, el *(ehl oh-'breh-roh)* laborer
obstruir *(ohb-stroo-'eer)* obstruct (to)
ochenta *(oh-'chehn-tah)* eighty
ocho *('oh-choh)* eight
octavo *('ohk-'tah-boh)* eighth
octubre *(ohk-'too-breh)* October
ocupado *(oh-koo-'pah-doh)* busy
odiar *(oh-dee-'ahr)* hate

oeste *(oh-'eh-steh)* west
oferta, la *(lah oh-'fehr-tah)* offer
oficina, la *(lah oh-fee-'see-nah)* office
oído, el *(ehl oh-'ee-doh)* ear
oír *(oh-'eer)* hear (to)
ojo, el *(ehl 'oh-hoh)* eye
oler *(oh-'lehr)* smell (to)
olla, la *(lah 'oh-yah)* pot (cooking)
olmo, el *(ehl 'ohl-moh)* elm
olor, el *(ehl oh-'lohr)* odor
olvidar *(ohl-bee-'dahr)* forget
ombligo *(ehl ohm-'blee-goh)* navel
once *('ohn-seh)* eleven
onza, la *(lah 'ohn-sah)* ounce
operadora, la *(lah oh-peh-rah-'doh-rah)* operator
operar *(oh-peh-'rahr)* operate (to)
oportunidad, la *(lah oh-pohr-too-nee-'dahd)* opportunity
orden, el *(ehl 'ohr-dehn)* order
ordenar *(ohr-deh-'nahr)* order (to)
organizar *(ohr-gah-nee-'sahr)* organize (to)
orina, la *(lah oh-'ree-nah)* urine
oro, el *(ehl 'oh-roh)* gold
oscuro *(oh-'skoo-roh)* dark
oso, el *(ehl 'oh-soh)* bear
otoño, el *(ehl oh-'toh-nyoh)* autumn
otra vez *('oh-trah behs)* again
oveja, la *(lah oh-'beh-hah)* sheep
paciente, el *(ehl pah-see-'ehn-teh)* patient
padre, el *(ehl 'pah-dreh)* father
padres, los *(lohs 'pah-drehs)* parents
pagar *(pah-'gahr)* pay (to)
pago, el *(ehl 'pah-goh)* payment
país, el *(ehl pah-'ees)* country
pájaro, el *(ehl 'pah-hah-roh)* bird
pala, la *(lah 'pah-lah)* shovel
palabra, la *(lah pah-'lah-brah)* word
palmera, la *(lah pahl-'meh-rah)* palm
palo, el *(ehl 'pah-loh)* stick
pan, el *(ehl pahn)* bread
pan tostado, el *(ehl pahn toh-'stah-doh)* toast
panadería, la *(lah pah-nah-deh-'ree-ah)* bakery
pañal, el *(ehl pah-'nyahl)* diaper
panecillo, el *(ehl pah-neh-'see-yoh)* roll
pantalla, la *(lah pahn-'tah-yah)* lampshade
pantalones, los *(lohs pahn-tah-'loh-nehs)* pants
pañuelo, el *(ehl pah-nyoo-'eh-loh)* handkerchief
papa, la *(lah 'pah-pah)* potato

papel de lija, el *(ehl pah-'pehl deh 'lee-hah)* sandpaper
papel, el *(ehl pah-'pehl)* paper
papel higiénico, el *(ehl pah-'pehl ee-hee-'eh-nee-koh)* toilet paper
paquete, el *(ehl pah-'keh-teh)* package
par, el *(ehl pahr)* pair
para, por *('pah-rah, pohr)* for
parachoques, el *(pah-rah-'choh-kehs)* bumper
parada de autobús, la *(lah pah-'rah-dah deh ow-toh-'boos)* bus stop
paralelo *(ehl pah-rah-'leh-loh)* parallel
paramédico, el *(ehl pah-rah-'meh-dee-koh)* paramedic
parar *(pah-'rahr)* stop (to)
pared, la *(lah pah-'rehd)* wall
pareja, la *(lah pah-'reh-hah)* couple
pariente, el *(ehl pah-ree-'ehn-teh)* relative
parque, el *(ehl 'pahr-keh)* park
parrilla, la *(lah pah-'rree-yah)* grill
parte, la *(lah 'pahr-teh)* part
pasa, la *(lah 'pah-sah)* raisin
pasillo, el *(ehl pah-'see-yoh)* hallway
pasta de dientes, la *(lah 'pah-stah deh dee-'ehn-tehs)* toothpaste
pasta, la *(lah 'pah-stah)* paste
pastel, el *(ehl pah-'stehl)* pie
pasto, el *(ehl 'pah-stoh)* grass
patear *(pah-teh-'ahr)* kick (to)
patio, el *(ehl 'pah-tee-oh)* backyard
pato, el *(ehl 'pah-toh)* duck
pavo, el *(ehl 'pah-boh)* turkey
peces, los *(lohs 'peh-sehs)* fishes
pecho, el *(ehl 'peh-choh)* chest (body)
pedazo, el *(ehl peh-'dah-soh)* piece
pediatra, el *(elh peh-dee-'ah-trah)* pediatrician
pedir *(peh-'deer)* ask for (to)
pegamento, el *(ehl peh-gah-'mehn-toh)* glue
pegar *(peh-'gahr)* glue (to)
peine, el *(ehl 'peh-ee-neh)* comb
pelar *(peh-'lahr)* peel
pelear *(peh-leh-'ahr)* fight (to)
película, la *(lah peh-'lee-koo-lah)* film
peligro, el *(ehl peh-'lee-groh)* danger
peligroso *(peh-lee-'groh-soh)* dangerous
pelirrojo *(peh-lee-'rroh-hoh)* red-headed
pelo, el *(ehl 'peh-loh)* hair
pelota, la *(lah peh-'loh-tah)* ball
peluquería, la *(lah peh-loo-keh-'ree-ah)* barber shop
pene, el *(ehl 'peh-neh)* penis

penicilina, la *(lah peh-nee-see-'lee-nah)* penicillin

pensar *(pehn-'sahr)* think (to)

pepino, el *(ehl peh-'pee-noh)* cucumber

pequeño *(peh-'keh-nyoh)* small

pera, la *(lah 'peh-rah)* pear

perder *(pehr-'dehr)* lose (to)

perdido *(pehr-'dee-doh)* lost

perejil, el *(ehl peh-reh-'heel)* parsley

perezoso *(peh-reh-'soh-soh)* lazy

perfume, el *(ehl pehr-'foo-meh)* perfume

perico, el *(ehl peh-'ree-koh)* parakeet

perilla, la *(lah peh-'ree-yah)* knob

periódico, el *(ehl peh-ree-'oh-dee-koh)* newspaper

perla, la *(lah 'pehr-lah)* pearl

permiso, el *(ehl pehr-'mee-soh)* permission

permitir *(pehr-mee-'teer)* permit (to)

perno, el *(ehl 'perh-noh)* bolt

pero *('peh-roh)* but

perro, el *(ehl 'peh-rroh)* dog

persianas, las *(lahs pehr-see-'ah-nahs)* blinds

persona, la *(lah pehr-'soh-nah)* person

pesadilla, la *(lah peh-sah-'dee-yah)* nightmare

pesado *(peh-'sah-doh)* heavy

pesar *(peh-'sahr)* weigh (to)

pescado, el *(ehl peh-'skah-doh)* fish

pescar *(peh-'skahr)* fish (to)

peso, el *(ehl 'peh-soh)* weight

pestillo, el *(ehl peh-'stee-yoh)* deadbolt

petirrojo, el *(ehl peh-tee-'rroh-hoh)* robin

picante *(pee-'kahn-teh)* spicy

picar *(pee-'kahr)* chop (to)

pico, el *(ehl 'peh-koh)* pickax, mountaintop

pie, el *(ehl 'pee-eh)* foot

piedra, la *(lah pee-'eh-drah)* rock, stone

piel, la *(lah pee-'ehl)* fur, skin

pierna, la *(lah pee-'ehr-nah)* leg

pijama, la *(ehl pee-'hah-mah)* pajamas

pila, la *(lah 'pee-lah)* battery

píldora, la *(lah 'peel-doh-rah)* pill

piloto, el *(ehl pee-'loh-toh)* pilot

pimienta, la *(lah pee-mee-'ehn-tah)* pepper

piña, la *(lah 'pee-nyah)* pineapple

pino, el *(ehl 'pee-noh)* pine

pinta, la *(lah 'peen-tah)* pint

pintar *(peen-'tahr)* paint (to)

pintura, la *(lah peen-'too-rah)* paint, painting

pinzas, las *(lahs 'peen-sahs)* pliers, tweezers

piscina, la *(lah pee-'see-nah)* pool

piso, el *(ehl 'pee-soh)* floor

plancha, la *(lah 'plahn-chah)* iron

planchado permanente *(ehl plahn-'chah-doh pehr-mah-'nehn-teh)* permanent press

planchar *(plahn-'chahr)* iron (to)

planear *(plah-neh-'ahr)* plan (to)

plano, el *(ehl 'plah-noh)* plan

planta, la *(lah 'plahn-tah)* plant

plantar *(plahn-'tahr)* plant (to)

plástico, el *(ehl 'plah-stee-koh)* plastic

plata, la *(lah 'plah-tah)* silver

plátano, el *(ehl 'plah-tah-noh)* banana

plato, el *(ehl 'plah-toh)* plate, dish

plato hondo, el *(ehl 'plah-toh 'ohn-doh)* bowl

playa, la *(lah 'plah-yah)* beach

plomero, el *(ehl ploh-'meh-roh)* plumber

pluma, la *(lah 'ploo-mah)* pen

plumero, el *(ehl ploo-'meh-roh)* duster

pobre, el or **la** *(ehl or la 'poh-breh)* poor

poco, un *(oon 'poh-koh)* a little

pocos *('poh-kohs)* few

podar *(poh-'dahr)* prune (to)

poder *(poh-'dehr)* be able to (to)

poder, el *(ehl poh-'dehr)* power

podrido *(poh-'dree-doh)* rotten

policía, la *(lah poh-lee-'see-ah)* police

polilla, la *(lah poh-'lee-yah)* moth

polvo de hornear *(ehl 'pohl-boh deh ohr-neh-'ahr)* baking powder

polvo, el *(ehl 'pohl-boh)* dust, powder

poner *(poh-'nehr)* put (to)

por ciento *(pohr see-'ehn-toh)* percent

por favor *(pohr fah-'bohr)* please

por qué *(pohr keh)* why

por todas partes *(pohr 'toh-dahs 'pahr-tehs)* everywhere

porque *('pohr-keh)* because

portal, el *(ehl pohr-'tahl)* porch

portón, el *(ehl pohr-'tohn)* gate

poste, el *(ehl 'poh-streh)* post

postre, el *(ehl 'poh-streh)* dessert

potro, el *(ehl 'poh-troh)* pony

práctica, la *(lah 'prahk-tee-kah)* practice

practicar *(prahk-tee-'kahr)* practice (to)

pre-cocido *(preh-koh-'see-doh)* pre-cooked

precio, el *(ehl 'preh-see-oh)* price

precioso *(preh-see-'oh-soh)* cute

preferir *(preh-feh-'reer)* prefer (to)

pregunta, la *(lah preh-'goon-tah)* question

preguntar *(preh-goon-'tahr)* ask (to)

prender *(prehn-'dehr)* ignite (to), turn on (to)

preocupar *(preh-oh-koo-'pahr)* worry (to)

preparar *(preh-pah-'rahr)* prepare (to)
prestar *(preh-'stahr)* lend (to)
prevenir *(preh-beh-'neer)* prevent (to)
primavera, la *(lah pree-mah-'beh-rah)* spring
primero *(pree-'meh-roh)* first
primeros auxilios, los *(lohs pree-'meh-rohs aw·ook-'see-lee·ohs)* first aid
primo, el *(ehl 'pree-moh)* cousin
privado *(pree-'bah-doh)* private
privilegio, el *(ehl pree-bee-'leh-hee·oh)* privilege
probarse *(proh-'bahr-seh)* try on (to)
problema, el *(ehl proh-'bleh-mah)* problem
procedimiento, el *(ehl proh-seh-dee-mee-'ehn-toh)* procedure
producto químico, el *(ehl proh-'dook-toh 'kee-mee-koh)* chemical
profundo *(proh-'foon-doh)* deep
prohibir *(proh-ee-'beer)* prohibit (to)
prometer *(proh-meh-'tehr)* promise (to)
pronto *('prohn-toh)* soon
pronunciar *(proh-noon-see-'ahr)* pronounce (to)
propina, la *(lah proh-'pee-nah)* tip
puente, el *(ehl 'pwehn-teh)* bridge
puerco, el *(ehl 'pwehr-koh)* pig
puercoespín, el *(ehl pwehr-koh-eh-'speen)* porcupine
puerta, la *(lah 'pwehr-tah)* door
puesta del sol, la *(lah 'pweh-stah dehl sohl)* sunset
puesto, el *(ehl 'pweh-stoh)* position
pulga, la *(lah 'pool-gah)* flea
pulgada, la *(lah pool-'gah-dah)* inch
pulmón, el *(ehl pool-'mohn)* lung
puño, el *(ehl 'poo-nyoh)* cuff, fist
punta, la *(lah 'poon-tah)* end
purificar *(poo-ree-fee-'kahr)* purify (to)
puro, el *(ehl 'poo-roh)* cigar
qué *(keh)* what
quebrado *(keh-'brah-doh)* broken
quebrar *(keh-'brahr)* break (to)
quemadura, la *(lah keh-mah-'doo-rah)* burn
quemar *(keh-'mahr)* burn (to)
querer *(keh-'rehr)* want (to)
queso, el *(ehl 'keh-soh)* cheese
queso crema, el *(ehl 'keh-soh 'kreh-mah)* cream cheese
queso parmesano, el *(ehl 'keh-soh pahr-meh-'sah-noh)* Parmesan cheese
quién *(kee-'ehn)* who
quieto *(kee-'eh-toh)* quiet

químico, el producto *(ehl proh-'dook-toh 'kee-mee-koh)* chemical
quince *('keen-seh)* fifteen
quitar *(kee-'tahr)* remove (to)
quizás *(kee-'sahs)* maybe
rábano, el *(ehl 'rah-bah-noh)* radish
radio, el *(ehl 'rah-dee·oh)* radio
raíz, la *(lah rah-'ees)* root
rallar *(rah-'yahr)* grate (to)
rama, la *(lah 'rah-mah)* branch
rápido *('rah-pee-doh)* fast
raro *('rah-roh)* strange
rasguño, el *(ehl rahs-'goo-nyoh)* scrape
raspador, el *(ehl rah-spah-'dohr)* scraper
raspar *(rahs-'pahr)* scrape (to)
rastrillar *(rah-stree-'yahr)* rake (to)
rastrillo, el *(ehl rah-'stree-yoh)* rake
rata, la *(lah 'rah-tah)* rat
ratón, el *(ehl rah-'tohn)* mouse
rayos equis, los *(lohs 'rah-yohs 'eh-kees)* x-rays
raza, la *(lah 'rah-sah)* race
receta, la *(lah reh-'seh-tah)* prescription
recibir *(reh-see-'beer)* receive (to)
recibo, el *(ehl reh-'see-boh)* receipt
recoger *(reh-koh-'hehr)* pick (to)
recomendar *(reh-koh-mehn-'dahr)* recommend (to)
reconocer *(reh-koh-noh-'sehr)* recognize (to)
recordar *(reh-kohr-'dahr)* remember (to)
reemplazar *(reh-ehm-plah-'sahr)* replace (to)
referencias, las *(lahs reh-feh-'rehn-see·ahs)* references
referir *(reh-feh-'reer)* refer (to)
refresco, el *(ehl reh-'freh-skoh)* soft drink
regalo, el *(ehl reh-'gah-loh)* gift
regañar *(reh-gah-'nyahr)* scold (to)
regar *(reh-'gahr)* water (to)
registradora, la *(lah reh-hee-strah-'doh-rah)* cash register
regla, la *(lah 'reh-glah)* rule
reír *(reh-'eer)* laugh (to)
relación, la *(lah reh-lah-see-'ohn)* relationship
relámpago, el *(ehl reh-'lahm-pah-goh)* lightning
religión, la *(lah reh-lee-hee-'ohn)* religion
reloj de pulsera, el *(ehl reh-'loh deh pool-'seh-rah)* watch
reloj, el *(ehl reh-'loh)* clock
remedio, el *(ehl reh-'meh-dee·oh)* remedy
remendar *(reh-mehn-'dahr)* mend (to)
remojar *(reh-moh-'hahr)* soak (to)
remolacha, la *(lah reh-moh-'lah-chah)* beet

renovar *(reh-noh-'bahr)* renovate (to)
renunciar *(reh-noon-see-'ahr)* quit (to)
reparar *(reh-pah-'rahr)* fix (to), repair (to)
repartir *(reh-pahr-'teer)* share (to)
repetir *(reh-peh-'teer)* repeat (to)
repisa, la *(lah reh-'pee-sah)* shelf
repollo, el *(ehl reh-'poh-yoh)* cabbage
requesón, el *(ehl reh-keh-'sohn)* cottage
   cheese
resfriado, el *(ehl rehs-free-'ah-doh)* flu
   (cold)
respetar *(reh-speh-'tahr)* respect (to)
respiración artificial *(lah reh-spee-rah-*
   see-'ohn ahr-tee-fee-see-'ahl) CPR
respirar *(reh-spee-'rahr)* breathe (to)
respuesta, la *(lah reh-'spweh-stah)* answer
restaurante, el *(ehl reh-stah-oo-'rahn-teh)*
   restaurant
retirar *(reh-tee-'rahr)* retire (to)
retrato, el *(ehl reh-'trah-toh)* portrait
revista, la *(lah reh-'bee-stah)* magazine
revolver *(reh-bohl-'behr)* stir (to)
reyezuelo, el *(ehl reh-yeh-soo-'eh-loh)* wren
rico *('ree-koh)* rich
río, el *(ehl 'ree-oh)* river
robar *(roh-'bahr)* steal (to)
roble, el *(ehl 'roh-bleh)* oak
robo, el *(ehl 'roh-boh)* robbery
rociadora, la *(lah roh-see-ah-'doh-rah)*
   sprinkler
rociar *(roh-see-'ahr)* spray (to)
rodilla, la *(lah roh-'dee-yah)* knee
rojo *('roh-hoh)* red
romo *('roh-moh)* dull
romper *(rohm-'pehr)* break (to)
ropa interior, la *(lah 'roh-pah een-teh-ree-*
   'ohr) underwear
ropa, la *(lah 'roh-pah)* clothing
ropa sucia, la *(lah 'roh-pah 'soo-see-ah)*
   laundry
ropero, el *(ehl roh-'peh-roh)* closet
rosa, la *(lah 'roh-sah)* rose
roto *('roh-toh)* broken
rubio *('roo-bee-oh)* blond
ruido, el *(ehl roo-'ee-doh)* noise
sábado *('sah-bah-doh)* Saturday
sábana, la *(lah 'sah-bah-nah)* sheet
saber *(sah-'behr)* know (to)
saco, el *(ehl 'sah-koh)* coat
sacudir *(sah-koo-'deer)* dust (to)
sal, la *(lah sahl)* salt
sala, la *(lah 'sah-lah)* living room
salchicha, la *(lah sahl-'chee-chah)* sausage
salida, la *(lah sah-'lee-dah)* exit

salir *(sah-'leer)* leave (to)
salón de belleza, el *(ehl sah-'lohn deh beh-*
   'yeh-sah) beauty salon
salsa, la *(lah 'sahl-sah)* sauce
saltamontes, el *(ehl sahl-tah-'mohn-tehs)*
   grasshopper
salud, la *(lah sah-'lood)* health
sandalia, la *(lah sahn-'dah-lee-ah)* sandal
sangre, la *(lah 'sahn-greh)* blood
sapo, el *(ehl 'sah-poh)* frog
sartén, el *(ehl sahr-'tehn)* frying pan
sastre, el *(ehl 'sah-streh)* tailor
secador de pelo, el *(ehl seh-kah-'dohr deh*
   'peh-loh) hair dryer
secadora, la *(lah seh-kah-'doh-rah)* dryer
secar *(seh-'kahr)* dry (to)
seco *('seh-koh)* dry
secretario, el *(ehl seh-kreh-'tah-ree-oh)*
   secretary
sed *(sehd)* thirst
seda, la *(lah 'seh-dah)* silk
segadora, la *(lah seh-gah-'doh-rah)* lawn
   mower
seguir *(seh-'geer)* follow (to)
segundo *(seh-'goon-doh)* second
seguridad, la *(lah seh-goo-ree-'dahd)* safety
seguro *(seh-'goo-roh)* sure
seguro, el *(ehl seh-'goo-roh)* insurance
seguro social, el *(ehl seh-'goo-roh soh-see-*
   'ahl) social security
seis *('seh-ees)* six
selva, la *(lah 'sehl-bah)* jungle
semáforo, el *(ehl seh-'mah-foh-roh)* traffic
   signal
semana, la *(lah seh-'mah-nah)* week
sembrar *(sehm-'brahr)* sow (to)
semilla, la *(lah seh-'mee-yah)* seed
señalar *(seh-nyah-'lahr)* point (to)
señor *(seh-'nyohr)* Mr.
señora *(seh-'nyoh-rah)* Mrs.
señorita *(seh-nyoh-'ree-tah)* Miss
sentarse *(sehn-'tahr-seh)* sit down (to)
separar *(seh-pah-'rahr)* separate (to)
septiembre *(sehp-tee-'ehm-breh)* September
séptimo *('sehp-tee-moh)* seventh
serrucho, el *(ehl seh-'rroo-choh)* saw
servicio, el *(ehl sehr-'bee-see-oh)* restroom
servilleta, la *(lah sehr-bee-'yeh-tah)* napkin
servir *(sehr-'beer)* pour (to), serve (to)
sesenta *(seh-'sehn-tah)* sixty
setenta *(seh-'tehn-tah)* seventy
sexo, el *(ehl 'sehk-soh)* sex
sexto *('sehks-toh)* sixth
si *(see)* if

sí *(see)* yes
siempre *(see-'ehm-preh)* always
siesta, la *(lah see-'eh-stah)* nap
siete *(see-'eh-teh)* seven
silenciador, el *(ehl see-lehn-see-ah-'dohr)* muffler
silla de ruedas, la *(lah 'see-yah deh roo-'eh-dahs)* wheelchair
silla, la *(lah 'see-yah)* chair
sillón, el *(ehl see-'yohn)* armchair
simpático *(seem-'pah-tee-koh)* nice
sin *(seen)* without
sistema, el *(ehl sees-'teh-mah)* system
sobre, el *(ehl 'soh-breh)* envelope
sobrevivir *(soh-breh-bee-'beer)* survive (to)
sobrino, el *(ehl soh-'bree-noh)* nephew
sobrina, la *(lah soh-'bree-nah)* niece
sofá, el *(ehl soh-'fah)* sofa
soga, la *(lah 'soh-gah)* rope
sol, el *(ehl sohl)* sun
solamente *(soh-lah-'mehn-teh)* only
soldado, el *(ehl sohl-'dah-doh)* soldier
solicitud, la *(lah soh-lee-see-'tood)* application
solo *('soh-loh)* alone
soltero *(sohl-'teh-roh)* single
sombra, la *(lah 'sohm-brah)* shade
sombrero, el *(ehl sohm-'breh-roh)* hat
sombrilla, la *(lah sohm-'bree-yah)* umbrella
soñar *(soh-'nyahr)* dream (to)
sonreír *(sohn-reh-'eer)* smile (to)
sonrisa, la *(lah sohn-'ree-sah)* smile
sopa, la *(lah 'soh-pah)* soup
sorpresa, la *(lah sohr-'preh-sah)* surprise
sostén, el *(ehl soh-'stehn)* brassiere
sótano, el *(ehl 'soh-tah-noh)* basement
su *(soo)* her, his, their, your
suave *('swah-beh)* soft
suavizador, el *(ehl swah-bee-sah-'dohr)* fabric softener
subir *(soo-'beer)* climb (to)
sucio *('soo-see-oh)* dirty
sudaderas, las *(lahs soo-dah-'deh-rahs)* sweatsuit
suegra, la *(lah 'sweh-grah)* mother-in-law
suegro, el *(ehl 'sweh-groh)* father-in-law
sueldo, el *(ehl 'swehl-doh)* salary
suéter, el *(ehl 'sweh-tehr)* sweater
supermercado, el *(ehl soo-pehr-mehr-'kah-doh)* supermarket
sur *(soor)* south
tabla, la *(lah 'tah-blah)* board
tablero, el *(ehl tah-'bleh-roh)* dashboard
tableta, la *(lah tah-'bleh-tah)* tablet

taladrar *(tah-lah-'drahr)* drill (to)
taladro, el *(ehl tah-'lah-droh)* drill
talco, el *(ehl 'tahl-koh)* talcum powder
talla, la *(lah 'tah-yah)* size
tallo, el *(ehl 'tah-yoh)* stem
también *(tahm-bee-'ehn)* also
tambor, el *(ehl tahm-'bohr)* drum
tapa, la *(lah 'tah-pah)* cover
tapar *(tah-'pahr)* plug (to)
tarde *('tahr-deh)* late
tarea, la *(lah tah-'reh-ah)* chore
tarjeta de crédito, la *(lah tahr-'heh-tah deh 'kreh-dee-toh)* credit card
tarjeta de salud, la *(lah tahr-'heh-tah deh sah-'lood)* health insurance card
tarjeta, la *(lah tahr-'heh-tah)* card
tarjeta postal, la *(lah tahr-'heh-tah poh-'stahl)* postcard
taza, la *(lah 'tah-sah)* cup
té, el *(ehl teh)* tea
techo, el *(ehl 'teh-choh)* ceiling
tejado, el *(ehl teh-'hah-doh)* roof
tejer *(teh-'hehr)* knit (to)
tela, la *(lah 'teh-lah)* cloth
teléfono, el *(ehl teh-'leh-foh-noh)* telephone
televisor, el *(ehl teh-leh-bee-'sohr)* TV
temperatura, la *(lah tehm-peh-rah-'too-rah)* temperature
temprano *(tehm-'prah-noh)* early
tender la cama *(tehn-'dehr lah 'kah-mah)* make the bed (to)
tenedor, el *(ehl teh-neh-'dohr)* fork
tener *(teh-'nehr)* have (to)
tener cuidado *(teh-'nehr kwee-'dah-doh)* be careful (to)
tener que *(teh-'nehr keh)* have to (to)
tenis, el *(ehl 'teh-nees)* tennis
tercero *(tehr-'seh-roh)* third
terminar *(tehr-mee-'nahr)* finish (to)
termo, el *(ehl 'tehr-moh)* thermos
termómetro, el *(tehr-'moh-meh-troh)* thermometer
termostato, el *(ehl tehr-moh-'stah-toh)* thermostat
terraza, la *(lah teh-'rrah-sah)* deck, terrace
terremoto, el *(ehl teh-rreh-'moh-toh)* earthquake
terreno, el *(ehl teh-'rreh-noh)* land
tía, la *(lah 'tee-ah)* aunt
tibio *('tee-bee-oh)* warm
tiempo, el *(ehl tee-'ehm-poh)* time, weather
tienda, la *(lah tee-'ehn-dah)* store
tierra, la *(lah tee-'eh-rrah)* dirt, soil, earth
tijeras, las *(lahs tee-'heh-rahs)* scissors

timbre, el *(ehl 'teem-breh)* doorbell
tina de baño, la *(lah 'tee-nah deh 'bah-nyoh)* bathtub
tintorería, la *(lah teen-toh-reh-'ree-ah)* cleaners
tío, el *(ehl 'tee-oh)* uncle
tipo, el *(ehl 'tee-poh)* kind
tirador, el *(ehl tee-rah-'dohr)* handle
tirar *(tee-'rahr)* throw away (to)
título, el *(ehl 'tee-too-loh)* diploma
toalla, la *(lah toh-'ah-yah)* towel
tobera, la *(lah toh-'beh-rah)* nozzle
tobillo, el *(ehl toh-'bee-yoh)* ankle
tocador, el *(ehl toh-kah-'dohr)* dresser
tocar *(toh-'kahr)* touch (to)
tocino, el *(ehl toh-'see-noh)* bacon
todavía *(toh-dah-'bee-ah)* yet
todo *('toh-doh)* everything
todo el mundo *('toh-doh ehl 'moon-doh)* everybody
tomar *(toh-'mahr)* take (to)
tomate, el *(ehl toh-'mah-teh)* tomato
tonelada, la *(lah toh-neh-'lah-dah)* ton
topo, el *(ehl 'toh-poh)* mole
tormenta, la *(lah tohr-'mehn-tah)* storm
tornillo, el *(ehl tohr-'nee-yoh)* screw
toronja, la *(lah toh-'rohn-hah)* grapefruit
torta, la *(lah 'tohr-tah)* cake
tortuga, la *(lah tohr-'too-gah)* turtle
tos, la *(lah tohs)* cough
tostador, el *(ehl toh-stah-'dohr)* toaster
tostar *(toh-'stahr)* toast (to)
trabajar *(trah-bah-'hahr)* work (to)
trabajo, el *(ehl trah-'bah-hoh)* job, work
traducir *(trah-doo-'seer)* translate (to)
traer *(trah-'ehr)* bring (to)
tráfico, el *(ehl 'trah-fee-koh)* traffic
tragar *(trah-'gahr)* swallow (to)
traílla, la *(lah trah-'ee-yah)* leash
traje de baño, el *(ehl 'trah-heh deh 'bah-nyoh)* bathing suit
traje, el *(ehl 'trah-heh)* suit
trampolín, el *(ehl trahm-poh-'leen)* diving board
transporte, el *(ehl trahns-'pohr-teh)* transportation
trapeador, el *(ehl trah-peh-ah-'dohr)* mop
trapear *(trah-peh-'ahr)* mop, to
trapo, el *(ehl 'trah-poh)* rag
tratar *(trah-'tahr)* try (to)
trece *('treh-seh)* thirteen
treinta *('treh-een-tah)* thirty
tren, el *(ehl trehn)* train
tres *(trehs)* three

triángulo, el *(ehl tree-'ahn-goo-loh)* triangle
triste *('tree-steh)* sad
tronco, el *(ehl 'trohn-koh)* trunk
trueno, el *(ehl troo-'eh-noh)* thunder
tubería, la *(lah too-beh-'ree-ah)* plumbing
tubo, el *(ehl 'too-boh)* pipe, tube
tuerca, la *(lah too-'ehr-kah)* nut (bolt)
túnel, el *(ehl 'too-nehl)* tunnel
un (m.), una (f.) *(oon, 'oo-nah)* a
uña, la *(lah 'oo-nyah)* fingernail
una vez *('oo-nah behs)* once
uniforme, el *(ehl oo-nee-'fohr-meh)* uniform
unión, la *(lah oo-nee-'ohn)* joint
uno *('oo-noh)* one
usar *(oo-'sahr)* use (to), wear (to)
usted *(oo-'stehd)* you (sing.)
ustedes *(oo-'steh-dehs)* you (pl.)
uva, la *(lah 'oo-bah)* grape
vaca, la *(lah 'bah-kah)* cow
vaciar *(bah-see-'ahr)* empty (to)
vacío *(bah-'see-oh)* empty
vagina, la *(lah bah-'hee-nah)* vagina
vainilla, la *(lah bah-ee-'nee-yah)* vanilla
vajilla de porcelana, la *(lah bah-'hee-yah deh pohr-seh-'lah-nah)* china ware
valiente *(bah-lee-'ehn-teh)* brave
valioso *(bah-lee-'oh-soh)* valuable
valle, el *(ehl 'bah-yeh)* valley
válvula, la *(lah 'bahl-boo-lah)* valve
vapor, el *(ehl bah-'pohr)* steam
vaso, el *(ehl 'bah-soh)* glass (drinking)
vecino, el *(ehl beh-'see-noh)* neighbor
vegetal, el *(ehl beh-heh-'tahl)* vegetable
veinte *('beh-een-teh)* twenty
vejiga, la *(lah beh-'hee-gah)* bladder
vela, la *(lah 'beh-lah)* candle
venado, el *(ehl beh-'nah-doh)* deer
vendaje, el *(ehl behn-'dah-heh)* bandage
vendedor, el *(ehl behn-deh-'dohr)* salesman
vender *(behn-'dehr)* sell (to)
veneno, el *(ehl beh-'neh-noh)* poison
venir *(beh-'neer)* come (to)
venta, la *(lah 'behn-tah)* sale
ventana, la *(lah behn-'tah-nah)* window
ventilar *(behn-tee-'lahr)* to ventilate
verano, el *(ehl beh-'rah-noh)* summer
verde *('behr-deh)* green
veterinario, el *(ehl beh-teh-ree-'nah-ree-oh)* veterinarian
viajar *(bee-ah-'hahr)* travel (to)
viaje, el *(ehl bee-'ah-heh)* trip
vida, la *(lah -'bee-dah)* life
vidrio, el *(ehl 'bee-dree-oh)* glass
viejo *(bee-'eh-hoh)* old

viento, el *(ehl bee-'ehn-toh)* wind
viernes *(bee-'ehr-nehs)* Friday
vinagre, el *(ehl bee-'nah-greh)* vinegar
vino, el *(ehl 'bee-noh)* wine
violación, la *(lah bee-oh-lah-see·'ohn)* rape
violar *(bee-oh-'lahr)* rape (to)
visitante, el *(ehl bee-see-'tahn-teh)* visitor
vitamina, la *(lah bee-tah-'mee-nah)* vitamin
viuda, la *(lah bee-'oo-dah)* widow
viudo, el *(ehl bee-'oo-doh)* widower
vocabulario, el *(ehl boh-kah-boo-'lah-ree·oh)* vocabulary
volar *(boh-'lahr)* fly (to)
voltear *(bohl-teh-'ahr)* turn (to)
volumen, el *(ehl boh-'loo-mehn)* volume
vomitar *(boh-mee-'tahr)* vomit (to)
voz, la *(lah bohs)* voice
vuelo, el *(ehl 'bweh-loh)* flight
y *(ee)* and

ya *(yah)* already
yema, la *(lah 'yeh-mah)* yolk
yerno, el *(ehl 'yehr-noh)* son-in-law
yeso, el *(ehl 'yeh-soh)* plaster
yo *(yoh)* I
yodo, el *(ehl 'yoh-doh)* iodine
zanahoria, la *(lah sah-nah-'oh-ree·ah)* carrot
zancudo, el *(ehl sahn-'koo-doh)* mosquito
zanja, la *(lah 'sahn-hah)* ditch
zapatilla, la *(lah sah-pah-'tee-yah)* slipper
zapatillas, las *(lahs sah-pah-'tee-yahs)* tennis shoes
zapato, el *(ehl sah-'pah-toh)* shoe
zona postal, la *(lah 'soh-nah poh-'stahl)* zip code
zoológico, el *(ehl soh-oh-'loh-hee-koh)* zoo
zorrillo, el *(ehl soh-'rree-yoh)* skunk
zorro, el *(ehl 'soh-rroh)* fox